ADOLESCENCE: PSYCHOSOCIAL PERSPECTIVES

ADOLESCENCE: PSYCHOSOCIAL PERSPECTIVES

EDITED BY

Gerald Caplan *and* Serge Lebovici

BASIC BOOKS, INC., PUBLISHERS

NEW YORK/LONDON

© 1969 by Basic Books, Inc.

Fourth Printing

© 1969 by Basic Books, Inc.

Library of Congress Catalog Card Number: 68–54133

Manufactured in the United States of America

Designed by Sophie Adler

DEDICATED
TO THE MEMORY OF

FREDERICK H. ALLEN, M.D.

DECEMBER 6, 1890–JANUARY 15, 1964

PRESIDENT,
INTERNATIONAL ASSOCIATION
FOR CHILD PSYCHIATRY,
1948–1954

THE AUTHORS

W. H. ALLCHIN is the Medical Director of the Wessex Regional Adolescent Psychiatric Unit and consulting psychiatrist at the Southampton Child and Family Guidance Clinic. He was formerly Assistant Psychiatrist at the Portman Clinic and psychotherapist at the Middlesex Hospital in London.

JAMES ANTHONY is the Ittleson Professor of Child Psychiatry at the Washington University School of Medicine in St. Louis, Missouri, and a Professorial Lecturer at the University of Chicago Medical School. He was formerly Senior Lecturer in Child Psychiatry at the Institute of Psychiatry in London. Dr. Anthony has also taught and served as supervising analyst at the Chicago Institute for Psychoanalysis.

EDGAR H. AUERSWALD is Chief of Psychiatric Services and Director of the Applied Behaviorial Sciences Program at the Gouverneur Health Services Program, Beth Israel Medical Center, New York City, and is Associate Professor of Clinical Psychiatry at the Mount Sinai School of Medicine.

HILDE BRUCH is Professor of Psychiatry, Baylor University College of Medicine, Houston, Texas. She was formerly Clinical Professor of Psychiatry and, prior to that, Instructor in Pediatrics at the College of Physicians and Surgeons, Columbia University.

ALBERT BRYT is Assistant Clinical Professor of Psychiatry at the New York University School of Medicine, Training and Supervising Analyst at the William Alanson White Institute, Psychiatrist-in-Charge of the Adolescent Outpatient Service, Bellevue Hospital, and Psychiatric Consultant to the Division of Day Care, New York City Bureau of Child Welfare.

DONALD F. BUCKLE is consultant psychiatrist to the Victoria Government and Consultant in Clinical Psychology, Monash University Health Service, University of Melbourne. He was formerly Regional Director for Mental Health (Europe) of the World Health Organization.

GERALD CAPLAN is Clinical Professor of Psychiatry and Director of the Laboratory of Community Psychiatry at Harvard Medical School. He was formerly Psychiatric Director of the Lasker Mental Hygiene and Child Guidance Center of Hadassah, Jerusalem.

P. H. CONNELL is the Director of the Drug Dependence Clinical Research and Treatment Unit at the Bethlem Royal and the Maudsley Hospital in London. He is a member of the World Health Organization Expert Advisory Panel on Drug Dependence, and Consultant Advisor on Drug Addiction and member of the Advisory Committee on Drug Dependence to the Ministry of Health and the Home Office.

ROBERT J. CORBOZ is head of the Child Psychiatric Service at Psychiatrische Poliklinik für Kinder und Jugendliche in Zurich and Professor of Child Psychiatry at the University of Zurich.

ANNA FREUD is a psychoanalyst and child-analyst and Director of the Hampstead Child-Therapy Course and Clinic in London. She has been a training analyst, Director of the Hampstead War Nurseries, and a member of the Executive Committee of the International Psychoanalytic Association.

M. E. M. HERFORD is a specialist in industrial medicine and is the Appointed Factory Doctor for Windsor and Slough District, United Kingdom. He was a Colonel in the Royal Air Force Medical Corps and has held a Rockefeller Fellowship in Preventive Medicine.

ALEX H. KAPLAN is a Lecturer in Social Psychiatry at the Brown School of Social Work and Clinical Assistant Professor of Psychiatry at Washington University, St. Louis, Missouri. He was formerly Psychiatrist-in-Chief, Jewish Hospital, St. Louis.

ROBERT LAFON is Professor of the Faculty of Medicine at the University of Montpellier, France.

SERGE LEBOVICI is Director of Center Alfred Binet (Centre de Santée Mentale Infantile du 13e Arrondissement), Paris, President of the International Association for Child Psychiatry and Allied Professions, and Vice Chairman of the International Association of Psychoanalysis. He is a consultant for the World Health Organization. He has been the Director of the Institute of Psychoanalysis, Paris.

THEODORE LIDZ is Professor and Chairman of the Department of Psychiatry of the Yale University School of Medicine. He has been a recipient of a National Institute of Mental Health Career Investigator Award. He is a past president of the American Psychosomatic Society.

TSUNG-YI LIN is Medical Officer, Mental Health Unit, of the World Health Organization. He was formerly Professor and Chairman of the Department of Psychiatry and Neurology at National Taiwan University Medical School and Director of Taipei Children's Mental Health Centre, Taipei, Taiwan.

BRUCE A. MCFARLANE is Professor of Sociology at Carleton University, Ottawa, Consultant and National Rapporteur (Canada) to the Directorate for Scientific Affairs' Committee for Scientific and Technical Personnel of the Organization for Economic Cooperation and Development, Paris, and Member of the Minister's Advisory Committee in Dental Health.

ALEXINA M. McWHINNIE is a psychiatric social worker and was Director of the Child Care and Adoption Agency in Edinburgh, Scotland. Her research is primarily concerned with adoptive families and adopted children.

JAMES B. McWHINNIE is Consultant-in-Charge of the Adolescent Psychiatric Unit, the Warneford Hospital in Oxford. He was formerly Consultant in Adolescent Psychiatry in Glasgow, and Visiting Consultant to Borstals and Approved Schools in Scotland.

IRWIN M. MARCUS is Clinical Professor of Psychiatry, Louisiana State University Medical Center, Lecturer at Tulane University School of Social Work and Teacher Education Center, and member of the senior staff, Touro Hospital, New Orleans. Dr. Marcus is President of the New Orleans Psychoanalytic Institute.

JOSEPH L. MASSIMO is Chief Psychologist for the Newton Public Schools and Assistant Clinical Professor of Psychiatry at the Boston University School of Medicine. He was formerly Administrative Manager and Head of the Vocational Counseling Department, Judge Baker Guidance Center, Newton-Baker Project.

PAUL A. OSTERRIETH is Professor of General Psychology and Developmental Psychology at the University of Brussels. He has been Professor of Educational Psychology at the University of Liège and was founder and psychologist of a child guidance clinic in Brussels.

ULF OTTO is Head Physician of the Child Psychiatric Clinic of the Central Hospital, Kristianstad, Sweden.

JEAN PIAGET is Professor of Child Psychology and the History of Scientific Thought at the University of Geneva. He is Director of the International Bureau of Education and the Institut J. J. Rousseau.

FRITZ REDL is Distinguished Professor of Behavioral Sciences at Wayne State University, Detroit, Michigan.

JEAN ROUSSELET is Director of the Center for Research on the Work and Employment of Youth, Ministry of Social Affairs, France.

WILLIAM A. SCHONFELD is Assistant Clinical Professor of Psychiatry at the College of Physicians and Surgeons, Columbia University, Consultant in Curriculum, Mercy College, Dobbs Ferry, New York, Associate Attendant in Child Psychiatry at New York State Psychiatric Institute and Hospital. He is President of the American Society for Adolescent Psychiatry.

ROGER L. SHAPIRO is Chief of the Section on Personality Development, Adult Psychiatry Branch, of the National Institute of Mental Health. He is also a teaching analyst at the Washington Psychoanalytic Association and a Fellow of the American Psychiatric Association.

MILTON F. SHORE is Chief of the Clinical Research and Program Evaluation Section, Mental Health Study Center, of the National Institute of Mental Health. He is also lecturer at the University of Maryland and on the faculty of the Washington School of Psychiatry.

JOHN A. SOURS practices general and child psychiatry and is an Associate in Psychiatry at the College of Physicians and Surgeons, Columbia University, and at the Columbia Psychoanalytic Clinic. He was a National Institute of Mental Health Career Teacher in Child Psychiatry.

JAMES M. TOOLAN is Assistant Professor of Psychiatry at the University of Vermont, Psychiatric Consultant to Bennington and Marlboro Colleges, and Director of Medical Services, United Counseling Services, Bennington, Vermont.

GEORGE VASSILIOU is Director of the Athenian Institute of Anthropos and is on the Editorial Board of the *International Journal of Psychiatry*.

DON A. WINN is Supervising Psychiatrist at the Children's Unit, Creedmoor State Hospital, Queens Village, New York.

INTRODUCTION

THROUGHOUT HISTORY many generations have seen themselves living in an Age of Anxiety, and their writers have longed nostalgically for the "good old days" when problems were simpler and the future was predictable. Adults laboriously work out ways of grappling with the challenges of their time, but their children usually do not participate in nor realize the nature of their parents' struggles. Fathers bequeath to sons their patterns of coping, but although these may have been appropriate to the problems of the past, historical change leads to a new crop of stresses and challenges for which the old methods are not suitable. In fact, each generation must work out its own salvation and is helped by the traditions of its predecessors only insofar as the rate of situational change is minimal. Whenever social and technological change accelerates, the gap between the generations increases, and each succeeding generation is involved in the anxiety-inducing process of basic innovation.

This is especially marked in our own time. Whether or not we can validly say, as has so often been said before, that there has never in history been a time of such dramatic change, it is clear that recent developments in communication, transportation, and energy production, together with the major economic, social, and political consequences of increasing populations and productivity, have led to revolutionary changes. These confront us with many life problems fundamentally different from those of our fathers. In the Western world these changes have had some consequences for our infants and small children, whose lives, however, are largely protected within the family circle. They do impinge directly on the adults. We experience the strain of having to adjust constantly to novel situations, but at least we feel that we are playing a more or less active part in shaping the new world. The greatest impact of these changes is on the adolescent population, which in our time must make the huge leap from a relatively unchanged world of childhood to our very complex new adult world, in whose making they were not involved. We provide them with few guidelines and dependable role models, because we have as yet no clear answers to our own problems, especially the sociopolitical and ethical consequences of our technological revolution.

This situation is complicated by the fact that as participants in an evolving culture we adults have continually been adjusting to a succession of changes. We have developed selective perceptual distortions and ways of reconciling ourselves to discrepancies between feasible "reality" and our basic theories and stated values, which allow us to pursue our paths in life with relative equanimity, even though it may well be that these paths turn out to be unsuccessful. We communicate only our abstract concepts and values to our adolescents. And since they have not shared in the process whereby we insensibly adjusted these to our experience of reality, when they come relatively suddenly onto the adult scene, with open eyes they correctly perceive the discrepancies between our precepts and our practice. Moreover, they do not have our commitment to the ways of life we have worked out or our need to rely on them because of personal investment. Since adolescence is a developmental period marked by a rapid increase in the capacity for abstract conceptualization and an interest in active exploration and analysis of the world, adolescents often confront us with fundamental questions about our adult ways. Their lack of adult bias and stereotyped thinking may frequently result in their seeing a situation more clearly and truly than we do. They propose valuable innovative approaches precisely because they are not aware of those "facts of life" to which we, possibly ill-advisedly, have accommodated ourselves.

Whether or not there is merit in their questions, criticisms, and proposals, it is inevitable that these will often irritate and unsettle us, because they attack our defenses and our accustomed ways of thinking. It is also not unlikely that we will express our irritation in negative ways such as by the belittling of *ad hominem* arguments and suppressive behavior. This is aggravated by the common tensions that arise from the adolescents' need to repudiate the adults on whom they have been dependent as children in order to develop their own autonomy.

The problem is exacerbated in technologically advanced societies, such as in the United States and Europe, by the necessity to keep adolescents out of the labor market for as long as possible. This is partly the result of our current inability to adjust to automation without producing unemployment, and the consequent need to reduce the labor force by the crude method of restricting input. It is also the result of increased demands on the individual knowledge and specialized skill of workers who must manage ever more complicated machines and cope with their frequent changes. This means that the demand for unskilled or semiskilled labor, which in the past was supplied largely by the adolescent population, has been drastically reduced. The net result has been a policy of prolonging the schooling of adolescents. This has been rationalized as being for their own good, but it seems that this is only partly true. Moreover, the rapidity of rise in the school-leaving age and a natural lag in the development of our educational system to cope with the novel demands of the current man-power situation have resulted in an overburdening of our teaching resources and a prolongation, relatively unchanged, of a schooling process that was originally designed for late childhood and early adolescence. This is clearly unsuited to the needs of many older adolescents, and they perceive it as the denial of an opportunity for the meaningful participation in the activities of society for which their native capacities fit them, as well as a way of being arbitrarily held back from economic independence and personal autonomy.

Rapidity of change in the work field and increasing size and complexity of automated industry mean that few adolescents can utilize their parents or older family members as occupational role models, as was the case in the past; nor can these familiar adults offer much guidance in starting and shaping their work careers. We shall deal later in this book with some of the problems this presents us in trying to develop new ways to bridge the gap from school to work and to provide organized community services to fulfill a function that for past generations was largely accomplished privately by family and friends.

In the technologically underdeveloped countries of Africa, Asia, and South America, the situation of adolescents is different, but not less complex. In such countries rapid advances in public health have led to a recent dramatic lowering of infant and child mortality, so that the adolescent population has considerably expanded. Political independence and the communication and transportation revolutions have provided previously isolated and underdeveloped countries with a sudden opportunity to enter the modern world. The ecological upset and the new threat to survival consequent on the population explosion make this essential, but a relatively small number of the older adults in these countries are physically or educationally fit to fulfill the new demands. These burdens must be shouldered by the young adults and older adolescents. It is notable that in these rapidly developing countries much of the revolutionary leadership comes from student groups.

The significance of this situation for the patterning of adolescent development and for the emergence of mental health and psychiatric problems remains for the future to determine. Unfortunately, this book does not deal with the topic, since it has been based on the experience of practitioners and researchers from the technologically advanced societies, and even in these, it has focused mainly on problems usually seen by psychiatrists who work largely with middle-class patients in cities.

In addition to this restriction in focus, our book does not attempt to deal systematically and comprehensively with all the consequences for adolescents of living in our changing world. It does, however, deal with certain of those consequences which have current salience for child psychiatrists and for their colleagues in allied fields of clinical practice, program planning and administration, and biopsychosocial research. Some issues are meagerly represented in our book, not because they are unimportant, but because we lack the information to give valid answers to the questions. For example, are the special stresses and challenges of the present day responsible for a change (*a*) in the patterns of adolescent personality development or (*b*) in the frequency and type of psychiatric manifestations? The first section of the book provides some indication that we have noticed no basic change in patterns of personality development, although a later section suggests that antipoverty programs in the United States may result in significantly promoting the development of abstract thinking among hitherto deprived subpopulations in city slums. This may have important implications both for their personality patterns and for their vulnerability to delinquency. We also lack the necessary information to answer the second half of the question. We include a chapter on changes in suicide rates in various countries that seem to be related to changes in sociocultural factors, but we know of no valid data on changes in the incidence and prevalence of psychiatric conditions among adolescents over time in different cultures which would allow us to give a meaningful answer to this question. We also do not know whether our present-day conditions of life are producing new illnesses or syndromes, apart from the superficial coloring of symptoms which is obviously related to the cultural idiom of the day. One possible exception to this is the apparent increase in eating disorders, to which we devote special attention in Section IV, and which appears to be specifically related to the ready availability of food in affluent societies, so that conflicts about overeating take on particular significance. On the other hand, we have no comparison studies carried out in deprived populations to confirm that the ready availability of food is an important predisposing factor to increased prevalence of such syndromes.

It may be thought that drug abuse is a psychiatric condition dependent on environmental factors (for example, the availability of relevant substances to be used) and that there are indications that this condition is occurring more frequently and more severely among adolescents at present than in the past. We devote a chapter to a consideration of this topic, which is certainly arousing much interest today in the Western world. On the other hand, there have usually been intoxicating or hypnotic substances available in the past (in addition to alcohol, such substances as ether and chloral hydrate were once fashionable among young people), and we have no grounds for judging whether drug abuse is commoner today than in previous generations. In fact, we do not even have valid statistics on the incidence and prevalence of drug use at the present time.

The reason, therefore, that this book does not deal with many important aspects of our central theme is not that our writers are not interested, but that we do not have the necessary knowledge. We do not know what we should about changes in the nature and frequency of patterns of mental health and mental disorder over time and in respect to different life situations. We do, however, have a growing body of clinical information and insight and of research results derived from current studies of adolescents in their environmental settings in the United States and Europe, and our book is devoted to the description and discussion of this material by a group of leading clinicians and researchers drawn from eleven countries, who came together at the Sixth International Congress of Child Psychiatry in Edinburgh in July 1966.

The book is a successor to *Emotional Problems of Early Childhood* * and *Prevention of Mental Disorders in Children: Initial Explorations.*† Like them, it is not an edited version of conference proceedings, but a cohesive treatment of its subject derived from some of the papers originally prepared for a congress, many of which have subsequently been modified by their authors, and which have been welded together by editorial comments.

The continuity of themes has been obtained by appropriate selection from the very large pool of papers prepared for a major international meeting and also from the integrating activities of an International Preparatory Commission that met annually between 1962 and 1966 to study and circumscribe the topic and to choose the congress speakers. The Commission produced a book ‡ which was read by participants prior to the congress and provided a common frame of reference.

The editors are responsible for the final choice of papers and for asking some of the authors to contribute additional material. This has been no easy task and necessarily introduces an additional source of personal bias in our attempt to produce a valid picture of the range of international interest and opinion among child psychiatrists and allied professionals about present-day adolescents in relation to current trends in psychiatric theory and practice. We have made no attempt to impose a standardized format on our contributors and have done a minimum of stylistic editorializing, so as to preserve the individualized flavor of each author's chapter.

The book that has emerged consists of three main parts, subdivided into six sections. The first part (Sections I, II, and III) is devoted to a discussion of the healthy and unhealthy ways adolescents in our society develop, as they are influenced by and in turn exert an influence on the complex of forces—physical, affective, cognitive, psychosocial, sociocultural, and socioeconomic—which impinge on them. The emphasis of most of our contributors is on the need for a multifactorial approach to an understanding of adolescent normal and pathological development and for the realization that despite the emergence of general patterns which are related to psychosocial and sociocultural situational characteristics, each adolescent's rate and type of development has features that are idiosyncratic and can be understood only by a depth analysis of his own bodily characteristics, personality, and network of human relationships.

The second part (Sections IV and V) discusses psychiatric conditions and their treatment. It deals with topics such as depression, drug addiction, and eating disturbances among adolescents, which are arousing much current interest; with some very interesting studies of problems of communica-

* New York: Basic Books, 1955.
† New York: Basic Books, 1961.
‡ G. Caplan and S. Lebovici, eds., *Psychiatric Approaches to Adolescence* (Amsterdam: Excerpta Medica Foundation, 1966).

tion between adolescents and adults and their implications for treatment; and with new theoretical models that provide a basis for more effective and economical methods of treatment.

The final portion (Section VI) discusses the problems of organizing mental health services for adolescents in communities that are becoming committed to the right of every inhabitant to receive adequate treatment. We review the consequent need to plan services for an entire population and not just to organize clinics or hospitals that undertake responsibility only for selected patients who come for treatment. This shift to a population focus took place many years ago in the Communist countries of eastern Europe. In western Europe it has occurred in recent years as a consequence of developments in enlightened welfare-state legislation; and in the United States it has come most recently as a result of social security measures, the civil rights and antipoverty movements, and the democratic pressure on government of the consumer population. Whatever its origin, this change is exerting a major influence on the patterning of services for the promotion of mental health and the prevention and control of mental disorder among adolescents as part of a comprehensive program of health, education, and welfare services for people of all ages and classes.

Gerald Caplan

September 1968   Serge Lebovici

ACKNOWLEDGMENT

We are pleased to acknowledge our deep gratitude to the Grant Foundation of New York which financed the work of our International Study Group and helped defray the expenses of the Sixth International Congress of the International Association for Child Psychiatry and Allied Professions, Edinburgh, July 1966.

CONTENTS

SECTION III   THE TRANSITION FROM SCHOOL TO WORK

SECTION IV   PSYCHIATRIC DISORDERS

A. Eating Problems

B. Depression and Suicide

SECTION V   PSYCHIATRIC TREATMENT

A. Problems in Communication

B. Philosophies of Treatment

SECTION VI   COMMUNITY MENTAL HEALTH SERVICES FOR ADOLESCENTS

SECTION

I

DEVELOPMENT
ISSUES

EDITORS' INTRODUCTION We open this first section of our book with a chapter by Anna Freud which summarizes the manifestations of adolescence as an expectable transitional phase of upset between the relatively stable psychological worlds of childhood and adult life. She points to alterations in drives, ego organization, object relations, and social roles that characterize this period and force a move from the psychosocial equilibrium of the child within his family through a phase of inevitable developmental disturbance to adult independence.

This thesis is taken up and elaborated by Osterrieth in Chapter 2. He characterizes late childhood as a period of coherence and stability, in which the child has become well adapted to his family and to the outside world and pursues an integrated, harmonious, and unself-conscious existence. In contrast, he sees the adolescent in a state of psychological flux, many of whose manifestations can be understood as an active and usually self-conscious search for a new identity, different from that of childhood, but for some years not yet stabilized as that of adulthood. Osterrieth emphasizes the mutative importance of two principal developmental factors in the adolescent: changes in his body and in his intellectual capacities. He examines the significance of bodily development, not only the sexual but also the increase in size and muscle power, both in regard to the adolescent's self-concept and also in altering his status in comparison with his parents and other adults. He stresses the concomitant and equally dramatic increases in intellectual capacity, especially that of abstract reasoning. He interprets the

1

fundamental manifestations of the period as the active striving and searching for a new identity consonant with the new powers and with the reverberations of these in the adolescent's relationships with his family and the
adult world.

Osterrieth, like Anna Freud, sees the frequent crisis upsets of adolescence not as undesirable, despite the discomfort they cause all concerned,
but as necessary epiphenomena of the exploratory trials and errors of the
search for a new sense of self and social role. He sees the frequent opposition to the values of the adult world not as destructive rebelliousness, but as
both an exercise of newly developed powers of abstract thinking which
makes philosophical doubtings and debates an exciting pastime and also a
testing of the authenticity and worth of a position before one accepts it as a
part of one's self. He interprets the peer group and the adolescent subculture as an island of refuge where the adolescents can relax and take a
breathing spell in conforming to a code they all know is temporary, and also
as a base camp from which to renew their attempts to scale their mountains.

Chapter 3, by Piaget, describes and clarifies the details of the new attain-
ments of the adolescent in the realm of abstract thinking. This is contrasted
with the limited reasoning system of the preadolescent, which is pegged to
actual perceptions. The reasoning of the adolescent advances to a logic of
propositions by which he can reason entirely abstractly on the basis of verbal or symbolic statements. This frees him to manipulate ideas in themselves rather than restricting him to the manipulation of concrete objects.

Piaget ends his chapter by raising an interesting unanswered question. He
points out how the newly developed capacity for abstract thinking enables
adolescents in our society to take their place as independent actors in our
adult world, but he wonders whether the nature of the tribal organization in
underdeveloped societies, in which the adult roles are circumscribed by
conservative traditions and close social control, demands such abstract reasoning. He implies that if this type of logic is not needed it may not develop.
He points to the need, also, for comparative research on the cognitive development of adolescents in the lower socioeconomic classes of our own
society to see whether here, too, a possible lack of social necessity among
adults is associated with a reduced individual cognitive capacity among
adolescents.

Schonfeld, in the following chapter, provides us with an authoritative
review of current research on the physical aspects of adolescent development. He defines the stages of adolescence and links these with those of
physical development, or pubescence. He gives a detailed chronological account of expectable changes in boys and girls and emphasizes the normal
range of variations which are complicated by the fact that body tissues grow
at separate rates. This is a matter of importance to the clinician who is
often consulted by an anxious adolescent or his parents because development seems to them to be taking place faster or slower than their expectations, and they fear abnormality. Schonfeld also discusses the significance

to the adolescent of differing in rate of development from the norms of his peer group at a period when such difference is often equated with inferiority.

In the second part of his chapter, Schonfeld analyzes the reverberations in psychological development produced by the adolescent's subjective perceptions of his bodily changes and of the reactions to these changes by others. He discusses the concept of body-image as a core of ego identity or self-awareness and as a bridge involving body-percept and body-concept. He then describes some of the problems that result when the rapid physical changes of adolescence demand a major revision of body-image at the very time when the individual is in the midst of emotional turmoil because of the other psychological, psychosocial, and sociocultural forces with which he is involved.

Chapter 5, by Anthony, deals with another major influence on adolescent development which in the past we have tended to neglect, namely, the network of perceptions and expectations within which adolescents are held by the adults and which often forms the basis for self-fulfilling predictions. Anthony analyzes the elements of this network, which often take the form of ambivalent stereotypes that tend to force the adolescent to take on either of two unwelcome polar roles. He gives details of some of these, such as dangerous victimizer and endangered victim; sexually rampant and sexually inadequate; and emotionally maladjusted and emotionally freer than adults. He analyzes some of the psychosocial and sociocultural sources of the stereotypes and discusses their implications for distorting family relationships and disturbing the work of clinicians, who are often caught up in them. He discusses how unsolved problems from the adolescent phase of the adult's development or current personality problems of the adult become intertwined with these stereotypes and may complicate relationships with the adolescent. He ends with a plea that adults should recognize that adolescents are particular people and should make a special effort to dissipate their stereotyped perceptions and expectations that provoke adolescents to respond by setting up "barriers to communication, excluding the adult by a conspiracy of silence or by a language and culture of their own."

In Chapter 6, Redl brings this section to a close by analyzing the responses of adolescents to the attitudes and actions of the adults as well as to all the developmental forces and constraints discussed by the other authors. He begins by disagreeing with those who, like Osterrieth, see adolescence as a phase of emigration from the stability of late childhood and immigration to the stability of adulthood. He points out that the phase from which the adolescent moves is itself characterized by "organismic disorganization," and he lists the signs of "loosening of existing personality structure" of the latency child that immediately precede the changes of puberty. He points to the difficulty experienced by clinicians in differentiating the normal developmental phenomena of preadolescence from the apparently identical picture found in the early stages of serious mental disorder. He also emphasizes that already during preadolescence the old primary identification of the child with the family group weakens and is replaced by a new identification with the peer group. He then goes on to differentiate what he calls "the pure psychiatric core" of growth processes that are inherent in all adolescents, more or less irrespective of cultural and historical locus, and the specific pattern of the growing-up process that is based on the interplay of this with the influences of the current environmental reality, its cultural expectations, and its socioeconomic opportunities and constraints.

Redl discusses the complexity of the matrix of forces to which the adolescent is obliged to respond, and he lists a number of these, endogenous and exogenous, physical, psychosocial, and sociocultural. He then continues with a penetrating analysis of some of the special predicaments faced by adolescents in our culture, which are mainly based on the hypocrisy, the ambivalence, the prejudice, as well as the unfortunate side effects of helpful policies, of our adult world. Like Anthony, he points to the particular burdens that we adults often unthinkingly heap on our adolescents.

The remainder of the chapter is devoted to a discussion of some of the characteristic patterns used by adolescents in coping with these burdens and challenges. Redl focuses on those which have particular relevance to clinicians, because they complicate or obstruct our traditional patterns of analytic psychotherapy. He makes brief mention of the fact that many, if not most, adolescents also make use of coping patterns that do not come to the attention of clinicians, but enable them to master the crisis tasks of this period so that they emerge with relatively healthy adult personalities; but neither he, nor Anthony in the preceding chapter, is able to throw much light on these. We are left with the realization that the major task of uncovering the details of the healthy patterns of adolescent coping is still a matter for future research. The special merit of Redl's chapter is its very tentativeness, its thought-provoking emphasis on the tremendously complicated nature of the system of forces involved in adolescent development, and its plea to avoid oversimplification and to continue our search for further knowledge in this field.

1

Adolescence as a Developmental Disturbance

Anna Freud

THE PSYCHOANALYTIC VIEW
OF MENTAL HEALTH AND ILLNESS

Our psychoanalytic investigations of individuals have convinced us that the line of demarcation between mental health and illness cannot be drawn as sharply as had been thought before. Especially so far as the neuroses are concerned, neurotic nuclei are found in the minds of normal people as regularly as large areas of normal functioning are part of the makeup of every neurotic. Also, people cross and recross the border between mental health and illness many times during their lives.

There is the further point that the concept of health as it is derived from the physical field cannot be taken over to the mental side without alteration. Physically, we are healthy so long as the various organs of the body function normally and, via their specific action, contribute to an over-all state of well-being. Mentally, more than this is needed. It is not enough if each part of the mind, as such, is intact, since the various parts of our personality pursue different aims and since these aims are only too often at cross purposes with each other. Thus, we may be healthy so far as our instinctual drives are concerned; or our sense of reality plus adaptation to the environment may be well up to the mark; or our ideals may be considered admirable by other people. Nevertheless, these single items do not yet add up to the result of mental health. To achieve this, all the agencies in our mind—drives, reasonable ego, and ideals—have to coincide sensibly and, while adapting to the external world, resolve the conflicts inherent in the total situation. To say it in other words: mental health depends on work-

5

able compromises and on the resulting balance of forces between the different internal agencies and different external and internal demands.

THE CONCEPT OF DEVELOPMENTAL DISTURBANCES

It is implied in the view above that this balance and these compromises are precarious and easily upset by any alteration in the internal or external circumstances. It is obvious also that such changes are as inevitable as they are continuous and that they occur especially frequently on the basis of development. Every step forward in growth and maturation brings with it not only new gains but also new problems. To the psychoanalyst this means that change in any part of mental life upsets the balance as it had been established earlier and that new compromises have to be devised. Such change may affect the instinctual drives, as happens in adolescence; or it may occur in the ego, that is, in the agency whose function it is to manage and control the drives; or what undergoes change may be the individual's demands on himself, his aims and ideals or his love objects in the external world or other influences in his environment. Changes may be quantitative or qualitative. Whatever they are, they affect the internal equilibrium.

Developmental disturbances of this type are frequent occurrences, for example, in the area of sleep and food intake in early childhood. Infants may be perfect sleepers in the first half-year of life, that is, drop off to sleep whenever they are tired and when no stimuli from inside or outside their bodies are strong enough to disrupt their peace. This will alter with normal further growth when the child's clinging to the people and happenings in his environment make it difficult for him to withdraw into himself and when falling asleep thereby is turned into a conflictful process. Likewise, the disturbing food fads of childhood are no more than the impact on eating of various infantile fantasies, of dirt, of impregnation through the mouth, of poisoning, of killing. These fantasies are tied to specific developmental phases and are transitory accordingly, as are the feeding disorders based on them. In fact, in clinical practice with children, the concept of transitory developmental disturbances has become indispensable to us as a diagnostic category.

It is worth noting here that developmental change not only causes upset but can also effect what is called spontaneous cures. A case in point here is the temper tantrums that serve young children as affective-motor outlets at a time when no other discharge is available to them. This is altered by the mere fact of speech development that opens up new pathways and by which the earlier turbulent and chaotic behavioral manifestation is rendered redundant.

THE ADOLESCENT REACTIONS AS PROTOTYPES OF DEVELOPMENTAL DISTURBANCES

Let us return to the problems of adolescence that, in my view, are the prototypes of such developmental upsets.

Although in the childhood disorders of this nature we are confronted usually with alterations in one or the other area of the child's personality, in adolescence we deal with changes along the whole line. There are, as a basis on the physical side, the changes in size, strength, and appearance. There are the endocrinological changes that aim at a complete revolution in sexual life. There are changes in the aggressive expressions, advances in intellectual performance, reorientations as to object attachments and to social relations. In short, the upheavals in character and personality are often so sweeping that the picture of the former child becomes wholly submerged in the newly emerging image of the adolescent.

A. Alterations in the Drives

So far as the sexual drive in adolescence is concerned, I have found it useful to differentiate between quantitative and qualitative changes. What we see first, in the period of preadolescence, is an indiscriminate increase in drive activity that affects all the facets which have characterized infantile sexuality, that is, the pregenital, sexual-aggressive responses of the first five years of life. At this juncture, the preadolescent individual becomes, as a first step, hungrier, greedier, more cruel, more dirty, more inquisitive, more boastful, more egocentric, more inconsiderate than he has been before. This exacerbation of the pregenital elements is followed then, shortly after, by a change in the quality of the drive, namely the changeover from pregenital to genital sexual impulses. This new element involves the adolescent in dangers which did not exist before and with which he is not accustomed to deal. Since, at this stage, he lives and functions still as a member of his family unit, he runs the risk of allowing the new genital urges to connect with his old love objects, that is, with his parents, brothers, or sisters.

B. Alterations in the Ego Organization

It is these temptations of giving way, first to sexual-aggressive pregenital behavior and, next, to incestuous fantasies or even actions that cause all those ego changes which impress the observer as the adolescent's personal upheaval and also as his unpredictability. Serious attempts are made by the preadolescent to keep the quantitative drive increase under control as drive activity has been controlled in earlier periods. This is done by means of major efforts on the side of the defenses. It means bringing into play more repressions, more reaction formations, more identifications and projections, sometimes also more determined attempts at intellectualizations and sublimations. It means also that the entire defensive system of the ego is overstrained and breaks down repeatedly and that therefore the frantic warding off of impulses alternates with unrestrained upsurges of drive activity. When we approach a young adolescent at this stage, we never know which of these two aspects we are going to meet: his overstrict, highly defended personality or his openly aggressive, openly sexual, uninhibited primitive self.

C. Alterations in Object Relations

What serves the preadolescent as some protection against the quantitative pressure of the drives proves wholly inadequate against the qualitative change to a primacy of the genital urges, that is, adult sexuality proper. Nothing helps here except a complete discarding of the people who were the important love objects of the child, that is, the parents. This battle against the parents is fought out in a variety of ways: by openly displayed indifference toward them—by denying that they are important—by disparagement of them since it is easier to do without them if they are denounced as stupid, useless, ineffective; by open insolence and revolt against their persons and the beliefs and conventions for which they stand. That these reactions alternate also with returns to helplessness and dependence on the part of the young persons does not make it any easier for the parents. Obviously, the task imposed on them is a double one: to be thick-skinned, self-effacing, and reserved, but also to change over at a moment's notice to being as sympathetic, concerned, alert, and helpful as in former times.

The closer the tie between child and parent has been before, the more bitter and violent will be the struggle for independence from them in adolescence.

D. Alterations in Ideals and Social Relations

The adolescent's change in social relationships follows as the direct consequence of his stepping out of his family. He is not only left without his earlier object ties. Together with the attachment to his parents, he has thrown out also the ideals that he shared with them formerly, and he needs to find substitutes for both.

There is a parting of the ways here which, I believe, produces two different types of adolescent culture. Some adolescents put into the empty place of the parents a self-chosen leader who himself is a member of the parent generation. This person may be a university teacher, a poet, a philosopher, a politician. Whoever he may be, he is considered infallible, Godlike, and is

followed gladly and blindly. At present, though, this solution is comparatively rare. More frequent is the second course where the peer group as such
or a member of it is exalted to the role of leadership and becomes the
unquestioned arbiter in all matters of moral and aesthetic value.

The hallmark of the new ideals as well as of the new emotionally important people is always the same: that they should be as different as possible
from the former ones. In the remote past, when I myself was adolescent,
there had come into being in central Europe the so-called Youth Movement, a first attempt at an independent adolescent culture. This was directed against the bourgeois complacency and capitalistic outlook of the
parent generation of the period, and the ideals upheld by it were those of
socialism, intellectual freedom, aestheticism, and so on. Poetry, art, and
classical music were what parents did not believe in, although adolescents
did. We know how far the tide has turned in the last two generations. At
present, adolescents are hard put to set up new ideals—constructive or disastrous—which can serve to mark the dividing line between their own and
their parents' lives.

CONCLUDING REMARKS

To the abbreviated summary of the main theme given above, I add a few
concluding remarks that concern more general issues.

First, it has struck me always as unfortunate that the period of adolescent upheaval and inner rearrangement of forces coincides with such major
demands on the individual as those for academic achievements in school
and college, for a choice of career, for increased social and financial responsibility in general. Many failures, often with tragic consequences in
these respects, are due not to the individual's incapacity as such but merely
to the fact that such demands are made on him at a time of life when all his
energies are engaged otherwise, namely, in trying to solve the major problems created for him by normal sexual growth and development.

Second, I feel that the obvious preponderance of sexual problems in adolescence is in danger of obscuring the concomitant role of aggression that,
possibly, might be of great significance. It is worth noting that countries
which are engaged in a struggle for existence, such as, for example, Israel,
do not report the same difficulties with their adolescents as we do in the
Western world. The main difference in their situation is that the aggression
of the young people is not lived out within the family or community but
directed against the enemy forces that threaten the state and therefore use-
fully employed in socially approved warlike activities. Since this is a factor
outside the sphere of sexual growth, this should extend our thinking into
new directions.

Third and last, it seems to me an error not to consider the details of the
adolescent revolt in the light of side issues, disturbing as they may be. If we

wish to maintain the developmental point of view, it is of less significance how the adolescent behaves at home, in school, at the university, or in the community at large. What is of major importance is to know which type of adolescent upheaval is more apt than others to lead to a satisfactory form of adult life.

2

Adolescence:
Some Psychological Aspects

Paul A. Osterrieth

Adolescence can be considered in many different ways and in many perspectives. It is different at different times, in different cultures, and in different milieus. Less is known about adolescence than about childhood from the point of view of psychology, probably because of the greater variety of its modes of appearance. Any attempt at synthesis can easily be incomplete, and although it may appear acceptable to some it may be arguable to others.

Passing into Adolescence

It is so usual to consider adolescence as a particular stage that it may not be a bad thing to recall at the outset that it is above all and always the normal and unavoidable continuation of childhood. It would seem to be an exaggeration to see a hiatus, a break, between the two periods. There is little doubt that the psychic structure of the adolescent has its roots in childhood and that many of the characteristics that are generally considered as typical of adolescence appear and are already present during late childhood. In practice it is not easy to place a precise limit somewhere between the ages of 11 and 14; if the young person who shares our family life clearly appears to us one day as an adolescent, it is nevertheless impossible to state that the day before he was still a child.

Perhaps what seems to us most characteristic in the adolescent can best be distinguished in contrast to the period from about 9 to 12 years which some authors have justly qualified as "infantile maturity." The child of this age indeed shows, in general, a consistent and well-balanced psychic structure. His behavior is well adapted to the circumstances in which he finds

11

himself and to the goals he pursues; the individual is well integrated in the family group as well as in his group of friends of the same age; he is happy in his school life. He shows an active and self-assured interest in the surrounding world. The older child enjoys a well-established social status; he is capable of organizing himself and of confronting all kinds of circumstances with a real autonomy, whose limitations he can nevertheless accept. If some conflicts alter inevitably his relationships with others, with his equals, with adult authority, they do not generally give rise to profound disturbances. From the intellectual point of view, the projective subjectivism and the adualism of the first years have gradually given place to a more objective orientation, less self-centered, and to a logical structuring of the different sectors of concrete experience, making possible correct and generally coherent reasoning. The older child has at his disposition a considerable gamut of solutions and methods of coping that allow him to solve all kinds of problems, insofar as they present themselves in concrete terms. Proper emphasis is given to his intellectual availability, his curiosity, his thirst for information, his tendency to general classing of the diverse series of information that he receives in school, in the street, in his reading, or in the investigations of all kinds he pursues so arduously. Although he seems especially oriented toward the exterior world, toward people and things, there is nonetheless the development of an interior world within him, which he will know how to protect, if he has to, against incursions by others. His parents doubtless remain for him the preferential center of reference that they have been since the beginning, but the family is no longer his only pole of attraction; the older child moves about easily and in a coherent way in a relatively extensive material and social universe, which he explores with enthusiasm and about which he has learned that it is objective and exterior to him, but that he has his place in it. In short, he is a well-integrated, active, flourishing, happy small person who "has a good hold on himself" and demonstrates the existence of working organs of control. If he happens to be a dreamer, his behavior is nonetheless scarcely problematic.

It is in this willingly harmonious context that, between the ages of about 11 and 15, a whole series of profound modifications will take place, which will affect organic equilibrium as well as intellectual structure, the social and affective integration as well as the image that the individual has of himself and of his environment. It is not easy to describe with precision the order in which these different modifications will take place—modifications that continue to react on one another. What is certain is that they will bring about a questioning and upsetting of the psychic economy that was a result of the years of childhood. And because, as Maurice Debesse[1] has already pointed out so clearly, they take place in an individual already psychologically organized and structured and already integrated socially, they can only provoke in him an intense problemization of self and therefore an intense centering on self. It has been stated, in a very schematic manner, that the child lives in a way that is somehow exterior to himself, in the continual projection of an ego that is generally unaware of itself, whereas the adolescent, on the contrary, lives inside himself, relating everything to himself, continually taking stock of himself, seeking to find himself, so to speak, through others, being the main center of interest for himself. The statement is perhaps excessive and should be qualified; but it seems clearly to sum up something essential. The young adolescent who is changing watches himself change; he is attentive to his transformation. He is not content to undergo these changes: he is going to undertake them. How could he himself not be the center of his preoccupations?

PHYSICAL ASPECTS AND THEIR EFFECTS

At about the age of 10 for a girl, at about 12 for a boy, the somatic transformations of puberty begin to appear, and for most people they constitute the principal characteristic of entry into adolescence and the motivation of the other changes of this age. These phenomena are studied in detail in the chapter by Schonfeld, and we can dispense with further discussion here. But the enormous psychological effects, which do not always receive enough attention, should be pointed out. The fact already described by Dimock[2] is a good example. In studying muscular strength in the boy, Dimock found that it practically doubled between the ages of 12 and 16. It is easy to understand that such an increase in muscular strength will have obvious psychological effects. On the one hand, it is doubtless of a kind to bring about behavior that is more energetic, more expansive, that favors certain kinds of valuation and authorizes a greater self-confidence. New potentialities permit new, more spectacular feats, performances by means of which the young person is brought considerably closer to the adult. For the boy who is growing up, the possibility of being equal to and even of surpassing his father in the matter of physical performance is thus outlined and will soon be confirmed. It is not only his own image of himself that is modified but also the image he has of his father, who was previously prestigious and unsurpassable. On the other hand, one may also say—and it is not without importance for our thesis—that the father himself will doubtless also modify the idea he has of his son. The demands he makes on him, his willingness to help him, to protect or direct him, will be altered, as well as the image the father has of himself in relation to his growing boy. A whole scale of relations is transformed on the basis of a somatic modification apparently of secondary importance in our culture.

An analogous situation can be thought to exist for the whole series of organic transformations characteristic of puberty, whether it is a question of growth in stature and in weight, a refinement in the senses of smell, of taste, of touch, modifications in skin structure, the appearance of secondary sexual characteristics, the development of the genital system. Each of these changes has its effects on the behavioral level, leads to re-evaluations and to a shifting adjustment of attitudes, contributes to a modification of the individual's image of himself and the way in which he perceives others. Each of them, finally, because of its effects on the young person, is also susceptible of setting off new reactions in the people around him. The fact of "having" a body that changes, of being a body in the process of change, cannot help drawing the attention of the individual toward this changing body and therefore toward the ego. It is this meeting of the individual with himself that is expressed so well in the classic image of the boy or the girl studying himself in the mirror and trying to find out who he or she is. It must not be forgotten that for the former child, here is an event that is highly significant, that is of capital importance: the change that is taking place in his person constitutes the most obvious evidence of his gradual accession to the adult state that people have been dangling before his eyes for so many years as a kind of supreme goal.

However, these transformations are no longer simply undergone and carried out like those that take place in the young child. At the age of 13 or 14, one necessarily participates in the culture of the human group to which one belongs; these transformations also call for the adoption of an attitude, and they are judged and integrated in relation to a frame of reference that is intellectual, social, and moral. A good example can be found in the frequent phenomenon of masturbation, evidently associated with the pubertal "resensualization." Undoubtedly, the young person discovers in it, or rediscovers, certain specific satisfactions. But they now have a meaning, as is witnessed by the erotic fantasies or the more or less precise images that begin to accompany them and, as certain authors have pointed out, that in some way orient the young person in an anticipative manner toward the search for a sexual partner. Moreover, these practices and these fantasies are inseparable from the adoption of a moral position, from a judgment of oneself: either they are tolerated, even sought after, with all sorts of supporting justifications or else they arouse feelings of guilt and unworthiness, which we well know to be of a nature that is disturbing to the socioaffective adaptation of the young person.

INTELLECTUAL ASPECTS

This evaluation, this meeting with oneself, takes place simultaneously on another level—the level of intellectual development. We are especially indebted to the work of Jean Piaget and his colleagues[4, 5] for putting forth evidence of the profound evolution of the intellectual structures between the ages of 11 and 15. This evolution is known to be characterized by the appearance of logic in propositions, by the passage of the thought process from the concrete to the hypotheticodeductive level. The older child reasoned about present objects, concrete situations, by establishing relationships between these objects or these situations. The young adolescent becomes capable of reasoning about the relationships between relationships, thus raising himself above the concrete level. At the beginning of adolescence there takes place the building up of a network of combinatory operations, which are the crowning of the intellectual evolution and which, giving internal coherence to the thought process, will be the authority for a rigorous reasoning based on assumptions and hypotheses, without regard for their truth or their material reality and without resort to a control by experience and facts. A world constructed by the thought process will thus be superimposed on a world presented by the senses. On the specific and circumscript rules available to the older child is now superimposed a scale of laws and principles that govern the most varied domains: formal thought will be applied to every context and everything will be grist for logical organization. Thus, at about the age of 15, the structural evolution of thought will be achieved, precisely at the level of development where the authors of the classic scales in testing came up against the impossibility of finding proofs distinguishing two successive ages.

There is barely any doubt, as Piaget himself has shown, that this evolution of an intellectual order contributes profoundly to giving adolescent mentality its specific character. To reason is for the young person a need and a pleasure; the "constructs of the mind" are a delight. He reasons every which way, about subjects that are most unreal and farthest from his experience. Most positively, this evolution takes into account not only the interest that young people show in discussion but also their fascination with general questions, with artistic, scientific, political, philosophical, and social problems. The arrival at abstraction permits the individual to delve into the systems of collective representation that are offered to him by the culture in which he is growing up, and he will gradually become carried away by ideas, ideals, and values. This enthusiasm will probably at first have little order or system, as though it were really a game of ideas, of hypotheses, of systems; he will throw himself into it without much self-criticism, with hardly any sense of relativity. As one author has noted, it is the blooming of "exclusive certitudes that follow one another as they are discovered." Everything will be food for thought, for spoken thought, for passionate discussion, for endless discussions, for peremptory affirmation, and the adult, losing his footing a little in this tidal wave, will often fail to perceive that what he takes to be vain rehashing or sterile questioning of old worn-out problems corresponds in reality, for the youngster, to useful explorations and true discoveries.

But what the youngster discovers above all in this disordered and voluntarily chaotic exploration is himself in the process of thinking, his interiority. By getting away from the concrete, by reasoning, by "concentrating," by trying out hypotheses, he meets up with himself. Who is he, this person who thinks, who adopts an attitude, who speaks his opinion? What is he? What is it in him, what is this center where his ideas are shaped, where his thoughts are produced, where his assumptions are formulated? Is it not himself? And doubtless he will have an impression of interior freedom, of profound originality, of authenticity, and also, therefore, of responsibility:

he will feel himself involved by the fact of his freedom. It is apparent that intellectual transformations bring the youngster to ask himself questions about himself, to wonder, to acknowledge himself, just as much as do the physical transformations and just about at the same time. The values that the adolescent is "trying out," not without paradoxes and sophisms, the opinions that he defends sometimes with as much fire as thoughtlessness, are these not just so many ways of looking for himself, of defining himself, so many attempts to be and to become himself? The affirmation or the vigorous defense of self shows through very clearly in the attempts to convince, to astonish, or to shock the person he is speaking to, and Arnold Gesell [3] wrote of these attempts that, although the youngster loves to discuss, it is impossible to have a discussion with him! Finally, it is still himself that the adolescent meets in his dream world, in the gratuitous world of the imaginary where he loves to withdraw and which is like a relaxed and easy counterpart of rigorous abstract thought: whether he follows the steps of ordered thought or whether he dreams away while listening to his favorite record, it is always himself that he finds; it is on himself that he centers his thinking.

SOCIOAFFECTIVE ASPECTS

During the time that the transformations discussed above take place, the youngster has to face the many changes that appear in the attitudes of the people around him, in his position with regard to the social group, in the role that is presented to him. He is told that he is "growing up" and that new kinds of behavior are expected of him. Assuredly, certain rights, certain advantages, which did not belong to the child, are accorded to him; but, in return, new demands and new responsibilities are imposed on him, and certain former privileges are lost. The youngster changes schools or his school program; he is confronted with discipline and methods that are new to him; he must make decisions as to what will come after his studies, as to their orientation. His childhood friends are scattered; he enters new groups where he seems small next to the big ones, a novice, whereas he was formerly big among the little ones; he has to adopt the ways of the big ones so that he will seem to be "up to par." Advertising accentuates this changeover by telling the youngster that he is one of the "teen-agers," by soliciting his buying power, by awakening new desires, new interests.

Is it then surprising that after the assured competence of the older child come the hesitation, the awkwardness, the contradictions, of the adolescent? On the one hand, he is confronted with himself in the process of change and with a new way of looking at himself and at the things he does; on the other hand, he is confronted by circumstances and demands that he has not had to measure up to before. All his habits, all his old and tried assurance, are brought into question, not without a certain nostalgia at times; and although the seductions of novelty are vivid, they still have more than one disturbing aspect. In this respect, an important question confronts the individual in his ambivalence and his unsureness. Not always in explicit terms, of course, but with a nagging persistence, the questions worry him: who am I, what am I worth, am I good enough? It is probably in the context of this questioning, which is a kind of leitmotiv of the early years of adolescence, that one of the major behavioral characteristics of this age can best be understood.

First, there comes to mind the melancholic-bitter brooding of the young adolescent, self-doubting, disoriented by the change he perceives in himself and in his environment, disappointed at not being more than he is, just at the time he thought he was becoming an adult. Because of the tormenting feeling of inadequacy, he begins to turn inward on himself, to burn his bridges, to break off contacts in order to spare himself defeats. He does not understand himself, and he feels misunderstood; he is looking for himself, but finds nothing clear or sure inside himself; not knowing what kind of behavior to adopt, he refuses in a way to behave at all. But, almost at the same time he puts us off on a false scent: insofar as he doubts himself, he affirms himself noisily, in an arrogant and aggressive manner; he tries to make himself noticed by his prowess, his eccentricity, by adopting attitudes that are as shattering as they are clumsy and transient. To be himself, to affirm himself in his new status, he must get away from and differentiate himself from all that has to do with his old status; his parents, too, the family background, will have to pay for this affirmation, essentially oppositional in nature at the beginning. "What's wrong with parents," a 14-year-old youngster stated explicitly, "is that they knew us when we were little." Parents are a perpetual reminder of childhood, of what was before, so they are the ones to astonish, to shock; they are the ones who must be shown that one has changed, that one is no longer the same; for their benefit are the more or less boisterous displays of emancipation, which will sometimes give rise to guilt feelings and regression.

Most adults seem to have little tolerance for these displays that seem to them to imply a loss of adult prestige and a weakening of their authority. Often they react by irony or by coercive measures that can only arouse aggressiveness or reinforce the opposition of the youngsters. The youngsters come to judge adults with a growing perspicacity; they try to catch their parents in the act of contradicting principles that they uphold or to unmask the hypocrisies of adult society without making any bones about it. It is not unusual that they feel they have been deceived; they are disappointed in their parents. If the adult should happen to fail in understanding, in composure, or in generosity, violent tensions may appear. However, the "conflict of generations" is rarely all-out; far from it. Among the adults, some are going to find grace in the eyes of the young person: those who show themselves capable of listening to him, of taking him seriously, and who will reassure him about his own worth; those also who seem to him to represent new values, as against those he found in the family framework and which satisfy his own preoccupations. One can hardly exaggerate the importance of these older people whose behavior and attitudes awaken echoes in the consciousness of the young person and through whose example he can make his own aspirations clearer. By an out-and-out imitation of them, by identifying with them, he draws the outlines of his own personality. These identification objects are not, however, exclusively or necessarily within the domain of reality. The young person finds as many, and probably more, in literature and in the movies, not to mention the world of sports. Thus, through the intermediary of real or fictive personalities, belonging to the most diverse categories of humankind and at the most varied levels, the adolescent builds for himself a kind of ideal person that can range from Hamlet to the bicycle racer, from Cherubino to James Bond. During the time when he is opposing those around him, belittling them, trying to differentiate himself, it is striking to see the young person identify himself with other adults, his heroes, to see him reveal in this way, while "trying them on" and defining them, the attitudes and the values that appear of prime importance to him, thus working out a vision of the world and of life that is to express his essential preoccupations and to compensate for his inferiorities of the moment. It is as though he goes out supported by these successive personalities, so to speak, into a world and a society that are opening up to him.

He consigns his discoveries to an intimate diary that he keeps secret. This diary is a symbol of the stage he is at, in the same way as the mirror; it fills an analogous function. The young person notes down facts and events that impress him more or less, as well as quotations gleaned from his reading, then observations, personal reflections, confessions, attempts at self-analysis. Doubtless, in his writings he comes to pose as the character, as much for himself as for posterity; he thus reveals nonetheless the attention he pays to himself and the consciousness he has of the passage of time and of his own progression toward a new stage. The young person henceforth sets himself up as a witness of his own history, and it should not be surprising if it seems important to him! And he is not content with being the witness of his present; he is constantly anticipating, he sees himself as an adult, he dreams of the future opening up before him. Escaping in his reveries from a present that weighs on him heavily because of his studies or the many constraints to which he still must submit, the adolescent already sees himself grown up, famous, important, showered with adventures and honors or gratified by the favors of the other sex. The girl dreams of love, the boy of all kinds of prowess. They both make plans, build an ideal future. The development of their powers of abstraction is a strong support for this imaginary life. The child lives more in the present, like the adult, attached to his daily tasks.

But the seeking and the affirmation of self do not take place only in the framework of opposition to and identification with the adult, or of sulky or happy solitude. The group of peers is just as important, if not more so.

Among his peers, who are bothered by the same preoccupations as he is, the young person finds at the same time a security and a stabilizing rivalry; he also encounters quite a few burning problems concerning his status. It is doubtless in a perspective of security that the amazing conformism that characterizes the adolescent must be understood, the outright mimicry that is in such striking contrast to the attempts at emancipation that appear with respect to his family. Our recent anarchist shows himself to be a patent snob: he has fads, ways of dressing, mannerisms, ways of speaking, that he borrows wholly from his peers and by means of which he seems in some way to depersonalize himself. But these ways are just what give him such a reassuring feeling of not being isolated and at the same time permit him to differentiate himself as a young person from the group of ancient adults. At the same time, however, among his peers, by his bragging, his exploits, his eccentricities, and his peremptory views, he tries to make himself stand out and to distinguish himself with respect to those very ones with whom he confuses himself on so many points. As for group activities, they are of a diverse nature and differ from one milieu to another according to the intellectual and material possibilities; one can be assured, though, that discussion and arguments as well as shared daydreaming occupy a large place, but that some effective realization or other is not excluded.

In the group the adolescent will often meet his counterpart, the alter ego who is again a mirror: the chosen friend. Along patterns that are different according to sex and perhaps a little earlier in girls than in boys, the beginning of an intense attachment to a contemporary of the same sex develops. By means of common experiences and adventures, interminable conversations that are more or less intimate, the two partners, who are inseparable, do each other the mutual favor of helping each one to know himself; they examine themselves, placing in common their experiences, their plans, their ambitions, and their most intimate secrets. In the true sense, they explain themselves to each other, and in so doing, each explains himself to himself. We know how easily these friendships, whose narcissistic component is often evident, can in certain cases take on an exalted and passionate character, especially in girls. It is because the young person has finally found in the friend the person who really takes him seriously, the one who he feels understands him, the one he feels he understands—above all, the one with whom he does not need to defend himself, the one he does not have to deceive. In a large measure, solitude, the quest for the self, has come to an end, the nagging question has been answered: "Since he is fond of me, since he likes me, it means that I really am worth something." Maybe it is logical to see in these juvenile friendships, with the joys and disappointments that go with them, a kind of "rehearsal" of love. We must not, however, underestimate the proper function of this friendship: it has for the young person the value of a "confirmation" of his personality and his identity that contributes greatly to the fixing of its traits and to turning it toward the tasks and the positive realizations of existence.

However, the adolescent group will soon become mixed. Although, during the last years of childhood, boys and girls have rather kept their distance from each other and even to some extent avoided each other, this segregation tends to disappear during the course of puberty. Their approach develops first in a disguised and more or less unconscious way; they try to get each other's attention, they tease each other; the boys show off in front of the girls; the girls respond by all sorts of flattery, usually addressed to boys a little older than they are. In short, after having met the friend of their own kind, the friend of the same sex, they venture to find the friend who is different. A whole activity of seeking out and seduction of the partner of the other sex is carried out, sometimes under the guise of timidity, sometimes of daring. Heterosexual relationships are outlined and become more precise; the exploration of others and of oneself is pursued by means of common undertakings, flirtation, more or less transient relationships, in general in much less concrete form than adults fear, but sometimes much less ethereal than they think. All these attempts at an approach keep an undeniably playful character for a long time, but it is incontestable that they give the young person experiences that lead him to a greater maturity. "To have a boy friend, to have a girl friend" has a reassuring and stabilizing effect, contributes to situating the young person with respect to his peers, to giving him importance. But especially in friendship, affection, and love, he experiences sharing, giving, the solidarity that delivers him from his initial isolation and his interior solitude. By means of the ups and downs of an affective exchange with others, by the joys and disappointments of love, he discovers and structures the resources of his sensitivity.

The particular position of the adolescent, "caught," so to speak, between childhood and adulthood; the absence of a well-defined status of youngsters, who are sometimes treated as children, sometimes bound by the demands of the adult level; the prolongation of studies and the impossibility of assuming real responsibilities in society—all contribute to giving adolescence a character that is transitory, delayed, suspended, even fictive. And the adolescent sometimes has the impression that what he does is without reality, without consequences. He waits; he grows tired and revolts; he likes to play a role. He waits for something to happen. In the midst of vague yearnings, anxious nostalgia, or impatience, he waits for a revelation; he waits for the time when he will "really" live. Sometimes he tries to kill time; sometimes he becomes active, he becomes involved, he has the impression of really living. He knows wonderful joys and moments of exaltation, but often life weighs on him. He feels full of potentialities, but he has the impression that there is no place for him in society, that he is marginal. More than at any other age, the individual is in transition, in the process of change, going from discovery to discovery and from one disappointment to another. He discovers and intuits life, astonished and disgusted in turn. He carries out his explorations in all directions and wants to try everything. Doubtless, his interests, his activities, his investigations, will never again attain such extensiveness. He is reproached for his instability, the superficiality of his fads, the vanity of his undertakings, the ease with which he becomes involved without always having thought things out. But the prodigious richness of this age and the structuring power of these tryers of everything, as well as the relative poorness of what is offered to them by an adult society that is organized, policed, and commercialized, must be recognized. It is not at all astonishing that there is in the youngster inconsequentiality, anxiety, even panic, in response to the multiple aspirations that he finds in himself and to the innumerable demands of the exterior world; it is almost normal that, faced with so many unknowns and so many uncertainties, his behavior should sometimes become aberrant.

The outline we have just examined is doubtless quite incomplete and will perhaps seem partial. We have tried to center it on an element that experience has shown us to be truly crucial, that is, the challenging of the individual by the changes he undergoes, his finding himself as a result, the consequent questioning of the individual about his own worth with regard to a new world that has opened up to him. The anxieties and the errors of the young person, his behavior problems, his troubles, whether they be sexual, social, or metaphysical, even his mental aberrations, seem to us to be advantageously illuminated by being considered in this perspective, which, of course, does not exhaust the question.

References

1. DEBESSE, M. L'Adolescence. Paris: Presses Universitaires de France, 1942.
2. DIMOCK, H. S. "Research in Adolescence. I. Pubescence and Physical Growth," Child Development, VI (1953).
3. GESELL, A., F. L. ILG, and L. B. AMES. Youth: The Years from Ten to Sixteen. London: Hamish Hamilton, 1956.
4. INHELDER, B., and J. PIAGET. De la logique de l'enfant à la logique de l'adolescent. Paris: Presses Universitaires de France, 1955.
5. PIAGET, J. Six études de psychologie. Geneva: Gonthier, 1964.

3

The Intellectual Development
of the Adolescent

Jean Piaget

Psychologically, adolescence is the age when the individual becomes integrated into the society of adults, the age when the child no longer feels that he is below the level of his elders, but equal, at least in rights, to the adult and quite frequently above his level (because of a kind of resurgence of narcissism or egocentrism, which has frequently been stressed). This integration into adult society has many affective aspects, more or less linked with puberty, which I leave to be discussed by people who are much more qualified to do so than myself. But it also includes very profound intellectual changes on which (and this is rather strange) much less stress has been laid, possibly because arguments are frequently based on the postulate that affectivity explains everything, but no doubt also because the understanding of these intellectual changes requires detailed logical analysis as a necessary corollary to psychological analysis.

Let us first stress the fact that the intellectual or cognitive novelties that characterize the thought process of the adolescent do not constitute absolute novelties, which would be the result of a creation or an inexplicable emergence, but they represent in a way the achievement or the crowning of an entire process of evolution that originates at birth and whose stages can be observed throughout the development of the child. After the sensorimotor phase, during which the infant builds up action schemes in which the roots of future intellectual operations can already be found, the child from age of 2 to 7 then goes through a stage of preoperatory thought characterized by a progressive interiorization of the sensorimotor actions. Around the age of 7 or 8, the child discovers what we shall call concrete operations (classification, serialization, one-to-one correspondency features, numbers,

22

spatial operations, and the like), which already constitute a kind of logic because of their group structures. But this is a logic of a very limited scope, relating only to objects themselves which can be effectively or mentally manipulated. This logic leads only to restricted systems, corresponding to certain structures of classes, of relationships and numbers, but which do not include the general and formal logic that logicians call the logic of propositions, which in turn makes it possible to reason on assumptions and not merely on objects.

Now, the great novelty that characterizes adolescent thought and that starts around the age of 11 to 12, but does not reach its point of equilibrium until the age of 14 or 15—this novelty consists in detaching the concrete logic from the objects themselves, so that it can function on verbal or symbolic statements without other support. Above all the novelty consists in generalizing this logic and supplementing it with a set of combinations. This set of combinations is not radically new and merely extends, in a way, the classifications and serializations of the level of concrete operations. It is new, however, in that these are operations at one stage removed, or operations on operations. A set of combinations consists, in fact, in a classification of all the possible classifications, a serialization of serializations (permutations), and so forth.

The great novelty that results consists in the possibility of manipulating ideas in themselves and no longer in merely manipulating objects. In a word, the adolescent is an individual who is capable (and this is where he reaches the level of the adult) of building or understanding ideal or abstract theories and concepts. The child does not build theories. His ideas can certainly be coherent, and the psychologist who studies these ideas can easily compile and co-ordinate them into formal theoretical structures. But the child himself does not express them as theories. He is content to live in the present, in the domain of everyday reality. However, the adolescent is capable of projects for the future (of the *Lebensplan*), of nonpresent interests, and of a passion for ideas, ideals, or ideologies. This basic fact gives rise to a problem of psychology of intelligence and not only to a problem of affectivity.

Let us examine somewhat more closely how these new conquests are made possible. First, the novelty consists in the capacity of reasoning on hypotheses. This is the main feature that distinguishes adolescent intelligence from the intelligence of the child. Concrete operations relate only to objects or to perceptive events, and they proceed step by step without being able to become independent of the concrete and above all without being able to detach the form of reasoning from its material substance. On the contrary, the new operations that emerge around the age of 12 to 15 consist in the capability of reasoning on pure hypotheses, that is, on the basis of propositions, which are not taken as true or false but are experimentally formulated in order to derive from them all possible consequences, which are then checked by comparison to the facts. This reasoning on hypotheses will be a formal type of reasoning; that is, it will be governed by the structure of reasoning alone.

Moreover, these formal operations are more fertile than the few concrete operations of classes, relationships, and number that the child has had available to him in the preceding period. These new operations could be called propositional operations. In other words, they relate to the logic of propositions rather than to the logic of classes and relationships alone.

Indeed, the logic of propositions consists in combining propositions or hypotheses independently of their content and by a simple mechanism of logical combinations. These operations are, for example, the implication "if/then," or the disjunction "either/or," exclusive or nonexclusive, or incompatibility, and so on. These are operations that are used in a logical discussion, when, for instance, the assumption of a contradictory opinion is admitted in order to show the necessary consequences to which this opinion would lead.

These propositional operations (or they could be called hypotheticodeductive operations) present a whole series of new characteristics in contrast to the concrete operations. The first of these characteristics is that they constitute a set of combinations. Concrete operations proceed step by step, according to similarities, so that in a zoological classification, for instance, animals can be classified in a certain way only, but the combination aspects of a class that would include two noncontiguous subclasses like oysters and camels would have no natural significance. A set of combinations consists, on the contrary, in linking any element to any other element, according to all the possible combinations by groups of two, three, and so on. Now the propositional operations, as can be demonstrated in logic, assume such a technique of sets of combinations.

It is very interesting to note that the preadolescent and the adolescent reach this set of combinations of ideas and of propositions at the same age and at the same mental level as they are able to reach the power of combination in the handling of objects. For instance, if you give a child a number of red, blue, and green counters, and if you ask him to build up all the possible color combinations, two by two, three by three, four by four, he never reaches a complete system and in fact proceeds empirically. However, at the level of propositional operations, the subject is capable of these combinations of objects, just as he is capable of achieving combinations of propositions from the logical point of view. Again, when you give the subject a physical material that enables him to find certain elementary laws or certain elementary factors spontaneously, such as factors of flexibility or the factors that play a part in the frequency of oscillations of a pendulum, or the like, then you find a major difference between children at the level of concrete operations and adolescents who have reached the level of propositional operations. The first group proceed directly to action. They vary all the factors at the same time; they proceed by serialization and by direct relationships. The subject of 12 to 14 years of age, on the other hand, will try to dissociate factors by varying a single element at a time and by neutralizing all the others. He will try to compile a complete inventory of factors, in other words, of possible assumptions, which he will then check, and above all in this inventory and in this verification he will try to take into account all possible combinations. Thus, the logic of propositions is not merely a verbal logic but also an instrument of combinations for the analysis of external reality.

A second novelty of the propositional or formal operations is to constitute systems that synthesize in a single system the two forms of reversibility inherent in concrete operations. There is a reversibility by inversion or by negation—for example, $+ A - A = O$ or $+ N - N = O$—and a reversibility by reciprocity, as in the case in the logic of relationships; for instance, A is on the left of B necessarily results in the fact that B is on the right of A. These two forms of reversibility remain distinct in the field of concrete operations, one applying to classes and the other to relationships. However, in the field of the propositional operations, each operation has inherent in it its inverse and its reciprocal. Thus, it is possible to synthesize both in a single system. This system is rather complex and takes the form of what is called a group of quaternality, or of four transformations (Klein's group): the inverse transformation N, the reciprocal transformation R, the correlative C or inverse of the reciprocal, and the identical transformation I. This group, $INRC$, which was discovered in the logic of the adolescent, has since then been reidentified in the logic of propositions and constitutes one of the fundamental structures of logic.

Now, this system of two reversibilities makes possible the construction of a series of new concepts which all appear at about the age level of 12 to 14; without this logical analysis, however, it would be difficult to show the links that exist between them. This applies, for example, to the concepts of proportions, or to the concepts of the relation between action and reaction, or to the co-ordinations of displacement according to two simultaneous systems of reference (for instance, a snail moving on a plank while the plank is being moved the other way), and so forth.

In conclusion, it is apparent how these intellectual transformations typical of the adolescent's thinking enable him not only to achieve his integration into the social relationships of adults, which is, in fact, the most general characteristic of this period of development, but also to conquer a certain number of fundamental intellectual operations which constitute the basis for a scientific education at high-school level. The problem that remains unresolved, however, is the generality of these intellectual transformations, which we have stressed in the course of this chapter. It is probable that in underdeveloped societies which still have a tribal organization the individual remains throughout his entire life at the level of concrete operations, without ever reaching the level of formal or propositional operations that are characteristic of adolescents in our cultural environment. But in these societies the younger generations remain under the authority of the "elders" of the tribe, and the elders in turn remain subject to the conservative traditions of their ancestors. There is then a full circle between the social and intellectual processes, both being ruled by conservatism. In our societies, the as yet unresolved question is whether these intellectual transformations exercise a similar effect on all classes of society. Certain indices would seem to show that they do not, but we would wish to reserve our opinion because it is quite possible that, among manual workers and technicians, the same formal operations develop on the vocational level, but in a manner which is distinct from the verbal or experimental level found in adolescents with literary or scientific training. A large number of problems remains to be solved in this field, which is rich in promise for the analysis of the cognitive behavior of the adolescent.

4

The Body and the Body-Image in Adolescents

William A. Schonfeld

Adolescence is a dynamic phase in the continuum of life in which profound changes take place in physical, physiological, and biochemical as well as personality development so that the child is transformed into a sexually "attractive" adult capable of reproducing. There are biological, social, and psychological reasons for setting aside this broad span of life for special consideration. In this chapter we shall limit our concern to the biological changes and youth's reaction to them, namely, the body and the body-image, which must be understood by the psychiatrist, pediatrician, psychologist, social worker, and educator who are concerned with the mental health and personality problems of adolescents.

Definition of Biological Concepts

Adolescence is neither a homogeneous nor a precipitous period, but rather an evolving one, beginning with the earliest hidden changes in endocrine activities and continuing until sexual and physical development is relatively complete. Although subdivisions are artificial, since maturation is an interdependent fluid process, to facilitate description a variety of classifications has been used.[5, 18, 22, 36, 46, 47, 51, 52, 64, 68, 69, 77]

The terminology used in the literature describing the maturational phenomena associated with adolescence is often confusing. One area of confusion centers around the definition of puberty.[68] It has been defined first as the point at which an individual is capable of procreating; or second as menarche, the first menstrual period in girls and the time of the first seminal emission in boys; or third as a phase in which the major changes of adolescent development occur. This is further complicated

27

when adolescence is defined as starting with "puberty" and ending with maturity by those who accept either of the first two definitions or wrongly assume them to be synchronous; while others, who accept puberty as the phase of major changes, divide adolescence into prepuberty, puberty, and postpuberty.[5]

In light of our present knowledge and to avoid confusion, it would be desirable to limit the definition of puberty as that point at which the individual is capable of procreating, which is not synchronous with menarche or the time of the first emission. The term "pubescence" is used to delineate the phase in which the major changes in development occur and "adolescence" as the total period of sexual maturation. Adolescence may then be arbitrarily subdivided into three phases: (1) Early adolescence, or prepubescence, which is initiated by the first evidence of sexual maturation and terminates with the appearance of pubic hair. (2) Middle adolescence, or pubescence, which begins with the onset of pubic hair and ends when the pubic hair is completely developed. It is accompanied by the peak velocity of growth in height, menarche in girls, and the first emission in boys along with progressive development of the primary sexual organs. (3) Late adolescence, or postpubescence, which starts when the pubic hair growth is complete and is characterized by deceleration of growth in height, completion of maturation of the primary and secondary sexual characteristics, and fertility. Adolescence is preceded by childhood and followed by adulthood, although the phases of each, just before and after adolescence, are often referred to as pre- and postadolescence.

Fortunately, as far as effective work with youth is concerned, the precise definitions of these terms are only of academic interest. However, the understanding of adolescent personality development and the significance of specific behavior would be enhanced if the mental health specialists were to correlate their findings not only with the chronological age but also with the level of adolescent development, namely, early, middle, or late adolescence, since it is important to know where an individual youth stands in his passage through adolescence. An assessment of the phase of adolescence is surprisingly easy and useful, but rarely done by the mental health specialists.

THE BODY

Developmental Data

There is a wide range as to the age when normal adolescence begins, the speed with which it develops, and the pattern it follows. Adolescence usually occurs between the ages of 10 and 18 years in girls and 12 and 20 in boys. It essentially corresponds to the teen years, although the mean age in well-nourished European and American girls is 11½ years and about one and a half to two years later in boys. It ends between 13 and 20 years. The controlling factors, besides the inate capacity for growth, are still unknown. Contrary to popular opinion, neither climate nor race influences the onset of adolescence as greatly as do nutrition and associated socioeconomic factors.[5, 12, 69] Although the average age for each stage of development has no significance for the individual youth, knowing the range of normal does help to evaluate whether there is any justification for the youth's concern over his development.[54] It is essential to have a clear picture of the wide variation which is still within normal limits and to understand that "normal" connotes neither optimum nor ideal. [17, 53, 69, 77]

To evaluate the youth's developmental status, most psychiatrists prefer to have a pediatrician or endocrinologist examine him and to limit their own evaluation to information obtained by direct questioning and obvious appearance, but some psychiatrists do examine the youth when indicated.[31, 34, 58] At times, to obviate the need for physical examination, the author has gone beyond the projective technique of the Draw-a-Person test and has asked the youth to draw a picture of his whole body as he looks nude when he "gets out of a bath," on a full-length piece of paper attached to a door or wall "as if it were a mirror." The boy may have to be urged to indicate the size of his penis, and the girl, the size of her breasts, and in both the pubic, auxillary, and facial hair distribution as well as the fat distribution. Most adolescents co-operate; however, youths with a great deal of anxiety over their body-image may resist both the questioning and the drawing because of what D. Cappon has called a "veil of inhibition."

Adolescence does not initiate but only intensifies sexual behavior, which is an exceedingly complicated learned phenomenon that starts in infancy, and directs it usually into heterosexual patterns with reproductive significance. If the learned process was distorted because of an inability to identify with the parent of the same sex, and thus the individual is unable to relate effectively to members of the opposite sex, gonadal function may direct the sexual behavior into homosexual patterns. We must differentiate this latter group from the large number of youths who early in adolescence are merely apprehensive about relating to members of the opposite sex and feel more comfortable with their own sex, which often leads to anxiety about homosexuality. This group invariably modifies its self-concepts as experiences with the opposite sex increase. Homosexual practices at boarding schools and institutions have a still different significance and relate to availability rather than preference.

I. *Primary and Secondary Sexual Characteristics*

(a) IN BOYS [10, 47, 51, 52, 53, 64, 67, 69, 73, 75]

The earliest manifestations of adolescence come in close sequence; there is progressive enlargement of the testicles, with enlargement and reddening of the scrotum and increase in length and circumference of the penis.

Table 4–1. Normal Maturational Sequence in Boys

Phase	Appearance of Sexual Characteristics	Average Ages	Age Range*
Childhood through Preadolescence	*Testes* and *penis* have not grown since infancy; no *pubic hair;* growth in *height* constant. No spurt.	—	—
Early Adolescence	*Testes* begin to increase in size; *scrotum* grows, skin reddens and becomes coarser; *penis* follows with growth in length and circumference; no true *pubic hair,* may have down.	12–13 yrs.	10–15 yrs.
Middle Adolescence	*Pubic hair*—pigmented, coarse and straight at base of penis becoming progressively more curled and profuse, forming at first an inverse triangle and subsequently extends up to umbilicus; *axillary hair* starts after pubic hair; *penis* and *testes* continue growing; *scrotum* becomes larger, pigmented, and sculptured; marked spurt of growth in *height* with maximum increment about time pubic hair first develops and decelerates by time fully established; *prostate* and *seminal vesicles* mature, spontaneous or induced *emissions* follow but *spermatozoa* inadequate in number and motility (adolescent sterility); *voice* beginning to change as *larynx* enlarges.	13–16 yrs.	11–18 yrs.
Late Adolescence	*Facial* and *body* hair appear and spread; *pubic* and *axillary hair* become denser; *voice* deepens; *testes* and *penis* continue to grow; *emission* has adequate number of motile *spermatozoa* for fertility; growth in *height* gradually decelerates, 98 per cent of mature stature by 17¾ yrs. ± 10 mo.; indention of frontal *hair line*.	16–18 yrs.	14–20 yrs.
Postadolescence to Adult	Mature, full development of *primary* and *secondary* sex characteristics; *muscles* and *hirsutism* may continue increasing.	onset 18–20 yrs.	onset 16–21 yrs.

* Normal range was accepted as 1st to 9th decile (80 per cent of cases).

The histological picture of the testes is highly variable in its transition to a mature state. With adolescence the lumen of the seminiferous tubules enlarges, the undifferentiated cells become Sertoli cells, androgen-producing Leydig cells appear in the interstitial tissue, and the spermatogonia give rise to the germinal cells—primary and secondary spermatocytes, spermatids, and, by late adolescence, spermatozoa.

Middle adolescence, or pubescence, begins during the year following the first manifestation of sexual development. The pubic hair, downy at first, becomes pigmented, but sparse and straight or slightly curled at the base of the penis. It progressively becomes more curled and profuse, forming an inverse triangle and subsequently spreading up to the umbilicus in the characteristic male distribution. This usually requires two or three years and designates the end of middle adolescence. During this phase the testes continue growing; the scrotum becomes larger, sculptured, and pigmented. The penis also grows progressively in length and circumference and now becomes erect not only in response to local stimulation, as in childhood, but also to sexually provocative sensations and thoughts. This is accompanied by a desire for sexual release. The breast nipples also become pigmented and often a subareolar nodule may appear, which may erroneously be diagnosed as gynecomastia but which disappears spontaneously during the following year or two. The deepening of the voice, associated with growth of the larynx, is a gradual one. It starts in middle adolescence and is often not complete until adolescence is practically over. Axillary hair usually first appears about two years after the appearance of pubic hair. At about the same time, hair first begins to grow on the upper lip.

Concomitant with the growth of the penis, the prostate, the seminal vesicles, and the bulbourethral glands enlarge and develop, forming seminal fluid. The boy has his first ejaculation, either induced or spontaneous, in middle adolescence. The average age for the American boy is just under 14 years, with 90 per cent of a large sample falling between 11 and 16 years.[30] The time of the first emission is to some extent determined culturally as well as biologically but occurs as a rule about one year after the onset of accelerated penis growth. At this point the youth is usually sterile; only in a year to three years does spermatogenesis advance far enough for sufficient numbers of motile sperm to appear in the ejaculate so that the boy is fertile.[39]

In late adolescence, primary and secondary sexual characteristics continue to mature. The ultimate size of the penis and testes varies a great deal in different individuals. The relative size of the relaxed and erect penis also varies in different ethnic groups. Although the beard usually starts to grow in this phase and is followed by thoracic and abdominal pilosity with extension to the extremities, there is a conspicuous ethnic difference in the distribution of facial and body hair.

At 17 to 18 years of age most of the boys studied by the author reached full maturity, although a few achieved this level at 15 years of age and a few not before 20 years. The final secondary sexual characteristics to develop in most of the males studied is the bitemporal indentation of the hair line, which is absent in adolescent girls.

(b) IN GIRLS [5, 10, 46, 64, 68, 69, 73]

Although adolescence usually begins on the average of about two years earlier in the girl than the boy, this is not always true. The first histological manifestation of adolescence in a female is enlargement of the ovary, with the ripening of one of the 200,000 to 250,000 primary graffian follicles; but since the size of the ovaries cannot be evaluated clinically, we must depend on secondary changes, namely, the rounding of the hips or the more readily discernible breast development, as the first visible criteria of the onset of early adolescence.[68] The rounding of the hips is due in part to broadening of the bony pelvis, but more particularly to increased deposition of subcutaneous fat. In early adolescence breast development is usually characterized by an elevation of the areola surrounding the nipple, which produces a small conical protuberance and is known as the "bud" stage. In middle adolescence there is a deposition of fat under the areola with further elevation, which is referred to as the "primary breast," and in late adolescence there is an enlargement of the breast tissue itself and further fat infiltration, forming the "mature" breast which varies greatly in size and shape. The breast is most frequently in a primary stage at menarche and takes several years to develop fully.

Pubic hair, at first downy, becomes coarse, pigmented, straight or curly along the labia, initiating middle adolescence. As this phase progresses the pubic hair becomes more abundant and curly, spreading over the mons to develop the characteristic female inverse triangular pattern by the end of this stage. By late adolescence, pubic hair spreads to the medial surface of the thighs. Axillary hair usually begins to grow in middle adolescence about two years after the onset of pubic hair.

In middle adolescence, as a result of the hypertrophy of the uterus and cyclic changes in the endometrium, menstruation results. Menarche has been reported by various observers in the United States to occur at a mean age of 12.9 ± 1.4 years.[46, 64, 68, 69]

Bouterline-Young[5] reports the age of menarche in several ethnic groups with a mean of 12.5 years in the Florentine girls he studied, while Duché[14] reports a mean age of 13.5 years among girls in France. Chan, Chang, and Hsu[12] found the mean age to be 12.8 among girls in Hong Kong. Thus we can state that menarche is considered to occur normally in the age range of 10 to 17 years with a mean varying from 12.6 to 13.0; 80 per cent of girls fall into the range of 11 to 15 years. Menarche almost invariably occurs after the apex of the height spurt has passed. The variations in age are the result of genetic factors and nutrition associated with socioeconomic determinants and not caused by climate or race. Repeated studies indicate that the menarche has been occurring earlier by four months per decade in western Europe over the period of 1830 to 1960, and there is no evidence that the trend has stopped.[69] This again may be the result of improved nutrition and decrease in debilitating illnesses. Initially menstrual periods are not accompanied by ovulation, so that the early adolescent girl is usually sterile. Ovulatory menstruation and the ability to conceive (puberty or nubility) start one year to three years later.[39] The uterus does not usually attain adult size until 18 to 20 years of age. The histology of the uterine endometrium and the vaginal epithelium undergoes cyclic changes reflecting the hormone milieu. Lactic-acid-producing bacilli replace the previously mixed and scanty bacterial flora present in the vagina, changing the vaginal secretion abruptly from an alkaline reaction in childhood to an acid reaction in adolescence.

In adolescence the vulva enlarges as a result of the marked development of the labia majora, which in childhood are practically nonexistent. The clitoris also enlarges somewhat, probably as a result of the circulating adrenal androgens, and becomes erectile.

Table 4–2. Normal Maturational Sequence in Girls

Phase	Appearance of Sexual Characteristics	Average Ages	Age Range*
Childhood through Preadolescence	No *pubic hair; breasts* are flat; *growth* in height is constant, no spurt.	—	—
Early Adolescence	Rounding of *hips; breasts* and nipples are elevated to form *"bud"* stage; no true *pubic hair,* may have down.	10–11 yrs.	9–14 yrs.
Middle Adolescence	*Pubic hair:* pigmented, coarse, straight primarily along labia but progressively curled and spreads over mons and becomes profuse with an inverse triangular pattern; *axillary hair* starts after pubic hair; marked *growth* spurt with maximum *height* increment 18 months before menarche; *menarche: labia* become enlarged, *vaginal secretion* becomes acid; *breast:* areola and nipple elevated to form "Primary" breast.	11–14 yrs.	10–16 yrs.
Late Adolescence	*Axillary hair* in moderate quantity; *pubic hair* fully developed; *breasts* fill out forming adult-type configuration; *menstruation* well established; *growth* in height is decelerated, ceases at 16¼ ± 13 mo.	14–16 yrs.	13–18 yrs.
Postadolescence to Adult	Further growth of *axillary hair; breasts* fully developed.	onset 16–18 yrs.	onset 15–19 yrs.

* Normal range was accepted as 1st to 9th decile (80 per cent of cases).

2. *Physical Growth*

Growth is not synchronic, in that the different body tissues grow at separate rates. Neural tissue has a rapid postnatal growth which slows down in childhood and stops before adolescence, while lymphatic tissue grows rapidly in childhood and atrophies during adolescence. The reproductive system in turn does not grow during childhood, but grows rapidly in adolescence.[69]

(a) STATURE

The characteristic adolescent cycle of growth in height starts abruptly in early adolescence with a rapid acceleration in rate of growth. This increases progressively for about a year, reaching the point of maximum increment in middle adolescence, about the time when pubic hair first develops. This is followed by a progressive reduction in velocity of growth during late adolescence until the rate of growth reaches the level normal for earlier childhood. Subsequently the rate of growth tapers off still further so that virtually all growth (98 per cent) ceases in boys at 17¾ years ± 10 months and 16¼ years ± 13 months in girls.[5, 67, 69]

The timing of the onset of accelerated growth is the principal factor accounting for the extreme differences in size in different youths of the same age. This spurt characteristically starts earlier in girls than in boys because of the earlier onset of adolescence. At about 8 or 9 years of age girls enter the period of accelerated growth, with the result that they catch up with and later pass boys, so that from 11 to 13 years they are often taller and heavier.[33] However, boys soon enter a phase of more rapid development, usually surpass girls, and continue to enlarge the difference until maturity. Both the intensity and the duration of the growth spurt are greater in the male than in the female. The ultimate height which any individual attains depends not only on the rate at which growth occurs but also on the age at which the growth spurt starts and the age at which epiphyseal fusion occurs and thus the duration of growth. Bayley[3] has developed tables for predicting adult height based on sex, chronological age, present height, and skeletal age.

Adolescents are taller today than they were a hundred years ago as a result of many factors. Children grow more rapidly, there is an acceleration of the maturational process so that the growth spurt is earlier, the rate of growth is greater, and the maximum height is reached earlier. Statistics point to the fact that youth mature four months earlier each decade so that they reach their adult height two years younger now than two or three generations ago. Thus, although men are on the average some 10 cm taller than men were a century ago, indicating that the trend for adults is about a 1 cm increase per decade, the spurt is occurring earlier so that youth tend to be 2½ cm taller each decade.[69]

During this growth the skeletal proportions are modified, so that in the late adolescent the measurement of the lower extremities equals that of the sitting height, while in the child the extremities were proportionately shorter. The ratio of the biacromial diameter to the bitrochanteric diameter changes considerably in middle adolescence, so that in boys the thorax becomes wider and the pelvis remains narrower, as opposed to that of girls, in whom the reverse is true. Characteristic changes in the shape of the pelvis, differentiating the sexes, occur during adolescence. Changes of proportion can likewise be seen in the face. Now the lower portion of the head begins to grow; the nose and the chin take the lead and the forehead appears small by contrast. Similar disproportionate growth of the eyeballs accounts for the increased incidence of myopia evident in adolescents.[64]

(b) OSSEOUS DEVELOPMENT

Evaluation of epiphyseal fusion by roentgenologic evaluation of "bone age" can be helpful in determining the general developmental status of an adolescent.[22, 69, 74] This is basically expressing qualitative aspects of development by quantitative units of measurement, using chronological time as a standardization device. Bone age thus indicates the average chronological age at which the epiphyseal development present occurs. It is a more reliable criterion of "biological age" than is chronological age and thus may help in predicting a youth's ultimate height and in evaluating the adequacy of sexual maturity. In boys, the beginning of the spurt of growth usually occurs when the skeletal age reaches what is average at 14 years. In girls, menarche and the growth spurt occur at an earlier bone age. Growth ceases when the epiphyses fuse.

Athletic coaches should be made aware that serious injuries result from a sudden and excessive muscular pull on the epiphyses before they are fused; thus it would be best to avoid strenuous sports in 13- to 15-year-old boys.

(c) BODY MASS

(1) *Fat.* Weight changes are considerable during adolescence. There is often a very striking increase in subcutaneous fat in preadolescence or early adolescence preceding the growth spurt. This gives rise to a configuration in some boys which has been incorrectly considered evidence of hypogonadism and diagnosed as Froehlich's syndrome, although actually these well-nourished boys mature earlier.[8, 17, 51] However, in the male after the growth spurt the increment in deposition of body fat tends to decrease again. In contrast, the adolescent girl seems to add more subcutaneous fat.[25] A second and greater increase in weight usually follows the growth in height.[45]

(2) *Muscles.* A greater part of the weight increase in the second phase of the bimodal weight gain is the result of an increase in skeletal growth and musculature, only partly because of the deposition of fat.[5, 18] As muscles grow strength virtually doubles between early and middle adolescence in boys. This is much less so in girls. Motor skill in general increases in step with motor strength, with some elements such as balance not showing an adolescent spurt, but increasing continually with age.[62] Present data do not support the concept of an "overgrown, clumsy age." According to longitudinal data, the clumsy adolescent is likely to have been the clumsy child. A

youth may appear awkward, in response to sudden stimuli, because of the lack of learned patterns, since his body changes may be so rapid that he is unfamiliar with his own body. However, when a pattern is established through learning a technique, whether it be athletics, dancing, driving, and so on, the ability to co-ordinate becomes evident.[28] There is a lag of about a year between achieving full body size and the development of full musculature power, so that the youth should not be subjected to pressures beyond his capacity. However, adequately controlled exercise appears to be more effective in stimulating muscle development at this age of rapid muscle growth than at any other time.[69]

3. Skin

The skin is also involved in the adolescent process, by an increase of the sebaceous secretion especially noticeable in the nasolabial folds. Acne is present to some degree in 75 to 80 per cent of adolescents by the time they reach late adolescence. The primary lesion is the plugged sebaceous gland or comedo which becomes secondarily infected; pustular formation results often as a result of a lack of cleanliness and the effects of habitual manipulation of the skin.[18] The sweat glands, especially in the axilla and the anogenital and palmo-plantar regions, become hyperactive with the ensuing hyperidrosis.

Neuroendocrine Mechanisms of Adolescence

To understand the mechanisms of morphological and physiological modifications which take place in adolescence we have to look successively at parts of the central nervous system, the anterior-pituitary, the peripheral endocrine glands, and the end organs. The initial releasing factor for the mechanisms associated with adolescence is still unknown, but it appears that the changes are initiated by maturation of nuclei in the limbic system[43] which in turn stimulate the hypothalamus, although some neurophysiologists feel it counteracts an inhibiting factor. Rather than being "cerebral centers" they are links in an important circuit for complex behavioral and endocrinological responses. The release of adolescence parallels the earlier development of motor and speech function. The hypothalamus, in turn, either through neurohumoral secretions or nerve impulses, incites anterior-pituitary secretion of hormones. The pituitary has been considered to be the primary controller of all endocrine gland functions. It now appears that the hypophysis is more of a mediator between the brain and the target glands and contributes important elements of amplification, stability, and homeostasis to the mechanism. The hypophysis and the hypothalamus are also subject to regulation by circulating hormones elaborated by other endocrine glands, resulting in cyclic interplay.

Wilkins[75] felt that the initiation of adolescent processes must also depend on the maturity of the end organs as evidenced by the fact that ossification must reach a prescribed level before the growth phenomena associated with adolescence can occur.

Except for the growth hormone (somatotropin), which acts directly on the somatic tissues, stimulating the rate of growth, and is involved in regulating fat metabolism,[66] the other hormones of the hypophysis are trophic hormones, stimulating their respective specific "target glands": the thyroid (thyrotropin), the adrenal cortex (adrenal cortical tropic hormone ACTH), and the gonads (gonadotropins-follicular-stimulating and luteinizing hormones).[10, 19] In the male the follicular-stimulating hormone acts on the spermatogenic cells in the testes and promotes growth of the seminiferous tubules. The gonadotropins also promote secretion of androgens by the Leydig cells of the testes. In the female the follicular-stimulating hormone which promotes maturation of the graffian follicle and the small amounts of luteinizing hormone released stimulate the secretion of estrogens. After ovulation, induced by a sudden discharge of luteinizing hormone, the newly formed corpus luteum begins to secrete progesterone. The steroid biosynthesis follows the same basic pathways in testes, ovaries, and adrenal cortex. The character of the principal final product is probably determined by quantitative differences in enzyme concentrations in the steroid-producing tissues. The estrogens and androgens thus secreted affect the "sexual end organs": the penis, scrotum, seminal vesicles, and prostate in the male; the uterus, vagina, and breasts in the female; and hair and skin in both. Androgens initially stimulate the rate of linear growth and muscle development, but eventually both androgens and estrogens limit the duration of growth by stimulating skeletal maturation with fusion of the epiphyses.[10, 19] Prior to adolescence the gonads exert little or no influence on hormonal mechanisms.

The popularization of oral contraceptives brings to the fore the need of understanding how estrogens and progesterone influence pituitary function. It is believed that in the proper level they inhibit follicular-stimulating and luteinizing-hormone production by their negative feedback action on the hypothalamus-pituitary axis, modifying the ovulatory surge of luteinizing hormone so that ovulation fails to occur. They have also been used in some cases of menstrual disorders without apparent deleterious effects on the adolescent process.[35]

In some animals, the afferent stimuli from genital stimulation also play a part in initiating the neural-endocrine-gonad mechanism, but this has not been proved in man. Numerous studies in the literature related to the effect of starvation on the maturity mechanism indicate that this complicated process depends not only on an inherent genetic factor but also on a variety of extrinsic factors. The effect of emotional stress on this regulatory mechanism has not been established beyond the fact that it may precipitate or delay menstrual flow and that it may vary the time of ovulation. There are also clinical observations which suggest that failure in growth may be associated with emotional deprivation.[44, 72]

Types of Variation in Adolescent Development

There is characteristically a wide range of normal variation in adolescent development. Although pathological deviations do occur, they are infrequent. However, the adolescent, his family, and even the doctor are often unreasonably concerned about normal deviations in maturation, a concern which may either be caused by or result in disturbances of body-image. Developmental studies reveal that 4 per cent of boys who subsequently become normal adults start adolescence as young as 10 years, while 1 per cent do not start their adolescence until 16 years.[60] Similarly in girls, some few have their menarche at 9 years; others, not until 17 or 18 years with adolescence beginning a year or two before. It is important to differentiate these extremes of constitutional variations from the endocrinopathies.[74]

1. *Early Maturation versus Precocious Puberty*

Earlier-maturing adolescents, that is, girls with menarche between 10 and 12 and boys beginning adolescence between 11 and 13 years, have distinct social advantages in most cultures over late-maturing youths, namely, girls with menarche at 15 to 17 and boys with onset of adolescence between 16 and 18 years; but youths who mature "too early" may manifest personality difficulties.[41, 63]

One variation in the pattern of sexual maturation occurring more often in girls is early appearance of pubic hair (premature pubarche), without other manifestations. This is the result either of an increased sensitivity of the pubic hair follicles to normal preadolescent levels of androgens or of the premature increase of adrenal androgens. In the latter group the height and bone age are also accelerated.[65]

There are some girls below 9 years of age with idiopathic sexual precocity beyond the appearance of pubic hair. They have breast development and even menarche with an advance in height, dental, and bone ages as well as sexual maturation age, although their intellectual and "social" age, as well as their level of sexual interest, according to most authors,[24] corresponds to their chronological age and creates marked discordance. Although it is usually of functional origin it is necessary to differentiate youths with ideopathic precocious development from those who have an adrenal neoplasm, endocrinopathy, or the results of hormone administration. There are also boys and girls who mature early presumably because of cerebral pathology, probably in the hypothalamic region resulting from neoplasms, encephalitis, or birth injuries.[49]

2. *Delayed Adolescence versus Sexual Infantilism*

Delayed adolescence is one of the most common complaints that confront the endocrinologist. Although it is encountered in both sexes, it seems to be a greater concern of the parents of boys. By the time they reach the age of 13 to 14 years, most boys show at least some signs of adolescence. However, some fail to show any enlargement of their genitalia or presence of pubic hair and continue to grow at a slow preadolescent rate. They lag behind their contemporaries in height, muscular development, and personality maturation. Often, these are the boys who have been smaller than the average throughout childhood and show a delay of two to four years in their epiphyseal maturation. Although beginning later, adolescence, once begun, will progress either rapidly, with a sudden spurt of growth, or by a slow continuous process.

Such delays in the maturation process are usually constitutional, depending on genetic mechanisms, and are not due to a specific endocrinopathy. However, extreme nutritional deficiencies, as in anorexia nervosa or starvation, may be responsible for a delay in maturation. The problem is to distinguish patients with merely delayed adolescence from the very few who may remain permanently dwarfed or sexually infantile as a result of hypophyseal, gonadal, neurogenic, or chromosomal defects. Hormone assays and cytogenic studies[48] help in some cases, but we must still depend on clinical acuity. In many of these cases, the earliest evidences of adolescence are present but not recognized. Most of the youths who express concern over their sexual adequacy merely have delayed adolescence or are within normal limits of development with disturbances of the body-image.

The use of hormones in this group depends a great deal on the convictions of the endocrinologist or pediatrician.[74] There is always the question of when to give hormones to advance adolescence and when it would be judicious to resist the temptation to try to alter constitutional differences. Psychotherapy ranging from merely reassurance and explanation to intense psychotherapy may be required, depending on the needs of the individual.

3. *Short Normal versus Dwarfism*

Delayed onset of adolescence with the absence of the growth spurt at the anticipated age accounts for most of the youths seen with complaints of short stature. The etiology is usually either genetic or the result of a nutritional disturbance. In these youths the bone age more than the chronological age parallels the height and sexual ages. There are some youths, however, who are maturing adequately but are shorter than their associates because of hereditary factors and are classified as constitutionally short normals. Only rarely is there a failure of both sexual maturation and growth because of primary hypophyseal pathology leading to the development of a true midget.[70] Short stature is more acceptable in girls than in boys. Commercially available growth hormones have not been effective in either group, but recently available experimental data on the use of human-growth hormones have been more promising. Androgenic hormones are being used by some clinicians because of their anabolic action to stimulate growth.

4. *Adolescent Obesity*

In countries where food is plentiful, obesity is a distressing problem for body-conscious adolescents, particularly girls. A great deal has been already written in this area.[71] Data have been presented to the effect that obese children are advanced in statural growth and maturation, so that earlier than average adolescent development is the rule with obese girls and boys. This is contrary to the long-held fallacious concept that obesity in adolescence results from an endocrine disorder—either hypothyroidism, hypogonadism, or hypopituitarism. Often a diagnosis of hypogonadism is made in the male adolescent merely because the penis, normal in size, appears small because it is imbedded in the suprapubic fat. The concept of obesity resulting from overeating caused by a psychological regression or compensation is primarily the work of Newburgh[42] and Bruch.[7, 8] However, we must keep in mind that the consistent inactivity characteristic of many of these youths often plays an important role.[25]

Treatment of an obese adolescent means, therefore, more than calculating a reducing diet or giving her diuretics and amphetamine. Often she needs help for her personal difficulties. Actually the extensive use of amphetamines often creates a secondary problem that is even more distressing than the overweight, namely, psychological dependency on amphetamines.

5. *Menstrual Disorders*

Primary amenorrhea as evidence of delayed adolescence versus sexual infantilism has already been discussed. Dysmenorrhea is a common symptom and only rarely is caused by some organic condition. Usually the incapacitating cramps are an indication that the girl has difficulty in adjusting to adolescence or has a low threshold to pain.[16] Secondary amenorrhea is also common in adolescence because menstrual irregularities are the rule during the first few years after menarche. Metrorrhagia and menorrhagia are not common but demand prompt treatment, for they may indicate the presence of systemic disease, a failure of ovulation, or unusual emotional tension. Girls with menstrual disorders should be reassured and gynecological examination undertaken only when truly indicated.[20] A variety of medications and hormone therapy including thyroid has been used effectively[35] at times, in all these conditions, but often supportive reassurance or more intensive psychotherapy may be indicated, depending on the accompanying personality structure. It is because of this personality structure and the chronicity of the condition such as dysmenorrhea that the physician must be particularly wary of prescribing any drugs which may be potentially addicting.

6. Intersex

There are seven variables of sex which may go awry in problems of sexual development: the chromosomal, gonadal, and hormonal sex; the sex of the internal and external organs; the sex of assignment and rearing; and the gender role and identity.[23] Although incongruities in sexual development may be apparent before adolescence, it is often at this age that the pseudo-hermaphrodite, the eunuchoid, or the individual with abnormal chromosome disorders such as Klinefelter's or Turner's syndrome is first recognized.[23, 37, 38, 61] Attention has been called to genital abnormalities in infants, particularly enlargement of the clitoris in girls following the administration of progesteroids to mothers during their pregnancy.[76]

7. Abnormalities of the Mammary Gland

Enlargement of the breast is an occasional concern of adolescent boys. It is important to differentiate the physiological subareolar nodule and the pendulous pectoral region due to obesity or muscular development from true gynecomastia. Treatment should be directed to the personality problems created by the disturbed body-image, although, if gynecomastia is present, plastic surgery should be considered early. Subareolar nodules are usually absorbed, and pectoral obesity will respond to the usual weight-reduction regimes. The personality adjustment and body-image disturbances associated with gynecomastia have been reported in previous publications.[55, 56]

The size of adolescent girls' breasts varies a great deal and is dependent largely on genetic factors, but also on obesity, mammary glands, and hormone status. Hypertrophy of one or both breasts may occur, but this is rare. The usual anxiety of girls as to the size of their breasts relates to their self-concepts of sexually appropriate development and their concepts of the ideal, which are often unrealistic.[54]

8. Undescended Testicles

It is important to differentiate cryptorchidism from migratory testes, in which one or both testicles are at times palpable in the canal or scrotum but at other times are not palpable but can be manipulated into the scrotum.[51] These testicles usually descend into the scrotum after they enlarge with the advent of adolescence or following hormone therapy.

In cryptorchidism the testes do not descend into the scrotum at any time and may be fixed either in the canal or in the abdomen. Orchidoplexy should be performed at 5 or 6 years of age, to avoid the irreversible semini-ferous tubule degeneration which occurs during adolescence.[2]

Bilateral cryptorchidism should also be differentiated from eunuchoid-ism, in which the primary problem is failure of development of the testicles. In cryptorchidism secondary sexual characteristics develop with adoles-cence, although not in eunuchoids.[53, 54] Gonadotrophic hormones may be used to test the viability of the testes.

When a boy with undescended testes reaches later adolescence, surgery should not be performed unless there is a history of trauma, pain, tender-ness, or a hydrocele formation. Intra-abdominal testes are no more prone to malignancy than testes in the scrotum.

To avoid body-image disturbance some surgeons insert a plastic ball into the scrotum if it is necessary to perform an orchidectomy.

9. *Hirsutism*

Excessive hirsutism in girls is usually idiopathic and is often familial in origin and should be managed through cosmetic means. Only very rarely is hypertrichosis of endocrine origin, and in these cases it is associated with other symptoms.[10, 37]

BODY-IMAGE

The body-image, as a psychiatric concept, can aid in the understanding of the problems of the adolescent, for whom the body takes on a new sig-nificance. Every facet of social and personality adaptation is affected by body configuration and function: first, the impression a person makes on others, and second, how his body appears to himself, namely, the body-image. The idea of body-image was developed by Schilder[50] in his effort to integrate biological and psychoanalytical thinking and was further elabo-rated by Kolb.[32]

The body-image was defined as the "image of our body which we form in our mind—the way in which our body appears to ourself." Kolb has further divided body-image into two components: the body-percept and the body-concept.[31] The individual develops the former through the integration of multiple percepts related to his body, while the latter depends on the inter-nalized psychological processes and sensations coming from within. Each of us carries around a mental image of our own appearance which is more than a mirror image and may or may not closely approximate our actual appearance. In fact, the body-image, although wholly a psychological phe-nomenon, embraces our view of ourselves not only physically but also phys-iologically, sociologically, and psychologically. It has also been referred to in the literature with minor variations as self-awareness, self-concept, the self, body-ego, self-identity, ego identity, and body-schema. In adolescence this awareness of the self is particularly intensified because of the radical physical changes which occur, the increase of introspection, the emphasis assigned to physical traits by the peer group, and the increased tendency to compare one's self with culturally determined standards.

The rapid changes of adolescence require a revision of the body-image at the very time when youth is in the midst of emotional turmoil, so that even the normal adolescent often feels his body to be strange to him and is overly concerned about how he compares with his or her companions. Repeated studies[13, 63] have shown that the more emotionally disturbed an adolescent is, the less tolerant he is of his physical self. There is a fairly high correlation between difficulties in psychological and social adaptability and excessive interest in the body.[8, 11, 58] Many adolescents who are well within the normal range of development find that they cannot accept themselves for a variety of emotional reasons and will project concern over themselves to some aspect of their appearance or achievements.[73]

A common area of concern is whether their development is sexually appropriate. When the sexual development is atypical in comparison with the standards of the group subculture to which the adolescent belongs, whether it be stature, configuration, absence of breasts or menarche in girls, or enlarged breasts or small penis in boys, there is a loss of self-esteem, often an agonizing self-consciousness, and unwholesome adaptations because of a disturbance in body-image.[58]

Disturbances of body-image may be manifested through direct concern over appearance and function as well as through a variety of unacceptable patterns of behavior, adaptation, anxiety, and depression. The complicated constellation of physical, psychological, and social components which determine the structure of the body-image on both the conscious and unconscious levels can be evaluated through anamnesis, a variety of inventories, direct questioning, and psychological testing.

The structure of the body-image[57] is determined by:

(1) *Subjective perception of appearance and ability to function.* Ordinarily, during childhood and preadolescence the body-image changes slowly. Gradual alterations in appearance and height are easily absorbed in the prevailing picture the child has of his own body. Then, with the upheaval of adolescence, the tempo of change is greatly accelerated.[68, 69, 72] Curran and Frosch[13] call attention to the need for the radical reconstruction of the body-image during normal adolescence because of the rapid changes taking place with pubescence in size, body proportions, and primary and secondary sexual characteristics. The body attains a new value in adolescence, so that any abnormalities which may have been present since childhood develop a new significance. Growth during pubescence often tends to be discordant, so that the physical changes associated with sexual development do not always occur at the same time. Boys who experience "delayed" adolescence with an associated deficiency of height, obesity, lack of muscular development, and inadequate secondary sexual characteristics may interpret this as evidence of impaired virility; while in the girl, delayed

menarche and small breasts create equal concern about sexual adequacy. Obesity and minor aberrations in appearance such as size or shape of the nose, ears, hair texture, or certain skin conditions may become important determinants in personality adjustment. Adolescents feel that being different implies being inferior. Observable incongruous sexual development such as gynecomastia or eunuchoidism, or congenital defects such as pseudohermaphroditism, have particularly deleterious effects.[37, 53, 55, 56] Greenacre reaffirmed Schilder's contributions regarding the importance of body-image as a factor in the picture one has of one's own identity.[21] In the male the paramount features are height, the concept of strength and muscular development, the length of the penis, the presence of testes, and hirsutism. Menarche, size of the breasts, and hip development are typical of the female identity.

Stolz and Stolz[67] found that 7.5 per cent of a group of 93 normal adolescent boys appeared to be disturbed by their shortness and 13 per cent of 83 adolescent girls showed signs of worry over their tallness. At some time during adolescence, 22 per cent of the boys were unhappy about certain aspects of their physiques. Jones and Bayley[27] reported that two-thirds of the adolescents they studied expressed a desire for some change in their physique. Other studies[40, 69] revealed that late-maturing boys are more likely than their early-maturing peers to encounter a generally unfavorable sociopsychological environment resulting in an adverse effect on their personality adaptations. Sexually inappropriate development during adolescence creates disturbances of body-image. However, not all adolescents with actual defects in maturation have a body-image disturbance.[11] Therefore, it is important to evaluate to what degree obvious distortions of body configuration are actually creating a disturbed body-image and not merely assume an interrelationship of structure and behavior.

(2) *Internalized psychological factors.* Adolescents who lacked relative stability as children as a result of disturbances of the parent-child relationship, with problems of personality development and adjustment, frequently fail to develop a wholesome frame of reference for self-concept and find it difficult to cope with the social, academic, or vocational demands of adolescence. The less effectual their adaptations were in early childhood, the poorer are their adaptations to even normal adolescent body changes and even more so to real or fantasied deviations in maturation or body configuration. We must keep in mind that it is the personality which experiences the perceptions and creates the concepts that make up the body-image. Thus previous emotional experiences influence the individual's observations and interpretations. Body-image is a condensed representation of the individual's current and past experiences of his own body, real and fantasied. It has both conscious and unconscious aspects.

Although most of the essential components of the personality do take shape during childhood, their interrelationship is not fully established until late adolescence. Some of the components we must evaluate are the individual's concept of his own importance: his aspirations for self-enhancement, the sources from which he desires status, the degree of independence characterizing his relationship with others, his method of assimilating new values, his concepts of his own capacity for doing things for himself, his self-esteem and feelings of security, his ability to withstand frustration, his ability to judge himself realistically, his need for pleasurable and immediate gratification, his sense of moral obligation and responsibility, and the type of defenses he uses when his security or self-esteem is threatened.

During childhood these components are aligned according to the capacities of the child and the demands and needs of childhood. With adolescence the alignment is disrupted, creating confusion in the youth's modes of response. Before the individual can be comfortable in an adult world he must realign the components of his personality and create a new equilibrium, a new picture of himself. It seems logical to suppose that adolescence, which ushers in such tremendous change in the anatomic and physiological structure of the body with consequent emotional reactions, would also bring with it modified attitudes toward the body. The first sign of psychological change is probably an increased pressure toward maturation.[29] Very shortly, the more aggressive attack on life problems, the need for independence from parental control, the striving for maturity, and the struggle for heterosexual adjustment become fused into the so-called typical behavior of the adolescent. Many adolescents are somewhat overwhelmed for a short period by the effects of the physiological maturing process, so that some degree of body-image disturbance frequently results.

The biological differences of the sexes influence their psychology. The menstrual cycle and the role of childbearing in the female, the difference in distribution of fat and muscle in the two sexes, as well as the availability of the male genitalia for visual and tactile perception in contrast to the largely hidden female genitalia, influence the body-percept. However, the sexual differences in body-image and self-concept result not only from biological differences but also from variations in the prevailing culturally assigned gender roles.

Every adolescent has a need for a sense of his own worth, and anything that tends to make him feel inadequate or inferior is apt to be met promptly with some kind of defensive reaction. My findings agree with those of Ackerman[1] that behavioral aberrations in both boys and girls in the second decade of life are frequently caused by an inadequate adjustment to the feeling of being different. To a youth, being different usually implies being inferior.

Adolescents with a variety of personality disorders manifest their psychopathology through distortions of body-concept. Some express their feelings of smallness or inferiority of self as compared to their father through unrealistic concern over the size of their penis; others see the minimal pubertal hyperplasia of the breast or delay in onset of adolescence as evidence of actualization of a castration anxiety.

(3) *Sociological factors.* An individual in the course of his development is exposed to a variety of pressures from his environment, and he learns to adjust or adapt himself to them. Both the pressures and the adaptation occur in a social environment, so that the person is at the same time exposed to the reactions of others and by implication their evaluation of him, on the basis of which the individual may alter his behavior or reinforce it. At times the stress in the environment triggers a "feed-back mechanism" whereby primary tensions are fed by secondary ones, often leading to a vicious cycle of reverberations.

The attitude of the parents or parent substitutes imparts an indelible impression on the child's concept of himself—his body and its functions. From earliest infancy, the mother conveys her attitude toward her child's body by the way she holds him, feeds him, touches him, and attends to his needs. Later her approval or disapproval is also conveyed verbally. Bruch[9] presents a concise conceptual model of how parental attitudes are transmitted to the child.

The child's assessment of his body reflects the values of those who take care of him. Children who are accepted by their families usually neither overvalue nor undervalue their bodies. On the other hand, when the child feels that his body fails to come up to the expectations of those about him he frequently develops self-deprecatory feelings. In turn, families which tend to exploit the significance of the body's appearance and function often convey to their children an overevaluation and reliance on security through the "body beautiful" or "muscles." Adolescents with such security reliances are less able to accept or adapt to any deviation in body configuration than those who have been taught by the family to respect the uniqueness of the individual.[61]

Parents have often created the adolescent's initial anxiety about his sexual adequacy by a look, a statement, or intensive persistence in their concern over their son's genital status or height or their daughter's delayed menarche or excessive weight, transferring their concern over their own inadequacy to their children. Many parents in the series studied were overtly or covertly rejecting of their children for a variety of reasons. At times, however, their attack is unconsciously malicious and directed toward satisfying their own psychopathological needs.[26, 59] We must remember that unconscious motivations of parental behavior toward the child may be in contrast to the conscious ones, thus creating further confusion for both the adolescent and the parent.

Many of the youngsters we studied were obese children and fitted into the category investigated by Bruch.[6, 7, 8] She stated that the "outstanding pathogenic factor in the families of these obese children is the fact that the child is used by one or other parent as a thing, an object whose function is to fulfill the parents' needs, to compensate for their failures and frustrations in their own lives. The child is looked upon as a precious possession to whom is offered the very best of care." The overprotective measures which inhibit the development of muscular skills and interfere with adequate social learning and the excessive feeding are part of this "special care." Many parents openly express their dissatisfaction with the sex of the child because the other sex would have better fulfilled their hopes and dreams. The severe confusion in sexual identification, so characteristic of this group of obese boys particularly, can often be directly traced to such unfortunate parental attitudes.

When deviant maturation and inappropriate sexual development do exist, they may intensify and further complicate a previously existing hostile parent-child relationship. The anxiety associated with this inappropriate sexual development is superimposed on and interwoven with previous and current frustrations of the child's need to be loved for himself regardless of his appearance. The adolescent may feel that unrelated difficulties are caused solely by his disfigurement.

Adolescents reveal extraordinary sensitiveness about their concept of self. They react with instant responsiveness to what they think of themselves and what others think of them. Since their image of self is in a state of flux, they are especially vulnerable to other persons' judgments. The issue of whether one is approved or disapproved by others assumes a critical importance.

More significant than the objective handicap of inappropriate sexual development is the social disadvantage at which it places the deviant adolescent. Deviancy from the group elicits a highly negative response from his peers and almost guarantees that he will be treated unlike his fellows. Adolescents accord highly discriminatory treatment to persons with physical handicaps. Such persons hold lower status in the group, are frequently ostracized, fail to receive their share of attention from the opposite sex, and are often treated with open contempt and hostility. Adolescents take competitive advantage of the shortcomings of their rivals in the race for status in the group and for favor in the eyes of the opposite sex. The individual's response to his own maturational deviation is largely a reflection of the social reaction to it. During adolescence, when he is so dependent on a peer group for status, he tends to accept as real the value that the group places on him.

The physician, in turn, through his attitudes may reinforce or relieve the anxieties of the adolescent. He must be particularly careful in assessing the status and prognosis of individuals in the extremes of normal maturation.

(4) *Ideal body-image.* An ideal body-image is formulated by the adolescent derived from his experiences, perceptions, comparisons, and identifications with other persons, both real and fantasied.[29] Throughout his childhood he has been compared to others in height, weight, and intelligence. Now the adolescent finds himself inadvertently comparing himself to his age mates. The mass media contribute to his stress by overemphasizing unrealistic standards, glorifying the ideal body and degrading the deviant.

To add to his confusion, the adolescent finds that the ego ideal, the abstract concept of the person he strived to be throughout childhood usually based on identifications with the parents of the same sex and the conceptualization of the ideal by the parent of the opposite sex, often fails as a model of what he, as an adolescent, would like to be. To attain individuality he must be different, creating an amorphous self-concept.

During this period in which the ego ideal is so unstable, the adolescent may feel very anxious and may turn to his own age group. The gang or group is just one of the many examples of the effort of adolescents to find a satisfactory self-image through an interchange with others struggling for the attainment of the same goal.

CONCLUSION

Psychiatrists, pediatricians, endocrinologists, educators, psychologists, and social workers who deal with adolescents must understand the numerous changes in body structure and function which take place as a result of the adolescent process. These changes occur normally over a wide range of chronological ages and at different rates. Developmental status and chronological age are significant for the understanding of the specific behavior and attitudes of a youth. Thus it is helpful in any case study to delineate whether a youth is in early, middle, or late adolescence. Physicians working with youth must also be able to differentiate the clinical syndromes associated with adolescence.

Many of the problems of adaptation in youth are due to disturbances of body-image or self-concept associated with real, exaggerated, or fancied deviations in maturational status, which are often interpreted as inappropriate sexual development. Youths with actual developmental problems must be differentiated from those who are well within the range of normal. If the defect is real and can be modified, it may be desirable to do so through such means as are available: hormones, plastic surgery, medication, diet, or exercise. However, if it cannot be modified we must foster in the youth an acceptance of himself. Other youths merely focus on a minor physical aberration as a rationalization of a profound emotional problem.

Many adolescents with disturbances of body-image or self-concept often require intensive psychotherapy. Others merely require reassurance, continuing interest, and help in developing an insight into the difference between being abnormal and not being average. The adolescent is concerned about his body and wants his physician to take his worries seriously. It is not enough to tell an adolescent that he is within the statistical limits of normal or that he will "outgrow it."

Disturbances of body-image may be manifested through a variety of unacceptable patterns of behavior, anxieties, or depression as well as through direct concern over appearance and function. Sometimes the behavior is a reflection of the body-image disturbance; at other times it is a reaction to it.

Through a knowledge of the factors which are involved in determining the "structure" of the body-image—namely, the individual's actual appearance, the internalized psychogenic factors, the sociological factors, and his concept of the ideal—the mental health specialist is able to help the adolescent to understand his needs and thus develop acceptable adaptations.

References

1. ACKERMAN, N. W. "Adaptive Problems of the Adolescent Personality," in *The Family in a Democratic Society*. New York: Columbia University Press, 1949, p. 85.
2. BAKER, R. "Treatment of Cryptorchism," *Medical Tribune*, November 9, 1966.
3. BAYLEY, N. "Tables for Predicting Adult Weight from Skeletal Age and Present Height," *Journal of Pediatrics*, XXVIII (1946), 49.
4. BOUTOURLINE-YOUNG, H., and G. TESI. "A Standardization of Raven's Progressive Matrices," *Arch. Psicol. Neurol. Psychist.* (Milan), XXIII (1962), 455.
5. BOUTOURLINE-YOUNG, H., A. ZOLI, and J. R. GALLAGHER. "Events of Puberty in a Group of 111 Florentine Girls," *American Journal of Diseases of Children*, V (1963), 451.
6. BRUCH, H. "Obesity in Relation to Puberty," *Journal of Pediatrics*, XIX (1941), 365.
7. BRUCH, H. "Psychiatric Aspects of Obesity in Children," *American Journal of Psychiatry*, XCIX (1943), 752.
8. BRUCH, H. "Puberty and Adolescence: Psychologic Consideration," *Advances in Pediatrics*, XXXI (1948), 219.
9. BRUCH, H. "Falsification of Bodily Needs and Body Concept in Schizophrenia," *Archives of General Psychiatry*, VI (1962), 18.
10. BURNS, T. W. *Syllabus for the Endocrine Lecture Series*. Columbus, Mo.: University of Missouri School of Medicine, 1964.
11. CAPLAN, H. "Some Considerations of the Body-Image Concept in Child Development," *Quarterly Journal of Child Behavior*, IV (1952), 382.
12. CHAN, S. T., and K. S. F. CHANG. "Growth and Skeletal Maturation of Chinese Children in Hong Kong," *American Journal of Physical Anthropology*, XIX (1961), 299.
13. CURRAN, F. J., and J. FROSCH. "The Body Image in Adolescent Boys," *Journal of Genetic Psychology*, LX (1942), 37.
14. DUCHÉ, D. J., W. A. SCHONFELD, and S. TOMKIEWICZ. "Physical Aspects of Adolescent Development," in G. CAPLAN and S. LEBOVICI, eds., *Psychiatric Approaches to Adolescence*. Amsterdam: Excerpta Medica Foundation, 1966.
15. FRANK, L. K., *et al.* "Personality Development in Adolescent Girls," *Monographs of the Society for Research in Child Development*, XVI (1951), Serial No. 53.

16. GALLAGHER, J. R. "Dysmenorrhea and Menorrhagia in Adolescence," *Connecticut State Medical Journal,* XIX (1955), 469.

17. GALLAGHER, J. R., and C. D. GALLAGHER. "Some Comments on Growth and Development in Adolescents," *Yale Journal of Biology and Medicine,* XXV (1953), 335.

18. GALLAGHER, J. R., F. P. HEALD, and R. P. MASLAND. "Recent Contributions to Adolescent Medicine, Medical Progress," *New England Journal of Medicine,* CCLIX (1958), 24, 74, 123.

19. GARDNER, L. I. "Biochemical Events at Adolescence," Symposium on Adolescence, *Pediatric Clinics of North America,* VII (1960), 15.

20. GRAY, L. A. "Gynecology in Adolescence," Symposium on Adolescence, *Pediatric Clinics of North America,* VII (1960), 43.

21. GREENACRE, P. "Anatomical Structure and Superego Development," *American Journal of Orthopsychiatry,* XVIII (1948), 636.

22. GREULICH, W. W. "A Handbook of Methods for the Study of Adolescent Children," *Monographs of the Society for Research in Child Development,* III (1938), Serial No. 15.

23. HAMPSON, J. G. "The Case of Management of Somatic Sexual Disorders in Children; Psychological Considerations," in *Human Reproduction and Sexual Behavior.* New York: Lee and Febiger, 1964.

24. HAMPSON, J. G., and J. MONEY. "Idiopathic Sexual Precocity in the Female," *Psychosomatic Medicine,* XVII (1955), 16.

25. HEALD, F. "Obesity in the Adolescent," *Pediatric Clinics of North America,* VII (1960), 207.

26. JOHNSON, A. M. "Juvenile Delinquency," in S. ARIETI, ed., *American Handbook of Psychiatry.* New York: Basic Books, 1959, Vol. I.

27. JONES, M. C., and N. BAYLEY. "Physical Maturing among Boys as Related to Behavior," *Journal of Educational Psychology,* XLI (1950), 129.

28. JOSSELYN, I. M. "The Adolescent and His World," *Family Service Association of America* (1952).

29. JOSSELYN, I. M. "Psychology of Adolescents," in M. LEVITT, ed., *Readings in Psychoanalytical Psychology.* New York: Appleton-Century-Crofts, 1959, p. 79.

30. KINSEY, A. C., W. B. POMEROY, and C. E. MARTIN. *Sexual Behaviour in the Human Male.* Philadelphia: W. B. Saunders, 1948.

31. KOLB, L. C. "Body Image in the Schizophrenia Reaction," in A. AUERBACK, ed., *Schizophrenia.* New York: Ronald, 1959.

32. KOLB, L. C., "Disturbance of the Body-image," in ARIETI, *op. cit.*

33. KUHLEN, R. G. *Psychology of Adolescent Development.* New York: Harper, 1952.

34. LEVY, D. M. "Method of Integrating Physical and Psychiatric Examination with Special Studies of Body Interest, Overt Protection, Response to Growth and Sex Difference," *American Journal of Psychiatry,* IX (1929), 121.

35. McARTHUR, J. W. "Use of Newer Steroids in the Treatment of Adolescent Bleeding and Cramps," *Clinical Proceedings, Children's Hospital* (Washington), XVIII (1962), 123.

36. MASTERSON, J. F., JR., K. TUCKER, and G. BERK. "Psychopathology in

Adolescence, IV: Clinical and Dynamic Characteristics," *American Journal of Psychiatry*, LXX (1963), 357.

37. MONEY, J. "Hermaphroditism, Gender and Precocity in Hyperadrenocorticism: Psychologic Findings," *Bulletin of Johns Hopkins Hospital*, XCVI (1955), 253.

38. MONEY, J. "Problems in Sexual Development, Endocrinologic and Psychologic Aspects," *New York State Journal of Medicine*, LXIII (1963), 2348.

39. MONTAGU, M. F. A. *Adolescent Sterility, U.S.A.* Springfield, Ill.: Charles C Thomas, 1946.

40. MURSEN, P. E., and M. C. JONES. "Self-Conceptions, Motivations and Interpersonal Attitudes of Late and Early Maturing Boys," *Child Development*, XXVIII (1957), 243.

41. MUSSEN, P., and H. BOUTOURLINE-YOUNG. "Relationships between Rate of Physical Maturing and Personality among Boys of Italian Descent," *Vita Humana*, VII (1964), 186.

42. NEWBURGH, L. H. "Obesity; Energy Metabolism," *Physiological Review*, XXIV (1944), 18.

43. PAPEZ, J. W. "A Proposed Mechanism of Emotion," *A.M.A. Archives of Neurology and Psychiatry*, XXXVIII (1937), 725.

44. PATTON, R. G. "Growth and Psychological Factors," *Report of the Fortieth Ross Conference on Pediatric Research.* Columbus, Ohio: Ross Laboratory, 1962.

45. REYNOLDS, E. L. "The Distribution of Subcutaneous Fat in Childhood and Adolescence," *Monographs of the Society for Research in Child Development*, XV (1950), Serial No. 50, No. 2.

46. REYNOLDS, E. L, and J. V. WINES. "Individual Differences in Physical Changes Associated with Adolescence in Girls," *American Journal of Diseases of Children*, LXXV (1948), 329.

47. REYNOLDS, E. L., and J. V. WINES. "Physical Changes Associated with Adolescence in Boys," *American Journal of Diseases of Children*, LXXXII (1951), 529.

48. ROSS, G. T., and J. H. TIJO. "Cytogenetics in Clinical Endocrinology," *Journal of the American Medical Association*, CXCII (1965), 977.

49. ROTHBALLER, A. B. "Some Endocrine Manifestations of Central Nervous System Disease," *Bulletin of New York Academy of Medicine*, XLII (1966), 258.

50. SCHILDER, P. "The Image and Appearance of the Human Body," *Studies in the Constructive Energies of the Psyche.* London: 1935.

51. SCHONFELD, W. A. "Management of Male Pubescence," *Journal of the American Medical Association*, CXXII, No. 3 (1943), 177.

52. SCHONFELD, W. A. "Primary and Secondary Sexual Characteristics," *American Journal of Diseases of Children*, LXV (1943), 535.

53. SCHONFELD, W. A. "Inadequate Masculine Physique as a Factor in Personality Development of Adolescent Boys," *Psychosomatic Medicine*, XII (1950), 49.

54. SCHONFELD, W. A. "General Practitioners' Role in Management of Personality Problems of Adolescents," *Journal of the American Medical Association*, CXLVII (1951), 1424.

55. SCHONFELD, W. A. "Personality Effects of Gynecomastia in Adolescence," *Archives of General Psychiatry,* V (1961), 46.
56. SCHONFELD, W. A. "Gynecomastia in Adolescence, Effect on Body-Image and Personality Adaptation," *Psychosomatic Medicine,* XXIV (1962), 379.
57. SCHONFELD, W. A. "Body-Image in Adolescents, a Psychiatric Concept for the Pediatrician," *Pediatrics,* XXXI (1963), 845.
58. SCHONFELD, W. A. "Body-Image Disturbances in Adolescents with Inappropriate Sexual Development," *American Journal of Orthopsychiatry,* XXXV (1964), 493.
59. SCHONFELD, W. A. "Body-Image Disturbances in Adolescents, Influence of Family Attitudes and Psychopathology," *A.M.A. Archives of General Psychiatry,* XV (1966), 16.
60. SCHONFELD, W. A., and G. W. BEIBE. "Normal Growth and Variation in the Male Genitalia from Birth to Maturity," *Journal of Urology,* XLVIII (1942), 759.
61. SCHUTT, A. J., and A. B. HAYLES. "Intersex," *Mayo Clinic Proceedings,* XXXIX (1964), 363.
62. SEASHORE, H. G. "The Development of a Beam-Walking Test and Its Use in Measuring Development of Balance in Children," *Research Quarterly, American Association of Health,* XVIII (1947), 246.
63. SEIDMAN, J. M. *The Adolescent—A Book of Readings.* New York: Holt, Rinehart, and Winston, 1960, pp. 140, 150, 168.
64. SHUTTLEWORTH, E. K. *The Adolescent Period: A Pictorial Atlas,* Monographs of the Society for Research in Child Development, XIV (1949), Serial No. 50, No. 2.
65. SILVERMAN, S. H., et al. "Precocious Growth of Sexual Hair without Other Secondary Sexual Development: Premature Pubarche, a Constitutional Variation of Adolescence," *Pediatrics,* X (1952), 426.
66. SOBEL, H. "Factors Regulating Growth," *Report of the Fortieth Ross Conference on Pediatric Research.* Columbus, Ohio: Ross Laboratory, 1962, p. 55.
67. STOLZ, H. R., and L. M. STOLZ. *Somatic Development of Adolescent Boys.* New York: Macmillan, 1951.
68. STUART, C. "Normal Growth and Development during Adolescence," *New England Journal of Medicine,* CCXXXIV (1946), 666, 693, 732.
69. TANNER, J. M. *Growth at Adolescence.* Springfield, Ill.: Charles C Thomas, 1962.
70. VAN GEMUND, J. J., F. J. BEKKER, and N. VAN BOKHORST. "Psychosocial Sequelae of Dwarfism and Retarded Maturation," Lisbon: *Tenth International Congress of Pediatrics,* September 1962.
71. WALLACE, W. M. "Why and How Are Children Fat," *Pediatrics,* XXXIV (1964), 303.
72. WIDDOWSON, E. M. "Mental Contentment and Physical Growth," *Lancet,* I (1952), 1316.
73. WILKINS, L. "Abnormalities and Variations of Sexual Development during Childhood and Adolescence," *Advances in Pediatrics,* III (1948), 159.
74. WILKINS, L. "Tools and Methods of Diagnosis and New Trends in the Treatment of Endocrine Disorders," *Pediatrics,* XIII (1954), 393.

75. WILKINS, L. *The Diagnosis and Treatment of Endocrine Disorders in Childhood and Adolescence,* 3d ed. Springfield, Ill.: Charles C Thomas, 1965.

76. WILKINS, L., *et al.* "Masculization of the Female Fetus Associated with Administration of Oral and Intramuscular Progestions during Gestation: Non-adrenal Female Pseudohomaphroditism," *Journal of Clinical Endocrinology,* XVIII (1958), 559.

77. World Health Organization, *Health Problems of Adolescence,* Report of a WHO Expert Commission, Technical Report Series No. 308, 1965.

5

The Reactions of Adults to Adolescents and Their Behavior

James Anthony

A QUESTION OF STEREOTYPES

"In recent years," remarks a contemporary psychologist, "the adolescent has come to weigh oppressively on the American consciousness" and to occupy "a peculiarly intense place in American thought and feeling." [1] This was in contrast to earlier times when he was generally regarded with tolerant condescension as a simple-minded character living "outside the world of adult happenings" and inhabiting "an Eden of pre-responsibility." Now, he had "invaded the adult world" in two antithetical stereotyped forms. In one, he was the victimizer, "leather-jacketed, cruel, sinister and amoral," the carrier of society's sadistic and sexual projections, replacing the gangster and Negro in this role. In the other, he was pictured as the victim, passive and powerless in the face of adult corruption that sought to exploit his gullibility.

These were not the only adolescent stereotypes available to the adult population, but they presented an element of ruthlessness and sadism that resonated disturbingly in the minds of the older group and were seized upon as shibboleths in the ongoing "conflict of the generations." So powerful have been these oversimplified preconceptions and so resistant to rebuttal by opposing facts that they have made their influence felt even within the family circle, causing parents to respond to their adolescent children as if they were embodiments of negative ideas rather than real people.

To compound the mischief even further, the stereotypes have also functioned as mirrors held up to the adolescent by society reflecting an image of himself that the adolescent gradually comes to regard as authentic and according to which he shapes his behavior. In that way, he completes the circle of expectation. The adult is convinced of the validity of his stereotypes since the predicted behavior does in fact occur; the adolescent is convinced that he is simply doing what everyone is expecting him to do; and society at large is convinced that it has a problem on its hands by the daily news of incidents chronicled luridly by its reporters.

The response of any individual adult to any given adolescent may therefore be dictated by a collusion of three factors: a collective reaction as represented by the stereotype, an idiosyncratic reaction based on the personalities and experiences involved, and the "transference" reaction in which pre-existing factors from an earlier phase of life exert an influence unbeknown to the participants on their attitudes, affects, and actions, often to the detriment of the relationship. There is probably no human transaction in which any of these occurs uncontaminated by the presence of the other two, and the situation to a large extent determines which one predominates. As a general rule, the more negative the relationship, the less operative is the person-to-person response and the more conspicuous the stereotypic and irrational, unconscious modes of transacting.

In the next section follow various contemporary polarities of stereotypic thinking in their nascent form, unmodified by personal considerations. The adolescent will be seen as victimizer and victim, as dangerous and endangered; as sexually rampant requiring restraint and as sexually inadequate needing encouragement; as emotionally maladjusted crying out for treatment and as emotionally free emitting a breath of fresh therapeutic air onto stale adult conflicts; as an enviable object to cut down and as a repository of the adult's unfulfilled ambitions to be built up; as a redundant family member to be extruded with as much haste as decency will permit and as a lost object to be mourned in passing. Both adult and adolescent oscillate between these extreme images, and when the pair are not in phase, the resulting interaction may occasion a high degree of perplexity with the bewilderment evident in the inconsistent communications that then flow between the participants.

The inherently dichotomous nature of the stereotype is reflected in the good or bad images created. The behavior of the adolescent is more of a continuum with the reactions distributed along a Gaussian curve, the extreme manifestations occurring with lesser frequency. However, because they tend to gain greater publicity, the impression is created that they are the statistically expectable modes of teen-age behavior. The "headline intelligence" characteristic of the public mind has come to consider adolescence and delinquency as synonymous, interchangeable labels. The clinician does little to correct this misconception since he himself is constantly confronted with extreme reactions and may eventually be led to regard them as typical rather than atypical and infrequent. The "good" adolescent, although representing perhaps three-quarters of the adolescent population, is so effectively camouflaged by his conformity to the standards of a given culture that he is scarcely credited with existence. Instead of victim to victimizer, his role with respect to the adult has a special and satisfying quality to it that was not present in his dependent status as a child and will not be present in his ultimate status as an adult. In large measure, it can be viewed as a learning experience in which the adolescent is constantly practicing the adult role under the experienced tutelage of a friendly and encouraging adult. The relationship is regarded as basically helpful and trustworthy, even if a little avuncular and out of date. Since this chapter is directed mainly toward clinicians, it must be understood that the clinical viewpoint, with its more pathological emphasis, will be salient. Since the stereotypic reaction and the vicious misunderstanding it engenders are felt to make a major contribution to pathology, the two factors, the clinical and the stereotypic, will be interwoven in the account that follows.

THE STEREOTYPIC REACTION TO THE ADOLESCENT AS A DANGEROUS AND ENDANGERED OBJECT

The image of the "victimizer," slowly, relentlessly, and ruthlessly stalking the terrified adult, calls attention to a surprising metamorphosis in the life of the individual through which the weak and helpless child is transformed into a potent and menacing figure that can now threaten the adult on whom he once depended for his security and sustenance. Every period of human history has accorded recognition to the potential dangerousness of this transitional period, and complex procedures have been instituted to control the situation. In the Darwinian and later Freudian speculation on the "primal horde," the threat to the father with the supervention of adolescence ended with the killing and eating of the father. It was never clear in the theory to what extent such a termination was inevitable and "natural," but one would expect that when the primal hordes banded together in the form of communities, the fathers would begin to legislate in favor of their own survival, perhaps resorting to the extrusion of the adolescent male as a first resort and then eventually subduing him by means of institutional techniques. In this context, it is interesting to note that adolescent male monkeys when caged with a typical monkey family—father, three or four wives, and one or two adolescent females helping to care for a few infants—are often slain by the father at the onset of puberty.

The later institutional methods of dealing with the same problem by means of initiation rites, secret adult societies, and prolonged apprenticeships were generally effective in subduing any revolutionary trends present in the adolescent and in suppressing any inordinate wishes he might entertain for possession of the women, the work, and the food of the adults.

There is another side to the adult's reaction other than this preoccupation with the dangerousness of the adolescent. It takes the form of marked concern for the safety of the younger person and may express itself in practical measures to safeguard him against premature exposure to the physical and emotional stresses of the adult world. The minor is protected legally against exploitation by the unscrupulous adult and may react to the protection as "overprotection," regarding the prohibitions imposed as ways of thwarting his normal and necessary drives. He is quick to detect the hostility behind the solicitude, and he is often inclined to react to the former rather than to the latter component of the adult's ambivalence.

The same mixture of intention is present in the reactions of primitives. In many parts of the world, girls are suspended between earth and sky, inside a dark, airless, and filthy contraption at the time of their first menstruation not only because there is a fear that they will blight the crops, blunt the weapons, sour the milk, and cause cattle to miscarry but also because they themselves, if exposed to light, may suffer from sores, grow blind, or shrivel up into skeletons. The precautions taken, therefore, to isolate and insulate them are activated as much by concern for their safety as for the safety of the adults.[9]

As far as constitutional measures go, the more advanced societies appear to ignore adolescence almost as completely as the primitives recognize it, but the sense of danger still remains. In the words of one anthropologist: "We prescribe no ritual; the girl continues on a round of school or work, but she is constantly confronted by a mysterious apprehensiveness on the part of her parents and guardians. . . . The society in which she lives has all the tensity of a room full of people who expect the latest arrival to throw a bomb." [18]

Psychotherapists, confronted by the adolescent, have put forward as many reasons and rationalizations as parents and adults in general for treating him at all. They have argued cogently in favor of treatment, but by other therapists and in other institutions. Many have concluded, on the basis of sound reason, that it is better to leave adolescents psychotherapeutically alone during adolescence because of their well-known proclivity to act out and drop out. The vivid metaphors they have coined possess a strong deterrent quality. "One cannot analyze an adolescent in the middle phase," says one prominent author; "it is like running next to an express train." [10] Another likens adolescence to "an active volcanic process with continuous eruptions taking place, preventing the crust from solidifying." [12] Once the psychotherapist gets it into his head that he has to deal with a bomb that might explode or a volcano that might erupt or an express train that will outpace him, he will approach the treatment situation with very mixed feelings. If one adds to this array of stereotypes the reputation that even the mildest adolescents have for resorting to slight delinquencies at the least provocation, then the psychotherapist's reason for by-passing adolescence is easier to understand, if not to condone. The teen-age patients that do come to therapy and remain in therapy generally have severe passive character disorders that are developmentally preadolescent in their make-up. They behave with the co-operativeness of the average adult and child patient, but they remain largely untouched by the therapeutic process.

Within the last decade, these various considerations, plus a growing sense of responsibility toward a neglected group, have led clinicians to conclude that adolescents are best dealt with by psychiatrists who, whatever their major affiliations are, wish to deal with adolescents. There are child psychiatrists as well as adult psychiatrists who have a "built-in" flair for resonating sympathetically and empathizing deeply with the "in-between" situation. This gives them a sufficiency of comfort and confidence in coping with even tempestuous teen-agers and dampens down the fluctuations between the cautious and the carefree. Adolescents are especially sensitive to the "phony" attitudes and mannerisms of adults who are not sure whether to talk "down" or "up" or "on the level" with them, and they are liable to exploit this uncertainty to the full by taking up provocative counterpositions.

THE STEREOTYPIC RESPONSE TO THE ADOLESCENT AS A SEXUAL OBJECT

Even in these pseudosophisticated days, when information on infantile sexuality can be purchased in every drugstore and vivid accounts of prepubertal, heterosexual activities have been reported in the press, the emergence of biological sexual maturity in children invariably seems to take the family off guard as if it were completely unprepared for this natural and long-expected event. It would appear that early manifestations of the sexual impulse are in some way disregarded or depreciated as "child's play" and therefore not to be taken seriously. With the development of the secondary sexual characteristics and the occurrence of seminal emissions and menstrual flow, the family becomes uneasily aware of the new sexual object in its midst. The response varies from family to family. In some, the succession of pubertal events may be shared by the family members as in the manner of other achievements, whereas in others it is hushed up and confined to the privacy of the bedroom and bathroom.

Parental reactions to puberty are closely correlated with the extent to which sexuality has found a comfortable acceptance in the household as gauged by the affectionate demonstrations between the members and the level of accurate biological knowledge possessed by the children. There are parents who regard it as the consummation of their own psychosexual development, rounding off the cycle of the generations. There are others who are pruriently intrigued by the shy and groping sexuality of the novitiate and obtain vicarious enjoyment in stimulating its appearance and mocking its ineptness. A third group of parents, with a high degree of sexual repression, may react with dismay and displeasure at the slightest display of erotic feeling. The frigid woman, psychosexually infantile, insists on maintaining an asexual status not only for herself but also for her children.[22] She is blind to the pubertal indices and repulsed by any form of adult heterosexuality. On the other hand, she is not greatly perturbed when the adolescent displays homosexual tendencies, symptoms indicating oral and anal fixations or incestuous concerns. The hostile reactions to maturity contrast with the overflow of pathological tenderness occasioned by immaturity, so that the children are caught up in a vortex of changing attitudes and behavior that bewilder them even more than the biological events taking place in them. Unable to accept her own femininity, the frigid woman is inevitably led to sabotage the sexual development of her adolescent daughter. As long as the little girl is a "neuter," the mother remains on good terms with her; but with puberty, a dynamic conflict comes into focus and a fierce hostility takes hold of the mother. She cannot and will not allow her daughter to become a woman, and the resulting conflict around the sexual identity in the daughter reactivates her own identity problem. It is difficult for any child to develop beyond the neurotic inhibitions of its parents, but nowhere is this truer than in the development of sexual identity. The transition from "asexual" child to sexual adolescent may not only put the parent's psychosexual maturity to the test but also tax her relationship with the child. "The very individual toward whom the parent was able to show overt signs of love during childhood has now become a sexually stimulating and taboo object. As a result parents must mobilize defenses to handle the anxiety provoked by their own incestuous fantasies." [2]

Another effect of adolescence on the adult is the reactivation of his own adolescent struggles with overt autoerotic, homosexual, and oedipal conflicts with the development of what amounts to an adolescent decompensation in retrospect. Not infrequently, this upsurge of suppressed adolescent feeling may drive the parent into psychotherapy. A given family may therefore have two crises occurring concomitantly: the crisis of adolescence in the child and a reactivated adolescent crisis in his parent.

These roused sexual impulses may confine themselves to the realm of psychopathology, but a break-through into everyday life is not uncommon, especially in homes where there is a general degradation of living conditions as a result of economic privations, alcoholism, and mental illness. A weak incest barrier may give way under these circumstances and a spate of miscarriages and pregnancies may result. In one survey at an obstetrical hospital, it was calculated that at least one-third of the illegitimate pregnancies were the products of incestuous union, mainly with the father. It is surprising that the figure is not even greater when one takes into account the prevalence of "Lolita" fantasies in middle-aged men with adolescent daughters, as revealed in psychotherapy. It is also characteristic of fathers who have near-incestuous relationships with their daughters to react to any adult heterosexual interests on the part of the girls with prudish indignation.

The ambivalence noted in the parent's response to the adolescent as a dangerous object is equally true of the present consideration. An analysis of transactions between parents and adolescents around a covertly sexual conflict can illustrate how both sides play out their conscious and unconscious roles in response to wishes and fears that are implied, but seldom verbalized. At one level, the parent may react with justifiable anxiety in keeping with his cultural standards, and the adolescent, in turn, may behave in a way appropriate to the codes prevalent in the peer group. Underlying this reaction, there may be another less conscious one in which the parent may be provoking the adolescent to act out some of his own urgent repressed fantasies, at the same time punishing him for attempting to do so. The child may be dimly aware of this unconscious manipulation and may respond to the conflicting communications of the two levels with a double-bind communication of his own. For example, he may deny that he has done anything bad, indignant at the suspicion, and at the same time, he may "blow up" the experience and make a sexual mountain out of an ignominious molehill. On still another level, the parent may be reacting to a deep dissatisfaction with his own sexual lot in life and envious that his child is getting something while he is being deprived. The adolescent, in turn, may react with anger because he is being accused of engaging in activites the like of which he has often desired but cannot bring to pass because of his own inhibitions or the inhibitions of his partner. Under these circumstances, both parents and child may feel that his biological drives are setting up an insuperable barrier between them.[20]

The way in which a mother and adolescent daughter may play out their conscious and unconscious roles in a critical transaction involving sexuality is beautifully illustrated in Spiegel's account [21] of a 16-year-old daughter of an Irish-American family who, after being instructed to be home at 11:30 P.M. following a dance, eventually arrives home at midnight and explains to the mother that she and her date had gone for coffee and doughnuts with some others and had not been served right away. Her mother glares at her and asks in an accusatory voice what she has been up to. The mother proceeds to smell her breath, getting her to exhale in order to detect any trace of alcohol. She then carries out a minute examination of her clothes, all of which are accompanied by the daughter's protestations in the form of: "Oh, Mother, why do you behave like this? I didn't do anything. I just couldn't get home in time; there is no reason to get excited about it. . . ."

Spiegel then sets about analyzing the nature of the persuasion implicit in the various operations. The daughter's intention is to show mother that she is steering herself in the direction of conventional behavior for adolescent girls. The mother's third-degree technique is aimed at casting the daughter in a particular role, that of a girl who has already carried out the mother's fantasy that she was a bad girl. Practically the only way that the daughter can understand the mother is by seeing her as a disppointed and indignant parent of a bad girl. On an implicit level, mother is heavily but unconsciously involved in steering her daughter into an impression of deviant behavior, as a result of which the daughter assigns her the role of a mother who is overanxious, inappropriately disturbed, and overinvolved in her morbid fantasies about her daughter. The girl perceives what underlying pleasure it is to the mother, and she assumes the role of the bad girl. In terms of double-bind theory, the mother is making a contradictory set of statements, wanting her daughter to be good and at the same time wanting her to be bad. The mother's unspoken statement, "I want you to be good," can be coupled with a similar response from the daughter, saying, "I have been good." The mother's unspoken statement, "I think you have been bad, and, in fact, I am sort of expecting that you have been bad," may be linked to the daughter's unspoken response, "I am sort of expecting that you would expect that because of your nasty mind. In fact, I might just as well be a bad girl. You think I am so awful that I might just as well make you happy." Spiegel interprets the mother's unconscious motivation as a wish that her daughter act out the mother's urgent but repressed sexual fantasies. The situation at this point clearly reaches an impasse. Spiegel then speculates as to what the daughter or mother *might* have said in order to avoid falling into this state of pathological equilibrium. For example, the daughter might have responded to the mother's opening inquiry by bursting into tears and saying, "I am terribly sorry. I know you told me what I shouldn't do, but the boy was so attractive that I thought it wouldn't hurt if we just sat in the car a little bit before we came in." A confession like this would have assured mother that her message had been adequately received by the daughter, adequately understood, and adequately returned. The mother, for her part, might have responded to her daughter's tardiness by simply inquiring, "What happened?" meaning you might have been doing something exciting that would interest a mother whose romantic life has passed but who can live it again in her daughter. The daughter would then offer some minor little sin within the framework of the world's moral system that would satisfy her mother without upsetting her.

The half-conscious knowledge of the girl is constantly responding to the mother's unconscious feelings and fantasies. Neither of them can express what they really want to say, and for this reason misunderstanding grows on a manifest level until it reaches the moment of assault. The state of pathological equilibrium becomes established, and there appears to be no way out of the situation. The daughter is almost aware that her mother is involved in her own personal drama and that much of what is happening does not belong to her and the situation at all. The mother's unconscious motivation leads her to suspect and expect sexual misbehavior on the part of the child.

This type of "driven" suspiciousness is not confined to mothers and daughters. Fathers, who have established the same type of intimate and possessive relationship with their children, can also behave with disturbing intrusiveness when adolescent sexuality threatens their regime. Gosse, in this sensitive autobiographical study of son and father drawn too closely together,[14] tells of the way the boy is "bombarded" with letters from the father while attending school in London away from home. (It is pathognomonic of the relationship that he both read and responded to these with such intensity of persuasion and protest.)

My father's anxiety about what he called "the pitfalls and snares which surround on every hand the thoughtless, giddy youth of London," became extremely painful to himself . . . he worked himself up into a frame of mind which was not a little irritating to his hapless correspondent.

In response to his son's protests, the father writes back:

You charge me with being suspicious, and I fear I cannot deny the charge. . . . I rejoicingly acknowledge that from all I see you are pursuing a virtuous, steady, worthy course. . . . Holy Job suspected that his sons might have sinned. . . . Was not his suspicion much like mine, grounded on the same reasons and productive of the same results?

The son, internally rebellious if outwardly obedient, groans under the moralistic tyranny:

I was so docile, I was plausible, I was anything, but combative: if my father could have persuaded himself to let me alone, if he could merely have been willing to leave my subterfuges and my explanations unanalyzed, all would have been well.

But the father, like the mother of the girl on the date, cannot, in the nature of things, leave the son alone. The pruriency occasioned by his own repressed wishes, combined with his possessive protectiveness, compels him to probe and pry frantically to the point where all rational perspective is lost.

The capacity for such sexually inhibited parents to stifle the growing wonder and curiosity of their pubescent children is based on stratagems for which the children have no response at all, since they exploit a technique that emphasizes an apparently vast psychological distance between the child's naïveté and the adult's experience and know-how.

The sexual rivalry appearing in the family at this time can have disruptive effects on marriage. An attractive daughter may become a serious rival to a mother who has been thwarting her husband for many years. The father begins to take notice of his daughter and finds reasons for taking her out in place of her mother. He may also begin to respond to other "dates" in a jealously hostile matter, either sulkily ignoring their existence or referring to them in terms of scathing criticism. (One young girl amusingly referred to her father as suffering from an attack of "oedipops.")

The development of a strong love relationship, almost exclusive in its attachment, with one parent can sometimes shut out the other parent altogether and leave her mourning the loss of a child. This is clearly shown in an extract from the *Diary of Anne Frank*.

Friday, second of April, 1943, Dear Kitty, Oh dear: I've got another terrible black mark against my name. I was lying in bed yesterday evening waiting for Daddy to come and say my prayers with me and wish me goodnight, when Mummy came into my room, sat on my bed, and asked very nicely, "Anne, Daddy can't come yet, shall I say your prayers with you tonight?" "No, Mummy," I answered. Mummy got up, paused by my bed for a moment, and walked slowly towards the door. Suddenly she turned and with a distorted look on her face said, "I don't want to be cross. Love cannot be forced." There were tears in her eyes as she left the room. I lay still in bed, feeling at once that I had been horrible to put her away so rudely. But I knew, too, that I couldn't have answered differently. It simply wouldn't have worked. I felt sorry for Mummy; very, very sorry, because I had seen for the first time in my life that she minds my coldness. Just as I shrink at her hard words, so did her heart when she realized that the love between us was gone. She cried half the night and hardly slept at all.[8]

The mother-daughter rivalry has its most extreme expression within the setting of the "menopausal-menarche" syndrome, when the mother's waning reproductive life is confronted with the flowering sexuality of the girl. The interaction stirs up considerable anxiety and depression in both, and the nagging relationship of prepuberty is transformed into an open warfare in which the Geneva conventions are abandoned. The father often carries a "diplomatic immunity" in these situations. The bread-and-butter battles are waged between mother and daughter at the same time as the daughter retains her romantic attachment to the father. An example of this was given by the mother of a young college freshman. The two were screaming at each other over the long-distance telephone, locked in a fierce argument about allowance, clothes, and so on. At the height of the quarrel, the father came to the phone and asked the girl how things were going. In her sweetest, most agreeable style, she informed him that everything was going very well and that she was very pleased with herself and with life in general. After he had had his say, his wife took up again, and the battle was resumed at its former pitch. There is a two-sided masochistic-sadistic tendency in adolescent parental quarrels, and it is a strange fact that the quarrels may often take on the color of love scenes with tender reconciliations.

The reactions of adults to the sexual pressures produced by their adolescent children may run the gamut of sexual psychopathology from the autoerotic to heterosexual "acting out" so that unfaithfulness may enter the marriage for the first time. There is no doubt that the sexuality of the adolescent is a stimulus for the sexuality of the parent. This is well demonstrated again in the primitive situation, when the adolescent is initiated into sexual life and the adult seizes upon the occasion to be openly sexual. "The use of obscene language, expressions of desire for prohibited sexual relationships, public mention of the sexual act and its mechanics, immodest exposure and hip movements—all these ordinarily shocking acts are expected and performed by women leading the novices back from the initiation ceremony." [16]

In psychotherapy with adolescents, the countertransference feelings may become erotic and disturbing, especially when the therapeutic alliance is a heterosexual one. The incest barrier is not as strong in the transference relationship as it is in real life, and the adolescent can be as seductive and charming as with the parents. The therapist has techniques for dealing with children and with adults, but he is often at a loss to know what to do therapeutically with the adolescent. For want of anything better, he may simply combine the child and adult approach or move from one to the other. He may find himself defeated, whatever his approach. When, for example, he treats the adolescent girl with the open friendliness he reserves for his child patients, she may react disconcertingly like a mature woman, so that his innocent maneuvers take on the guise of seduction; and when he retreats to the adult position and keeps her at a distance, she melts away, leaving behind a little girl who cannot understand why she may not be loved in the old way.

The therapist may also find himself reacting as indignantly as the parents to reports of sexual misdemeanors and even adopting a strategy of moral expediency. He may warn against boys who proceed beyond "third base" and confront the defiant patients with threats of pregnancy and venereal disease in the name of the reality principle.

The following clinical illustration will indicate how far this can go.

The girl, age 16, comes in, sits down, and crosses her leg over a knee. Her short skirt slips up and exposes her thigh. The therapist quickly looks away into the far corner of the room, but some cue leads her to pull her recalcitrant skirt down. It slips up several times during the interview, and each time the same looking-away, pulling-down sequence follows. At one point, he is deliberating whether to interpret her seductiveness, but for some reason cannot bring himself to do so.

She says: "Well, if you must know, I went out with Charlie last night."

He lights his pipe carefully while she watches him. Eventually he says: "You want to tell me something about it."

"I didn't say I did." He is silent for a while, but a vague annoyance about Charlie begins to grow.

"He is not the best person for you to go out with, but you know that."

"Yes, I know that." She looks at him silently.

"The problem is not that you'll do something that you'll regret, but that you'll fill yourself with anxiety and guilt that will set you back to the point when you first came to me."

"You're taking it for granted that something happened."

"I'm taking it for granted that you'd be upset if something happened, and you are upset."

"In your mind, I can only be upset about sexual things?"

"That's what has always upset you in the past, but I admit I am making an assumption. Are you going to tell me I'm wrong?"

She is silent for a moment.

"You really want to know all about it, don't you? But you're not going to know, so put that in your pipe and smoke it."

Her skirt has slipped up again, and he feels an erotic tug.

Such difficulties have led many to conclude that adolescents should be treated by therapists of their own sex. When this happens, the situation is different, but no less disturbing. The blatant homosexuality of the adolescent under conditions of treatment may evoke countertransference responses in the therapist that may take the form of outright rejection.

THE STEREOTYPIC RESPONSE TO THE ADOLESCENT AS A MALADJUSTED INDIVIDUAL

In one of the many current portraits of the adolescent, the author refers to "a fluent, loosejointed restlessness alternating with catatonic repose." [5] A puzzled teacher likened the experience of his contact with adolescents to a ride on the big dipper: "Sometimes you are up and sometimes you are down, but you never knew for certain when the next swing was coming." The adult in our Western culture has apparently learned to expect a state of acute disequilibrium and anticipates the "storm and stress" in his adolescent child as he once anticipated the negativism of his 2-year-old. The expectation has seemingly been incorporated into the literature of psychological development, and it may take methodical research and many years of endeavor to remove it from the textbooks. There is, however, growing anthropological and sociological support for the concept that society gets the type of adolescent it expects and deserves, and this is true of even those members who come into daily contact with the ordinary teen-ager. In a recent poll of teachers, for example, more than 80 per cent of them subscribed to the opinion that adolescence was a phase of "great emotional disturbance," and more than half of them believed that the child at this time underwent a complete personality change.[5]

It is not surprising, from what we said earlier, that adolescents themselves begin to share this opinion and to assume that their mood swings and waywardness are signs of incipient insanity. The referral to the psychiatrist may help to confirm this inner apprehension, and it is at this age that the fear of the psychiatrist is at its greatest. It is at this age that the altered body-image, the alienation of parts of the psychic structure, and the intense masturbatory conflicts all give rise to the same terrible speculation with the panic-stricken reaction, "I'm not nuts; I don't need a nut doctor."

The immature, unstable parent, like the sexually inhibited one, helps to aggravate these feelings of inner looseness and unco-ordination. In fact, the unstable parent may respond to the increased pressures introduced by adolescence by regressing into helplessness himself and may invite and obtain a protective, solicitous, almost therapeutic response from the adolescent. This "reversal of generations," which can be looked on as a natural development

of life when the parent figures shift into the helplessness of old age, is sometimes prematurely in evidence at this early stage. In his "therapeutic" role
the adolescent may be burdened with many of the adjustment problems of
the parent. "At last I've got someone to talk to. I've never been able to say
this to anyone else. I have never been able to tell anyone what a sexual
brute your father really was. Now that you know all about sex, you can
realize what I have been through with him. . . ." And in like measure:
"Your mother never really understood me. She aged so quickly, whereas I
managed to remain comparatively young. Poor old dear, she's only half the
woman she once was. I suppose you and I have to hold up the fort now
together. She's not going to be much help to us now. . . ."

Adolescent feelings persisting in the parents do not always work negatively for the adolescent child. They can and do often lead to greater sympathy, empathy, and understanding. The parent with a better recollection of
his own adolescent difficulties can use this constructively in dealing with his
child and, in so doing, may be able to help himself. The capacity to identify
with the adolescent will permit parents to handle the usual type of
adolescent problem with a lighter touch. They may react, as one author
puts it, with "a felt nostalgia for the youthful exuberance, fresh love impulses, and a sneaking adoption of the rebellion." [19] This "ectopic youthful-
ness" enhances the sensitivity of the individual in relationship to younger
individuals.

The fluctuations characteristic of adolescence demand flexibility on the
part of the parent, the changing mood and manners calling constantly for
changing attitudes and behavior toward them. It is not easy for even the
average parent to shift comfortably in rhythm with these emotional swings
since he is so often left completely in the dark as to what has occasioned
them. For example, a transient depression may reflect an intercurrent scholastic or vocational difficulty, a setback in a love affair, a nostalgia for the
lost world of childhood and its love objects, or an upsurge of guilt from a
reactivation of unconscious sexual and aggressive urges leading to a hostile
retreat from the world. On the other hand, it may be no more than a phase
of introspection, as the adolescent stops to take stock of himself. The same
variety of causes may underlie states of happiness, and it is therefore not
surprising at all that the psychologically untutored parents, however devoted, may find themselves exasperated by the unpredictable nature of the
affect.[16] When they do shift successfully in rhythm with the children, a sense
of harmony pervades the family, at least for a while. Jacobson gives an
example of such flexibility.

"Last summer," I was told by the mother of an attractive, lively intelligent
girl of seventeen, "nothing but poetry existed for June. During the winter her
only interests were dancing, flirtations, and boys. This summer she has spent
sitting alone on the rocks, gazing dreamily at the ocean . . . but, after all,"
the mother added thoughtfully, "what are rocks for?" [16]

The therapist, like the parent, has his own special problems in fitting himself and the adolescent into the same therapeutic situation. What disturbs him, as it disturbs the parent, is the "unsettled state" of the adolescent ego and the sheer intensity of the libidinal and aggressive impulses. He may show a similar sensitivity to the swings in object relationships. The adolescent's continued need to experiment with his object world, cathecting and decathecting without too much rhyme or reason, can interfere in the therapeutic situation with the establishment of a stable transference state that can proceed to a workable transference neurosis. In fact, the therapist is treated in the same "transitional" way as the other objects in the adolescent's life, and the countertransference of the therapist may take the form of inner resentment at the "fickleness" of his patient as he struggles to break away from the reactivated infantile tie.

A great many therapists find it highly uncomfortable to treat children during the earlier phase of adolescence when they neither play nor talk nor look to a friendly adult for help, but seem merely bent on escape. The patients are bored and restless, may yawn openly in response to a well-thought-out interpretation, and, when the therapist attempts to focus on the relationship, they will counter with a description of their passionate involvements at school and elsewhere. The therapist finds himself put on the shelf with a hundred other objects currently competing for the adolescent's attention. He will be irritated, and parents will readily recognize and sympathize with the essence of his irritation.

> Most of the young adolescents I have seen consider all adults their natural enemies. If they say anything at all, they will barely state a complaint, and then defiantly wait for you to magically do something about it. I have never found any way to handle this, and the only children of this age I have treated are those who started with me at an early age or were quite immature. . . . A great deal of environmental manipulation is usually required, and as soon as external pressures are relieved, the patient tends to drop out of treatment.

The high dropout rate in psychotherapy has given adolescents a bad name in therapeutic circles, and therapists are wary of taking them on for any form of intensive treatment. The main complaint is that they do not seem to form a stable working relationship; but this is like saying that the seasons vary throughout the year and that you cannot depend on having warm days and blue skies for picnics in the middle of March. It is in "the nature of things." Once the therapist has accepted the fluctuating responses and the irregular attendance as a "natural" part of the general variability of the period, he can settle down to incorporating them into his technical approach, even to the extent of regularizing anticipated breaks from treatment.

THE STEREOTYPIC RESPONSE TO THE ADOLESCENT AS AN OBJECT OF ENVY

It is clear that "psychologically speaking" the adolescent is on his way up when the caretaking adults are on their way down. This basic anabolic-catabolic distinction understandably provokes in the adult envy for the adolescent's youthful vigor with all its freedom, freshness, and joyful foolishness. The envy may show itself in a contrast derision at the simplicity and awkwardness of the younger person and at his lack of experience in worldly matters. At its worst, it can take the form of highly sadistic measures disguised in the form of initiation rites and rituals.

A frequent cause of disturbances in the family is the narcissistic parent in competition with the adolescent of the same sex. He has long been better at doing some things than his son, and he can hardly conceive that the latter is now overtaking him. At this point, the better-adjusted parent will retire gracefully from the scene, acknowledging the new state of affairs, while his immature counterpart will attempt strenuously to outdo his rival in every activity, even to the point of a coronary attack, as occurred in one case recently when a father undertook to beat his teen-age son in ten different athletic events and was rushed to hospital at the end of the eighth.

The envious response to the biological events of puberty may take a variety of forms. A woman analyst has discussed the sadistic manifestations of the mother in her treatment of the girl at her first menstrual period: "We should reflect that many mothers do their best to keep young and to deny, even to themselves, the fact that they are growing older and find an adolescent daughter an uncomfortable reminder of what they are striving to forget or to hide from others. It often happens that the first menstruation may coincide with the mother's menopause, and this will greatly magnify her reactions." [3]

The complex emotions involved in the adult reaction—the hatred, the ambivalence, the sadomasochism, the envy and jealousy, the resentment, the reproachfulness, and (most difficult for the adolescent to endure) the dramatized martyrdom—are all condensed in the mother-daughter relationship described by Helene Deutsch.

> Dorothy is so cruel to her. The mother supposes that Dorothy must grow away from her and that this is part of it, but it is not right. Sometimes Dorothy says that she hates her mother. The mother tells her right back that she hates her. Then the mother begins to cry. "And I mean it! She is so wicked. If I had a choice, I would send her to the army instead of John (her son). He is good. Why should the good ones have to go and the mean ones remain? Of course, I love her, too. But why must she act that way to me? It's not right." She continues to complain that Dorothy is "unfair" to her, and that she is "cheap" and "ungrateful." She can't endure it. She will tell the whole

world and punish her daughter. "You want me to forgive her, but I can't," she says resentfully and hatefully; she will not be a doormat for Dorothy. "I don't say anything. I keep my feelings inside me, and they pile up, and then I can't keep them back any longer. I let them out on her, and then she is angry, and it happens all over again. . . . It's not right for her to act so, and I resent it, and I cannot keep from showing it." The mother had pushed her daughter into a stage career from early childhood as a personal fulfillment for herself, and she now resents and is frightened of her daughter's sophistication, independence, and defiance. Above all, she is strongly envious of her. She contrasts her own lot with Dorothy's. She was never liked; nobody ever cared for her; this was not "right," because she was a conscientious hard worker. Things never came easily and effortlessly to her as they have come to Dorothy.[6]

In primitive communities, the attack on the pubertal child is institutionalized and, therefore, more open. An anthropologist offers this description of the reaction of the mothers to the removal of the clitoris at a ceremony for female initiation: "As soon as the piece of flesh has dropped to the ground, the crowd of women begin trilling loudly, gaily screaming and shouting, and in some cases dancing individually." [17]

The conflict of the generations is, therefore, directed in some part at keeping upcoming youth with all his enthusiasm, his drive, his developing skills and knowledge, his relatively open mind, and his colossal capacity for assimilating new ways and new ideas from overthrowing the "establishment" and upsetting the adult roles. Initiation rites help to keep him in his place, and so do qualifying examinations.[23] The examiner may regard the examination as a means of "getting his own back on his father" or of getting his own children to "toe the line" and do exactly what they are told. The hostility of some examiners on these occasions has passed into the student folklore, but it does lead to a great deal of impotent counterhostility on the part of the students. It is interesting to recall that following examinations during the Middle Ages, the candidate was required to take an oath that he would not "take vengeance on the examiner."

The mechanisms of envy in the adult frequently feed on the differences between the child's experience of life and what the parent himself had to go through as a child. "I never had a car at your age, and I don't see why you should. You get more allowance in a week than I got in a year. I had to work my way through high school, but you go to a private one." The feelings are exacerbated by grandparents, once so hard on the parents and now so intent apparently on "spoiling" the adolescent grandchild.

One way the parents have developed of dealing with these scarifying feelings of envy is by identifying with the newcomer and making his future narcissistically their own. He can then carry the parents' unrealized ambitions and aspirations, and the energies are thus harnessed to pushing the adolescent up rather than keeping him down, although the process may generate as much conflict and resentment in the younger person. Henry quotes from a letter written by a 16-year-old girl, "I have problems in turning down dates with boys because I would rather do something with just girls rather than go out with any boy I don't like. My parents don't think I should feel this way—my parents think I don't go out with enough boys." [15] And from a 16-year-old boy, "My parents tried to make me into a boy who would impress them if they would meet me for the first time." Many parents, still smarting from recollections of an unpopular adolescence, preach that fun is of paramount value and that "youth should be a swirl of fun."

The complex cluster of emotions involved in this particular adult reaction—the hatred, the ambivalence, the sadomasochism, the envy and jealousy, the resentment, the reproachfulness, and (most difficult for the adolescent to endure) the dramatized martyrdom—is usually not so manifest in the workings of the therapeutic alliance, especially if the therapist has undergone some treatment himself. Nevertheless, there are certain transient manifestations of envy that crop up from time to time in the course of treatment and stem from a "comparison of lots." In one instance, a therapist found himself becoming increasingly angry with an adolescent boy whom he had been treating for some years. On carrying out a little self-analysis, he found himself deeply envious of the boy's progress as a patient and unable to derive any satisfaction whatsoever from the excellent outcome. Not only did he feel that the boy was getting much more out of the treatment situation than he himself ever did, but moreover he had had to wait until well into adult life for his help. He recalled struggling hopelessly and despairingly with his adolescent predicament to the point of contemplating suicide, and now he was confronted with this rich child who obtained it as he needed it. Having undone the severe inhibition impeding his patient, he had watched the unfolding of a delicate and tender adolescent romance which had filled him with pain at the thought that he himself had never and would never experience such young love. At that time of life, he had been racked with unfulfilled desires for which masturbation and fantasy were no compensation. He even envied the good relationship that the boy had established with his parents, which was again so unlike his own experience. At the time that he had felt his first angry countertransference response, his patient had been given a Thunderbird by his father and had taken his girl for a trip through the countryside. In his self-analysis, this immediately evoked one of his adolescent fantasies. His father had suddenly broken through the barrier of their bad relationship and had presented him with a motorcycle. Full of a new confidence, he was riding through the countryside and encountered a young hitchhiker. He picked her up, and they passed an idyllic day in the country.

The deep clash lay between the unfulfilled adolescent fantasy of the therapist and the consummations achieved by the patient, resulting in an overpowering surge of envy that almost brought the treatment to a premature ending.

THE STEREOTYPIC REACTION TO ADOLESCENTS AS LOST OBJECTS

Many writers have commented on the depression that invades the earlier part of adolescence when the children are decathecting their childhood objects. The children lose their parents, but the parents also begin to lose their children, and it is this depression that may evolve into a serious clinical melancholia. The parents experience a sense of emptiness about the home and an absence of goals that had motivated them so strongly and consistently throughout the childhood of their children.

The attempt to recapture the vanishing object can be strenuous. With every artifice at their command, certain parents will attempt to close the doors and raise the drawbridges and dig deep moats to keep their burgeoning offspring in, for they cannot bring themselves to realize that the loss entailed is almost as inevitable as death and almost as irreversible. They may offer themselves as apparently new objects, disguised as adolescent playmates, but the adolescent readily detects the old object in the new and struggles to escape even more strenuously. They may attempt to keep pace with the young and wear themselves out in so doing, or at least for a while they may successfully deny entrance to any new object.

It may take some time to discover that gaining new objects and losing old ones go hand in hand in the course of normal adolescent development and that their only chance of preventing the escape of the adolescent is to set about systematically enslaving the child from his earliest years, so that by the time he reaches adolescence, the incestuous enthrallment is complete. This is the type of child who never seems to enter adolescence. Childhood is prolonged indefinitely, and the parent certainly has possession of the child. However, the ambivalence involved in the fixation is so severe, and the pathological developments of the child so extreme, that the conservation is associated with little real happiness for the parent.

A surer way of retaining some part at least of the lost child is by helping the process of separation and individuation to its completion and culmination in the adult child. A new relationship then becomes possible in which two adults, linked by mutual happy memories, find to their surprise (not knowing the strength of the identification processes) that they have many interests in common and discover a new mature pleasure in each other as people. This pleasure is no longer derived from the old anaclitic model, but depends on the rediscovery of the child as an adult object, the parent having gracefully relinquished the child at the start of adolescence.

The problem for the therapist is also a major one which, unless resolved, can result in one form of interminable treatment. Termination may become a crucial problem for the therapist with patients of all ages, but particularly so at adolescence, when it may reactivate separation difficulties experienced by the therapist during his own adolescence. This is, once again, a counter-transference issue. As previously affirmed, it is part of normal development for the adolescent to wish to break away from the regressive treatment relationship, and it is in the nature of the countertransference based on parental identification that the therapist can constantly find rational reasons why it is always too early to do so. There is an inevitable struggle between these two opposing forces, culminating in the guilty escape of the patient and in angry depression, often masked, in the therapist. It may take several incomplete terminations for the patient finally to end his treatment and for the therapist to feel satisfied that it was really the right moment. Some of his termination anxiety may go underground to be reactivated, as in a recent instance when a former adolescent patient sent her therapist a wedding invitation which promptly precipitated a depression in him.

STEREOTYPIC REACTIONS OF SOCIETY TO THE ADOLESCENT

There are recent indications that an organized teen-age subculture is undergoing rapid development in the United States and that the products of this culture are producing mixed reactions in the adult population. Books and articles give a good indication of the way in which adult opinion is consolidating around the adolescent problem. The literature seems fairly evenly divided between those who are for the adolescent and say so and those who are against, but find it difficult to express their hostility directly. A few sentences from *Teenage Tyranny* will convey the flavor of this latter attitude.

> Teenage, like birth and death, is inevitable. It is nothing to be ashamed of. Nor is it a badge of special distinction worthy of a continuous party. . . . We are not against teenagers nor are we particularly for them. It would be dishonest for us to claim that some of our best friends are teenagers. . . . We are not writing this book to declare war on teenagers. . . . What worries us is not the greater freedom of youth but rather the abdication of the rights and privileges of the adults for the convenience of the immature. . . . The pages which follow are not intended as a declaration of war; . . . we do not want to be cantankerous. But we strongly believe that . . . American civilization tends to stand in such awe of its teenage segment that it is in danger of becoming a teenage society, with permanently teenage standards of thought, culture, and goals. As a result, American society is growing down rather than growing up. . . . This is a creeping disease, not unlike hardening of the arteries. It is a softening of adulthood.[20]

Looking at the past, the authors of *Teenage Tyranny* feel that two magic words have dominated child development and child education; these are "self-expression" and "child-centered." They ascribe much of the growing conflict among teen-agers to the combined scholastic maneuvers of intellectual postponement and social speed-up. They are ready to blame the adults for much of the trouble brought about by adolescents. Their major concerns are with the uncontrolled and often adult-instigated dating and mating patterns and the pseudomaturity behavior accompanying them. The adults, they feel, are giving their children too much license and too much money. The authors question to what extent the emerging generations are likely to be "predecayed" as a result of the constant indulgence and taken-for-granted luxuries that surround them all their lives.

There is some feeling on the opposite side for the "vanishing" adolescent.[11] The adult's response to adolescent activity is recognized as being more influenced by the adult's own unconscious needs and tensions than by what the adolescent is actually doing. It is noted how often the adolescent personality generates a major conflict in the adult, characterized by too much anxiety and hostility (usually disguised as concern) and giving rise to a whole complex of feelings, attitudes, and influential, unconscious trends. Friedenberg feels that the primary response is invariably to adolescent sexuality, but that the total reaction is then maintained by the irrational vigor of the adult's libidinal energy. He thinks that adults are threatened first by the fear that adolescents will grow out of control situations and second by the fear of aging with concomitant envy of a life not yet squandered. The adolescents themselves react to the adult's reactions and act out the rituals imposed by an anxious culture.

The advice offered to teen-agers in special newspaper columns sounds as if it all comes from the same fashionable textbook. The counselors oscillate between the stereotypic response to adolescents as victims and victimizers. For example, parents may be told to view their teen-ager's hostility without any reaction other than sympathy and understanding. The permissiveness accorded currently to early childhood is merely pushed up one notch into adolescence. Having been pals rather than parents during childhood, they now become a mixture of part-time providers and part-time social workers.

In a different column or in the same column, at a different time, they may be advised instead to stand firm, set limits, forbid excesses, practice a little old-fashioned discipline, and never to leave teen-agers of opposite sexes unchaperoned. There is a growing feeling that adults have made life too exciting for the adolescent and that the "sorcerer's apprentice" has got out of hand. The treatment for this is by no means certain except to devise legitimate sublimations. All in all, the parent is being forced as usual into the dilemma of doing too much or too little, of giving too much or too little, and his resulting uncertainty is recognized and exploited by the adolescent.

The commercial groups have discovered the teen-ager and are lyrical about their latest customer. In his comments on advertising and marketing to young people, a well-known advertiser has this to say: "Just look at youth; no established pattern; no backlog of items—youth is the greatest force in the community. It has definitely been established that because he is open-minded and desires to learn, he is often the first to accept new and forward-looking products." [13] The adolescent of commerce is seen, there-fore, not only as a grand spender on his own account but also as a pied piper who sets the style and the trends for adult society to follow. The switch of major interests to the adolescent and a subtle cultivation of his narcissism, his age-specific anxieties, his wish for acceptance, and his strug-gling sexual consciousness are fully exploited in thousands of advertise-ments in newspapers and journals.

Teenage Tyranny offers some amusing verses to illustrate the new facts of commercial life:

> Thrice the Univac hath spoke;
> Sell your goods to younger folks;
> Thrice its tubes and tapes did purr:
> Make each kid a customer;
> Thrice its twanging clocks hath struck;
> Bobby-socks have got the buck.[20]

The interest is not without good foundations. In her study of "The Up-beat Generation" with regard to influence and affluence, Cox[4] has esti-mated that teen-agers are now spending up to ten billion dollars a year and that companies are by-passing parental preferences to study the fond likes and dislikes of the younger group. One adult response to this found expres-sion in a pathetic newspaper article entitled "The Displaced Generation" in which the author laments "the glories of the past" when adults were adults and teen-agers were still just children. Nowadays, the distinction between the adult and adolescent, he complains, has become as narrow and nebu-lous as the distinction between male and female. Youngness has become a goal in itself, and many of the adults spend a great deal of time on proce-dures designed to allow them to hold onto their youngness. It is not surpris-ing, therefore, that adolescence has become a kind of cultural arbiter in the United States. As Erikson pointed out,[7] few men in the United States can afford to abandon the gestures of the adolescent, as witnessed by the behav-ior of the American Legion, convention rituals, and New Year's Eve revel-ries.

REACTION TO THE ADOLESCENT AS AN OBJECT OF RESEARCH

As indicated in previous sections, therapists have been passing through a crisis with respect to how the adolescent should be treated, at what stage of adolescence this should occur, and by whom the treatment should be car-ried out. The research worker, too, has specific problems when investigating the adolescent. In the past, research in this area has been relatively sparse, owing to the fact that the developmental phase was poorly described and lacked guiding constructs that would help to raise meaningful questions.

When the concept of identity formation was first introduced as a specific problem of adolescence, research gained a new impetus. Work began to be done in the developmental features that fit into the sense of identity and the pathological factors that interfere with its formation. However, this in itself is not sufficient to sustain any large-scale research program.

The impression derived from surveying the total field of investigation directed to this stage of life is that researchers are still staying away from it as much as therapists and are often as confused in their approach as the therapist. It was found that research techniques that appeared suitable for use in childhood or during adulthood failed to elicit meaningful data during adolescence. In a recent longitudinal study conducted in the United States, researchers had shown an interest in extracting something more from the developmental scene than simple physical and psychological measures of differences. Until puberty they had managed to satisfactorily elaborate hypotheses and procedures that threw light on the adapting and coping processes of the child. When they tackled adolescence, the research and the researchers underwent a strange crisis that reflected itself in many disturbing and disrupting meetings between the investigators. They betrayed uncertainty as to how to approach the adolescent as a research object, being convinced that their previous strategies could no longer apply to this new situation. They could not agree among themselves as to what they wanted to investigate or how they wanted to investigate, and many were in favor of by-passing the adolescent phase, leaving it "silent," and postponing their research activity until early adulthood. Those who looked at this particular research crisis from the outside felt that a number of complex issues were involved and that the catastrophic reaction of the participants mirrored not only the usual uncertainty of the adult with respect to adolescence but also an unconscious resistance against reactivating the basic adolescent conflicts. Some of the investigators, who had been very much at home with the child, felt "disoriented" when confronted with the adolescent.

THE "GOOD" REACTION TO ADOLESCENCE

Normality, in psychology and psychiatry, is a concept difficult to define in operational terms. One can point to the fact that the majority of adolescents seem to come through adolescence and develop into average adults with average reactions as an indication that things cannot be as bad as they look under a closer clinical scrutiny. Although we might be dissatisfied with the finished products and aware that many of them will eventually find their way into mental hospitals, divorce courts, coroner's courts, prisons, and homes for alcoholics and addicts, the larger group who achieve statistically average lives must have been subjected to "good enough" reactions.

The "good" reaction or "good enough" reaction is one in which the stereotypic response is minimal or absent, the adult responding on a person-to-person basis. It is a reaction which is relatively free from the irrational influence of "transference," so that, once again, the adult responds not in terms of the there-and-then, but of the here-and-now. The third ingredient to a "good" reaction is the element of sympathy originating in a satisfactory adolescent experience—not satisfactory in the sense of being free from conflict, but satisfactory in the sense of having gone some distance toward making these conflicts conscious and resolving them. The acceptance of the once adolescent provides a sounding board to test out all future reactions for adolescent consumption.

Much the same applies to the therapist whose "good" reactions are also intimately bound up with his experiences of childhood and adolescence. His special hazard is the "Pygmalion" fantasy which besets all therapists but especially those who treat teen-agers. These may feel a strong urge to mold the soft, pliable substance of adolescence into a form reminiscent of the therapist's, the theme song being, "Why can't the patient be more like us?" The therapist who is not in love with his own personality can offer the adolescent the opportunity to emerge from the struggles of the transitional period with an identity that he himself can respect and, above all, with an identity that he can call his own.

CONCLUSION

The deflating and controlling techniques used by adults with adolescents are generally not the ones they employ in interpersonal relationships with other adults or even children. The shaming, reproaching, guilt-provoking, and stereotyping techniques have a peculiarly destructive and sadistic element to them. As an Indian once remarked to Erikson in the same context: "You white people seem bent on destroying your youth." [7]

It is peculiarly appropriate to set a well-worn cliché against the stereotype and insist that adults need to recognize that adolescents are people, and particular people at that. It is important to remember that the stereotypes they have cultivated are not necessarily even true of a minority of adolescents and that adolescents are not all delinquent, irresponsible, hypersexual, or simple-minded creatures in pursuit solely of a good time. As long as these stereotypes persist, adolescents will respond by setting up barriers to communication, excluding the adult by a conspiracy of silence or by a language and culture of their own. The adults are then narcissistically affronted that the youth want to act and look and talk differently from them, and then interpret this as rebellion, overlooking the fact that the adolescents also want to act and look and talk differently from the children and are as deeply engaged in delineating their identities as in revolting against authority. The principle of secrecy and silence adopted by the adolescent culture toward the adult is, according to Simmel, a universal phenomenon appearing in all cultures and can be understood as a counterresponse to the secrets and silences that adults have preserved in the face of insistent childhood curiosities and interests. The secrets and silences tend to produce glaring cultural discontinuities which intensify all the problems of transition and force the adolescent into a largely informal system of intimate relationships appearing to have no connection whatsoever with past or future, thus incurring the indignation and displeasure of the seniors.

As an adult author has remarked with tired patience, "Adults have to face it; adolescents are here to stay." One can only hope that the attitudes of adults are not here to stay, although they have been saying the same sort of things about adolescents for a very long time. A good example of this is the following:

> Our adolescents now seem to love luxury. They have bad manners and contempt for authority. They show disrespect for adults and spend their time hanging around places gossiping with one another. . . . They are ready to contradict their parents, monopolize the conversation in company, eat gluttonously, and tyrannize their teachers.

It sounds familiar and contemporary, but it is a comment by Socrates dated 2,500 years ago.

Parents need to look at their children in the context of their total development and to respond sensitively and appropriately in their attitudes and behavior according to the age and stage of the child. The identifications that accumulate during childhood reach their peak at adolescence, so that the warring factions are very like each other, however much they would appear to differ and disagree, exemplifying a facet of the conflict related by Freud to "the narcissism of small differences." If the adult remembers how much of himself has gone into the making of the adolescent, he will be able to sympathize and empathize to an extent that should make for a partnership based on mutual respect and affection. The matter was well summed up by BenHaMelikVehaNazir Hasdai in 1230: "Your son at five is your master, at ten your slave, at fifteen your double, and after that, your friend or foe, depending on how you bring him up."

References

1. ADELSON, J. "The Mystique of Adolescence," *Psychiatry*, XXVII, No. 1 (1964), 1.
2. BELL, A. "The Role of Parents," in S. LORAND and H. SCHNEER, eds., *Adolescence*. New York: 1961.
3. CHADWICK, M. *The Psychological Effects of Menstruation, Nervous and Mental Diseases*. New York: 1932.
4. Cox, C. *The Upbeat Generation*. New York: Prentice-Hall, 1962.
5. DENNY, T., J. FELDHAUSE, and C. CONDON. "Anxiety, Divergent Thinking and Achievement," *Journal of Educational Psychology*, LVI, No. 1 (1965), 40.

6. DEUTSCH, H. *Psychology of Women,* Vol. I. New York: Grune & Stratton, 1944.

7. ERIKSON, E. *Childhood and Society.* New York: Norton, 1950.

8. FRANK, A. *The Diary of Anne Frank.* New York: Random House, 1956.

9. FRAZER, J. *The Golden Bough,* abridged ed. London: Macmillan, 1949.

10. FREUD, A. "Adolescence," in *Psychoanalytic Study of the Child,* Vol. XIII. New York: International Universities Press, 1958.

11. FRIEDENBERG, E. J. *The Vanishing Adolescent.* Boston: Beacon Hill, 1959.

12. GELEERD, E. R. "Some Aspects of Psychoanalytic Technique in Adolescents," in *Psychoanalytic Study of the Child,* Vol. XII. New York: International Universities Press, 1957.

13. GILBERT, E. *Advertising and Marketing to Young People.* New York: Printers, Inc., 1957.

14. GOSSE, E. *Father and Son.* New York: Scribner, 1907.

15. HENRY, J. *Culture against Man.* New York: Random House, 1963.

16. JACOBSON, E. "Adolescent Moods and the Remodeling of the Psychic Structrue," *Psychoanalytic Study of the Child,* Vol. XVI. New York: International Universities Press, 1961.

17. LEVINE, R. A., and B. B. LEVINE. "Nyansongo: A Gussi Community in Kenya," in B. B. WHITING, ed., *Six Cultures.* New York: Wiley, 1963.

18. MEAD, M. "Adolescence in Primitive and Modern Society," in V. F. CALVERTON and S. SCHMALHAUSEN, eds., *The New Generation.* New York: Macaulay, 1930.

19. MILLER, E. "Individual and Social Approach to the Study of Adolescence," *British Journal of Medical Psychology,* XXXV (1962), 211.

20. HECHINGER, G., and F. HECHINGER. *Teenage Tyranny.* New York: Morrow, 1962.

21. SPIEGEL, J. P. "Interpersonal Influences within the Family," in B. SCHAFFNER, ed., *Group Processes, Transactions of the Third Conference.* New York: Josiah Macy Foundation, 1957.

22. STEKEL, W. "Frigidity in Mothers," in CALVERTON and SCHMALHAUSEN, *op. cit.*

23. STENGEL, E., in J. D. SUTHERLAND, "Three Cases of Anxiety and Failure in Examinations," *British Journal of Medical Psychology,* XIX (1941), 73.

6

Adolescents—
Just How Do They React?

Fritz Redl

I. ARE WE SURE WE ARE ALL TALKING ABOUT THE SAME THING?

I take it that these chapters are not meant to summarize or substitute for all books and articles written on adolescence. I go on the assumption that their main purpose is to start a fruitful discussion of the most pressing current problems that confront the psychiatrist. In addition, they should be oriented also toward the problems that come to him, not only in individual therapy, but also in his role as a helper of the young and an adviser to their parents and teachers and to the community at large. In that case, it might be wise to remember briefly the most important blocks to communication we are likely to run into when we deal with a topic as comprehensive and elusive as "adolescence."

A. Adolescents Are People Who Go through a Particular Developmental Phase

Not everything they do or are is directly an outcome of the fact that they happen to be "in their adolescence." In recent discussions in the United States—and I am now not talking about lay audiences—I have been shocked to notice how fast any discussion of adolescence drifts into the topic of delinquency, schizophrenia, juvenile crime, and so forth. We should all remember that there is a difference between talking about underaged crooks, premature schizophrenics, classical neurotics biding their time until they are old enough for the couch, and the problem of "adolescence"! In fact, to know just where sickness begins and adolescence as a phase—genu-

79

ine phenomenon—ends seems to me one of the as yet rather thinly explored issues well worth our special concern.

B. Adolescents—Which Age?

The very custom of using a single term for as wide a stretch of development as we do, reaching from "latency" into young adulthood, leads to a most misleading and dangerous abbreviation. Usually, although we are well aware of this risk, we forget about it in the course of a discussion and then end up not talking about the same people at all. It is true that it would not be easy or even advisable to draw the demarcation line too sharply and that in the case of the specific adolescent youngster we may have before us, sometimes such distinctions may seem superfluous. Yet, there seems to be no question that the difference between the young adolescent at the onset of his puberty and the older adolescent blurring into the picture of the young adult is enormous. The young adolescent faces entirely different tasks from the older one, no matter how great the similarities otherwise may be.

In the United States we have suffered from an additional complication: the handy term "teen-ager"—an incidental linguistic trick which encompasses the ages from 13 to 19—has obscured this difference within adolescent subphases even more. On top of this, we run into another unfortunate hang-over from earlier years of psychoanalysis: the old idea that "adolescence" directly follows "the latency years" may have had some truth in it for some of the children of the Vienna of the 1920's; but for our youngsters in the United States this is pure nonsense. Not that I have any objection to the latency concept as such, however. What irks me is only the degree to which an inexact use of the term has made us ignore an entirely different and most important developmental phase which squeezes itself between latency proper and the onset of puberty. Labeling it for the time being as the "preadolescent phase," I would like to postulate that a number of very important changes occur which neither fit directly into the picture of later childhood nor, in all cases, relate directly to the onset of puberty. I am happy to see that finally this fact is also being taken more seriously analytically, as is evidenced by the article by Martin James in the October 1964 number of the *International Journal of Psychoanalysis*.[5] Only, since he is mainly dealing with rather special problems of therapeutic technique, I want to point out in a few strokes what the behavioral picture of this phase is likely to be, on the level on which it puzzles those who have to deal with it in daily life. The following is a brief attempt to sketch in rather overstated and undifferentiated terms what I perceive to be characteristic of the phase from which the youngsters step into their early adolescence.

There are behavioral clusters around the process of "organismic disorganization." Some of the confusion of the preadolescent phase frequently blends imperceptibly into the picture of the "young adolescent." This seems to me due to the fact that the structure of the organism seems to *loosen up a bit,* just before major pubertal changes occur, and this very "loosening of existing personality structure," which is developmentally necessary, has in its wake similar phenomena, as a real disease-conditioned personality decay would show. As most visible evidence of such temporary loosening of the already achieved personality structure of the latency child, the following illustrative examples may serve, implying that any one of the behavior trends mentioned may, during this phase, be a perfectly normal developmental phenomenon, regardless of how sick or frightening it may look at the time:

(1) Increase in physical restlessness.

(2) Shortened attention span, but also shortened holding power of any one activity engaged in.

(3) Irrealism about one's own self in terms of what one can and cannot do.

(4) Ambivalence increase around issues of dependency, irritability toward former love objects.

(5) Partial return of already discarded infantile patterns (bed-wetting, nail-biting, old anxiety in the dark, all sorts of fantastic phobias).

(6) Appearance of a whole armamentarium meant to cope with this onrush of old and new anxieties (compulsive tics and rituals, magic, symbolic gadgets as anxiety protection and power symbols such as flashlight, knife), collectomania as fear assuagement and as safe territory from adult invasion, and so on.

(7) Return to earlier theories about sex in spite of sex information given in the meantime.

(8) Increase in sex body-play on a sporadic excitational level and quite different from later adolescent masturbation.

(9) Regression to earlier libidinous phases, especially a lot of anal joking and sadomasochistic fantasies often combined with technological daydreams (torture machines).

(10) Pregenital evaluation of "the other sex": girls sissies unless good fighters or tomboyish, devaluation because of lack of penis—misinterpretation by both sexes—of female sex as being "castrated" with all the subsequent hullabaloo of fear and guilt.

(11) And of course the well-known avoidance of intimate body contact with parents, which may show up considerably before actual puberty has set in.

There are also behavioral clusters around the phenomenon of a "group psychological break." By this I mean to imply that besides the usual and well-reported libidinal changes preparing themselves and the already mentioned loosening of personality structure, another change happens which is societally just as important, but cannot easily be subsumed under the usual framework of libidinous movements, namely: the old primary identification of a child with the family group as a group psychological base weakens, while a new identification with the peer group and its inherent code assumes full swing. This change happens, where I live, frequently considerably earlier than the actual libidinous changes are meant to occur, but the subsequent confusion in behavior and the internal conflicts produced further complicate the picture.

Developmental phenomena of this sort find expression in the following behavior clusters:

(1) Conflict of double standards: individual child still parent-loyal, peer-group code basically "anti-adult." Result: new waves of guilt and shame in both directions.

(2) Embarrassment about open submission to adult politeness and good-manner codes.

(3) Shamelessness in language and behavior, bravado through flouting of health and safety rules, special joy in risk-taking.

(4) Avoidance of too open acceptance of adults in official roles, even of those very much liked (teachers and parents, for example).

(5) Loyalty to peers and risk-taking in their favor, even where they are personally despised or feared.

(6) Openly displayed "freshness" against authority figures.

(7) Deep-seated revulsion toward any form of praise or punishment which seems to be perceived as "infantilizing."

(8) Safety in homosexual groupings; view of the other sex as "hunter's trophy" rather than in terms of interpersonal relationships.

(9) Negative loading of any form of official acceptance of help from adults; pride in "taking it bravely" at any price.

(10) Low prestige of verbal communication with the trusted adult; hesitation about communicating about feelings and emotions.

(11) Apathy toward adult as partner in play life, unless it is a group game situation (what a problem that one raises for our playroom therapy!).

(12) Increase in contagion power of behavior by peers, especially those five degrees tougher and a few years older than one's parents would feel comfortable about.

In short, although any one of the behaviors listed above may also occur at other ages or as a result of misdevelopment or pathology, the point here is: during "preadolescence" such phenomena may be perfectly "growth-appropriate" and may be part of the normal way of going through a developmental phase.

The reason why I think it worth while to remind ourselves with an abbreviated listing of this sort is that this is what preadolescents are like when "puberty" hits them. In fact, much of this is much more likely to continue way into the adolescent phase, but it all started much earlier. Or, in other words, what an "adolescent's reaction to his adolescence will be like is also determined by the preceeding phase from which he steps into his adolescence, not only what that adolescence itself does to him."

In other words, by analogy with the phenomenon of "emigration" and "immigration," which I shall elaborate later, the point I want to make is this: adolescents certainly "emigrate," but not from latency. The developmental place from which they emigrate is their preadolescent phase. And, if we stick to our analogy for a moment longer: growing youngsters certainly have some similarities with "immigrants." But what they immigrate into is not, as commonly assumed, the adult world. Their first goal of immigration is the adolescent peer society, with its peculiar peer-group culture and all that goes with it. But more about that later.

All this raises the painful question: how do we know which of these phenomena are the hang-over of an earlier phase or the reaction to a new one, and at which point does any one of them stop being "phase-characteristic" and become a clear signal of disease? Besides, what all this does to our armamentarium as therapists, surrounded by earlier childhood toys or forced into therapeutically rather unfertile but group-accepted play forms, might well keep a discussion going for some time.

C. Adolescence—And What Else?

Besides the problem of differentiating between what is Johnny's adolescence and what is his disease, discussions on adolescence also seem to get hung up at times at yet another point, namely, on the difference between what is the "psychiatric core" of a problem and what is due primarily to the geographical and social locus and the historical time at which a given adolescence occurs. It may be interesting to remember that even as far back as 1929, Siegfried Bernfeld [1,2] within the framework of so-called "classical psychoanalysis" tried hard to make the very point psychoanalysts have since been so customarily accused of ignoring. In fact, at a time when neither cultural anthropology nor sociology had itself reached the stage of development they have both impressed us with since then, Bernfeld tried to establish two items, most relevant to our discussion today:

First, ignoring for a moment what is supposed to happen during adolescence, especially in terms of libido development, it might be worth while to see how youngsters react to their adolescence as such. Looking at it this way, Bernfeld suggests we might find three major types of "reaction":

(1) That of youngsters whose first reaction to the self-perception of pubertal stress and strain is characterized by avoidance, wish for delay and fear ("neurotic-like reaction").

(2) That of youngsters whose first reaction is not only not one of fear and anxiety, but, on the contrary, a welcoming of what happens to them "at last" and a rush to get to the end point of the line. Welcoming the first secondary sex characteristics as a happy promise, they try to make that promise true faster than they or the society in which they live may be ready for.

(3) That of youngsters who are torn back and forth between both of these types of "reactions to becoming adolescent" (manic-depressivelike reaction).

Bernfeld's point about all this: any one of these may be entirely "normal"; it depends on where they end up, not on how they start; and it is important to avoid classifying each one of them as "neurotic," "wayward," or "manic-depressive" as such.

The second, even more important, point which Bernfeld tried to get us to take more seriously long before anthropologists, culturalists, and psycho-analysts (who hoped to get rid of the unconscious and of the sexual part of Freud's teachings) made similar requests, is that the question with which of these "reactions" a youngster greets his oncoming puberty may not be en-tirely a matter of libido development. It may have to do with the *sozialer Ort* (*sic*—liberally translated: socioeconomic subcultural value system) within which the youngster experiences his adolescence. For the society of the Vienna of 1929, this is what Bernfeld suggests: If you are a 14-year-old in a worker's family, it may be quite normal for you to start your adoles-cence as the "rushing" type. In fact, you are lucky if you happen to do so, for your subcultural environment is much happier with this: you go out, are proud of working for a living, and therefore are also looked on with much more indulgence as far as your psychosexual experimentation is concerned. If you happen to be a 14-year-old son of a highly "educated" family who expect you to sit in a "gymnasium" classroom obediently for years to come, you are better off if your adolescence does not start with a bang, but with a panic. For your parents and teachers are quite willing to put up with a lot of neurotic display on your side (they may even try to talk a psychoanalyst against his better insight into taking you on as a case) than they would be to put up with a school dropout.

Jumping from this somewhat abbreviated and oversimplified reminder of what Siegfried Bernfeld tried to tell us in 1929, long before Karen Horney and others descended on Libido Theory, to my specific topic, the following seem to me to be the lessons to keep in mind.

Whenever we talk about "adolescence," we had better differentiate sharply between two issues:

(1) The pure "psychiatric core" of growth processes which will have to take place "within," no matter where people grow up—at least as long as

we do not jump too far away from the type of cultures we are familiar with.

(2) The specific form the task of growing up takes, depending on the specific "environment," its sociocultural expectations, its psychoeconomic properties and so forth, and a wide array of other "sociocultural givens" which we so easily take for granted to the point of forgetting to put them back into our equations.

As far as the "psychiatric core" is concerned, we are lucky to have at least the psychoanalytic part of it clearly put together in one place: there is nothing psychoanalysts have said in print that could not be checked on by opening the recent book of Peter Blos.[3] We are not as lucky for all other psychiatric aspects of the problem of adolescence and for the cultural-socio-logical-ecological and similar angles of the problem. Fortunately, much of what these sciences have to teach us has long found its way into our own professional lore to the point at which we even forget where we got it from. In fact, some of this we have accepted so much that I am not getting worried about it's having been too stereotyped, and some of the concepts we have borrowed from sociologists earlier are by now beginning to get outdated and stale. In fact, the danger we seem to be running into now does not seem to me the worry that we as psychiatrists might forget what the behavioral sciences have warned us about, or that we might ignore the immense difference between growing up in New York or Moscow versus some hick town in the prairies or the steppes, but that we might oversimplify things on the other end of the line. In reference to this problem, and for those among us who may be tempted to be too heavily caught in the impact of recent sociological debates, I should like to add especially one warning which may come in handy when we talk about youth:

Let us never forget that children of all levels in our society—even in a so-called "clean delinquent subculture"—still have to live under a double standard. Even the youngster in a Detroit slum of the most delinquency-stuffed neighborhood is not supposed to use the same sexual invectives in the presence of adults, until he is old enough to do so, even though he may hear them thrown around by those very same adults all day long. In short, even the most "value-infraction slap-happy superego" of a young adolescent in a tough neighborhood still harbors the germ of possible neurotic value conflicts, which we are so well aware of in the more neighborhood-protected youngster of the middle class.

D. Reaction—To What?

And this leads me to another danger spot built into a theme like this one: if we want to discuss the adolescent's reactions, the question to be laid out as clearly as possible will be, of course: reaction to what?

The way they react to their own adolescence might be the preferred theme, but how am I to know whether whatever I have before me is it? And even if they reacted to "something in their environment," how do I know whether the *way* they reacted was due to the fact that they were under the impact of their "adolescence" or whether it was really a simple case of reaction dictated by the experiential input to begin with? Theoretically, this may be an obvious issue, and hardly worth debate. Yet, our professional discussions—and maybe even parts of our chapters in books—are full of the "case of the misnamed variable." So George hit his father heavier than he should have; hadn't the old man come home drunk and beaten his wife within an inch of her life as many times before? In the counterrage of defense, the slaying took place. How do I know what I have before me? Of course, it might be just a "typical adolescent crime"—outward-directed defense against inner incestual wishes, stirred up by the scene and fed into by the revived oedipal struggle of earlier years—and all that sort of thing. On the other hand, wouldn't *you*? I mean: wouldn't anybody, whether adolescent or not, be decent enough to defend a woman in such a predicament and therefore, not skilled enough in combat, deal a blow more murderous than intended? So how do I know of this whether it was characteristic of "teenage" rather than of the miserable things that should not happen to dogs but are being done to children?

In short, as we go along discussing "reactions" of adolescents, let us remember that each time we use such a term, our concept of "reactions" may have to be looked at more closely. Crudely speaking, we might subclassify their "reactions" into the following categories: Reactions to:

(1) Libidinous events, released or revived by "the adolescent process."

(2) The noise their childhood superego makes about gratifications which are normally adolescent, but still tinged with childhood guilt.

(3) People who happen to be the leftovers of their childhood-stage personnel—father, mother, siblings—but whose role has to be seen in a changing light.

(4) Their own self-image, confused by the struggle of establishing an identity for later life.

(5) The way people *feel* toward them anyway.

(6) The way people *act* toward them, the life experiences which they expose them to.

(7) All the intangibles of: group atmosphere, cultural milieu, social expectations floating in mid-air, general subcultural mores, and specific behavioral and ritualistic expectations.

(8) Space and things: the cars, knives, books, transistor radios, wide-open terrain, or chokingly narrow bed space in a crowded slum.

(9) Special life events and unusual circumstances: birth and death of a sibling, divorce, unemployment, sudden wealth, movement into new neighborhood, and so on.

(10) The work market and what it holds and does not hold for them.

(11) The philosophy of life or religion they or the people around them seem to be engulfed in, including the wide array of value systems which may meet them at different points.

(12) The confusions about "youth" which the adult generation of their orbit seems to exude.

Now, it is obvious that in this chapter of "reactions" I cannot treat even a fraction of what counts. So rather than attempt to cover the topic itself, let me bombard our field with enough irritating statements to start a good discussion. In short, as my reaction to the reaction theme, I shall try for the remainder of my space to select just a few themes illustrative, I hope, of what we really ought to take a much closer look at.

II. PREDICAMENT CLUSTERS OF THE YOUTH OF OUR TIME

A. Moratorium without Oxygen

I take Erikson's concept of a "moratorium" [4] for granted here: the leeway any society has to give the young for a reasonable amount of "consequence-and-commitment-tax-free" experimentation with life, so as to develop the characteristics they will need as adults and to find out which societal niche they really could fit into. We, in the United States, are quite vocal about the wide moratorium we say we give our young and, if anything, worry at times whether we might not be led too far astray on the path toward permissiveness. Yet, the following facts need to be looked at, for the moratorium we say we let them have seems to me to be chokingly void of what it takes to breathe in, at times.

With all the richness in gadgetorial equipment and technical abundance, our young find themselves sometimes squeezed into a frame of life which for them certainly implies unbearable degrees of infantilization. To wit:

(1) At the very time when autonomous mobility rates high not only because of its inherent gratifications but also as a symbol for independence, urban youths have to return to the "motorized baby buggy." Having roamed their close neighborhood quite freely as younger children, they now need to be chauffeured by mother even to their own peer-group affairs.

(2) Most "jobs" available to the younger adolescent in an urbanized surrounding invariably are soaked in the flavor of artificially created excuses for some pocket money. Meaningful contributions to the life of the family are invariably degraded into token conditions for the handing out of some more dole.

(3) The increasing demand for prolonged and overspecialized education, although meaningful for some, implies for many primarily the price of unbearably prolonged infantilization. For a school situation, compared with a contribution on the open market, invariably assumes that flavor (and this is even true for the interminable training seminars for the young psychiatrist).

(4) One of the most important coping devices the youth of our pioneer days had available was, of course, the constructive and therapeutic runaway —leaving home or unbearable conditions and "making something of oneself." In the young adolescent years, even the best attempts of this sort are now out. Even well-intended and reasonably "mature" attempts at this sort of self-cure invariably and ingloriously end at the desk of that nice lady from Traveler's Aid at bus, railroad, or air terminals.

(5) With the concept of automation looming impressively on the horizon, the chance for meaningful and creative occupational opportunities seems limited to the few who can meet the expectation of overspecialization and specific skill. For the many, who are neither socialized enough for that much specialization or whose training and native skill will not match with the specific job needs created, it is bound to make the usual vocational motivation acrobatics their adult advisers shower on them sound rather flimsy, indeed.

B. A New Prejudice Has Been Added

Maybe this is a special phenomenon, assuming its extreme forms primarily in the United States, but for our youngsters, anyway, this is the problem:

Even if you happened to live, as a child, far away from where prejudices hurt, upon entering the teen-age phase you become quite noticeably part of a discredited minority group. For, no matter how well the particular adults in your life may like you as a person, whenever they speak, write, and act as representatives of the adult generation of their time they view teen-agers with a jaundiced eye. Of course, some of my best friends are teen-agers; but, never mind, as such they are a bad lot, guilty or at least not to be trusted until proved innocent.

The variations of this theme are, of course, many and could hardly even be listed in a reasonable amount of space. But there are two comments I must make.

(1) A prejudicial stereotype thrown at any group finds, of course, its reaction by prejudicial stereotypes that are reinforced on the other side. Thus, what many teen-agers react to is not only their teen-age problem but also the stereotype of expectations that hit them as a barrage from adult mouthings and writings on practically every newspaper page. The reinforcement of a natural teen-age stereotype against "those adults" is one of the invariable and easily noted consequences of this stance.

(2) For some youngsters, especially at present among the American Negro youth, the recently stepped-up movement toward "pride in chucking old prejudices and proving it" creates a somewhat novel situation: expecting to be viewed with a scapegoat stereotype and used to it, they suddenly find themselves selected on the basis of a *mascot-stereotype:* the very fact of race plus class that made them ineligible before finds some of them singled out for special advantages, primarily in order to prove that outfit A or B is "free of prejudice."

However, before we wax too lyrical about new chances offered our youth, let us remember two facts of life with all the bitterness this issue deserves: for one, this chance reaches only a very few; for the rest the stepped-up selection of some makes it worse rather than easier. Then, let us not forget the price that has to be paid by one who is thus used as demonstration object for nonprejudicial policies: it consists of estrangement from a major portion of his previous compatriots and is added to by the fact that even prejudicial stereotypes of the "mascot" type are personally an insult. For it means: "It isn't me they want, they only use me to prove a point." What this implies hardly needs to be repeated for those who are sure to have read Freud.

C. New Highlighting of the Barriers of Race, Caste, and Class

Over and beyond the issue just singled out for comment, our youth find themselves in a period of a peculiar mixture of contradictory trends and the frantic attempt to do something about it. It is irrelevant here which side of an issue a given youth selects. My point is that the very fervent concern about the issues as such, laudable as it may be as a general trend, also highlights the barriers of race, caste, and class and sharpens them for those who are doing their growing up right now. Again, let me list only a few illustrations.

(1) The new emphasis on a fight against racial prejudice offers the young a chance to take up a cause—for or against, as the case may be— and has both implications: that of making life more "meaningful" for some and bringing lure of "risk and adventure" to others. This draws more youth, on a variety of levels, and not all desirable, into the orbit of "life in the service of a cause" than ever before in peacetime.

(2) The same fact, however, may for others simply increase the awareness of the unlikelihood of seeing any real change in their lifetime and make them even more sure of the hopelessness of their specific station in life than they might have been without this flare-up of public interest.

(3) No matter how well intended in basic "philosophy" adults may be, the increased technicalization, plus the need for early specialization in training, creates new outcast groups, now not because one would mind their race

or poverty, but because, as a secondary result of either or both, they are ineligible for the highly demanding tasks. In fact, one may wonder what is "easier" to react to: to be told one is not eligible for a job because one is Negro or because one does not have what it takes to do it.

(4) The highlighting of the issue of race, caste, and class, as presently exemplified by the fight against discrimination as well as by the new antipoverty campaign, holds additional challenge for our young, which is only slowly emerging into visibility right now. The newly opened mobility also creates added guilt feelings or defensive hostility toward those left behind, and for those left behind, it aggravates angry estrangement through envious hostility toward their more fortunate former cause-mates. This problem is by no means new, but we feel that it is being sharpened, and it certainly constitutes one of the "reactions to be expected" which deserve more detailed analysis than a mere listing here.

D. Destiny Complex Reinforced

In the United States the dream of "unlimited opportunities" has been preached to our young presumably from the day on which the first immigrants landed on these shores. Life is what you make of it; the sky is the limit. If you do not reach it, you have no one to blame but yourself. No doubt, this philosophy has always proved a special stimulant to most, a nightmare to some; and it must have sounded like a bad joke to the disinherited at any historical time. The fact is that one part of our adolescent population, especially the part given to advanced learning and career motivation, is now caught in a peculiar dilemma. For them, this dream is still a psychological reality. Not to reach the college of one's choice, the "best" education one could get, makes life hardly worth living, and for their parents it is a shame hard to bear. On the other hand, even they, adult-oriented though they are, cannot help but realize that "we" are bequeathing a mess to the young. Although we are still eager to do anything we can to sharpen up their brain waves and raise their I.Q.'s, they can hardly miss the fact that we failed to build enough seats for them in college. The adult generation meets this challenge with the usual bureaucratic procedures, besides taking some genuine steps for eventual improvement, but of much too long a range. For our younger, education hungry teen-agers, this is what it means: whether you will or will not get the education you want may depend on little matters of chance; on that failing grade you got in seventh-grade French, which at that time nobody, including yourself, took very seriously, or whether your puberty made you temporarily a less desirable pupil, even though you snapped out of it all right in a year or two.

Their reaction to this, in the extreme, is easy to see. For some it means just giving up; for all that is "destiny beyond your reach," so what's the good of worrying about it? For others it means the opposite: a totality of effort far beyond what the normal ups and downs of healthy adolescence should be loaded with—terrific anxieties, guilts, self-doubts, including a rise in the suicide rate.

In fact, sometimes I wonder whether we are not just about to produce, in this country, in larger amounts again the very types of neurosis with which we were so familiar in the Vienna of the 1910's and 1920's with all that this implies, and the absence of which puzzled us so much when we arrived on the American scene.

E. The Group: Emigrant's Refuge or Immigrant's Base?

The young adolescent finds himself faced with a double task: he has to emigrate from "family life," as he has known it as a younger child, and to immigrate, not into the world of adults, but into the social system of teenage society. This comparison of adolescence with emigration and immigration syndromes, by the way, might yield valuable leads which cannot, of course, be followed here. Suffice it to say, as in real emigration and immigration (and who should know better than Americans, who, after all, are all descendants of both?), "the group" obviously plays an impressive role on both counts. "Imbeddedness-feeling into one's group," whatever specific content such a phrase may imply, is well known to help in coping with the stress and strain of living and the shocks of adaptational struggle. How this may range all the way from offering people temporary acceptance feelings by their peers to immersing oneself into something like the "group womb" has been amply described in the literature. For others, the group seems to play yet a different role: rather than being a refuge, it seems to function rather as a home base from which to foray aggressively, and sometimes predatorily, into territories to conquer.

Anyway, the young adolescent of today finds himself confronted (a) with a wide range of needs on either side of this ledger; (b) with a most confusing array of "group phenomena" surrounding and engulfing him; (c) with the painful need to shift his own group belongingness needs from family to the larger society or to subgroups in which he will do his living and working for some time to come.

Although fifty-minute-hour psychiatry remained shocked for a time by the new complexities which the various fields of group psychology, sociology, cultural anthropology, social psychology, and so forth—and later even group therapy—have forced it to take seriously, these "facts of life" have by now been fully recognized as important factors in our patients' lives, even where we wanted the actual therapeutic inroad to remain limited to the two-individuals pair situation as traditionally perceived. However, while we know that we have to take "group psychology and group processes" seriously where they play a role in our youngsters' lives, we are far from knowing what to do with it all. In this respect, we find ourselves in a predicament not different from that of our young adolescents themselves.

III. COPING SYNDROMES THAT HAVE US STUMPED

Even if we limited ourselves only to reactions to those "predicaments," listed here, in which our young adolescents find themselves, we should end up with a sizable and most confusing volume. If we now mention only a few ways in which adolescents cope with their predicaments, it needs to be clearly understood that the selection is one of desperation, not of choice. Maybe its role here is primarily that of giving a flavor of what we ought to talk about, more than of the actual issues we ought to list for our agenda. By the way, the term "coping syndromes" tries to preserve the original charge of talking about "reactions," but hopes to get away from the all too two-dimensional concept that is usually involved in a list of "reactions" and hopes to point at their complexity, depth, and multifacetedness by the very choice of term.

A. Allergy toward Life-Space-Detached Situations and Life-Space-Detached Adults

I know this sounds funny, but I do not know how to say it faster in cramped space. Here is what I am trying to remind ourselves of with this clumsy headline.

Although, for classical therapy of a classical neurosis, the detachment of the therapeutic situation from the usual interventions of daily life is an essential ingredient, for some other tasks in our youngsters' lives it seems more appropriate if the people who try to counsel them are right there and have a decisive power over the situations in which both parties find themselves. Now, it so happens that there are some disturbances, such as, for instance, those of the so-called "acting-out type of child," where little progress can be made in individual therapy, unless many life events are at least also handled carefully and with clinical caution, when they happen in daily life, right then and there, and sometimes by people who are the natural teachers, group leaders, parents, and so forth. I have given this specific design of talking with youngsters in the style of the psychiatric interview but within the geographical and role framework of "daily living" the name of the "Life Space Interview."

The point to be made here is this: Even normal adolescents, to say nothing of their action-prone compeers, seem to have increased their resistance to the very situation that for the more classical anxiety neurotic seems such an advantage, namely, the "therapy or counseling hour" as separate from the turbulence of daily life. Contrary to the widespread assumption that the adolescents' resistance to this style of therapy is primarily due to their trouble in trusting adults to begin with, we really think there is more to it than that. For many adolescents, even the trusted adult loses his value in a role of therapist or counselor, unless he is somewhere built into the normal power hierarchy in which youngsters operate and unless he is close to the scene where life events occur and available when they do. We might want to speculate about reasons for this trend and in doing so might think of many, such as, for instance, the greater safety from introspection and from the emergence of transference fantasies; or we might even think of the degree to which the "therapy hour and the couch" have been made symbols of rather specific diseases by our popular literature; or we might remember the fear of too deep a commitment of so many youngsters, which would be reduced in the more familiar terrain of behavioral struggle. Whatever other explanations we might think of, the fact remains that a considerable number of our adolescents find it hard to make use of our traditional forms of fifty-minute-hour counseling and treatment, even where other factors do not contraindicate it.

If any of this is even partially true, this should certainly change our present system of support for the adolescent considerably.

(1) It puts heavy weight back on the shoulders of Junior's natural educators and play leaders at school and at home.

(2) It puts heavy weight back on how people in the trenches of daily life behave right then and there and challenges the psychiatrist to make a major effort to learn how to guide those "other adults" who so prominently figure in the life space of our young.

(3) It might even change our concept of the "office or clinic" hour in favor of a much more flexible and "crisis-geared" availability in the youngster's natural habitat, or at least a much more flexible contact design.

In short, the usually complained-about "resistance" of many of our adolescents against accepting help, even when they obviously need it so badly, might be the well-known resistance not only against therapeutic change but against the specific design of time and space and role distribution which has become part of our traditional professional armamentarium and may need revision for those cases for which it does not fit.

B. Shifts in the Overcharging of Reality Situations and Life Events with a Surplus of Symbolic Valence

The phenomenon as such is well enough known and hardly needs elaboration in this context. Only, as psychiatrists we are likely to assume that the need to overcharge daily life situations and reality issues with symbolic content would be one of the differentiation criteria between "healthy" and "sick." While this still holds true in the extremes, it does not hold in the median ranges. In fact, it is not so much the phenomenon as such that concerns me here as the unexpected and unpredictable way in which the very same youngster may react to an issue, well within its realistic weight at one time, and stuffing it full with irrational meaning at the next moment.

Also, the range of life situations and life events selected for such symbolic overcharging varies, of course, from age to age, subculture to subculture, setting to setting, and is also highly capricious in terms of the fashions of the times. Even worse, it seems that the degree to which any given youngster is tempted to supercharge not only depends on him and his proclivitity to do so but also is a function of that situation itself and the "irrationality pull" contained in the way the adult on the spot is handling it. To illustrate crudely: pants are pants, knives are knives, cigarettes are cigarettes, bedtime rules are bedtime rules, and a chow line is an unavoidable part of large-number reality for everyone to see. Whether any of these issues suddenly leads to an irrational flare-up, whether it is symbolically loaded with castration fear or is perceived as an insult to personal integrity, an unbearable violation of self-esteem, or what not, may depend on many details, among them the way in which the adult acts in such confrontational moments and the extra message that is packed into the communication between the adolescent and him.

If that is so, not only does the psychiatrist need to pursue his already lively interest in the question of just which life situation or reality issue becomes symbolic for what, but he needs, in addition, to spend extra effort to find out (*a*) what it depends on whether adult behavior tempts the adolescent into overcharging, or gives him ego support against just that, and (*b*) how one helps adults who are important figures in the natural habitat of adolescent life to avoid such temptation toward overcharging. On this issue, by the way, our textbooks are quite thin; it seems we have concentrated one-sidedly on exhausting the range of interpretations as to just what all this means and have not looked sharply enough in the direction of doing something about it with enough specificity so as to give the adolescents in turmoil some in-situational support.

C. Ego Collapse under the Influence of Group Psychological Intoxication and under the Impact of a "Dare"

Let me just briefly illustrate which life events I have in mind.

(1) The phenomenon of group psychological intoxication is well enough known. In fact, that the ego easily collapses under similar conditions has long been pointed out in connection with mass phenomena under extreme situations. But we know now that it does not take a "mass" phenomenon, and that such situations need not be "extreme" at all. Our case histories of adolescents are full of such mass-psychologylike phenomena in a teacup. Or, in other words, under some conditions adolescents are likely to "react" as adults usually do when they go to a convention in somebody else's town. Only they do not even need alcohol or other drugs to get themselves in-

ebriated; they can do it by just "watching each other goof off." Now, this in itself is also well known. What we, as psychiatrists, are likely to miss is this: The ability of the ego to sustain its reality-testing and impulse-control function in such moments is not simply a function of "ego strength" per se. Even the most wonderfully functioning ego of the most wonderful youngster sometimes finds itself totally helpless under such group psychological conditions. Thus, the ego's ability to maintain its role under the impact of group psychological intoxication is an independent variable in its own right. The old theory that the "nice kid with a good superego and a well-functioning ego" would be safe from collapse under the above-mentioned condition, while his less value-oriented and ego-weak compatriot would, of course, succumb, needs to be thrown onto the junk heap of early assumptions long obsolete. The latter assumption is easily disproved by the case of the toughie with high skills of group psychological manipulation; although he is much less value-identified than his more adult-oriented compeer and endowed with a much less well-functioning ego in most respects, group psychological intoxication does not throw him. On the contrary, he is the one who sets it off and even has reality sense enough to disappear before things get too hot. It is, on the contrary, often the otherwise well-functioning youngster who finds himself helpless in a moment when the whole group seems to have lost its sense. If this is so, I think we owe the educator an answer to the question: just what is required for adolescent egos to manage such group psychological predicaments? And we owe ourselves an answer to the question: just what does all this do to our theories about character, responsibility, and ego function to begin with?

If we remember how much of the life management of adolescents, with their expanding autonomy and unsupervised functioning in so many new and untried situations, depends on this very issue, it is clear how important it is to get this independent variable under better scrutiny and control.

(2) The same is true for another variable, namely, the ability of the adolescent to react halfway reasonably to situations implying a "dare."

This one, though, is an issue of much longer standing, but it did not hit us as hard universally and seemed limited to smaller select groups during specific periods of historical stress. Anybody who is familiar with the German fraternity system of the late nineteenth century will immediately know what I am talking about. No matter what a given individual is like, once he finds himself enveloped in the group psychological bind of a dare his way of reacting is prescribed by a clear-cut ritual and is practically in the hands of fate. Next to the somewhat milder forms of the same psychology in our fraternities, especially at initiation ritual time, we find ourselves reminded of the highly organized tough neighborhood gang which is in a feud with other gangs of the same area, where similar dare psychology has been well studied and documented. My contention of importance to our theme is this: this phenomenon, though less dramatically visible, is just as pervasively relevant for adolescent life, even where, on the surface, it does not look or sound like what we used to expect an open dare to look and sound like. However, once a situation is marked as a dare in an adolescent's life, he finds himself in a similar predicament, and his reaction is of prime importance. The danger of the total abandoning of any reality testing is omnipresent; the chance is high that he finds himself helpless unless certain ritualistic alternatives of working his way out of it can be found; and the price the individual pays for ignoring the dare in terms of shame, fear of reprisal, lowering of self-image and self-esteem, or self-imposed loneliness and group estrangement is considerable.

This problem of finding proper reactions to a dare, by the way, is not limited to the usually well-described events in peer-group life. Many behaviors which outwardly do not seem connected with this issue at all, which may look like a personal struggle between the adolescent and his teacher or like the usual type of "resistance to therapy," may really fall into this category at times. This is especially so if the adult in charge of the situation is not familiar with the peculiar kind of dare situation and does not perceive how far his own behavior, though quite normally educationally motivated, has really led into one.

In short, of all the "reactions" of adolescents, the ego's ability to deal appropriately with the moments of dare belongs to the issues that would rate high on my lists of preventive psychiatry, for even otherwise well-stacked superegos and egos do not seem to be very good at this particular task.

D. The Gang under the Couch

The general assumption in psychiatry seems to be that group psychology is, of course, an important item in groups, but it had better stay there. Unless, of course, one invites it in specifically by doing group therapy, whatever we know about group processes would be considered relevant for group life only. The idea that group psychology should be rampant, while Junior and I sit in a well-soundproofed cabin in a treatment interaction, sounds plain silly. However, it is not. In fact, it seems to me that the degree of frequency with which group psychology elements force themselves into the privacy of the interindividual situation has increased when we deal with the adolescents of our time. To come straight to the point:

(1) Even while alone in a room with one adult, the "group psychological mirror" is omnipresent, and the fear of showing up badly—or the hope of showing up well—if one's "group" saw one right now may be a strong motivating factor, far beyond anything else we have learned to take seriously in a therapeutic interaction.

(2) There is a clear-cut "dueling code" that a given adolescent subsociety develops, which makes a struggle between youngster and adult a

"clean" one, and there are special rituals which make losing in the battle with the adult and yielding to common sense, reason, or advice tax-exempt from group blame or ostracism.

There is another set of adult-youth interactions which make the advisee's behavior inexcusable and tantamount to "ratting" or betrayal of the group code or to cowardly surrender to advice from without which can result in his losing face with his group or downright ostracism.

(3) Much of what looks like "resistance," especially in the opening gambits of a treatment situation with adolescents, is not what we usually assume it to be, namely, personal distrust, lack of proper transference, or downright resistance to change. Some of it can be shown to be due to the fact that, even though invisibly, the "group is listening in" and the youngster can never afford to think himself really "alone."

Now, if we deal with youngsters who are known to be highly involved with gang life, we have no trouble remembering all this. However, I have found the same basic situation pervading interviews with youngsters of suburbia, who did not belong to any gang, but were as heavily resistance-encrusted in terms of the "teen-age code of their subsociety" against giving in too easily to parental or psychiatric advice or risking their prestige by being too confidential with the enemy.

The issues that become group-code relevant vary, of course, with country, terrain, social class, neighborhood style, age, and what not. The phenomenon itself remains the same. This issue of group psychological resistance, even during group absentia, becomes especially hot where an adolescent is "sent into treatment" by parental dictum, although the peer-group code of the other adolescents of his orbit contains a special clause against accepting any "parent-flunkies under psychiatric disguise." However different in detail, some such situations are practically identical with that of the prison psychiatrist who knows that his patient's co-inmates just wait to find out whether he "ratted" in that interview with his "doc" or not.

Needless to say, resistance flowing out of this group psychological corner needs entirely different countertechniques as compared to those so well established for the usual type of resistance—a chapter which as yet remains to be written.

E. Astounding Degrees of Ego Resilience

Most of our writings in psychiatry are still focused on the attempt to understand why people break down. Actually, we often have reason to be equally puzzled about the fact that they hold up so well under circumstances whose traumatic weight would surely make one expect that it would be human to collapse.

Although we seem to drift into the same custom as far as the young are concerned, I would like to abandon that habit and remind all of us of an equally surprising fact: a huge number of youth do not surprise me by breaking down, but by the incredible feat of their egos in holding up, where anything but health seems to be supported by the conditions to which they are exposed. Although these are happy incidents, and perhaps not so much a cause for worry, they should worry us if we cannot understand why. For something is wrong with our theories as long as unexpected health is not as easily conceptualized as expected disease.

My reference to "ego resilience" limits itself to two situations, which should be enough for the remainder of this chapter, though it certainly is not enough in terms of the phenomenon as such:

(1) I refer by this term to the capacity of an ego to stand up even under pressures which we usually assume to be pathogenic.

(2) I also imply the capacity of an ego to "recover" from temporary collapse fast, without much outside help, and bound back to a high degree of normalcy.

It is my contention that an unusually large number of our adolescents seem to tell us, "Look, Sigmund, no trauma even in situations where such would be expected," and that even the peer-group code lures I have just complained about seem to find some youngsters "resilient" enough to remain unaffected. One of the problems we face is that such ego resilience is often considered a negative issue by the adults in charge and that the full picture of what really happens may be hard to unveil. To wit: some of the "beatniklike" stances constitute a healthy rebellion against the anti-anti-intellectual stance of parents or peers, just as we know that some of the vehement rebellion of some youngsters displayed in their battle against a teacher or parent may actually be only the other side of real courage and devotion to a "cause" or rather unselfish service to a "pal" one considered wronged.

Although we know all this in general, I think we need to spend more downright clinical time to explore the demarcation line between the ego that loses control and the ego that sticks up for a cause, the ego that covers escape into a fad and the ego that courageously maintains an unpopular or misunderstood stance.

For preventive work, the puzzle of just how to support egos to be more resilient, especially under crisis impacts, remains the problem most worthy of our attention.

References

1. BERNFELD, S. "Der sociale Ort und seine Bedeutung für Neurose, Verwahrlosung and Pädogogik," *Imago,* Vol. VII (1938).
2. BERNFELD, S. "Types of Adolescence," *Psychoanalytic Quarterly,* Vol. VII (1938).
3. BLOS, P. *On Adolescence.* New York: Free Press of Glencoe, 1962.
4. ERIKSON, E. H. *Childhood and Society,* 2d ed. New York: Norton, 1963.
5. JAMES, M. "Interpretation and Management in the Treatment of Pre-Adolescents," *International Journal of Psychoanalysis, London,* Vol. XLV (October 1964), Part 4.
6. REDL, F. "Strategy and Technique of the Life Space Interview," *American Journal of Orthopsychiatry,* XXIX (1959), 1–18.
7. REDL, F. *When We Deal with Children.* New York: Free Press of Glencoe, 1966, pp. 35–67.

SECTION

II

THE ADOLESCENT
AND HIS FAMILY

EDITORS' INTRODUCTION   This section continues the developmental themes of its predecessor. It opens with a chapter by Lidz, who analyzes in detail the expectable conflicts within the family group that occur as an adolescent strives to overcome the dependency of his childhood, free himself from parental control, and work out a separate identity that will be all his own. One source of difficulty for the adolescent is that he must give up the security of his childhood "nest" in the family before he has developed the alternative security of a stable adult identity. He may try to bridge the gap by using peer-group support, which he has begun to build during pre-adolescence, but during periods of stress this may not be enough; and then he may wish to return temporarily to the warmth and security of his previous childhood reliance on his parents. Unfortunately, this impulse conflicts with his dominant wish for freedom and entire self-reliance, which often impels him aggressively to seek flaws in his parents and to devalue them. Provocative behavior not infrequently leads to a crescendo of mutual disparagement. Both the adolescent and his parents are then surprised by his sudden reversions to the loving and dependent role.

Lidz discusses the common complication of this process by possible disharmony between the parents and by their being currently involved in their own crises of middle age. Like Anthony, he emphasizes the significance of stimulation of parental sensitivities by the flowering sexuality of the adolescent at a time when the parents are with difficulty coming to terms with their own waning powers.

Lidz goes on to discuss the needs of the adolescent for the parents to set up consistent limits against which he can struggle in his attempts to burst his bonds. If these are missing, the adolescent often feels neglected and unloved. He must continue seeing his parents as basically valued role models, no matter how much he rebels against them. His eventual identity is considerably influenced by identification with them, so that his adult self-esteem will be linked to his esteem for his parents in the world of reality, no matter how much he may devalue them in fantasy or in his rebellious phases. Lidz ends his chapter by discussing the special difficulty faced by an adolescent who makes the discovery, sometimes as an acute traumatic experience, that a parent has inferior value in the real world. This may destroy the parent as a feasible identification model and leave the adolescent floundering. Such a situation will be aggravated if the parent responds to the revelation by counterattacking and belittling the adolescent. Lidz points to the even more disastrous effect of such a problem's coming up in therapy and the therapist's dealing with it by trying to deny its reality or its profound significance for his patient, rather than by mobilizing all possible measures to support the adolescent in his painful predicament.

Chapter 8, by Shapiro, throws some interesting light on the three preceding chapters. It describes research on the family interaction of disturbed adolescents, based on observations of weekly family therapy sessions together with research interviews and psychological testing of the adolescent and his parents. Shapiro focuses on the failure in age-appropriate development of relative ego autonomy in adolescents and relates this to corresponding impairment of ego autonomy in one or both parents. His study demonstrates the causal links between these two factors. From an analysis of the formal content of the records of family therapy interactions he shows that the image the parents have of their son, which he calls their "delineation" of him, has a fixed stereotyped quality and is inconsistent, constricted, and distorted. It shows the adolescent as an incompetent, dependent, impractical person and communicates to him a view of himself that undermines the development of his independence and autonomy. Shapiro's study presents us with a microscopic picture of the process, described macroscopically by Anthony and by Redl, of the effect of stereotyped parental perceptions and distorted expectations in molding the adolescent's behavior and self-image. Shapiro takes this analysis a step farther. His research demonstrates that the distorted delineations of the adolescent are produced by defenses of the parents against similar problems in their own personalities, which are characterized by identity confusion and lack of ego autonomy. In addition to molding the adolescent's behavior and self-image by their verbal and nonverbal communications, the parents also serve as role models influencing him by identification to incorporate similar patterns of sickness.

It is interesting to compare the stereotyped distorted delineations of the adolescents by their parents in Shapiro's study with the stereotypes discussed by Anthony, which he ascribes not to personality disorder in parents, but to dominant themes in our culture. It is likely that Shapiro's research reveals the details of the process whereby parental perceptions and expectations affect the behavior and self-image of the adolescent. But it is probable that there is an important difference between the stereotypes which emerge from major personality disorder in the parents, leading to similar disorder in their children, and those that are the common heritage of many healthy adults in our culture. Shapiro's sample, which was drawn from a pool of severely ill adolescents at a treatment institution, must represent one end of a continuum. What the differences are between this and the more usual situations described by Anthony, Redl, and Lidz still remains to be studied.

Further light is thrown on this question by Vassiliou in the following chapter. Vassiliou describes the effects of recent economic and sociocultural changes in Greece on general patterns of functioning of men and women and on their complementary role relationships in marriage. On the basis of a series of studies, he traces the effects of these factors on the commonly occurring patterns of relationship between parents and children, especially during adolescence. He paints a picture similar to that described by Shapiro. He provides some examples of adolescent cases seen in his clinic which appear to illustrate the findings of his researches on the population at large. These show parents forcing their children into dependent roles and attitudes by overprotection coupled with constant and severely inhibiting criticism of any sign of autonomous behavior. The personalities of the clinical cases show the defect in autonomous ego development described also by Shapiro. Vassiliou then raises the question of whether Greek culture today is "sick," with the implication that it should be expected to produce a high incidence of personality disorder among its adolescents. Unfortunately he ends his chapter without providing data to answer this question. On the other hand, Vassiliou does express an opinion which, although not buttressed by research data as are the earlier statements in his chapter, nevertheless has some face validity. He points out that his clinical cases are probably a skewed sample and that it is not valid to derive from studying them the conclusion that the stereotypes, attitudes, roles, and patterns of family life which have led to mental disorder in the adolescents who come to a clinic for help have the same pathogenic effect as the apparently similar patterns that impinge on the bulk of adolescents in the population. He does not document this, but it seems plausible that parents who overprotect their children and keep them dependent because of culturally based attitudes and values affect their superficial behavior, but not necessarily their personality structure, whereas parents who behave similarly because of their own idiosyncratic disorder exert a deep pathogenic effect on their children. Vassiliou ends his chapter with a statement that is consonant with this. He emphasizes the special threats to personal survival inherent in the ecological situation in Greece and postulates that "very often even biological survival throughout life is secured through the interdependences of the in-group [which consists of] family, friends, and friends of friends." He cites studies which have shown that an essential core of behavior in these "in-groups" is a warmly nurturant relationship with its members similar to a mother's relationship to a young child. Vassiliou then points out how important it is, therefore, for a Greek to be trained to be dependent on such a protective group and how this training is effectively carried out by the overprotective nurturant transactions in the Greek family. What we need in order to deepen our understanding of Vassiliou's thesis is studies that compare the personality structure of the well-adapted dependent Greek who fits neatly into his role in the protective in-group and the Greek with defective ego autonomy who comes to Vassiliou's clinic. We also need studies that utilize the methods developed by Shapiro to analyze the essential differences between the parent-child relationships in the two families and how each affects the behavior and self-image of the adolescent.

The last chapter in this section, by Alexina McWhinnie, reports a study of the development of adopted children during adolescence. It deepens our understanding of the point made by Lidz that despite all his active rebellion, the adolescent needs the actuality of his parents as identification objects in the molding of his adult identity. McWhinnie provides us with a sensitive description of the tribulations of these adolescents who do not know their biological parents and are therefore particularly confused in their search for identity. She reports that during adolescence many adopted children make a special effort to find out about their biological parents so that almost self-consciously they can use this as a basis for developing their identity and resolving doubts about inferiority inherited from parents who abandoned them. On the other hand, the adolescents feel that it is their adopted parents who represent for them the nurturing figures who foster their dependency and from whom they must separate themselves in order to achieve autonomy. This is often complicated by the attitude that they should be grateful to people who made a conscious choice to adopt them and that they should therefore suppress their rebellious feelings and behavior. McWhinnie discusses the way these struggles of the adolescent are often further complicated by the effect of unresolved feelings of the adopted parents about the adoption process and about expectations that during adolescence sexual arousal will impel the children to follow in the footsteps of their aberrant biological parents. She ends her chapter by pointing to the implications of her research for the therapy of adopted children who have psychiatric disturbances during adolescence and for the organization of preventive programs of anticipatory guidance for adopted children and their parents.

7

The Adolescent and His Family

Theodore Lidz

Anna Freud has written, "While an adolescent remains inconsistent and unpredictable in his behavior, he may suffer but he does not seem to me to be in need of treatment. I think that he should be given time and scope to work out his own solution. Rather, it may be his parents who need help and guidance so as to be able to bear with him. There are few situations in life that are more difficult to cope with than an adolescent son or daughter during the attempt to liberate himself." [1] Indeed, it is during adolescence that the parents' faith in the child they have reared receives its most severe test; but it concerns their confidence in what they have provided and conveyed as well as trust in the child. The parents must rely more and more on what they have instilled in earlier years, for now the youth must begin to direct his own life, to try out what he has gained during the more protected years, and to find himself as an individual in his own right. Yet, Anna Freud's statement has its limitations. Although it is salutory to recognize that parents can need help as much as or more than the adolescent in coping with the anxieties and frustrations created by the child's transition into adulthood, it is during adolescence that casualties begin to appear in number and require treatment if catastrophic outcomes are to be averted.

We should like to offer clear guidelines concerning when an adolescent can be left to his own devices, to know when advice to parents will suffice and when treatment is indicated. Rules and even guidelines are difficult to establish, but I believe that through considering the nature of the problems that adolescence presents to the youth and his family, we can have a better grasp of how things go wrong and what might help set them aright.

It has been customary to consider the problems of adolescence in terms of what went amiss during preceding developmental phases. Indeed, since Ernest Jones's classical paper, it has been customary to examine the nature of the youth's oedipal transition and seek to understand his adolescent

105

problems largely as recrudescences of the oedipal difficulties.[3] Such genetic
concepts have been extremely valuable; the proper transition through any
developmental phase rests on solving the tasks of preceding periods. The
intense sexual drives of adolescence tend to follow earlier attachments in
seeking outlets, and the oedipal configurations must be reworked and once
again resolved. However, each development period has its unique tasks
and problems.

It is natural for the adolescent and his family to be in conflict. The essential problems for both the youth and his parents arise because the youth is
confronted by the critical tasks of overcoming his dependency on his parents and of containing and redirecting his sexual drives away from the persons who had been the primary objects of his affectional and sensuous
attachments. Only after these tasks have been accomplished can he consoli-
date his identifications and role models to integrate as an adult, find an
identity of his own, and combine sexual and affectional strivings in an intimate relationship with another. Adolescence is a lengthy and far from homogeneous period during which a number of crucial issues must be worked
through. The needs of the 11-year-old, pubescent, fifth-grade school child
and the 18-year-old college sophomore are very different, and parents must
meet them differently even though the early teen-ager may seem convinced
that he is already emancipated.

At the onset of puberty the child's life still has its center in the family.
The problems of the oedipal period were concerned with overcoming the
intense erotically toned attachment to the mother to find a reasonably
conflict-free area *within* the family. Adolescence, in contrast, involves finding an identity as an individual outside the family. Much of the critical
preparation for adolescence takes place during the latency period when the
child begins to move beyond the confines of his family. He becomes part of
a peer group where even at his very young age he is judged as an individual,
and he enters the schoolroom social system where he is increasingly judged
on the basis of his achievements rather than by ascription. He also usually
forms an intense friendship with a child of the same sex—his first strong
investment of a peer and a person outside his immediate family. His horizons broaden, his family-centered orientation diminishes, and he begins to
take on peer-group values and moral evaluations. Without such movement
into peer groups at play and in school, serious difficulties are likely to ensue
during adolescence. Still, the latency child's security lies within his home,
and he still needs to feel that he will receive ascribed acceptance and affection while he begins to test out his capabilities.

The equilibrium established between the child and his family during the
latency period is almost inevitably disturbed by the events of puberty, and
many of the ensuing difficulties arise because the child must now begin to
move out from the shelter of the family that has always provided his basic
security and away from the parents who have formed his cardinal interpersonal relationships. Let us consider the changes of early adolescence and

why they require a reorientation of the child's relationships with his family.

The prepubertal spurt in growth requires the child to reorient himself to his own body and to others. As he begins to proximate adults in size he cannot blithely continue to relate to them as a child. Then the upsurge of genital sexuality with its unfamiliar sensations and impulsions preoccupies, and it requires strengthening of ego controls to contain them. The adolescent sexuality is not simply a rearousal of oedipal strivings, for the hormonally driven impulsions have not existed earlier. The sexual drive, however, directs toward the oedipal attachments, but the strivings are no longer easily repressed and must be directed away from the family members. The potential for ego control of the id impulsions are enhanced by the qualitative changes in cognitive abilities that enable the youth to conceptualize and, in Piaget's terms, carry out formal operations.[2] These cognitive developments strengthen the ego capacities for self-direction and also heighten the imagination and lead to adherence to ideals and ideologies. The adolescent's superego thus changes as he can rely less on parental injunctions and depend more on his own concepts and on the ideologies he embraces. Other revisions of the superego must occur to help guide adult rather than childhood behavior and eventually to permit sexual expression. In moving toward adulthood the boy must reverse his position toward females. He has been dependent on his mother, but now he prepares to have a woman become dependent on him and to provide for her as well as to become more sexually aggressive. The girl now completes the resolution of her oedipal attachment. Earlier she has overcome the primary attachment to her mother, but has found a new object within the family in her father. With the onset of her puberty the father moves away to frustrate the attachment, and the girl's fantasies lead her to repress it. She is often left with the feeling that in becoming a woman she has become unattractive to her father.

Occasionally a youth remains calm and considerate toward his parents without being pathological; but adolescence is usually a time of revolt— and conformity. The violence of the revolt is often a measure of the wrench necessary to overcome the ties to the parents rather than an indication of the youth's hostility toward them. He must convince himself as much as his parents that he does not need them and that they and he are very different from when he was a mere child.

Although freeing the self from dependency on parents, loosening the libidinal attachments to them, and modifying the superego for adult living are largely intrapsychic tasks, they are usually carried out via alterations in behavior toward the parents whose directives were the original sources of the superego. The parents' standards, values, and concerns are derogated as old-fashioned, stupid, unreasonable, and far different from those of the more modern and intelligent parents of friends. Even more conducive to intrafamilial strife is the devaluation of the parents themselves. To gain more latitude for himself, the youth seeks flaws in his parents' behavior and personalities, particularly in their ethical standards and actions. He is likely to magnify what he finds for several reasons. He must devalue a parent to counter his renewed oedipal strivings. He establishes rigid standards to maintain his own impulsions, and he judges his parents in the same ascetic terms. He has become disillusioned when learning of the sensuous nature of the parental sexual relationship and considers them deceitful in forbidding him what they permit themselves, but he seeks parental defects that he can openly condemn and rationally resent as a displacement from his anger over their sexual behavior. The attacks can constitute a severe blow to the parents' self-esteem, and a parent may counterattack against the upstart and ingrate, and retributive behavior can heighten the hostilities.

Matters become even more complicated when the adolescent becomes guilty about his hostile feelings toward his parents, fearful of retribution, and anxious about his inabilities to manage the independence he seeks. The rebelliousness gives way to displays of affection and regressive strivings for renewed dependency. The alternations in behavior and shifts in attitudes can perplex the parents. They also perplex the youth, who then tries to overcome ambivalences by proving that he does not want what he wants and by a contrariness that prevents his parents from providing the support he may need and would like to be able to accept. It may be easier for a youth, particularly during middle adolescence, when parents take a firm stand and provide something to fight against and thus provide a focus for the rebelliousness.

Still uncertain of himself and without definite internalized values of his own, the adolescent turns to the youth culture and embraces its standards. His loneliness when bereft of the ties to his family directs him to seek acceptance by his peer group, and he displays his loyalty by conforming to its mores—at times, through an overconformity to nonconformity that fosters conflict with his parents. He also modifies his superego by taking on the ideologies of those he idealizes—teachers and other adult leaders, but also the admired leader of the gang who may be admired because he is most defiant of adult values.

The adolescent's difficulties with his parents are not all caused by the youth's problems and behavior. The phase-specific tasks of the parents involve progressively permitting, and even encouraging, greater latitude of action and decision making to the youth and, concomitantly, requiring more responsibility. Parents not only may find it difficult to relinquish authority but also to contain their anxieties over a teen-ager's ability to take care of himself. Anxiety leads to anger and may be vented as rage against a child who arouses the anxiety. Parents distrust their child's new standards derived from the youth culture and abhor the image he creates in modeling himself after an ideal who flouts adult values. They find themselves involved in bitter arguments about the youth's new ideology, which runs counter to their own. The difficulties of the parents are often heightened because commonly they are passing through a critical phase of life themselves as they are confronted by middle age. They are seeking to come to terms with the limits of their own lives, the frustrations of their ambitions and ideals, just when their adolescent child feels life opening before him; and the blossoming of youth with its upsurge of sexuality heightens awareness of their own fading physical capacities and waning sexual abilities. The expansiveness of adolescence confronts the conservatism of middle life, and the youth's idealism irritates the cynicism of middle-age disappointment.

Conflicts between parents can also arise as a result of having an adolescent child. A family may be disorganized when a father flees from the sexual attractiveness of his daughter into some extramarital involvement. A mother envious of her daughter's attractiveness may seek to demonstrate her greater ability to charm young men. Dissent over the amount of freedom permitted the adolescent child can further divide a couple. At times old homosexual tendencies of a parent that had been contained by the marriage are reawakened by the presence of an attractive youthful boy or girl within the home, seriously threatening the equilibrium of the family.

A parent's ability to accept a child's adolescence and foster his independence are influenced by the satisfactions gained from the marriage. A parent who gains little gratification from the spouse often uses a child as a substitute source of emotional gratification and has difficulty relinquishing it. A father who has lavished much on a daughter and needs her admiration may be unable to tolerate ceding the child he has raised to another man.

A serious source of family discord derives from keeping an adolescent boy from practicing an instrumental role within the family. Adult roles are properly tried out within the family, and assuming an instrumental role is a cardinal aspect of being a man. Yet within the family even a late adolescent is a member of the childhood generation, and the exercise of leadership and decision making by the youth can afford a direct challenge to parental and particularly paternal prerogatives. Still, when a male adolescent's instrumental assertiveness is squelched he seeks to break up the family social system. Herein lies a major source of intrafamilial conflict and of behavior that is antipathetic to the family, if not clearly antisocial. Not only may the youth attack and sabotage but he may also rouse his siblings to rebelliousness and defiance. Whereas the ensuing conflicts seem to focus on matters of obedience of the child and the restrictiveness of the parent, they derive in large measure from failure to permit adequate scope for a boy's exercise of instrumental functions (and, perhaps, also for a girl to live out the feminine expressive-affectional role) within the family.

On the other hand, the youth may also deeply resent the parents' failures to set limits. He fights against delimitation, but at times he also wishes to be relieved of the responsibility of deciding what chances he can take, how far to go along with the gang, how far to venture sexually. The boy or girl can interpret parental compliance and their willingness to accede to his wishes as lack of interest. The youth may correctly guess that the parent gains satisfaction from his or her acting out. He begins to test the parental limits and is soon beyond his depth. In the study of sociopathic youths, we find many who have felt seriously neglected in having been permitted to follow their own wishes—at times, permitted by parents who feared the child would become as hostile to them as they had been to their parents, and sometimes by parents who enjoyed the behavior they stormed against. Many accepted their therapist's restrictions as the first evidence that someone really cared what happened to them.

Adolescence is the source of many types of intrafamilial discord, but in a well-knit family with reasonably adaptable parents the troubles begin to subside when the late adolescent realizes that the time for trying out is approaching an end and he must come to grips with finding a way of life for himself. His view of the world becomes less egocentric, and he begins to see his parents as individuals with lives of their own and with functions other than those of parenthood. He begins to understand that they have been caught up in their own fates and were not free to live out their own aspirations and expectations. The world becomes a very large place that can be very lonely without a family. He recognizes that achievement in reality is not as simple as in fantasy. He begins to delimit himself and seeks a small but real segment of life in which he can find his way and amount to something, and he searches for another person to whom he will be all-important, who can serve as a replacement for the parents whom he is relinquishing, and in whom both his sexual and affectional needs can find fulfillment. He settles down to be responsible for himself and to himself and unwittingly soon takes on the ways of his parents that he has so recently been repudiating.

Now, to emerge from adolescence and gain an identity of his own, the youth, despite his rebelliousness and need to loosen his bonds to the family, still requires a positive image of his parents and their relationship to one another. He may need to derogate his parents, but he does not wish to destroy them as models. His self-esteem is closely linked to the esteem in which he can hold his parents. He needs to overcome his childhood image of his parents as omniscient and perfect, but he also continues to require one parent with whom he can identify and who will serve as a model to follow into adulthood, and the other parent as an object whose affection and admiration is worth seeking. Further, the parents are internalized not only as individuals but also in their relationship to each other. A parent who is treated with contempt by the spouse or replaced as a sexual partner by the spouse is unlikely to seem an object worthy of emulation, and if such an identification should be made the other parent must be considered worthless or cruel.

From among the many types of difficulty that can arise between an adolescent and his parents, I wish now to consider one that can escalate to destroy the relationship and sometimes virtually to destroy the youth or the family. The danger arises when the youth seeks flaws in his parents to lessen the hold of superego injunctions. As noted above, the adolescent's attacks on his parents' behavior and, even more, his attacks on their character can lead to counterattack and retribution by the parent that lead to further mis-understandings and heighten the hostilities, but such problems are usually eventually overcome. There is, however, considerable difference between fantasy and reality, and there is a difference between the adolescent's exaggerations of his parents' shortcomings and his uncovering of a disillusioning reality. All too often, the youth gains a pyrrhic victory that shatters the parental image but also disrupts his own progress toward integration. The image of the parent cannot be restored sufficiently to serve again as an internalized guide for future relationships. A 17-year-old boy learns that his father, whom his mother had always idealized, not only is despised by his colleagues as an opportunist but is having an affair with a high-school girl. An upper-middle-class girl who ran away from home to become a call girl had learned that her mother had not really been the main support of the family through running an insurance agency but rather by being the mistress of a man who rewarded her with his firm's very lucrative insurance business. A girl who had become openly promiscuous and was a drug addict at the age of 14 had uncovered newspaper articles that showed photos of her mother being caught in bed in flagrante delicto and learned that her parents' divorce had been spread across the tabloids for weeks.

Such discoveries can destroy parents as identification models and useful models of love objects, but an even more injurious step can follow. The parents insist that their child's perception and understanding are erroneous. The girl whose mother was the mistress of the man who bought the insurance policies sought to talk with her parents about the drunken parties they attended. She was seeking a way of restituting her mother as an idealized person, but she was met by sharp rebuff and told to stop lying and defaming her parents to the hospital personnel. On their next visit, the parents told their daughter that they had become convinced that she would receive better treatment in a state mental hospital. Such parental behavior places the adolescent in a bind that can lead to psychosis, as it did in this girl, or into flagrant sociopathy. On occasion another step follows that can virtually seal the youth's fate. When he obtains psychotherapy and hesitantly ventures to discuss his parents' behavior, the therapist who is treating him because he is sociopathic or psychotic either discounts what he says about his parents, or considers that it has no pertinence, or seeks to focus on what and why the youth projects his own tendencies onto his parents. The youth is not only pushed further into unreality but despairs of ever being understood and becomes thoroughly disillusioned with the adult world, which he then feels like smashing completely.

Before closing this brief excursion into one of the more complex aspects of psychiatry—and of contemporary living—I wish to remark on how changing societal conditions have heightened the problems of adolescence. In an industrial and scientifically oriented society the essential preparation for living often extends beyond physical maturation. Further, the youth must, more than ever before, find his identity independently from his family with little reference to a family profession, business, or career pattern. The family itself—the isolated nuclear family of today—is a relatively unstable social organization with minimal foundations in traditional ways of living and of child rearing. We have recently passed through a period when many parents have been led to believe that their own lives had been blighted by repression and that their children must be permitted freedom of self-expression. The principles of child rearing have placed little emphasis on realizing that proper integration requires delimitation and channeling of drives and interests and that the complexities of the modern world may require parents to provide more rather than less guidance to their children. Perhaps, too, because a youth has less opportunity to follow parental patterns into a career, he may have a greater need to be able to identify with parents who manage to find that life is worth living and who through their example have taught that interdependence is desirable and that marriage and parenthood are goals worth pursuing.

References

1. FREUD, A. "Adolescence," in *Psychoanalytic Study of the Child,* Vol. XIII. New York: International Universities Press, 1958.
2. INHELDER, B., and J. PIAGET. *The Growth of Logical Thinking from Childhood to Adolescence.* New York: Basic Books, 1958.
3. JONES, E. "Some Problems of Adolescence," in *Papers on Psycho-Analysis.* London: Bailliere, Tindall, and Cox, 1922.
4. LIDZ, T. *The Family and Human Adaptation.* New York: International Universities Press, 1963.

8

Adolescent Ego Autonomy and the Family

Roger L. Shapiro

Efforts to specify the determinants of adolescent personality disorder have led recently to intensive investigation of the families of disturbed adolescents.[15] At the National Institute of Mental Health we have studied thirty adolescents of diverse diagnoses together with their families. In an attempt to define dynamic and stylistic regularities in the psychological organization of adolescents and their parents, our investigation has focused on observations of interaction between parents and adolescent in weekly family therapy meetings, research interviewing of adolescents and parents, and extensive psychological testing of family members.

Adolescent disturbance is conceptualized in this study as a failure in age-appropriate development of relative ego autonomy.[8, 9, 12] In another paper[14] I have proposed that adolescent maturation involves a new increment in ego autonomy and have suggested the relation between this formulation and Erikson's discussion of ego epigenesis in adolescent identity formation.[2, 3, 4] In this chapter I shall discuss evidence in support of the hypothesis that failure in the development of relative ego autonomy in the adolescent is related to ego impairment in his parents. The relation between parental ego structure, including its manifestations in behavior with the adolescent, and the adolescent's personality structure is the center of our study. More specifically our effort is to identify dimensions of impairment in ego functioning and autonomy in the parents which are manifested in behavior with the adolescent and may be related to impairment in the development of relative ego autonomy in the adolescent. Our study includes investigation of the

This chapter is based on work done in association with Winfield Scott, John Strauss, and Carmen Cabrera.

113

personality characteristics of the parents, of the identity problems of the adolescent, and of interactions within the family group. Our aim is to clarify the relationships among these.

The striking differences between the ego of the adolescent and the ego of the child have been accounted for in a variety of ways in psychoanalytic theory.[1-7, 11] I have previously proposed [13, 14] that these changes in the ego are a consequence of primary autonomous development in the cognitive ego functions at puberty leading to a sharp increase in the relative ego autonomy of the adolescent. The findings of Inhelder and Piaget[10] of a systematic development in the capacity for abstract thinking between ages 11 and 14 is evidence in support of the formulation of autonomous ego maturation during this period. We postulate a relationship between parental ego functioning and behavior and the realization of ego potentialities maturing autonomously in the adolescent.

Data regarding family interaction come from observation of conjoint family therapy sessions. In these sessions the ongoing relationship between the adolescent and his parents can be observed in a relatively unstructured setting, and its evolution in a therapeutic situation can be studied. We analyze transcripts of tape recordings of these sessions through use of the concept of delineation. By delineation we mean the view or mental image each parent has of the adolescent as it is revealed in his behavior with the adolescent.[15] Our interest is particularly in those persistent delineations of the adolescent which are, in our judgment, biased, inconsistent, constricted, or distorted. We consider these to be defensive delineations. We postulate that defensive delineations are related to parental defensive structure and to impaired ego autonomy in the parent. We relate this to evidence of impaired ego autonomy in the adolescent manifested in a clinical picture of identity confusion.

Our focus on family interaction in group sessions leads to questions which we investigate further in other situations. Individual interviewing of the parents provides a definition of their individual vulnerabilities and evidence of their defensive structure. This is one source of evidence for our inferences of defensive delineation. Individual interviewing of the adolescent is conducted with inquiry into organization and integration of self-definition, from which we define the identity problem. Dr. John Strauss has been conducting these interviews and making an assessment of various dimensions of cognitive style in the parents and the adolescent as they can be determined from a research interview. Cognitive style involves dimensions of ego functioning which seem to hold great promise for establishing regularities between parents and adolescent. These evidences of specific characteristics of ego functioning in parents and in adolescent may be isolated and subsequently related.

Dr. Winfield Scott has approached the problem of cognitive style through utilization of psychological test data of the family members. He has been able to match blindly projective-test protocols of adolescent to parents in sixteen out of sixteen families attempted, using a method developed in consultation with Dr. Margaret Singer.[16] These matchings were successful for each family in which they were attempted and were done on four groups of four families each where the marital couples were identified as couples and the adolescents identified as to age and sex. The basis of the matchings was complex, but involved great emphasis on the formal elements in the projective-test protocols, with particular attention to various aspects of cognitive style.

Excerpts of family interaction containing delineations of the adolescent are assessed for evidence of the dimensions of cognitive style which are characteristic of family members' performance in research interviews and psychological tests. This assessment allows us to evaluate not only content of delineations but the various styles of delineations in each family and provides a basis for discussion of dimensions of ego functioning of parents in relation to adolescents which may affect adolescent ego functioning.

Parental delineations of adolescents with disturbances in ego autonomy reveal regular characteristics both of content and of formal structure. The content of delineations is frequently discouraging and undermining to independent behavior of the adolescent. The parents often communicate a view of the adolescent in which he is explicitly defined as dependent, incompetent, impractical, and lacking in discernment. The formal characteristics of delineations frequently suggest impaired ego autonomy in the parents. Their style of thinking is frequently highly concrete, meaning may be ambiguous, and thinking may be stereotyped, inflexible, or blatantly unrealistic. The adolescent's independent thinking and action often generate particular anxiety in these parents and mobilize defenses which are expressed in the behavior of delineations. The content and style of these have the effect of containing the adolescent and militate against the adolescent's easy exercise of new capacities for autonomy.

A brief case example will illustrate our method and findings. In this family there was a dramatic personality change in the adolescent, a boy of 18, during his first year of college, with feelings of confusion, of merging with or being controlled by others, withdrawal, extreme shifts in mood, and rage episodes which resulted in his hospitalization. The following excerpt from a family session which occurred ten months after the patient's admission to the hospital is highly characteristic of the interaction of the patient and his parents over issues of autonomy. The patient has been working part-time outside the hospital and has been talking in recent family sessions about returning to college in several months. He raises the issue of college again in this session, but this time it is coupled with a new and more immediate project. He states that he wants to leave the hospital as soon as possible, but to move into an apartment of his own rather than live again with his parents.

EXCERPT 1

ALLEN: . . . I'm thinking of leaving here and getting an apartment on the outside—and I think I've found that [*pause*] for my *own* good, the approval I want is the absence of disapproval.

FATHER: That I don't understand. I don't know what the absence of disapproval means.

MOTHER: Either you approve or you disapprove.

ALLEN: Well, you don't disapprove or don't approve. You can . . .

MOTHER: In other words, you're going to do this regardless of how we feel? Is that it?

FATHER: No, no, no, no—that isn't what he's trying to say——

MOTHER: The absence of disapproval [*pause*]——

ALLEN: That's probably true, though, anyway. But that's not what I said. It's *your* interpretation.

MOTHER: Well, I'm interested in hearing what your plans are.

THERAPIST: I wonder how you arrived at that conclusion, though——

MOTHER: At *what?*

THERAPIST: From what Allen said.

MOTHER: That it means whether we approve or disapprove, he's going to go ahead anyway—with his own plans? Is that what you're referring to?

THERAPIST: Well, what Allen said originally, I thought, was that he—merely hoped for the absence of disapproval. That it meant something to him, more than approval. I wonder how you made the move—from *that*—which to me, at least, implied he was very sensitive to disapproval—to your statement which was that he's going to do what he wants to do whether you approve or not.

MOTHER: Well, that's what I got from the fact of [*pause; short laugh*] from the absence of disapproval. Of *dis*approval [*pause*] I mean if we don't say anything about—not wanting to, not approving of the fact of his going into the apartment—he's going to do it *anyway*. That's the way it sounded to *me.*

FATHER: I mean getting to the point of absence of disapproval—I mean I just don't—get it! He—even if we sat and didn't say a word about it, you would *know* whether we approved or disapproved.

ALLEN: How? [*pause*] How?

FATHER: I think you lived with us long enough and know our thoughts and our ways and——

ALLEN: [*quickly*] And you—you haven't changed any of them!

FATHER: Huh? Basically I don't think so.

ALLEN: I was afraid of that.

FATHER: I don't think you've changed eith— [*pause*] basically either.

MOTHER: [*after brief silence*] But in order to give you our approval or disapproval, we have to know what it is you're planning.

THERAPIST: It doesn't matter—that he doesn't want it [*pause*]—he'll get it anyway?

MOTHER: You mean he doesn't want our disapproval? If I disapprove I'll let him know anyway! If I approve I'll [*pause*] I'll also let him know.

Delineations of Allen by Parents (Excerpt 1)

FATHER: Allen is bewildering in his feelings about parental disapproval.

MOTHER: Allen is going to get an apartment regardless of how his parents feel and despite his parents' opposition.

FATHER: Allen is not going to act regardless of his parents' feelings.

MOTHER: Allen is saying he will act regardless of his parents' approval.

MOTHER: Allen is expected to discuss his plans with his parents.

MOTHER: Allen's moving into an apartment is disapproved of; he is going to do it anyway.

FATHER: Allen is aware of his parents' feelings whether they say anything or not.

FATHER: Allen is aware of his parents' thoughts and ways.

FATHER: Allen hasn't changed basically.

MOTHER: Allen is subject to his parents' approval whether he likes it or not.

Inferences of Defensive Delineation (Excerpt 1)

The mother's delineation of Allen as someone she has the unquestioned right to control is exemplified in this interaction. She defends her definition with great energy, insisting that she know Allen's plans in order to register her approval or disapproval. She assumes that she will not approve of his autonomous actions and seems to feel that unless she exerts great force he will ignore her disapproval. Her need to operate as a constraint on her son is arbitrary, automatic, and unyielding, and the inference of defensive delineation is based on the evidence of anxiety and exaggerated need for control in her response to him.

The father's delineation of Allen as someone who knows what his parents think without asking and who must still be controlled by this is exemplified in this interaction. He communicates an extremely pessimistic attitude about the possibility for change and for greater independence. The inference of defensive delineation is based on the apparent projection in this interaction. The father attributes to Allen feelings of inevitable compliance which are his own, at a time when Allen is actively attempting an alternate kind of behavior.

EXCERPT 2

MOTHER: If you go into an apartment . . .

ALLEN: . . . it's a way of defending myself.

THERAPIST: Against what?

FATHER: What are you defending against?

ALLEN: Against both of you.

MOTHER: [*rather vehemently*] I want to know that if you go into an apartment that you're going to live like a human being.

THERAPIST: Which is . . . ?

MOTHER: Which is—knowing that he's going to have three meals a day, because I know how negligent he has been about his meals, even being here . . .

ALLEN: [*low voice*] I don't get three meals a day here either.

MOTHER: Well, that's your own fault! I know that he gets up late and he hasn't been eating breakfast—and he has his lunch maybe 3 o'clock, maybe not. Then he has no supper! [*pause*] And *that's* under proper supervision. Now what's he going to do if he's in an apartment by himself???

THERAPIST: He'll need a supervisor, won't he?

MOTHER: [*brief pause*] Well, that's what I mean! Those things concern me. He's—unless he realizes that these things are important—to his health, and his maintenance—he has to know that he's—that he has to sleep on time, if he doesn't get enough sleep, which he feels isn't important, at least he didn't—and I had hoped already that he had thought that eating was important. [*This speech spoken with much feeling.*]

ALLEN: I'm surprised you haven't brought this up earlier. It's the first time you've mentioned this since . . .

MOTHER: And if he goes into an apartment . . . I mean, when you say an "apartment," you can get a one-room apartment, you can get a two-room, three-room apartment . . . I want to know that he's with somebody!

Delineations of Allen by Parents (Excerpt 2)

MOTHER: Allen is likely not to live like a human being if he goes into an apartment.

MOTHER: Allen cannot be relied upon to provide satisfactorily for his own basic necessities.

MOTHER: Allen requires supervision and even then does not take proper care of himself.

MOTHER: Allen refuses to recognize the importance of sleep and nutrition for his health and maintenance.

MOTHER: Allen must live with somebody if he is to maintain himself—he cannot do this unsupervised and on his own.

Inferences of Defensive Delineation (Excerpt 2)

The mother's clear definition of Allen as unlikely to be capable of caring for even his basic physical needs, as well as her insistence that he needs a supervisor, is contradicted by much current evidence that he can in many ways care for himself. This evidence is ignored in her delineation of him, and the inference of defense is made because of the incomplete and strikingly limited view of Allen she communicates. The view is derogatory of his ability to maintain himself independently and, in its emphasis on his need for a supervisor, supports the view that he is still very much in need of her supervision. Her repeated expressions of mistrust of Allen and insistence on his need for supervision seem unjustified in light of his current actual improvement and self-sufficiency and seem determined more by the mother's need to remain necessary to him than by realistic evaluation of him.

Defensive delineations repeatedly serve clear defensive needs in these parents. The mother manifests a striking need to contain and to control Allen. This seems related to a poor differentiation of Allen from herself and an anxious need to control feelings or actions which deviate from a narrow, highly conventional, and rigidly defined code of behavior and morality in him or in herself. The father's attitude suggests a characteristic dependency, compliance, and pessimism about the possibility of independent thinking or action which he projects upon Allen. It is suggested that his own wishes for greater freedom generate anxiety and guilt and that he discourages his son's developing autonomy out of projective delineation and hostile competition.

These excerpts of family interaction demonstrate some characteristics of content and formal style of parental delineations of the adolescent in a family where the identity problem of the adolescent is an evidence of impairment of ego autonomy. The adolescent complained of confusion, of feeling controlled by others, of feeling uncertain about his separateness from others, of subjective feelings of merging with others. We consider these complaints to be manifestations of impaired ego autonomy resulting in disturbance in identity formation. When we examine parental delineations of the adolescent, we find characteristics of content and of cognitive style which we consider to be determinants of the adolescent ego impairment. We find that the content of delineations by both parents challenges the adolescent's right and ability to make independent and sensible decisions and actions. His need for parental approval and inability to deal with disapproval is explicit in his own statements and reflects delineations of him by his parents. His effort to deal with his need for approval by requesting an absence of disapproval is ignored by his mother and regarded as futile by his father, who presumes that he is already controlled by what his parents think. His mother's delineations explicitly call into question his ability to care for himself and to exist independently from his parents. We suggest that the patient's own profound doubts about his ability to function independently, his uncertainty about his separateness from others, and his feelings of being controlled by others reflect parental delineations of him. Here a clinical picture of defective ego autonomy, specifically of an impairment in the ego's autonomy from objects in reality, is found in a family where the content of parental defensive delineations of the adolescent do not contain the potentiality for the adolescent to become autonomous. Family experience does not support the maturing cognitive capacities of the adolescent's ego to promote independent development. On the contrary, cognitive development crystallizes an identity in accord with the parent's view of him, in which the adolescent sees himself as highly vulnerable to the approval and control of others, dependent and lacking in competence and strength.

Characteristics of parental cognitive style as they appear in delineations are also of great interest. The mother's thinking is seen to be highly concrete, lacking in subtlety, and relatively impervious to the ideas of others. She responds in black and white terms to the situations under discussion and defends with great energy against any other definition of the adolescent than her own. The father is imprecise and vague in his thinking, expressing difficulty in grasping the issues under discussion and manifesting difficulty in clarifying his own ideas or making them understood. We relate these findings to the adolescent's own difficulty in defining his position and his inability to achieve clear and explicit thinking in his effort to formulate plans for independent functioning. Lack of an adequate model of mature cognitive functioning in either parent is therefore another area in which family experience does not support the maturing cognitive capacities of the adolescent's ego.

In summary, our findings suggest that in the families of adolescents with identity confusion both dynamic factors determining content of parents' defensive delineations of the adolescent and structural factors determining style of delineations are important determinants of impaired ego autonomy in the adolescent.

References

1. BLOS, P. *On Adolescence: A Psychoanalytic Interpretation.* New York: Free Press of Glencoe, 1962.
2. ERIKSON, E. *Childhood and Society.* New York: Norton, 1950.
3. ERIKSON, E. "The Problem of Ego Identity," *Journal of the American Psychoanalytic Association,* IV (1956), 56–121.
4. ERIKSON, E. "Reality and Actuality," *Journal of the American Psychoanalytic Association,* X (1962), 451–474.
5. FREUD, A. *The Ego and the Mechanisms of Defence* (1936). New York: International Universities Press, 1946.
6. FREUD, A. "Adolescence," in *Psychoanalytic Study of the Child.* New York: International Universities Press, 1958, XIII, 255–279.
7. FREUD, S. "Three Essays on the Theory of Sexuality" (1905). *Standard Edition of the Complete Psychological Works.* London: Hogarth, 1957, VII, 123–245.
8. HARTMANN, H. *Ego Psychology and the Problem of Adaptation* (1939). New York: International Universities Press, 1958.
9. HARTMANN, H. "Comments on the Psychoanalytic Theory of the Ego," in *Psychoanalytic Study of the Child.* New York: International Universities Press, 1950, V, 74–95.
10. INHELDER, B., and J. PIAGET. *The Growth of Logical Thinking from Childhood to Adolescence.* New York: Basic Books, 1958.

11. JACOBSON, E. *The Self and the Object World*. New York: International Universities Press, 1964.

12. RAPAPORT, D. "The Theory of Ego Autonomy: A Generalization," *Bulletin of the Menninger Clinic*, XXII (1958), 13–35.

13. SHAPIRO, R. "Adolescence and the Psychology of the Ego," *Psychiatry*, XXVI (1963), 77–87.

14. SHAPIRO, R. "Identity and Ego Autonomy in Adolescence," in J. H. MASSERMAN, ed., *Science and Psychoanalysis*, Vol. IX. New York: Grune and Stratton, 1966.

15. SHAPIRO, R. "The Origin of Adolescent Disturbances in the Family: Some Considerations in Theory and Implications for Therapy," in G. H. ZUK and I. BOSZORMENYI-NAGY, eds., *Family Therapy and Disturbed Families*. Palo Alto: Science and Behavior Books, 1967.

16. WYNNE, L., and M. SINGER. "Thought Disorder and Family Relations of Schizophrenics, I–IV," *Archives of General Psychiatry*, Vols. IX, XII (1963 and 1965).

9

Aspects of Parent-Adolescent Transactions in the Greek Family

George Vassiliou

The Greek family is in transition. All the variables that shape its structure, its life, and its activities are changing rapidly. Political instability and a slow-moving bureaucracy hinder the family's functions in numerous ways. Despite the remarkable rise of living standards in the metropolitan Athens area and in a few other urban centers, improvement is slow in the rest of the country. Per capita income was officially reported to be $484 in 1965 and $535 in 1966.

Cultural traditions are slowly being replaced by imported customs. Stereotypes are losing their absolute value. They are questioned critically. Prearranged marriage and the dowry system are on the decline. Social values are changing. In the middle of these developments family roles are undergoing significant changes.

Fathers are mainly responsible for securing the family's income, but in ways that are becoming progressively less attuned to the Greek national character. Ideal working conditions for a Greek are found in independent work, such as in a private office, a small shop, a home industry, or cultivation of one's own field. The Greek male finds that employment in large organizations or factories, where he must adapt to regimentation, discipline, teamwork, and smooth relations with authority figures, proves to be particularly stressful. Consequently his role requirements are changing both quantitatively and qualitatively.

On the other hand, official statistics[2] show that women are already a substantial proportion of the economically productive Greeks. One out of three financially active Greeks is a woman. Two out of every seven employees of governmental or private organizations are women. And one-third of all professionals in both applied and theoretical fields are women.

This change is all the more dramatic since in the near past the woman never ventured from her family and household duties. The new female role requirements are particularly stressful.[6] A woman competes with a man on unequal terms. Given the same credentials and abilities, a man will be preferred for employment or advancement. For instance, one organization has been employing women for almost fifty years, and presently 50 per cent of its employees are women; however, only 1.2 per cent of its department directors are women.

On the other hand, a gradually increasing scarcity of domestic help and a still prevailing cultural pattern that perceives her as housewife—"the Queen of the House"—place the Greek woman in perennial conflict. Occupational obligations conflict with family obligations. Professional role requirements conflict with cultural feminine role requirements.

Role change is even more strenuous in adolescents. The development of a role perception according to the cultural patterns accepted by the family is even more difficult when adolescents are flooded with contradictory, imported roles, alien to the culture, but widely and effectively advertised by mass media. They vacillate from one set of role demands to the other, faced by increasingly strenuous adaptational tasks in the middle of the rapid socioeconomic developments.

This picture emerges from a review of a few statistics and from qualitative observations.[2, 7] One can speculate about the efforts that are required from the family unit in order to survive in the middle of all these changes and the subsequent strain on all involved. Under the circumstances, what would the transaction in the family be?

We were confronted with this question from the moment we began our interdisciplinary effort within the framework of the Athenian Institute of Anthropos in 1963. In order to secure a broader perspective first we undertook studies of sociopsychological variables entering the dynamics of family life with macroscopic techniques. We started investigating stereotypes, attitudes, and roles by using questionnaires that included a variety of techniques such as fixed-alternative and open-ended questions, sentence completion, Cantril's Self-Anchoring Scale, the Semantic Differential, and the Behavioral Differential. Our samples were usually 400 to 800 subjects, representative of the adult population of the major Athens area 18 years and above (23 per cent of Greece's population), similar representative samples from the Thessalonike area (4.4 per cent of Greece's population), and at times larger samples, representative of larger areas of the country. A modified probability sampling technique was used. In addition, the Institute for Research in Communication, an affiliated center for applied research, made available to us data from public opinion research, mass media research, and market research. These economic, political, and economic-consumer patterns aided our understanding of the variables—other than the psychological—that contributed to family patterns in the milieu under study. This understanding proved very helpful in securing the desired broader perspective. Guided and safeguarded by this perspective, we started using microscopic depth techniques. Findings from the studies above have already been presented.[4, 7, 8, 9, 10, 11] We shall summarize here briefly the most relevant to the present topic.

As one moves from the provinces to the capital the extended family changes into the nuclear family type. In Athens 66 per cent of the families are already nuclear. The average number of children is two to three. Consequently family transactions involve smaller numbers of people.

Getting married is an event to which great social importance is assigned. It is the most frequently mentioned single event considered to make one happy in life. In order to fit the stereotype of the Proper Man or the Proper Woman one should provide well for his family and household. All this indicates that considerable pressure exists for the preservation of marriage, independently of possible future disagreement. When asked what makes a successful and happy marriage, responses stating that such a marriage depends on mutual understanding, agreement of character, and mutual concessions were three times more frequent than responses referring to love. This might be a result of the still existing but quickly declining custom of arranged marriages.

Further findings concerning husband-wife relations from both surveys[8] and cross-cultural studies on role perception[3] indicate the following: The wife is not supposed to make as many demands on the husband as he on her, or she should have no demands at all. She should give love and care and should not expect reciprocity. She should obey and assume the responsibility or blame if something goes wrong. It is expected that interpersonal conflict will be resolved without discussion and explanation through the wife's submission to the husband. The husband is not expected to submit to the wife.[7]

The same line is followed with the findings concerning man-to-woman relations.[3] The Greek man-to-woman roles reflect a more superordinate position of men than of women when compared to American roles. Women are perceived to be ingratiating and contemptuous in their relations to men (be they fathers, husbands, brothers, grooms). They are seen as giving affect, but at the same time as cheating the male while fearing him. Men, on the other hand, are expected to demand subordination and to relate to women from a position of strength and superiority. Although women (be they daughters, wives, sisters, or brides) are *not* supposed to compete, to rival, or even grow impatient with males, men may annoy, quarrel with, scold, or reprimand women. They help, admire, enjoy, feel sympathetic toward the woman when she is in a "mother" or "daughter" role, but do not show love or express understanding when she is in a "woman" role. On the contrary, they are expected to express hostility. This is clear evidence of ambivalence.

Of relevance also is the fact that the stereotype of the woman was found to be loaded with negative characteristics.[7] The fact that both male and female respondents attributed equally negative characteristics to the woman indicates that this negative stereotype has been reinforced so strongly by all the variables involved that it has been accepted by women as well.

It is interesting to compare these findings with those of a normative Rorschach study conducted with a sample of adults, representative of the major Athens area.[10] Women were found to be more productive and resourceful.

At this point, we should like to emphasize that we present statistical data. Consequently we talk about abstractions and trends that although prevalent are not universal. One has to keep in mind that there are large segments of the population who do not share the prevailing trends. We consistently find that education is the variable that differentiates among respondents with high statistical significance.

Under the circumstances, one can see that marriage makes necessary a number of checks and balances, in order to fit into the sociocultural context as a social institution and remain "happy and successful." Duties of husband and wife and mutual demands should be clearly delineated.* [7] Members of the family have to use a number of maneuvers in order to obtain what they desire; otherwise the family could be turned into a battlefield. In such cases the outcome would be either divorce or pathology.

However, the rate of divorce is officially reported as low. Delinquency is less frequent than in other comparable and geographically close cultures. Addictions, in general, have not been reported as presenting a problem. And there is no evidence of other mental pathology occurring more frequently in the milieu under study. One is led to the conclusion that the regulatory systems of the form of marriage described above are sufficient for the development of a transaction within normal limits.

One way to study the regulatory systems in the prevailing form of family interaction is to investigate further role perception of family pairs within the culture.[3]

A particularly revealing finding is that although Greeks tend to show more intimacy in their role perception in general than Americans do, they see *less* intimacy than Americans in the wife-husband role. Another relevant finding from the same study is that the wife-husband role in general is less central in the Greek culture and contains less meaningful behaviors. There are no role demands for intense affect exchange, helpful intervention, or admiration among spouses. On the other hand, parent-child interaction as revealed by role perception includes intense affect, helpful intervention on the part of parents, and strong admiration. Also the parent-child roles in Greece involve greater friendship and less rejection than in America. The highest respect among all Greek roles is found in the mother-son role. In general, parent-child roles are found to be *the central roles*. More specifi-

---

* In fact, they are. Comparative findings concerning Athens in Greece and Detroit in the United States show that the percentage of respondents assigning a duty to both husband and wife is low in Athens (from 0 to 30 per cent) but high in Detroit (from 23 to 76 per cent).

cally, father is perceived as greatly admiring and actively assisting both son and daughter. To the latter he gives in addition positive affect.

In the case of the father-son relationship, the father is perceived as on the alert to punish insubordination. However, he is perceived only in a controlling but not in a commanding position. The son is perceived to respond with subordination, which is expressed as gratitude. He asks for help and advice and fears the father. There is no role demand for the son to express positive affect to the father.

The daughter is perceived as responding to the father by ingratiating herself with contempt without reciprocating for affect—caresses, cries with, or has fun with him—but also cheats and lies to him, fearing him at the same time.

The mother is perceived as giving to the son positive affect, admiration, and active assistance, which the son is perceived as reciprocating with positive affect and subordination; he asks for advice, help, studies and co-operates with her, expresses gratitude, admires, has fun with her.[3]

The data above indicate clearly that in the culture the parent-child relationship is more meaningful than the wife-husband one. Consistent with these findings is that with a sentence-completion technique and from representative samples of large areas of the country, one gets responses indicating that the parent is often viewed as something highly ideal and absolute, the mother more frequently so.[7]

The reciprocity of intense affective exchange that is attributed only to the mother-son role,* on the other hand, makes this relationship particularly meaningful in the culture.

Before proceeding to examine further indications of family transaction, one should point out that the family system in the milieu under study operates in the middle of particularly stressful conditions resulting from social, economic, and political variables.

Survival proves often to be an impossibility. In order to be achieved it requires efforts straining resources to the limit. Under these circumstances one can expect an increased preoccupation with the future. It is natural that under these conditions the family develops a closer alliance of interests. Interests become more family than individual interests. There is, strictly speaking, no individual achievement. The aspired achievement of any member becomes a family matter. It is expected to raise the whole family up to higher socioeconomic levels.

In this context the central position assigned to the parent-child role acquires a more specific meaning. The child is a personification of the future. Consequently parental aspirations will become interrelated with the child's personal future and make it part of the total family's future in general.

One needs only to consider bare socioeconomic facts to see that the son

---

* It is unfortunate that data concerning the mother-daughter role pair are not as yet available.

will be a particularly welcomed child* and that the mother's aspirations will be particularly interrelated with the son's future.

Quite revealing is that we have often found that highly achieving Greek males recall being told by their mother during preschool age, "When you were born I saw our Lady in my dreams; who told me that you are going to become a great man," or, "When you were born I saw the stars moving in the sky and I heard a voice telling me that you are going to do great things in life."

Studying child-rearing patterns, we found mothers to be concerned with the infant from the very beginning.[1] The infant fills up the mother's life and becomes her main concern. The data indicate that she is on the alert to anticipate all needs and to gratify them, following faithfully the culturally defined patterns of proper mothering. This faithful observance goes at times to the extent of placing proper mothering requirements above the expressed needs of the child.

Child-rearing studies[1] reveal that breast feeding is both predominant and protracted in Athens and Thessalonike: 90 per cent of the children were reported by their mothers as having been breast-fed, and 54 per cent were breast-fed beyond 9 months of age. At the age of 16 months only 47 per cent of the children were reported to have been weaned.

On the other hand, toilet-training practices indicate that the mother is very demanding and strict in enforcing proper behavior. Later, during preschool years, following the prevailing cultural patterns, she permits little territorial freedom and carefully selects friends for the child. Consistent with these patterns, she treats sex as taboo and does not respond to the child's need for information.†

Concerning discipline of children, we found that women want to have this function exclusively. Half of the respondents, with women significantly prevailing, assign this task to the mother and only a quarter of them, with males significantly prevailing, assign this task to the father.[7]

The main ways of discipline are the accusation that the child has no philotimo—the highest Greek value which mainly means to respond to generosity with more generosity—the expression of parental dislike, deprivation of material things or affect, mobilization of divine authority to strengthen parental authority ("God will punish you").

Findings like these imply that this kind of mother-child relation will tend to foster dependence. In fact dependence becomes apparent in the profile portraying the motivational patterns of the 12-year-old as revealed by Story

---

* It is not accidental, of course, that in the rural parts of the country "child" has become synonymous with "son."

† A representative sample of Athenians reported that they were mainly informed about sexual matters by friends. Seventy-three per cent never dared ask their fathers any questions; 65 per cent never dared to ask their mothers. Half of those who did dare to ask their mothers reported that they were either punished, scolded, or misguided.[7]

Sequence Analysis.[5, 12] This profile is abstracted from a number of T. A. T. records of normal school children.

Concerning the dependence-independence dimension, the 12-year-old stays within dependence. He is aware that in order to achieve one needs hard effort. He wants to achieve, but from wanting to achieve he passes to having achieved, displaying no clear idea of how this can be done with self-initiated action. He finds no effective help from others, because he is told what he "must" do, but he is not shown the way to proceed. He feels that his self-esteem is not enhanced by the others and neither is his trust of himself and his abilities. However, resentment toward the other (authority) is not experienced, but only a tendency to act out or act on one's own. The consequence of acting out, though, is punishment, but forgiveness is granted and care provided when one asks for it. So one gives up independent action in exchange for protection. Since achievement is rather other-related than self-related, one expects the other to assist one actively.

At the eighteenth year of life we find the normal, adjusted adolescent to be achievement-oriented with the awareness that he owes this to himself, but also to the others who have done so much for him. The main difficulty he finds in achieving is how to break away from the others whose support, advice, and help he strongly needs. He feels that going away will break the other's heart. He is aware that staying will make achievement impossible, but going away raises in him fears of possible failure in the absence of the active support of the other. The decision to proceed is justified by the hope that eventual failure will bring consolation from the other.

As one can observe, at this age achievement has already become an expressed wish; however, there is no plan for independent action. The need for the other's active support is taken for granted, since the others have vested interests in his own achievement. He considers attempting achievement on the assumption that rescue is available in case of failure. Neither resentment toward the other is experienced nor tendency to act out. It seems that an alliance of interests has been signed.

Synthesizing these data, the investigator who takes into consideration only the psychological variable will be inclined to speculate along the following lines. Parents, within the framework of the family transaction implied by the data, will be left with mutually frustrated needs, wishes, and ambitions, the most frustrated being mother, of course. Consequently there is a strong unconscious motivation to use the child as an extension of the parents and to try to fulfill through the child—preferably the son—their own needs. For this reason mothers foster dependency and maintain their control throughout the child's development. In the presence of more than one child of the same or different sex, alliances will be formed and one subgroup will try to undermine the other and promote its own goals. The family becomes a battlefield, the result being manifest pathology.

We have seen such cases in clinical practice, of course. We should like to present here some examples.

GEORGE VASSILIOU   **129**

Parents having assigned to the child a role so all-important *for them* tend to overprotect and pamper their "treasure." Overprotection reaches extremes such as the father who would not permit his son even after his twelfth birthday to join the Boy Scouts because "they give knives to boys and he might hurt himself." This father came to us for help, complaining that his son was not respecting his parents, was lazy and disobedient, and used bad language. It took the mother's covertly hostile intervention to find out the true reasons for their worries about the boy. He was wearing his sister's underwear any time he had a chance to do so. Of course, the same father expected his son to study medicine and become a great scientist.

Overprotection manifested by mothers included an additional component. The child is induced in numerous ways to like and want only what the mother has to offer. He is induced to believe that only mother can offer it in such a way, and no other mothering can substitute for hers.

We find overprotection to be coupled with constant, severe inhibiting criticism of behavior which *the parents* consider as nonconducive to the desired outcome.

On the other hand, the child's personality growth is seriously impeded by a distorted, unrealistic parental evaluation of achievement. Insignificant, trivial achievements are overpraised by parents. It is obvious that under these conditions underachievement, or what the parents may occasionally feel is falling short of their expectation, is considered to be no less than "high treason." The child is not excused even when he is intellectually limited. Repeatedly we have found cases of boys and girls with borderline intelligence mercilessly pushed or patiently and sweetly persuaded to complete academic tasks beyond their abilities. One such girl, an 18-year-old with an I.Q. of 75, was convinced that the only possible existence for her was to succeed in the entrance examinations of our most demanding university, the Polytechnic, where competition is usually five or ten to one, and become an architect. She was brought to us suffering from "anorexia" which caused her to lose 10 kilograms in the months preceding her high-school diploma examinations. Her pushing father's diagnosis was that she was frustrated in a "romantic love affair." This father, beginning as a truck driver, had succeeded in founding his own small trucking company. When questioned as to why he wanted his daughter to go to the university, he answered furiously: "Everybody from the village where I was born has a child who is going to be a scientist. I am the most prominent man from that village. I want my child to be the first, too."

It is expected, of course, that a child under the described conditions will reach adolescence with a number of defects. Early fixations, unresolved conflicts of the triadic state of development, incomplete synthetic functions, not well-integrated internalized value system, and disturbed self-identity should be counted among them. And this is confirmed by clinical examination.

Such adolescents display certain patterns in transacting with their parents. When dependency needs are overwhelmingly strong and personality development seriously impeded, they capitulate, accept without resistance the parental demands, and take a direction leading to schizoid adjustment. In situations where, in spite of their strong dependency needs, they gather enough strength to attempt rebellion, they find themselves caught between anxiety, fear, and guilt. Their attempts take "silly," nonsensical forms. At the same time adolescents need desperately to hold to the parental hand. The adolescent tries to deny this threatening and humiliating attachment and reverses things. He perceives *his* parents as keeping him captive (which, historically speaking, is true, of course). He becomes vehement, accuses his parents of being "overdemanding," "overcontrolling," "unfair," "unreasonable," and so on. What usually happens next is that he makes living in the house impossible for everybody. At the same time he spoils his school progress, becomes an underachiever, and hits his parents where it hurts most. Yet at times he does not dare to do that openly. He does it covertly by developing "amnesia," "exam-shock," stuttering, psychosomatic reactions, and the like.

Characteristic is the case of a 17-year-old boy, son of a rich provincial merchant, who was pushed by his father to become a scientist. The boy became panicky during his high-school diploma examinations, forgot everything, went home, and, while attempting to explain to his father what had happened, suffered repeated global seizures that threw the father this time into a fright. His EEG was essentially negative. Psychological and psychiatric examinations revealed an immature, infantilized personality ridden by both intense aggression and guilt.

Parents in turn become vehement. They take the "child" to the psychiatrist, but it is obvious they do that as a kind of punishment, a social disgrace. They complain that their "child lets them down" and betrays their sacrifices. Such "betrayed" mothers and occasionally "betrayed" fathers spend hours talking about the incredible sacrifices they have made in order to raise "this ungrateful child." In cases with severely disturbed adolescents the parental attitudes bear little relation to reality and obviously intensify the adolescents' disturbance. We should like to quote here a case which we have reported already.[13]

An 18-year-old girl during an acute episode ruined her house by breaking almost everything. She was promptly hospitalized by her mother in a private mental hospital, where the girl was diagnosed as suffering from an acute psychotic reaction. One month later the mother decided it was time to take her daughter home. When she was told that it was against medical advice, she raised a storm. When a psychologist attempted to explain to the mother the seriousness of the patient's situation, the mother was shocked. Then she broke into tears and said, "Do you mean that my child is sick? I thought she did all that just to get even with me, and I sent her here to punish her. If I knew that my child was sick, I would never, never have had her hospitalized."

To return to our main discussion, we strongly feel that one is not justified in extrapolating from clinical cases and applying psychopathologic concepts in order to interpret data concerning the normal population of a given milieu. The fact that family conditions offer particularly strong stimuli for the parental, mainly maternal, unconscious processes to develop destructively for the child does not mean that this will necessarily happen.

We have, of course, found pushing mothers behind schizophrenics. But depth techniques show that overprotection and pushing are coupled with rejection in these cases. Behind every achiever in the milieu, however, there is also a pushing mother. But she admires him, fosters dependency, helps actively, and readily gratifies dependency needs. It is obvious that one needs to search for a kind of interaction between (a) type of mothering and (b) given milieu, an interaction which renders, under *certain conditions,* the mothering we have described conducive to adaptation.

We hope that the microscopic depth techniques we have started using in order to test relevant hypotheses will throw some light on this question.

Often, presentation of data concerning patterns of interaction in our milieu has been received by colleagues with remarks like, "But you describe a sick culture." We feel that this is due to the fact that the material presented is viewed in vitro and not in vivo. In other words, it is examined in the light of a personality theory and not in the context of the transaction of all the variables, social, economic, cultural, and psychological, that create the dynamic field in which the individuals under study function.

Without minimizing at all the importance of the psychological variable, we would like to keep in mind that powerful and strenuous cultural, historical, and socioeconomic conditions have contributed significantly to the formation of the stereotypes, attitudes, roles, and patterns of family life in the milieu under study.

By operating on the psychological variable only, one runs the risk of drawing the wrong conclusions. For instance, it is unquestionable that fostering of dependence such as the one we have seen results in maladaptation in other milieus.

In the milieu under study, however, very often even biological survival throughout life is secured through the interdependencies of the in-group. In-group is defined by Greeks as family, friends, and friends of friends, while in America it is defined as "people like me." [3, 4] The theoretical distinction between in-group and out-group has been found, in all comparative social-experimental psychological research, to make a significant difference in Greece but not in America.[3]

In-group behaviors in Greece have been shown by studies on role perception to be *extraordinary nurturant,* comparable to the nurturance involved in the *mother-child* relationship. Consequently the most important adaptive pattern for Greeks becomes how to learn to establish dependent and dependable relations and actualize dependency in securing help.

The Greek family has proved to be a particularly successful laboratory concerning such training. Three thousand stormy years of history illustrate vividly the miracles which the Greek in-group can perform. It is not playing with words if one says that up to the present, dependency on their mothers has been both the biggest liability for certain Greeks and the greatest asset for most of them.

References

1. KARATSIOLI, L., and V. VASSILIOU. "Patterns of Feeding and Toilet Training in Urban Greece," in preparation.
2. KAYSER, B., K. THOMPSON, et al. *Economic and Social Atlas of Greece.* Athens: The Social Sciences Center, 1964.
3. TRIANDIS, H., V. VASSILIOU, and M. NASSIAKOU. "Some Cross-Cultural Studies of Subjective Culture," *Technical Report No. 45.* Urbana, Ill.: Group Effectiveness Laboratory, 1967.
4. TRIANDIS, H., V. VASSILIOU, and E. THOMANEK. "Social Status as a Determinant of Respect and Friendship Acceptance," *Sociometry,* Vol. XXIX, No. 4 (December 1966).
5. VASSILIOU, G. "Story Sequence Analysis as a Tool in Research," *International Mental Health Research Newsletter,* Vol. V, Nos. 1, 2 (1963).
6. VASSILIOU, G., "Female Role Conflicts in a Developing Society," paper presented at the Fifteenth Annual Meeting of the European League for Mental Hygiene, Athens, September 12–16, 1965.
7. VASSILIOU, G., "A Preliminary Exploration of Variables Related to Family Transaction in Greece," *Technical Report No. 5.* Athens: Athenian Institute of Anthropos, 1966.
8. VASSILIOU, G., "A Transactional Approach to Mental Health: An Experiment in Greece," contribution to the International Research Conference on Evaluation of Community Mental Health Programs, National Institute of Mental Health, Warrenton, Va., May 17–20, 1966.
9. VASSILIOU, G., V. VASSILIOU, and G. GEORGAS. "Socioeconomic Determinants on Manifest Anxiety Scores," paper presented at the Fourth World Congress of Psychiatry, Madrid, September 5–11, 1966.
10. VASSILIOU, V., and J. GEORGAS, "A Normative Rorschach Study of Athenians," *Journal of Projective Techniques and Personality Assessment,* in press (1967).
11. VASSILIOU, V., J. GEORGAS, and G. VASSILIOU. "Variations in Manifest Anxiety Due to Sex, Age and Education," *Journal of Personality and Social Psychology,* in press (1967).
12. VASSILIOU, V., and H. KATAKI. "Motivational Patterns in Early and Late Adolescence, as Detected by Story Sequence Analysis," in preparation.
13. VASSILIOU, V., and G. VASSILIOU. "Attitudes of the Athenian Public Towards Mental Illness," *International Mental Health Research Newsletter,* Vol. XII, No. 2 (1965).

10

The Adopted Child
in Adolescence

Alexina M. McWhinnie

The purpose of this chapter is twofold. First, it presents details of the adjustment and reactions in adolescence of children who have been adopted when babies or very young children. This picture comes, not from the study of a group of disturbed adolescents, but from a research study[9] in which an unselected and representative group of adults who had been adopted as children was interviewed. The relevant findings from this research will be linked with evidence from the author's experience of group work over the past three years with parents of adopted children. The second object of this chapter is to discuss and suggest how these findings can be applied in therapy and in case work with adopted adolescents and their parents.

With regard to research in child adoption, this so far has largely been confined to studies of the problem as seen by the adopting parents or of cases where there has been a breakdown in the adoption and a referral to a child psychiatric clinic. It was thus planned to study adoption as it appeared to the person ultimately most concerned, namely, the child, and to do this it was necessary to meet and to interview a representative group of adopted adults, unselected in the sense of having no bias either toward being successful or unsuccessful adoption situations. Introductions to such a group, 52 in number, were made through family doctors in three administrative areas of the National Health Service in South East Scotland. The family doctors knew of the fact of adoption for a reason other than the adoption itself, and since the introduction of the National Health Service in the United Kingdom in 1948, they are in touch with all social and occupational classes in the community. In interview and assessment, the technique of "focused" interviewing was used. Interviewing was detailed with verbatim recording, and evidence was gradually built up over several interviews, from which retrospective life histories were then compiled and subsequently analyzed.

Of the 52 adopted adults, 6 of whom were originally placed as foster children but regarded by themselves and by their families as adopted, a classification of four grades of adjustment was made. There were 15 who had a good personal adjustment in all areas at the time of interview and had not experienced major problems as they grew up, either in their adoptive home or in their adjustment to the adoption situation. At the other extreme, however, there were 10 cases with poor or abnormal adjustment in many areas. There were a further 21 who had had or were experiencing severe problems in their upbringing, related directly to or complicated by their adoption situation, and there was a further group of 6 who came nearer to those who had no problems. Thirty-one out of the 52, then, had serious adjustment problems in adolescence, and all 6 children originally fostered also had adjustment problems, such difficulties being a reflection of the quality of their adoption or fostering situation.

This, as it stands, would suggest that adoption is a hazardous solution for the potentially deprived child. What emerged, however, very clearly was that there is a particular quality of total family and adoption situation which can lead to a good adjustment. Given this kind of situation, adoption presented few or no problems for the child. What also emerged, however, was that a wide range of factors had to be favorable before this was the case.[8, 9]

It was found that the adopted child can encounter problems in adolescence which are peculiar to such children and do not enter into the experience of adolescents growing up within their own biological family. Such situations arise in four main areas; learning about adoption, complications in the normal adolescent process at this time of the search for identity, how relationships with adoptive parents may be influenced by the parents' attitudes to all the facets of adoption, and reactions to parental attitudes about discussion of adoption. These situations were experienced, of course, by those found to be well adjusted in the research survey as well as the poorly adjusted cases, except that in the former these particular aspects of the adoption situation had not developed into problem situations, as they had done in the individuals with a poor adjustment.

First, with regard to learning about adoption, all the adults in this survey knew, of course, that they were adopted. Some had been told by their parents, and some had found out in other ways. Nowadays adoptive parents, at least in the United Kingdom and in North America, are advised to tell their children that they are adopted. Most adoptive parents try to do this, but not all succeed, for reasons discussed later. What the study revealed about this was that every child in its life is likely to learn that it is adopted, and this can happen in a large number of ways not even considered possible by their parents. For example, children who had not been told of adoption noticed even the slightest parental embarrassment if this were displayed when, for example, a birth certificate was required for school, employment, and the like. Others ruminated about overheard nuances in conversation between adults, and one girl observed from a cookery recipe book which was dated that her mother had gone to a cookery lesson three days after she was born, which suggested to her the possibility of adoption.

Having made such a possible discovery, the child or adolescent will not necessarily communicate this to the parents. Of those in the study who learned initially from an outside source that they might have been adopted (34 in number), only 50 per cent asked their parents if this were true. The others did not even mention it, but said to themselves, "If there is anything in it my mother will tell me." They were all emphatic that the source of information about adoption should be their parents, and by this they really meant their adoptive mother. Many who learned of their adoption initially from an outside source were resentful, and because of this some suffered lasting emotional trauma. This significant tendency to such one-way communication about adoption applied also to information about the biological background which, although desired by the adopted adolescent, could not on the whole be asked for. It was felt that to ask this would be unfair or disloyal to the adoptive mother. Throughout their life these adopted persons did not want to be referred to by their parents as "our adopted son or daughter" but as "our son or daughter." Often parents in our present society talk too much about adoption, wanting to stress that they are not ashamed of it and in fact may be proud of it. This does not coincide with the feelings and attitudes of their children, who, although they wish to know that they are adopted, want discussion of this to be confined to the immediate family circle. Adopted young people do not want to tell their peers and others of adoption unless under special circumstances. They appear, however, always to want to tell anyone whom they hope to marry.

Second, in their search for identity, it is with their adoptive parents that adopted adolescents primarily identify. In the series of 52 cases studied, almost all, however, wanted some factual information about their biological parents, that is, about their age and occupation, something about their personality, and also about why and how they themselves had been placed for adoption. They had all been curious about this at some time, many during their adolescence when they were giving thought to their own future employment and mode of life. In others such curiosity emerged or was reinforced during courtship or more immediate contemplation of marriage, or when having children of their own. Adolescent boys tended to be less curious about this than adolescent girls, but when the boys subsequently married, their wives were more curious. Where there was insecurity in the adoptive home, and where only fragments of information about biological parentage had been given, the frustration caused by the withholding of such information accentuated feelings of insecurity. Such adolescents talked of feeling "rootless" and of "being in a vacuum." Any fiction would have been viewed as better than the uncertainty which surrounded them. Some, lacking factual information, developed neurotic anxieties about the risks of inherited disease, or fantasied around the few facts which they knew. They feared to hear that they had been unwanted or rejected as children, and they were apprehensive about being given information which suggested that there were wide social and material differences between their biological parents and their adoptive homes.

As an example to illustrate these findings, the case history of a girl can be quoted who, although she knew that she was adopted, had found that her parents would not spontaneously offer her any information about her background. By persistent questioning of her adoptive mother during adolescence, she was able to obtain some factual information about her biological mother, but received only conflicting stories about her biological father, who was in varying ways reported as having died suddenly. The girl, who had a very poor relationship with her adoptive mother, but a good relationship with her adoptive father, fantasied that he perhaps was really her biological father. This girl's physical health was good, but she worried a great deal about her health, fearing that she might drop dead, as her biological father was reported to have done, and she wondered too about her racial antecedents. She sought out her biological mother, though "not as a mother who would understand her" as she felt her adoptive mother did not, but simply for accurate factual information, which she hoped would be reassuring about her antecedents, about the possibilities of inherited disease, and also morally and socially. With case-work help, she was able to institute inquiries at Register House in Edinburgh, this being the central government department in Scotland where all records of births, deaths, marriages, and legalized adoptions are kept. After finding out in this way where her biological mother lived, she found reassurance in learning indirectly that she and her family were "normal, healthy, and respectable."

There were many instances among those interviewed of the fear that they would learn that as babies they had been rejected. One woman reported that her adoptive mother had described to her in adolescence how her biological mother had "shuddered" when as a baby she had been handed to her. Years later she still wished that she need never have been told this. A man in the series felt that it was no help to him when he was considering his own career in adolescence to know that his alleged father was a medical student while his adoptive father's occupation was that of a skilled artisan. It was noteworthy that this man later was determined to send his own son to a private school which provided education for middle-class professional families, although he himself lived in a slum area of the city where such educational aspirations were unusual.

Although many in this study talked of wanting in adolescence to meet their biological parents out of curiosity, they were emphatic that they did not want these parents to know who they were. They would like, for example, to have seen their biological mother "walking down the street" and to have been able thus to observe her without themselves being observed. Only 5 out of the whole 52 looked on such a meeting as a way of finding a mother who would perhaps understand them as their adoptive mother did not; all these adolescents were very unhappy in their adoptive homes and estranged from their inadequate and neurotic adoptive mothers.

In all other cases, whether well adjusted and happy or the opposite, the adopted adolescents looked on the adoptive parents as their true mother and father, and they continued to do so in later life, even after years of estrangement from them. Relevant comments were, "Bearing a child does not make a mother," and "It is the people who bring you up who are your parents." In six instances where adopted children in adolescence or later life met their biological mother or father, all commented on how they were strangers to them, to quote, "just another human being" for whom they had no positive or negative feeling. Frequently, when talking about their own early history, they referred to "the baby" and "the mother of the baby" as if it were someone other than themselves. It also emerged that the few who sought information about their biological background from sources outside of their adoptive home found that it required great courage and determination to pursue such inquiries. Some, though initially determined to inquire, found that they hesitated at the last moment, fearing what they might find out. Others from desperation felt anything was preferable to doubt.

Such attitudes are in themselves potentially reassuring to adopters who fear giving their adolescent children information about their background. This has also considerable relevance when any kind of therapy or counseling is considered. Furthermore, when considered with the adopted person's observed genuine need for information about his or her biological background, it suggests that there is wisdom in the provision of Scottish law whereby an adopted adolescent, on reaching the age of 17, can have access to his original birth certificate at Register House. On average over the past eight years or so, some 60 persons do this each year, either by presenting themselves at Register House or through correspondence. The annual number of legalized adoptions in Scotland about seventeen years ago shows that there are approximately 1,500 adopted children of 17 years of age who could each year potentially make such an inquiry. The small number who do in fact inquire cannot be considered to represent the proportion of adopted adolescents who are curious about their antecedents, but merely those whose anxiety or desperation has been so great as to outweigh their fears of what they could find out. The research study suggests, of course, that some within their adjustment to adoption will feel secure with what they already know about their origins and not experience or require help with further curiosity. An ambivalent and apprehensive attitude in adolescence was illustrated, however, in the majority of cases interviewed, especially in those whose adjustment was considered to be poor. In England, under different law, an adoptee has to apply to a court for permission to obtain such basic information about himself. This more formal approach could deter many adolescents who might have a need for and be much helped by such knowledge.

The third facet to be considered of an adolescent's attitude to adoption is the fact that his or her relationship with the adoptive parents is a particularly compelling one. Among those who were well adjusted there was evidence of great devotion to and concern for their adoptive parents. For those who were poorly adjusted, there was evidence of marked ambivalence, of excessive devotion coupled with resentment that they were thus tied by conscience and feelings of duty. In the latter group, there were those who, although desperate to escape from home, stayed at home to care, for example, for invalid parents, commenting, "I felt I owed it to them," that is, because they had adopted them. There were cases, too, of excessive rebelliousness, leading to social deviation and delinquency or to leaving home. Where adoptive mothers feared that their adolescent daughters would inherit instability or immoral behavior patterns from their biological mothers, their mistrusting behavior toward these adolescents drove them into behaving in just the way that their mothers feared. One girl said, "As my mother did not believe me when I said I had not been out with boys, I felt that I might as well do what she feared I was doing."

The fourth area for consideration is parental attitudes to discussion of adoption. Telling a child of its adopted status emerged as much more difficult for many adopters than is generally assumed by social workers and others. It relates to their doubts about their adequacy as parents, their fear that their children will love them less if they know they are not biologically their own children, and concern that they may seek out their "other mother." It relates, too, to their fears, conscious and unconscious, about illegitimacy and immorality and of the possible inheritance of this kind of behavior. These fears are particularly acute as their children reach adolescent years, and such attitudes were apparent in the histories in the author's research study.[9]

That telling a child that he or she is adopted can be a difficult problem for adoptive parents is shown, too, by the findings of Brenner and Michaels,[1] Shaw,[13] and Goodacre.[2] Further evidence about the "genetic anxiety" of adoptive parents and their feelings of inadequacy is given in the study of Humphrey and Ounsted [4, 5] of a series of adoptive families referred for psychiatric advice and in the comparative study by Kirk[6] of fertile and nonfertile couples.

Further direct evidence of such feelings and difficulties experienced by adoptive parents has emerged in the group work that the author is currently undertaking with adoptive parents. The age range of their adopted children at the present time is from 3 to 9 years. The group meetings, with so far some twelve separate groups of up to eight adoptive couples, are held at intervals decided on by the groups in conjunction with the voluntary agency[3] concerned with the original adoption placement. All the groups have shown anxiety about the period of adolescence and about possible questions then from their children. One father was able to verbalize this in a particularly significant way. He saw the real crux of adoption as the dilemma for him of appearing to condone the behavior of the unmarried biological parents, yet having to teach adequate moral standards to his adolescent children.

Such a comment illustrates our need to consider the whole question of therapy with adopted adolescents and their families. It is not being suggested that all adoptive families or adopted adolescents require therapy, but research and experience show that many could be helped before psychotherapy as such is needed and that much more could be done in a preventive way, as is evidenced also by the findings of Nemovicher.[10]

First and obviously, careful selection of adoptive parents is imperative. This must include a careful assessment of their emotional attitudes to immorality and illegitimacy and of their possible fears about difficulties relating to the psychosexual development and behavior in adolescence of adopted children.

Second, even with very careful selection and interviewing at the time of assessment, it emerged that adoptive parents value and some urgently need counseling help as their children grow up. The author's group work with adoptive parents shows that for most parents group methods can effectively provide such support and in some ways have much more to offer than individual counseling. It was found that an appropriate time to provide such group counseling was when the adopted child is aged 3 to 5, a time when spontaneously it is asking questions and seeking information about how and where it was born. If the child is over 5, the parents may already have passed by such a phase of spontaneous questioning and may have missed these early opportunities of spontaneously giving simple factual information about adoption, the circumstances of the child's birth, and why the biological parents placed it for adoption.

Group counseling should be available again when the children are between 9 and 10, a time when discussion among peers about parentage and adoption reaches its peak and a time of potential crisis within the adoptive family. Many of the adopted children in the author's research study[9] had met comments from peers when aged between 9 and 10 about their possible adoptive status. As discussed by Lewis,[7] this can be related to the fantasies very common among children at this age that their present parents are not their real parents, and such fantasies have associations with age-old myths and legends of superior, royal, and heroic begetting.

When adopted children reach adolescence, group counseling could again provide support for their parents at a time when, as already discussed, their feelings of inadequacy as parents and anxieties about their children's psychosexual development are likely to be accentuated. Such fears of adoptive parents are described by Rosner,[11] in a report of case work with adolescent adopted girls, as a "crisis of self-doubt," during which the parents are preoccupied with an awareness that the adoptive family is created by a process of personal and social selection and when they doubt also whether they really qualify for the familial roles which adoption has conferred on them.

Such group counseling has been found to provide a helpful supportive case-work service to adoptive families which are functioning reasonably well, though experiencing some areas of anxiety. Adoptive parents in group discussions appear to find it much easier to verbalize and to gain insight into such anxieties when it is learned that these are shared by other parents in the group. In contrast, such discussion is observed to be more difficult with an individual case worker, and in particular with one who may have been involved in their original assessment for adoptive parenthood and toward whom they may have ambivalent feelings of gratefulness and a need for self-justification as parents. Where there are serious problems of adjustment, however, the adoptive parents either fail to continue with the group experience or else deny that there are such problems. Their needs are more likely to be met either in group psychotherapy in a different setting or in individual family psychotherapy.

Finally, in individual therapy with disturbed adolescents and their families, the evidence should be borne in mind that, although the adolescents may deny curiosity, they all need some information about their biological background. Winnicott, in describing psychotherapy with such adolescents, also stresses this, stating, "Adopted children find adolescence more of a strain than other children; and in my experience this is due to ignorance about their personal origin." [14] This "genealogical bewilderment" in children with substitute parents has been discussed also by Sants,[12] who comments that "very often in early adolescence, they will begin searching for clues" and that such a search can become a preoccupation. Where adopted adolescents lack information about their origin, or where information has been inadequate or conflicting, they need to know, as they have described it to the author, "the stock they came from," or they continue to feel "rootless" or even "lost in a flood and clutching at a straw." Rosner[11] describes how she found that disturbed adolescent girls needed help before they were able in this way to talk about adoption, and she found too that they were very commonly afraid of what they might find out. As soon as they felt comfortable enough with the case worker, however, "the questions tumbled out in a way that showed that they had been pent up and struggling for release."

In supportive case work and therapy with adopted adolescents, it thus emerges as important to establish as far as possible what are the facts of their natural origin. Some workers, however, may feel diffident about assuming an enabling role in discussion of the feelings and facts about biological background, possibly because they overidentify with the apprehensions of the adoptive parents, or possibly because they fear that for adolescents to learn of some aspects of their natural parentage may be traumatic. Since, as the author found,[9] adopted children prefer to learn details of their adoption from their adoptive parents, ideally work should be directed toward helping the parents to resolve with their adolescent child curiosity and fears about natural origins. In some cases, therapy within the family group may prove beneficial. The aim must be to help the inquiring adopted adolescent, in his crisis of doubt in the search for identity, to learn of his biological parentage in a positive, acceptable, and undamaging way, emphasizing what is known of the positive attributes of his natural parents and encouraging consideration of what may have been the difficulties in their human situation. Where some aspects of such information could be disturbing, as, for example, where the natural mother was a prostitute or the birth resulted from an incestuous union, such information can be discussed only as and when the child is able to come to terms with it and only as recognized in relation to the child's needs. The more secure and happily accepted the adopted child feels within his adoptive family, the more readily will he be able to accept such facts about his origins, although the less need will he have to seek them. This has obvious implications for initial adoption placement assessment.

In general, however, the needs for such case work or therapy with adolescents should be minimized by a preventive approach. This should start before adoption, first by the most careful assessment of how prospective adoptive parents can accept such potential conflicts in an adolescent child. Then, before and during adoption placement, adopters may require help to resolve their feelings of apprehension and inadequacy. They need also to be able to feel secure about answering the spontaneous questionings of the child about its origins from as early as the toddler years, receiving sufficient appropriate information to be able to do this. Of great reassurance to all concerned in this is the finding that it is with their adoptive parents that adopted children primarily identify and that they continue always to do this.

References

1. BRENNER, R. F., and R. MICHAELS. *A Follow-up Study of Adoptive Families.* New York: Child Adoption Research Committee, Louise Wise Services, 1951.
2. GOODACRE, I. *Adoption Policy and Practice.* London: Allen and Unwin, 1966.
3. Guild of Service, Edinburgh, *Annual Reports,* Vol. LIII (1964); Vol. LIV (1965).
4. HUMPHREY, M., and C. OUNSTED. "Adoptive Families Referred for Psychiatric Advice: Part I, The Children," *British Journal of Psychiatry,* CIX (September 1963), 599–608.
5. HUMPHREY, M., and C. OUNSTED. "Adoptive Families Referred for Psychi-

atric Advice: Part II, The Parents," *British Journal of Psychiatry,* CX (July 1964), 549–555.

6. KIRK, H. D. *Shared Fate: A Theory of Adoption and Mental Health.* Montreal: Free Press of Glencoe, 1964; London: Collier-Macmillan.

7. LEWIS, E. "Adoption Fantasies and Ancient Myths," *Child Adoption,* XLIX (1966), 13–14.

8. MCWHINNIE, A. M. *Adoption Assessments: A Team Approach Based on Research and Related to the Basic Needs of the Child.* Petersham, Surrey, England: Standing Conference of Societies Registered for Adoption, 1966.

9. MCWHINNIE, A. M. *Adopted Children: How They Grow Up.* London: International Library of Sociology and Social Reconstruction, Routledge and Kegan Paul, 1967; New York: Humanities Press.

10. NEMOVICHER, J. "A Comparative Study of Adopted Boys and Non-Adopted Boys in Respect of Specific Personality Characteristics." Doctoral thesis, School of Education, New York University, 1959.

11. ROSNER, G. *Crisis of Self-Doubt.* New York: Child Welfare League of America, 1961.

12. SANTS, H. J. "Genealogical Bewilderment in Children with Substitute Parents," *British Journal of Medical Psychology,* XXXVII (1964), 133–141.

13. SHAW, L. A. "Following Up Adoptions," *British Journal of Psychiatric Social Work,* II (November 1953), 14–21.

14. WINNICOTT, D. W. "Adopted Children in Adolescence," in H. LEWIS, ed., *Medical Aspects of Child Adoption.* Petersham, Surrey, England: Standing Conference of Societies Registered for Adoption, 1966, p. 42.

EDITORS' INTRODUCTION   This section opens with a spirited plea by Herford for the recognition of the transition from school to work as a complicated and important field to which more systematic attention should be paid by mental health workers and for which co-ordinated services involving schools, employment services, and industrial health programs should be provided to remedy major current hiatuses in our community facilities. He discusses the problems that are produced by the progressive raising of the school-leaving age, especially for those adolescents who are not verbally adroit and for those whose academic learning curve has leveled off so that they regard further schooling as enforced detention. It is indeed questionable whether our present-day school environment, which was developed to socialize younger children, is a suitable setting for the many older adolescents who are not destined for an academic career. Herford criticizes schools for not specifically preparing adolescent students for the working world, and he points to the ignorance of many educators and even guidance personnel concerning the realities of the demands and opportunities of the job market. The first steps in the adolescent's working career are often made without guidance or planning. Herford feels that parents should take a more active role in guiding their children and that their efforts should be supported and supplemented by services bridging the schools and the work field. He points to the potential value of the Appointed Factory Doctors in Britain as a network of care-givers who can follow the individual development of school-leavers and help steer them along adaptive paths.

He emphasizes the particular importance of supervision of populations at special risk such as the school-leavers whose intelligence falls in the lower half of the normal range. These are the populations where maladjustment in the work field with consequences for mental disorder is most likely in our urban society, and these are the adolescents who are currently neglected. Neglected, that is, by all except the mass media and advertising interests for whom they are vulnerable targets because their first jobs provide them with relatively large amounts of money which they are free to spend because they still have few family responsibilities.

Irwin Marcus, in the following chapter, enlarges on these points and discusses the implications for identity development of adjustment by adolescents to the work environment. He also refers to the other side of the coin: the specific disturbance of work performance by unsolved psychosocial problems, such as failing at work as a way of thwarting parental ambitions or in some other way using the work setting as a stage on which vicariously to work out problems with parents. He discusses the influence of peer-group values in molding an adolescent's work choice and level of functioning. And he concludes that there is a special need for practical guidance so that an adolescent can work out his career line based on his actual capacities and on the realistic opportunities of the employment field. He describes some examples of services in the United States which are designed to help adolescents make rational choices in the transition from school to work. There are opportunities at certain colleges for students to spend half-time working on an exploratory basis in a variety of different business and industrial settings. The Neighborhood Youth Corps is the analogue of such a program for unemployed youths from low-income families, who spend part of their time in special high-school courses and part in job training and work placements. And there are opportunities for regular high-school students to occupy part of their school day working in local business and industrial training situations. The purpose of these innovations is to provide the students with an opportunity to intersperse traditional classroom learning with experience in a real-life work setting, so that they can find out experientially what they like and are suited for and obtain meaningful training before starting their first job.

The final two chapters of this section report on researches that increase our understanding of these topics. Rousselet discusses the findings of a study of young workers in France who were questioned regarding their perceptions and feelings about the guidance they had received from their parents in choosing their first jobs; and their replies were correlated with their initial job adjustment and future prospects. The study validates Herford's emphasis on the importance of parental guidance. It suggests that in many cases adolescents felt that their parents showed little interest in their school studies or their job choice, and that this correlated with a relatively poorer adjustment in the work setting than was the case for adolescents whose parents had shown an interest in their studies and had actively guided them in choosing an appropriate job. Parental guidance or neglect was a matter of conscious concern for most of the young workers; and those who felt they had not been given adequate help by their parents were quite unhappy and bitter about it. It is of interest that Rousselet concludes that since it is unlikely that all parents can ever be expected to guide their children equally and effectively, such vocational guidance should be incorporated as a universal part of educational programs in school. He makes this recommendation on mental health grounds, having earlier in his chapter emphasized the noxious effects on personality development of maladjustment which is "the almost inevitable result of bad working conditions that offer no chance for personal fulfillment or real satisfaction."

While we agree with Rousselet's contention that poor initial vocational preparation and choice are likely to be correlated with continuing job maladjustment and consequent mental ill-health, and also that not all parents are likely to be equally effective in offering guidance, it may be open to question whether the best or the only remedy is to incorporate vocational guidance within the school framework. Drastic improvement along these lines, as suggested by Herford, is obviously needed. It involves, however, more than a mere addition to the school curriculum and will necessitate the building of effective bridges between the school system and the employment and industrial health systems—itself no minor challenge. Perhaps Rousselet's optimism in regard to achieving equal guidance for all children along this route may be linked to the culture of French education with its strong centralized tradition. A pluralistic society, such as the United States, however, provides school systems each of which has its policies and practices determined by its local community, and it might be easier to improve the vocational guidance of adolescents by focusing directly on parents through parent education and counseling. Moreover, it may well be that the meaning to the adolescent of parental interest rather than just the content of the advice and guidance he receives may be quite significant.

More research is needed to answer this question, but meantime it may be worth while for us to divide our efforts between stimulating improvements in specialized vocational guidance in schools and influencing parents to pay more attention to supervising and guiding their children's job preparation and job choice.

The next chapter, by McFarlane, reports the findings of a Canadian study of the initial occupational experiences of school-leavers in a town with a population of fifty thousand. It appears that in the final school years the girls in the unselected sample did better than the boys, but that educational achievement had little effect on the ease of finding the first job on leaving school. On the other hand, many more of the girls managed to make their initial job their permanent one, at least until marriage or pregnancy forced them to leave, whereas the boys, with their poorer educational background, had a much higher number of jobs per person and much greater periods of unemployment. This was related to the fact that in school the girls were taught clerical skills which they were able to use immediately in the white-collar occupations which they mostly entered, while the boys usually took blue-collar or manual work for which their schooling had given them no special preparation. Boys who had done well at school, even at vocational school, and went into a skilled trade had to start as apprentices for three to five years, whereas girls who had learned typing or bookkeeping at school could immediately start earning a full salary as secretaries.

McFarlane then reports the reactions of his study population to the vocational guidance they had received at school. These were almost universally negative. Guidance lectures and individual counseling in school appear to have been divorced from the realities of the outside world, whether that of the job market or even that of colleges and universities. Moreover, the students were told little by the school guidance personnel about the facilities offered by the National Employment Service for guiding the school-leaver into an appropriate niche in the work world. They did not find out about this service until they left their first job and were searching for another. McFarlane reports that by and large the school-leavers had to use their own initiative in making the transition to the work field, and many of them floundered.

This study validates our caution in relying on school guidance, at least as presently organized in many school systems. It also documents the necessity, as emphasized by Herford, to make a special effort to build organizational links between schools and outside community vocational guidance and employment services, so as to insure that the program of helping the school-leavers make the transition is molded by the current realities of the situation. Finally, this chapter once more raises the question of whether the content of instruction for adolescents in schools is sufficiently geared to preparing them for the problems they are likely to meet in the workaday world. We are used to hearing how our educational system for girls is currently designed to prepare them for unfeminine occupations rather than for their future roles as housewives and mothers. Perhaps this chapter validates this thesis; but it does show that at least school educates girls for their roles as long as they stay at work, whereas in the case of boys, at least at the lower end of the socioeconomic scale in Canada, even this is not being done very well.

In this chapter McFarlane makes one other point that has special relevance for us in child psychiatry. He discusses briefly the significance for marital adjustment of the situation his study has uncovered in respect to the differential job security of boys and girls. At the time when they are considering marriage, the girls on the whole have a higher occupational status and more stable employment than the boys. This is a continuation of the earlier picture in the senior grades of high school, where the girls thrived and the boys were failing. Such a pattern does not augur well for the development of a confident masculine self-image and for stability of husband-wife relationships in a culture where the man is expected to be the "master of the house" and a strong identification object for his children. Further research is clearly needed to obtain more information about such possibilities, which hint at very far-reaching personality consequences of the realistic opportunities for men and women in the labor force and the patterns of educational and guidance services we provide to prepare adolescents to take their adult places in the economy.

11

School to Work

M. E. M. Herford

Much anxious thought is being given to the purpose of education and the reconciliation of individual needs with social and administrative pressures. Often the chronological and biological time scales regrettably conflict. Raising the school-leaving age is chronologically simple, but biologically complicated. In man, mind is an increasingly important factor in biological evolution. Each individual has a biological pattern of development which on the chronological scale may be either early or late. The pattern differs for boys and girls.

There has been a tendency to consider problems of raising the school-leaving age merely chronologically. This ignores the biological changes which make a difference not of degree but of kind between the beginning and end of the adolescent period. It is therefore wrong to use the same arguments for raising the school-leaving age from 15 to 16 as were used for raising it from 14 to 15. The older age group contains more young adults with different needs. Staff, accommodation, and program requirements are quite different, and without proper facilities the extra year will represent, for many, detention in the name of education to be called a privilege and made compulsory. Their revolt will obstruct teaching for those who want to learn. The state of thwarted maturity is a real problem, exacerbated by the fact that in our present educational system many young people are filling in time, particularly in the last year, because they have already been cured of all desire to learn and are resentful of boredom and failure.

It is common to speak of the adolescent transition, which tends to mask the fact that there is a metamorphosis from the relatively undifferentiated prepubertal boy and girl to the highly differentiated, reproductively potent, intellectually and critically vigorous young adult man or woman. It is a change as great as that from water insect to dragonfly. The state has been described as a crisis of identity, a time of acute ambivalence when an indi-

149

vidual seeks a life pattern, a self-image to live by. New forces are at work, latent powers are awakening, and the crucial problems of psychosexual adjustment have to be faced. It is indeed a critical stage in life, rendered more or less difficult by cultural and social pressures. Three peaks are being approached.

First, the peak of maximum physical, Olympic achievement. One has only to look at the ages of gold, silver, and bronze award winners to see that the chronological age of maximum achievement has been getting lower. Second, the peak of sexual potency following the pubertal change is being reached, and, again, at an earlier age. Many factors are involved, of which the new social, psychological pressures are often undervalued. Third, there is the peak of dynamic creative intellectual achievement in every sphere. Maturation of these powers may be a long process, but the dynamic upsurge is manifest in these years. What chance of recognition do we give in any other sphere than athletics?

It is clear that the early developer not only may be of more powerful stock but certainly enjoys educational and biological advantages in capacity to make the most of opportunities offered. This may give a lifelong impetus to leadership and primacy. In reverse, those who have a poor start tend to fall further behind, so that biologically and educationally handicaps increase, with serious implications for society. At the same time, it is true that many late developers do catch up, or even pass ahead, by the end of adolescence. To overcome handicaps, support and motivation are important.

There is a tendency for early- and late-developing characteristics to run in families. Like father, like son, and if the late-developing son sees his father a normal or even larger than average man and is assured of catching up, he is not particularly worried. If he is not reassured in this way, he may be considerably upset. He will often benefit by an extra year at school. Some of the early-developing boys, on the other hand, under existing conditions of selection for grammar and technical school, have shot their bolt and after early success stay in the lower forms of their school and are among the early leavers with no academic success. Often they are upset by seeing smaller boys grow and pass them. The early developers at the statutory school-leaving age are often so much larger than their coevals and so little suited to being treated as children in a class that they are apt to resent school and form the hard core of rebellion and rowdyism that prevents those who would learn from being taught. They may carry resentment into their employment.

In the development of the individual, there is a vital nonverbal stage, when primary identity is established. This is a "body-sense," when physical relationship with the mother and space orientation are achieved; it is the primary "body-image." This precedes the verbal stage. In the development of the group, the culture, there is similarly a nonverbal stage. In the development of man, vital factors have been the power to communicate, to record, and to transmit. The verbal, the academic component, is a relatively late development. Many people are essentially nonverbal and think with their bodies and hands. Elementary drama, mime, painting, pottery, and craftwork preceded speech. These forms of expression may be described as physical literacy, and physical literacy must precede verbal literacy.

It was at one time thought that spastics were commonly in some degree mentally defective. Experiments have shown that if the spastic condition can be relieved near birth, thus facilitating physical movement and communication, mental deficiency appears to occur less often. In other words, the apparent mental defect arises from a block in communication which hinders mental development. We communicate with the body before we communicate through speech, and for full development the two must be combined.

In considering transition from school to work these factors are important, bearing in mind the two great illusions of beginning and of individuality, except in terms of relationship. Identity and personality evolve through relationships, individual and group; and lacking the stimulus of relationship, potential atrophies. Too early pressure toward the verbal may cause the child to opt out of the task, either because the attempt is made too early or because it is essentially nonverbal. The verbal stage must be approached through the nonverbal. As a result of omission or faulty timing, many young people leave school crippled in the capacity to use their nonverbal talents and cured of any desire to learn. They have opted out from education and are unable to use leisure creatively. In the modern world they are like those born spastic or dumb. It is not surprising that, frustrated in communication, they should show aggression, passivity, or delinquency.

At the other extreme, highly verbal children are often channeled too soon away from nonverbal modes of expression and are unbalanced. Verbally literate, they are physically illiterate or even dumb. Two stories may illustrate what is meant.

The first concerns a group of over thirty young men in the final year at a secondary modern school who had no further use for school. They were a nuisance and potentially delinquent, from frustration and boredom. They had opted out of learning. There was a good crafts master and there was ample accommodation, both vital factors in the situation. These leather-jacketed, heavy-booted lads were allowed to bring into the school three old cars and an assortment of motorcycles. There was equipment: drills, lathe, panel-beating, and spray gun. Instead of boredom they could all do something they wanted to do. In the process they learned English, mathematics, mechanical drawing, self-disciplined work, and the satisfaction of pulling as a team toward a desired objective. They could not be kept out of school. They matured because they found significance in participation and accepted responsibility. This was education and preparation for the creative use of leisure. Too many of our young people never reach this stage before leaving school and are therefore unprepared for the work situation. Their parents have too often said, "Please yourself; I want you to be happy." Home does not support school, and discipline is lacking; all children seek to find limits and may be disturbed and anxious if there are none.

The other story concerns a young man who graduated in mathematics. He had no real interest in the subject and no outside interests. He had wanted to leave at 15, but stayed for "O" level, then reluctantly for "A" level, and then went to university largely to avoid making a decision, able to earn his keep by performing his circus trick of juggling with mathematical problems. When he graduated, he was literally at a dead end.

At Keele University, where they have a foundation year for all students with topic teaching in place of subject teaching so that there is an opportunity to get some insight into a variety of subjects in a new setting, over 50 per cent of students change to a subject other than the one they originally chose at school. How many reach university like well-trained circus animals? How many at colleges and in industry take training for apprenticeships for which they are unsuited? How many make final choices too soon and stick in ruts?

In education we may learn something from the reactions of laboratory rats. Experimentally, it has been found that subjected to excessive strain, in seeking to learn and earn a reward, rats will react in one of two ways. Some will opt out of learning and become passive, repetitive conformists. Others will become aggressive or hysterical and rebellious. Surely, under the stress of inappropriate methods and excessive stress, one can see all stages of these two extremes manifested in our educational and social system.

My experience over fifteen years underlines the findings of many concerning the importance of parental influence and communication and the fact that in very many cases these are inadequate. Hence increased vulnerability to peer-group and cultural pressures, materialism, and sex, exploited by the mass media of communication. Adolescents realize the lack of preparation, particularly in problems of human relations, of which sex is a part. The psychosexual adjustment to society is probably one of the most difficult to make and cannot be left to random aid or none.

In too many cases of vocational choice the parents have said, "I don't mind what you do so long as you're happy." In the early years of employment the children have chosen the "cheese in the mousetrap" represented by high wages or "safe" jobs where they find themselves trapped without training or prospects, or else just drift; and resentment often follows.

Hence, in my view, the overwhelming need for better preparation at school and better continuity of tutorial supervision in the early years at work, during this metamorphosis. The school and the allied services must combine in stimulating a community growing-up process so that the young citizens and parents of tomorrow are better prepared by participation for their very responsible and vital jobs. We have lessons in driving and training for jobs, but none for adulthood, parenthood, and helping our children. This line of thought is behind everything I have tried to express here.

If little sense of responsibility has been learned at home or school, it is not surprising that employers commonly complain that a section of young people is unreliable. Employment is easy to obtain; wages are high and "easy money." Intermittent work can provide an "easy" living. In this country thinking is very muddled. There is no agency which can keep any continuous contact until the young person, having left school immature, or mature and rebellious, commits an offence and comes into the orbit of the probation service. Then salvage is attempted. Supportive advisory or psychiatric and hospital services are grossly deficient. Many adolescent crises are brief but acute, and like a slip on a mountain may, without support, lead to a fatal slide.

Let us look for a moment at the services in this country covering the transition from school to work of the less able. The Youth Employment Service, potentially vital, is generally impotent and marginal for this section. The vitally needed Careers and Counselling Service of schools is rudimentary. The School Health Service (which should be a *corps d'élite*) is again marginal, and like all school services ends with the clang of the schoolgates on leaving. The new training section for industry set up in the Ministry of Labour will not touch them; it is for the more able or conformist.

The only continuing link in this country is theoretically provided by the statutory duties of the Appointed Factory Doctor (A.F.D.), who is assigned to a particular district by the Factory Inspectorate of the Ministry of Labour. There are about 1,500 districts, and most Appointed Factory Doctors are also general practitioners. Their duties are to see young people in factories and civil engineering between the ages of 15 and 18 when they take their first job, every time they change jobs, and once a year up to the age of 18, if they remain in the same employment. It is the duty of the Appointed Factory Doctor, and for this purpose he possesses the rights of the Factory Inspector, to go into every place where these young people work and satisfy himself that the conditions are reasonable. If these duties were shared with the Youth Employment Service there would be the basis for a tutorial, stimulating service for the less able, equivalent to the student tutorial and health services for the more able.

The Youth Employment Service is potentially a senior extension of the educational service projecting into the early years at work on a tutorial basis. It is concerned with vocational guidance and stimulus to maturation over a period of time with changing individuals in changing circumstances. It should be essentially tutorial and stimulating. Change is so rapid in every sphere that for many it is not possible to look many years ahead, but only to say that basic skills and a capacity for self-disciplined mobility are essential. Anything that helps a young person to think of himself with respect, and his future with hope, promotes health, welfare, and citizenship.

The A.F.D. duties are unique and in fact should cover the section most at risk, the third and fourth quartiles of the secondary modern school, the subject of the "Newsom" Report, about which there has been so much talk.

This section contains a high proportion of the handicapped and problem cases. It is an extraordinary thing that while Student Health and tutorial services are being steadily developed for the more fortunate, it is proposed to abolish the unique opportunities of the Appointed Factory Doctor without survey or experiment, or even due consideration. Yet if the potential contributions of the A.F.D. were made a reality and linked with other services, a great deal could be done for the community, to phase out from school to work. At present all the services mentioned above work in relative isolation in different ministries, and even where in the same ministry, without any contact. There are rigid lines of demarcation and protocol. In fact, co-operation is deliberately refused.

The standards which the school has tried to inculcate are often in conflict with experience at work. Good placing, or the good intentions of managers, is often wasted because of poor handling at the workbench. Drift commences, and resentment and anxiety grow. The absence of any continuing link is a serious deficiency. The large and better-organized firms can be more selective in choice of employee. The less able and the unsettled are more likely to drift into the orbit of ignorant, less competent, or less desirable firms where they may be regarded as a nuisance and exploited as a form of cheap labor until they are 18 and can claim an adult wage, when they may be discharged. Many of the jobs in industry are more fit for the mentally handicapped than for the normal, and so boredom and frustration grow. The progress of automation renders continuity of employment less certain, and jobs more repetitive—mere machine-watching. Leisure hours are longer, and there is quite inadequate preparation for self-disciplined mobility and the creative use of leisure. Here the gap between school and youth services, which are still rudimentary, is a particular loss for the adolescent. In the youth service they should learn independence and democratic self-government, outside the family in their peer group, and develop a creative approach to social intercourse and the creative use of leisure. Too often schools are concerned with mere order and factual learning. There is too little attention to attitudes of mind to learning and living. This could be fostered by the development of youth services linking the school and the community. This is especially necessary because in the schools there are constant staff changes and what might be described as a turbulent turnover of young, inexperienced, and immature teachers, many of them girls getting married—"trousseau teachers," as they have been called. Too often the process of desocialization continues after leaving school and a sense of significance may be sought in antisocial ways. The image of the school is weak and group support lacking.

Many earn wages little less than their fathers, and beyond a nominal sum paid to their mothers for lodging, have relatively large sums to spend at will; this means power without responsibility, at a time when family relationships and values are in a state of flux. Money purchases mobility—motorcycles and cars—and more time is spent in areas of anonymity. The unsettled congregate and as a peer group are disruptive. Where a young person is unknown he is less restricted by convention. The press and mass media emphasize abnormality as if it were the commonplace, and the teen-age cult increases division between the generations, "we and they." At this stage, they are the target for mass media and advertisers, who exploit strong basic instincts, especially sex, for purely materialistic ends, which may be antisocial and contrary to the theoretical values of home and school. In no sphere of life is the knowledge of sex and psychology exploited more ruthlessly than in mass media and advertising. It has even been said that if advertising were stopped our society would collapse, for to survive we have to be molded to competition in material possessions and to rapid turnover and waste. In the great city of Minneapolis, in America, there was a printers' strike lasting 100 days. There were no papers of any sort, for all publications are local rather than national. The sale of all commodities dropped by from 10 to 20 per cent. The only individual who expressed unqualified satisfaction was the Commissioner of Police. Crime dropped 10 per cent. In reverse, in Montana they published the names of juvenile delinquents, and offences fell 50 per cent.

Suggestibility—hypnotism—is today receiving more attention medically. It is true that the adolescent, undergoing this crisis of identity, as it has been called, is particularly vulnerable to suggestion and subtly camouflaged seduction. The original meaning of "doctor" was teacher. As we gain control of the physical environment and the physical causes of ill-health, the relative importance of mental factors in health increases.

In Britain the figure of 300 million days lost from work through sickness, not including absences of less than four days, is often quoted. The important aspect of this vast total, approximating over 7 per cent of all working time, is that various surveys show that over one-third of the absences is due primarily to neurosis and that in a large proportion of all absence the functional element is large.

Since it is in the early years at work that attitudes to work are formed and hardened there is surely no need to stress the importance of planned induction to work from school. The idea is not to restrict but to stimulate. There is need for a communicating link to interpret school to work and work to school. If firms are aware of interest and supervision they are more likely to take some care of their young employees, and much can be done to enlarge insight into needs and responsibility on both sides.

CONCLUSION

Education and medicine are truly indivisible. Attitudes of mind to health and living are of vital importance. No medical examination of young people, in particular, can be without some element of health education even if it is no more than confirming an attitude toward doctors and health. By listening and learning and helping to link, insight may be increased and emotional stress alleviated. We need their help in order to gain experience to render help.

The young leave school at a vulnerable stage of metamorphosis. There is surely a vital need for adequate supportive, stimulating service for youth. There should be closer links, phasing out, between school and work. Services should be equivalent to lifelines across a pool, a Plimsoll line for safety so that they are not overloaded. Indeed, the aim is not to restrain, but to encourage, to help them to find their limits, to be their own best doctor, to know how to use a doctor, to realize responsibility and the joy of living and learning through participation and a sense of relationship (significance) which is essential for maturity. Not what to think, but to think that what they think is important. In an age of accelerating change and flux of values, where choice is taking the place of chance and power is infinite for harm or good, greater maturity is the price of survival. In the transition from school to work much can be learned and much can be done to help, both individually and to guide our educational system. I repeat: in this situation medicine and education are indivisible; youth and maturity meet in community.

12

From School to Work:
Certain Aspects of
Psychosocial Interaction

Irwin M. Marcus

In many instances adolescents are already preoccupied with a specific direction for future work while they are still experiencing developmental changes. An understanding of certain aspects of this important period of transition from school to work is a pertinent issue now and will continue to be for future generations. The problems under consideration cannot be dealt with entirely on a psychological basis, but require information and observations from many other sources, especially the contributions of sociology. If an individual pursues an occupation that is socially valued and accepted, he will receive varying degrees of approval and support from that society. The person's status and thereby his identity are intimately involved in these crucial decisions which must eventually be faced during a relatively early phase in life. Work decisions are, in a sense, social tension points, because they are made within a social context. Achievement through work will influence one's future social status and the many concrete and indirect rewards available in our society. As Erikson[4] stated the issue under discussion, identity "is never gained nor maintained once and for all." During a work career changes in social position affect personal identity, and behavioral stability in turn influences work patterns and institutional reactions. Knowing that this reciprocity exists, adolescents are particularly vulnerable to instability in their selection of occupational goals if momentous decisions are reached during periods of rapid transition in their development.

Old positions disappear and new ones arise in a work world that is constantly changing in its structure and direction.[1] People have to be prepared to reorient their ambitions and training. The many ways in which an adolescent's career interests are influenced, particularly during critical periods of this transitional phase, may irrevocably decide his future. In general, the scientific interest in these matters tends to focus on the maturation of the male in his quest for identity and fulfillment of his role in the world. I am currently engaged in a study of 110 student nurses at the Touro Infirmary in New Orleans, Louisiana, and it is apparent that females, too, are confronted with the many tensions associated with a transition from school to work.

These young women, who are no longer living in their family homes, experience a concealed resentment against the older women who are their supervisors and teachers. The conflict and accusations against adult authority and the struggle for psychosocial identity is present, as it is in the male. In their efforts at individuation and independence, they avoid intimate communication with their schoolmates, in contrast with the younger adolescent. When the hostility is more than they can handle, they become dropouts from the school and offer a rationalization as an excuse. Since this study was initiated, fourteen small groups were established with nonfaculty, adult group leaders. Communication among the student nurses is improving, and an outlet for verbalization of the hostility has been provided. Although this work is in an early phase, the faculty has reported a noticeable improvement in the learning and work attitudes. Most young adults and late adolescents prefer to "handle their own problems." The student nurses are in this transitional phase and resist seeking advice from the various possible sources available to them. Feelings of ambivalence regarding the career choice and inadequacy, or anger at authorities, and depression from daily contact with seriously ill patients may invoke unconscious defense mechanisms such as denial. Psychosomatic complaints are not infrequent, nor are neurotic patterns such as compulsive eating, withdrawal into unusual fatigue, or sleeping. The increased psychic stress may pass unnoticed even by the experienced faculty member; however, there may be enough disturbance to interfere with learning and progress toward the desired career. Group discussions should go beyond catharsis of anxiety and anger and aim toward improved self-understanding, thus providing a significant learning experience. The late adolescent must learn that sharing conflicts and feelings is not a threat to individuality and identity formation, but may constructively foster maturation, whereas a student's withdrawal from school avoids facing the problems in work adjustment and in turn may keep the identity struggle unstable and immature. The group experience appears to help the students scale down their adolescent fantasies of a frightening authority who will destroy their individuality. Furthermore, the group experience appears to help their inner security and stabilize their social work adjustments.

Family interaction influences adolescent patterns of development. I have reported on a pilot study exploring family interaction in younger adolescents with learning difficulties.[6] Here one sees the power held by adolescents to influence their parents' self-image by developing in an acceptable or unacceptable manner. As an example, I have heard the following expressions: (Male:) "If I become a bum, people will think my father is not so great either." (Male:) "Why should I get good grades to make my parents happy?" (Female:) "My mother wants me to do well so my father won't yell at her; he thinks I am her responsibility." Marriage problems of parents can envelop the adolescent so intensely that a chronic learning and work problem is created. Adolescents have a need to prove their own value rather than to certify the worth of their parents or supply them with vicarious fulfillment.

However, where family conflicts have revived oedipal struggles, the adolescent may strive to outshine the parent of the same sex or through guilt may withdraw into varying manifestations of failure. As an example, a young adult from a wealthy family had a professional education, but was preoccupied with gambling and avoided real work. His ambition was to make money faster and more easily than his father, since he could not hope to make more. His excellent education had no value to him because he was focused on father's financial power and their family conflicts.

The young man was lost because he was testing his strength with a magical concept rather than striving to find meaning in life for himself. Thus, the adolescent's need to grow by testing his abilities, by having a cause for assertiveness, can run aground if there are serious intrapsychic problems, a vague social order, absence of parental figures, distorted values in the family, or overwhelming control by the authority in his life.

The family situation does influence subsequent achievements, as well as the development of intellectual capacity and thus the educational experiences. Although Parsons[7] pointed out the role of schools in the United States in shaping achievement values, Halsey[5] notes that there continues to be a close relationship between filial and parental status. To cite one aspect of this complex problem, the housing situation is influenced by the economy, which in turn results in a type of residential segregation. Since an entire neighborhood is within a certain school district, the peer-group values will reflect the cultural ingredients of their own strata of society.

Peer-group values are frequently overlooked in the responsibilities of a school program and can be a potent influence on the developing adolescent. As an example, a local high-school class of senior students was particularly outstanding as a group. Inquiry into the situation revealed that, as one student stated, "In our class it is smart to be smart." One can contrast this with many examples where the group values are directed at being a good athlete, a good date, a good dancer, or, on the other side of the coin, being a "problem" or a type of "beatnik." Thus, the multiple overt or covert influences from the culture, the family, the peer group, and the personality structure of the adolescent all challenge the position of educational and vocational guidance. Obviously, decisions regarding vocational choice should not be made early in adolescence, because they are then strongly influenced by the class status of the environment. It is generally recognized that extended educational and vocational guidance is essential to meet the technological changes that are taking place, with its demands for skilled workers. However, longer-term education must not be misinterpreted to mean holding adolescents in school without an individualized goal. Secretary of Labor W. Willard Wirtz has suggested a Human Resources Development Program[10] which in certain aspects moves closer to the practices of many western European countries. The co-operation of schools, government, labor unions, business, and public and private training organizations would be involved toward the goal of preparing adolescents who are not going on to college for a useful and needed occupation.

Young women need more practical guidance to help them understand and have less conflict about their dual roles as housewives and workers.[11] Social attitudes tend to enhance the confusion for these women by viewing them as unfeminine, when in many instances they are striving to achieve their inner potential. The problem of identity becomes more complex and closer to the struggles of the male when the adolescent female feels unfulfilled if she restricts her role to mother and wife. As Bettelheim has pointed out,[2] our Western society stresses the goals of motherhood and homemaker for young women, whereas a higher education prepares them for self-realization in other fields of endeavor. The United States Office of Education conducted a study of about 4,000 high-school dropouts. One-half of the girls said they quit to get married, whereas the boys gave such reasons as dislike for school, failing grades, or request by authorities that they leave. Women tend to be judged a failure by others and themselves if they have not found a husband early in their adult years. In this regard, I have treated a number of female physicians and social workers who experienced considerable depression over their sense of failure in not achieving marriage. In many cases, the degree of mental distress interferes with their functioning in either direction. In contrast, young men generate considerable anxiety in their families if they do marry before a firm foundation is established in the area of their life's work. Here we can see one of the social roots of mental illness and divorce. Women who give up their quest for self-fulfillment and rely exclusively on motherhood and marriage tend to live vicariously through their children and/or husbands. Such women demand, in one way or another, that the family make them happy and life meaningful. The impossibility of these demands is obvious, and the consequences are well known.

Another strong force influencing the adolescent from the middle teens onward is the development of what Erikson[3] refers to as a "historical perspective." This useful term applies to the adolescent's capacity to perceive the irreversibility of significant events and, therefore, an urgent need to understand cause and effect. If the adolescent decides that his parental background will deprive him of achieving the identity he desires, he may reject his parents and whatever he feels they represent. He may also reject or belittle the authorities or social order, if he feels they are restricting his future. This search for his own identity and goals makes the developing adolescent vulnerable to individuals who can stir his imagination with ideologies. However, his need, which may take a potentially dangerous direction, can also respond in a constructive direction, if the teachers, vocational counselors, or members of industry and the professions are inspiring representatives of the adult world. Thus, the many facets of the adolescent's personality may present one pattern at one time and the opposite at another. When conforming, he may be like the acorn that falls close to the tree; however, in rebelling, he may be like the pollen that takes to the wind to grow in distant fields. In any event, the multiple forces interacting on the adolescent will influence the time and nature of his response to the transition from school to work.

CURRENT ACTIVITIES IN THE UNITED STATES TO AID THE TRANSITION

The co-operative education plan, which had its origin in 1906 in the engineering college at the University of Cincinnati, now has about 38 schools using this system. In recent years this growth has been stimulated by the formation of a National Commission for Cooperative Education in the United States.[8, 9] There are many variations in its practice. In the college setting, it is a five-year program with the work phase beginning in the second or third year. The student spends half-time on the job and the other half in school. Where the quarter system is used, thirteen weeks of work alternate with the same period of study. The participants may range from the entire student body to an optional or an honors program in one or more fields. A wide variety of businesses and industry employ these students, including newspapers, government agencies, automobile, insurance, marketing, and finance companies, and many others. The student receives the same pay scale as a regular employee for the job. The employer has recruitment in mind; the student is learning to test the reality of his interests and job requirements. The evaluation reports of the student by the employer become a valuable basis for more meaningful guidance by the school counselors. It is obvious that the success of this program is highly dependent on a wise and alert co-ordinator who will find the job opportunities and match them with the students. The co-ordinator must be flexible enough to allow certain students a variety of experiences when they may not be emotionally ready to commit themselves to a specific field. The reality testing for "job fantasies" stimulates maturation, for it involves accepting the responsibilities of work, the opportunities to develop real confidence based on mastering an assignment, and learning the importance of co-operation with co-workers. On the other hand, the school experience also becomes more real. Theories are more meaningful when the problems they relate to are practiced and faced in actual situations at work. Such students are more likely to participate in their education rather than passively sit back to listen and daydream. They can bring their experience back to the classroom to question and explore ideas, because they feel they have something to exchange with the instructor. They can challenge and test the theories and thereby contribute both to the study program and to their employer. One can readily see how helpful his approach would be to the low economic groups. These students, provided with a source of earned income, can pursue an education toward a more skilled occupation. The combination of experience and education and the acceptance by the employer that accompanies enthusiastic appreciation for the employment opportunity improve the students' self-image. The sense of worthiness and self-respect from gratifying employment diminishes self-hatred and the defense of turning hatred against others, thus fostering improved interpersonal relationships.

Direct benefits are gained by the educational institutions that use the co-operative education plan. Businesses get to know the institution better and develop a greater appreciation of educational goals; thus they are more likely to support the institution. The school can enlarge its student population within the same facilities because of the rotation into work situations, thereby saving considerable money in reduced per capita expense. For reasons stated above, the dropouts diminish, and the experience gained by both instructors and students improves the quality of the education.

Our government has also sponsored the Neighborhood Youth Corps (NYC) established under the Economic Opportunity Act of 1964 and directed by the Manpower Administration of the U.S. Department of Labor. This program is intended for unemployed youths from 16 to 21 years of age who come from low-income families. Students in school work about 15 hours a week; and those no longer in school work about 32 hours a week. They usually earn about $1.40 per hour. Their work placement may vary from clerical positions to jobs in hospitals, libraries, schools, government offices, or outdoor construction activities. The in-school youths who are encouraged to participate are frequently those who have shown poor educational attitudes or other personality problems. The out-of-school groups are usually the unskilled or underemployed with too little education, or rejectees from other programs. The recent figure on the foregoing program indicates an enrollment of about 250,000, of which about 75,000 are in the out-of-school category.

Many specific co-operative education programs are taking root in the United States. As an example, high-school students in their third and fourth years (this is usually the 16- to 18-year-olds) have participated in a distributive education program. This program teaches them marketing and distribution in the wholesale, retail, and service fields. They attend classes in the morning and receive related part-time job experience in the afternoon. Many businesses favor hiring distributive education students because of their interest in the job they are doing and their related school instruction in business. The automotive service field offers informal on-the-job training or formal apprenticeship. Courses are offered in high schools, vocational schools, and trade schools. Specialized areas in this field may require from two to four years of experience. For graduates of high schools, a' one-year on-the-job training program is available for work as a medical laboratory assistant. Many of these programs, which were established recently under the same Economic Opportunity Act referred to elsewhere in this chapter, are operated by hospitals.

There are presently five Job Corps Centers for Women and others at the planning stage for the future.* The first Center opened April 7, 1965. These centers are for girls from 16 through 22 years of age who have dropped out of school, are unemployed, and lack job skills. In general, these girls come from broken homes, schools that were inadequately equipped to meet their needs, and economically deprived communities.† Their intellectual capacity is usually average or above average, but they lack a healthy self-image to stimulate their development. Therefore, the training program includes basic remedial education, home and family life education, individual and group guidance, counseling and testing, health services, recreation, and student government. Within the framework of the entire program is the goal of education and training for a job skill, as well as becoming homemakers and responsible citizens. These Centers are exploring and experimenting with new teaching methods and materials that may have wide application in education. They are located in available urban buildings and are contracted to schools and colleges, private corporations, public education agencies, and national organizations. About 15,000 girls are now enrolled, with another 25,000 waiting to enter the program. Many of the girls have decided to return for continued education in college, whereas they were previously high-school dropouts. The Centers are residential settings with a staff of teachers and counselors, some of whom live in. The staff serve as examples of mature, responsible adults with whom the girls can identify and establish useful relationships. Characteristic of the program is the wide range of enrichment experiences designed to develop self-confidence and intellectual curiosity. In certain cases this is the girls' first experience in group self-government and thus a step closer to the feeling of independence so necessary for maturation.

Obviously, many adolescents have had great difficulty in meeting the challenge of a transition from school to work. Understanding the problems

---

* In November 1967, there were 84 conservation centers in rural areas for men (100 to 200 each); 10 men's urban centers (700 to 3,000 each); and 17 women's urban centers (400 to 1,000 each). The total number of trainees in the program was 41,000.

† I am grateful to Sister Francetta Barberis, Consultant to the Director of the Women's Centers Division of the Job Corps, for her personal communications to me.

in this important phase of life and helping youth meet the rapid technological changes in our society, *without sacrificing the all-important human values,* remains a central issue and responsibility for mankind.

References

1. BECKER, H. S., and A. L. STRAUSS. "Careers, Personality, and Adult Socialization," in M. STEIN, A. J. VIDICH, and D. M. WHITE, eds., *Identity and Anxiety.* Glencoe, Ill.: The Free Press, 1960, pp. 205–218.
2. BETTELHEIM, B. "The Problem of Generations," in E. H. ERIKSON, ed., *Youth: Change and Challenge.* New York: Basic Books, 1963, pp. 64–92.
3. ERIKSON, E. H. "Youth: Fidelity and Diversity," *ibid.,* pp. 1–23.
4. ERIKSON, E. H. *Childhood and Society.* New York: Norton, 1950.
5. HALSEY, A. H. "Youth and Employment in Comparative Perspective," in M. S. GORDON, ed., *Poverty in America.* San Francisco: Chandler, 1965, pp. 139–160.
6. MARCUS, I. M. "Family Interaction in Adolescents with Learning Difficulties," *Adolescence,* Vol. I, No. 3 (1966).
7. PARSONS, T. "The School Class as a Social System: Some of Its Functions in American Society," in A. H. HALSEY, J. E. FLOUD, and C. A. ANDERSON, eds., *Education, Economy and Society.* New York: Free Press of Glencoe, 1961, pp. 434–455.
8. RICHMOND, C. "Cooperative Education," *Occupational Outlook Quarterly,* Vol. X, No. 1. Washington, D.C.: Supt. of Documents, U.S. Govt. Printing Office, February 1966, pp. 14–18.
9. WILSON, J. W., and E. H. LYONS. *Work-Study College Programs: Appraisal and Report of the Study of Cooperative Education.* New York: Harper, 1961.
10. WIRTZ, W. WILLARD. "A Human Renewal Program," *Occupational Outlook Quarterly,* Vol. X, No. 1. Washington, D.C.: Supt. of Documents, U.S. Govt. Printing Office, February 1966, pp. 1–4.
11. Woman's Bureau of the U.S. Dept. of Labor and the U.S. Office of Education. "New Approaches to Counseling Girls in the 1960's." Washington, D.C.: Woman's Bureau, U.S. Dept. of Labor.

13

The Perception by Adolescents of the Role of Parents in Guidance and Job Choice

Jean Rousselet

In the course of various inquiries carried out among wide samples of young apprentices, of young people looking for work, and of young working people, the interviewers of the Research Center for Labor Conditions of Young Workers of the Ministry of Social Affairs asked adolescents, among other questions, for their opinion on the relative importance of the following: money, friends, work, parents, girls, leisure time, vacations, sports, politics, and everything other than work.

The responses of the adolescents were very similar. Nearly 70 per cent placed their parents first and work second, whether or not they considered work an inevitable necessity or morally or socially imperative.

These responses represent a hierarchy of values rather different from the often quite snap judgments made about today's juvenile population. However, the evidence of these responses corroborates frequent clinical judgments and most other observations made in other research work about these subjects.

It can be stated that in adolescents, at this very sensitive time of life, the way in which difficulties of orientation, of going to work, and of family relationships are resolved is of prime importance among the factors that condition psychological equilibrium.

Among tens of thousands of young people between the ages of 14 and 18 who were systematically examined in our services before their first entry into the working world, 10 to 15 per cent seemed to need special orientation measures. These measures were linked directly to pre-existing character difficulties. Three per cent of those examined needed psychotherapy. For many adolescents, whatever their previous educational or socioeconomic difficulties, going to work comes abruptly, before they are adequately prepared for it. It is natural that a sudden revolution of habits and responsibilities should aggravate previous imbalances or, as often happens, should itself cause various difficulties.

Investigations should not neglect the adolescents' experience of the working milieu any more than their initial entry into the working world. An examination of juvenile populations after six months of apprenticeship shows that some pathological conditions are improved just by an appropriate work environment. Other cases (and these are far more numerous) lack necessary, truly ergotherapeutic conditions and have become serious and often irreversible disorders.

Therefore it is understandable that work should hold such a prominent place in the preoccupations of young people. Because of their sociocultural milieu many adolescents are accustomed to derive most of their economic satisfactions and gratification from work. Work is also the source of most of their dissatisfaction. It is simultaneously dreaded and hoped for.

Their parents are still important to adolescents in spite of the age of the young people and their desire to be emancipated. One has only to look at the results of other inquiries. These show that 65 per cent of the adolescents from 14 to 18 years of age recognize that they are economically dependent on their parents, cannot live away from home, and cannot take sole charge of their own orientation. Sixty per cent of the same age group say that they are incapable of marrying, voting, or having real professional responsibilities before they are at least 20.

Taking these considerations into account, we have found it interesting to study the interaction of the two dominant interests—parents and work—in populations of young people who were about to begin working. The study was to measure the importance of these dominant interests and evaluate their effect on the psychotemperamental equilibrium of comparable groups of adolescents.

The subjective interpretation of each individual in this domain seemed to play a part more important than the nature of parental conduct toward him. Therefore the emphasis of this study was on the way adolescents perceived the role of their parents as it affected their orientation to work rather than on the role of the parents itself.

The study was carried out on three samples, each of 65 subjects under 20 years of age. The subjects in each sample happened to be in a different situation with respect to beginning work. The essential differences were a result of their levels of professional preparation and their chances of future social and occupational success. These two factors are obviously related and, as we know from other studies, are directly influenced by the socioeconomic and cultural characteristics of the adolescents' backgrounds.

The first sample was made up of young people seeking employment.

They were adolescents who had completed their compulsory education and, with no special preparation, were seeking immediate employment. They had little real chance to qualify more highly at a later date. It was almost inevitable that they would get dead-end jobs that rarely offered a chance for promotion.

The second sample was made up of young apprentices. These young people were preparing to obtain technical training in an environment suited to giving them such training. They would work toward a certificate which would authorize them to work as technicians.

The third sample was made up of young people, two or three years older than those in the first and second groups, who were preparing to obtain more advanced technical qualifications which would allow them to work as more highly skilled technicians or as industrial engineers.

The young people were interviewed directly and asked to answer individual questionnaires.

To keep within the scope of this book and to avoid too many figures, we have limited ourselves to a descriptive and comparative analysis of three main points:

(1) How young people perceive the role of their parents:
    (a) In their choice of work;
    (b) In the choice of the means used to decide on their choice of work (educational guidance, continuance of education, choice of technical or nontechnical education);
    (c) In their previous study (supervision of homework, learning lessons, interest in performance, visits to teachers, and so on).

(2) Reactions of satisfaction or dissatisfaction of these young people to their present personal situation.

(3) Evaluation of the role of the parents in these three fields (scholastic achievement, professional guidance, choice of job).

These three points seemed particularly important to us. The young people we studied were faced with the immediate and irreversible prospect of going to work and were in identical situations for reflection or eventual reevaluation. Furthermore, these points are among those that illustrate how the relation between parents and children was perceived during a limited, crucial, and rapid period of development.

ANALYSIS OF THE RESULTS

In relation to the perception of the role of parents in the choice of jobs, four different groups of attitudes could easily be discerned:

(1) No parental influence; instead a personal decision by the young person (46 per cent).

(2) Direct and authoritative influence of parents (18.5 per cent).

(3) Decisions taken together, with exchanges of opinion and discussion (18.1 per cent).

(4) Recourse to outside advisers (teachers, professional guidance people, and the like) (17.5 per cent).

These four groups resemble classic educational types: authoritarian, indifferent, liberal.

This distribution shows that almost half of these young people feel that they have decided their job choice themselves. It seems that those looking for immediate employment and the skilled technicians are most numerous in affirming their independence. Among those looking for immediate employment, independence sometimes implies being let down by the family, whereas among the skilled technicians independence smacks of excessive belief in their own autonomy. Perhaps their greater confidence is related to the greater age and higher cultural level of this group. This hypothesis finds support in the fact that the skilled technicians showed the weakest family ties.

The group looking for immediate employment did not seek professional guidance, interpreted as an explicit search for outside information. The two other groups, who are planning on some specialization, used about the same amount of professional guidance.

The analysis of parental influence on previous scholastic achievement shows that half the young people had neither help nor supervision in their studies. Those who made their own choice of career were mainly those who had received no help from their parents, whereas those who chose their future job after talking things over at home were mostly those who had been helped with schoolwork.

The fact that the group whose future was decided on the basis of outside advice (teachers, guidance counselors, and so on) includes a large number of subjects who were left alone to their scholastic pursuits suggests that recourse to outside help often indicates careless parents rather than an active search for information—a transfer rather than a widening of responsibilities.

A comparison between samples also shows that the first and third, those seeking immediate employment and the skilled technicians, experienced the greatest degree of abandonment, loneliness, and independence. Parental, and especially maternal, influence was felt most among the subjects of sample 2, the apprentices.

We decided to find out how the initial and determining steps were chosen which led to the circumstances in which each group began work, especially those circumstances that influenced their type of work and chances of promotion. In 75 per cent of the cases an agreement between parents and children seems to have been reached easily, whether the choice was a "technical education" or a decision to reject any previous training before actually going to work.

In 20 per cent of the cases the young people felt that they had decided alone and against the wishes of their parents.

In only 5 per cent of these cases did young people act on their parents' advice rather than their own inclinations.

Those who had decided alone on the choice of a career were also usually those who had made their own decisions about the preliminary steps. Those who claimed to have chosen their careers on the basis of discussions in the family also had a high percentage who had made their own decisions about preliminary steps. One may surmise that for many young people exchanges of opinion and discussion represent an effort to persuade rather than a truly mutual process of consultation.

When we compare samples we find again that the most individualistic behavior occurred among those seeking immediate employment. This group also disagreed most with their parents on the choice of channels through which to seek work. Among the apprentices the percentage of parent-child agreement increased.

Several hypotheses concerning parental influence on the choice of a job, preparatory study, and orientation procedures present themselves. These are obviously hypotheses that should be verified by other investigative methods or by interviewing larger samples. However, several observations seem interesting:

(1) Among young people looking for immediate employment, who must begin their careers without much training and with poor prospects, who start work in the worst social, occupational, and psychological circumstances, we usually find those whose parents have participated least in their children's education or choice of career.

(2) On the other hand, among apprentices of the same age, who have the better prospects and are probably less exposed to future risks of socio-occupational or other maladaptation, are usually those whose parental, and especially maternal, influence is perceived as relatively important. This influence is often accompanied by family discussions, interviews with outside guidance counselors, and support in previous scholastic achievement.

(3) Skilled technicians who may have had the same elementary training as the apprentices, but who look like an elite, capable of following a higher course of study, display greater independence. This can be seen as much in their choice of career as in the steps they take to attain it. This greater independence may be related to their being older (and therefore perceiving the role of the parents differently), to their higher cultural level, or to the intrinsic qualities that singled them out from their fellow students.

To conclude this part of our comparison between these samples, we may comment on their perception of the role of their parents in their choice of work and say that in the group of parents perceived as active we found no continuum of behavior that is authoritarian and at the same time effective. This applied equally to educational activities and to orientation decisions. On the contrary, a continuum of support is found in the group who discussed things with their families. A very marked continuum of isolation or abandonment is found in the group of young people who were left to themselves in the choice of a job.

We have already suggested that study of the group who made use of outside guidance shows habitual obedience to extrafamily structures rather than a real enrichment of family relationships.

To study how these young people evaluated their parents' roles, we investigated what they thought about their present situation. The greatest number, 65 per cent, said they were satisfied, and even very satisfied. However, optimism founded on such responses may be tempered by doubts raised by the context, which led us to suspect the nature and depth of these responses. The group of those seeking immediate employment, that is, the group doomed to a mediocre future, and the group of apprentices of the same age, whose future holds better prospects, expressed approximately the same degree of satisfaction. However, the degree of satisfaction expressed was much lower among the skilled technicians whose intrinsic chances for success are much greater. The level of satisfaction, as we already know, seems to be related to the level of ambition.

When we compare the sample groups, we find that the youths' perception of the role of their parents in the choice of their careers seems to yield a simpler interpretation.

Satisfaction was relatively weaker among those who perceived their parents' role as active, whereas it was very high (90 per cent) in the group that discussed matters within the family. It seems justifiable to say that an excess of family authority affecting a youth's choice of trade leads to dissatisfaction. On the other hand, the kind of influence closest to a liberal education gives significantly greater satisfaction.

To find out the main deficiencies the young people felt in their education, we asked them what they would have liked their parents to do if their education could be started all over again.

The results in this area seem particularly revealing. Only 10 per cent would have asked for more freedom, 27 per cent were sorry that their parents had not used more authority, especially in supervising their studies, and 36 per cent were sorry their parents had not sought more information before advising them.

Intergroup and intersample comparisons seem to be even more significant.

Absence of authority was criticized most by the young people who said they had decided alone or on the basis of an exchange of opinion. Lack of information was criticized most by those who had been passively influenced by their parents or gave in to outside advice. The largest percentage of young people who had no complaints about the educational guidance their parents had given them was found among those who decided after free family discussion.

These judgments seem to represent a very early insight into the exact nature of the relationships with their parents and into the consequences of these relationships on their future work. This impression is reinforced by a comparative study between the samples.

Those seeking immediate employment—who will probably always be marginal laborers—regretted the lack of concerned family authority most and asked least for an increase in freedom.

It seems that the young people doomed to the most mediocre futures regret that they were not obliged, even in spite of themselves, to acquire the minimal education compatible with a step toward professional training. It seems that the skilled technicians who can still receive higher qualifications, but will not attain the level of most academic and professional engineers, regret that because of the lack of information at the outset, they misused their energy and intelligence (a true conclusion in the eyes of informed observers).

The responses of the apprentice technicians were dispersed around the over-all average.

The clarity with which these young people assessed their situation is striking. One wonders about the future psychological consequences of estimates so simultaneously clear and severe.

To verify these opinions and to try to make them objective, we asked all these young people what they thought would be ideal parental behavior in these areas, work and education, and how they themselves expected to behave toward their own children.

More than half thought that parents should make it a prime duty to support their children in their studies; they also thought parents should show an unfailing authority.

One-third thought that parents should support children in their studies and leave them free in the choice of a career. Very few said they would allow complete freedom to their children.

When we compare the samples, we find that the first sample, those seeking immediate employment, were the most partial to authority. The third sample, the skilled technicians, on the contrary, showed the fewest defenders of complete freedom and the greatest number who hoped that as parents they would reconcile freedom of choice with help in studies.

As a whole, the results seemed to show that adolescents' conception of the role of their parents develops with their degree of maturity. Among young people who, for various reasons, have attained a low level of development, the conception of the role of their parents is global and entirely centered on authority. At a higher cultural level and a greater age, it gives place to a more complex conception whereby parents should help guide, should be informed, and yet should allow freedom in the making of basic choices.

CONCLUSION

This study, deliberately limited to young people about to start work, based on three relatively small samples, obviously does not permit us to formulate conclusions that can be applied to all young people and to all types of family background. However, it seems to us that it does justify a few hypotheses. We intend to verify these hypotheses in later studies, and we hope that they are of interest to all those already convinced of the importance of parent-child relationships to mental health.

When the analysis is limited to the period when young people begin work, influence on the adolescents' personality development can be analyzed in two perspectives.

The first concentrates on psychosocial aspects and refers to what we know of the consequences of a poor introduction to work on character, either immediately or in the long run. Indeed, it is obvious that maladjustment may be the almost inevitable result of bad working conditions that offer no chance for personal fulfillment or real satisfaction. Unskilled marginal workers, necessarily unstable in their jobs and ambitions, seem to be more vulnerable to all the factors of disequilibrium than those who, on the contrary, find their work a source of stability and fulfillment.

Among our sample, those seeking immediate employment, young people placed on the job market without preparation or hope of future success, seem to be by far the most threatened by either immediate or delayed pathogenic social maladjustment. These adolescents, as we have seen, perceived the role of their parents in supporting their studies, in giving informative advice, and when it came to elementary displays of authority, as least active.

The socioeconomic environments of our three samples were not very different, so it seems justifiable to surmise that family carelessness or shirking plays a decisive role in a bad introduction to the working world. Young people who are its victims feel parental insufficiency clearly and at an early age. It is significant that young people, when placed in circumstances that compare unfavorably with those of other youths of the same age, never blame society and socioeconomic factors for their situation. We know that these factors do have some effect, but the young people single out their parents' lack of interest in their studies, and they resolve that they will do better by their own children. In these cases we can see the beginning of conflict situations and reactions of frustration. As these tensions develop they can only aggravate the dangers of the existing social situation.

The second mode of analysis tends to be more psychological. It too studies situations that offer the greatest risk, on the personality level. It attempts an over-all analysis of the feeling of dissatisfaction. Thirty-five per cent of the subjects in all the samples said that they were disappointed, dissatisfied, or bitter but resigned. These subjects perceived the role of their parents in the choice of their work or in guiding their behavior as weak or nonexistent. Although these young people did not, any more than their peers, demand an increase in parental authority, they regretted especially that their parents did not make the necessary effort to inform themselves and their children sufficiently. The degree of dissatisfaction and the amount of blame expressed by these young people correlate more closely as the young people increase in maturity.

Finally, and to a very significant degree—perhaps the most significant percentage in our study—we find that those who are dissatisfied are those who were most alone in their studies. Their parents were not interested, did not have time to be interested, or did not have enough education.

Let us remember that almost all the young people questioned thought that in an ideal situation parental supervision of studies was among the most important of parental responsibilities. Second, let us remember that the young people destined to the worst social and occupational futures were the most neglected in this respect. Perhaps this factor is decisive in the role parents play in the formation of the occupational future of their children.

Taking into account the fact that it is materially and culturally impractical to expect all parents to help equally in this respect, we find in our study an additional reason to ask for an education that is entirely dispensed at school. In thus doing away with many sources of inequality and bitterness we might easily reduce the obvious sociological and psychological risks when young people find themselves in employment that they perceive as the result of chance or of parental shirking of responsibilities.

14

The Socialization of Boys and Girls at School and Work: A Canadian Study

Bruce A. McFarlane

This chapter is a report of a study carried out by Professor Oswald Hall,[3] of the University of Toronto, and myself under the auspices of the Canadian Federal Department of Labour. In large measure it constitutes an initial exploration of a murky area: the margin between school and work.

The study was in progress during a period when massive governmental funds were being expended on secondary education to meet the rising public demand in the early 1960's for secondary-school education and to help to supply society's demand for well-educated man power. It was also carried out at a time when there was a singular lack of information concerning the manner in which school-leavers solved the actual problem of locating themselves in the work world. There was also a lack of knowledge concerning the effectiveness of the various secondary-school courses as a preparation for the world of work. And, closely related to these two areas, there was a general lack of knowledge of the effectiveness of the various forms of vocational guidance provided, somewhat spasmodically, by the educational and other authorities. The latter is a particularly important point as an ever-increasing proportion of the whole population are able to attend secondary schools, and the parents of many of these students, because of their own limited education, will have only a vague notion, if any, of the occupational possibilities which this level of schooling makes available. In addition, the rapidly changing nature of the work world and the rapid introduction of new occupations and virtual disappearance of older well-known occupations, in content if not in name, make it difficult for even those parents with

174

a relatively good education to provide realistic concrete guidance for their offspring or supply anything other than vague generalizations about the value of a good education, and so on. Hence, the importance of the guidance teacher or officer to the social system is increasing, while our knowledge of what is actually taking place in this area is still very limited.

This study was an attempt to trace the experiences of young Canadians in Paulend, a "typical," albeit anonymous, Ontario community as they pass through the secondary-school system and enter the work world. The community chosen could not, of course, be "typical" in an absolute sense. It is relatively self-contained; it is large enough to represent modern industry, but it is not simply an industrial satellite of a large metropolis. At the time of the study it had a population of fifty thousand and had had no recent serious changes in population. While there we found no indication of a large postwar influx of non-English-speaking immigrants.

The initial plan was simple. In 1961 we selected a community in which we tried to contact the people born in 1940. We studied the school records of these 21-year-olds, to find out when they left school and what level they achieved there. We related these facts to whatever else we could discover about the backgrounds of the students such as sex, father's occupation, religion, I.Q. scores, experience with guidance counselors, and so forth. Wherever possible we traced these students into the work world to discover their sequence of jobs and periods of unemployment. We interviewed all who could be contacted and secured supplementary information about them from employers and the National Employment Service. In addition, wherever students had left the community subsequent to their secondary-school careers, we traced them, hoping to compare the work careers of the footloose types with those who remained at home. Similarly, we contacted, wherever possible, the 21-year-olds who had migrated into Paulend after terminating their school careers elsewhere.

By the end of the field work we had obtained the names of 816 persons who fitted our requirements. The total from whom detailed personal information was received was 527 persons, of whom 408 were interviewed personally and 119 completed self-administered questionnaires. Of the 527 respondents, 274 were girls and 253 were boys.

From these raw materials we tried to answer several questions. Who gets where in the school system, and how? How are jobs found by newcomers to the work world? How is school achievement linked to job opportunities? Who faces unemployment? How effective are guidance and counseling in the school system? Do boys and girls fare similarly in these matters?

Before looking at some of the more specific findings it should be noted that some of the general ones simply corroborated those of other workers. For instance, they were similar to the findings of Floud and Halsey[2] and those of John Porter[4] which are concerned with the "class chances" of entering and finishing secondary school and entering the university.

Twenty-two per cent of the respondents had parents or guardians in non-manual occupations, that is, white-collar or professional occupations, but 60 per cent of those in the study who went up to university had parents in this occupational grouping. In addition, family background appeared to influence school performance and eventual occupational opportunities in a more fundamental sense. Children from the homes of manual workers scored lower on the I.Q. tests administered on entry to the secondary schools than did those from the homes of white-collar workers. This is worthy of note in this context since the school authorities informed us that students are placed in the various courses at the secondary-school level largely on the basis of their I.Q. scores. Or, at least, it is recommended to the students and their parents that the students follow one course rather than another, that is, that they follow either a university preparatory course or a vocational course and hence are prepared for different occupational opportunities. Incidentally, we found that the parents in white-collar occupations as frequently as not ignored these recommendations if it meant placing their boy or girl in one of the courses which did not prepare them for university entrance. In fact, we found the students' social-class position to be a better predictor of success at school than I.Q. scores. It became clear to us in the study that students from working-class homes were easily discouraged from the academic side of secondary schoolwork, that is, from the university-oriented courses, and were readily directed into the vocational classes. Also, as far as teachers and other authorities who do the streaming are concerned, vocational courses are primarily and fundamentally the place for students of mediocre ability, poor study habits, lower-class parentage, and lower-class aspirations. (There is some evidence for this in the fact that students of limited potentialities from the middle-class families persevered in the academic course after the rebuff of failing several times along the way—these are the children of the middle-class parents who ignored the authorities' recommendations that their children should follow the vocational courses.)

Probably one of the most interesting findings, to the researchers at least, was the general ability of the girls in the sample to make their way through the various courses and grades in the secondary schools successfully when compared with the performance of the boys. Although it is true that there was a slight tendency for more girls to drop out of school than boys, they did so for different reasons. Of the male dropouts 80 per cent failed the last year which they spent at school, whereas less than 50 per cent of the female dropouts did so.

This higher academic standard on the part of the girls despite no significant difference in I.Q.'s was maintained throughout all the school years and in both the academic and the vocational programs. Seventy per cent of the girls who completed the final grade of secondary school did so in the minimum number of years, that is, in five years. On the other hand only 30 per cent of the boys fell into this category, the remainder taking six years and not infrequently seven years. This meant that, in general, the boys were one or two years older than the girls in their senior years at school. The consequences for the boys of the higher failure rates, of the repetition of years, and of association in class with girls chronologically younger than themselves are matters deserving much closer scrutiny. The negative attitudes and values toward educational achievement which may arise among boys under such conditions may have serious consequences, since in all likelihood they will be the major breadwinners at a point in time when there is increasing need and demand for males with a good educational background.

In addition to their proven greater ability to master the work at school there was the relative ease, when compared with the boys, with which they entered, left, and re-entered the work world. In part, of course, this was because 60 per cent of the total sample of girls who went to work in non-professional positions found jobs in white-collar occupations, a field of work which tends to provide greater job security and opportunities than the manual occupations, where 60 per cent of the boys found jobs.

The initial period of transition from school to work did not appear to be a very painful one for most of the respondents. Ninety per cent of both boys and girls found jobs within *one* month of leaving school. In the case of early dropouts, of course, this frequently meant that they left school because a particular work opportunity opened up. An additional 6 per cent found their jobs within three months after leaving school. Even here, one has to be careful, because from the end of the term in mid-June to the beginning of the next term in September many did not seriously look for work. Only the threat of a new school year caused some of the recalcitrant ones to "find" a job.

The educational background of the students appears to have had little or no bearing on the ease or difficulty with which they found their first job after leaving school, although it was very important in terms of finding jobs which offered an extended period of employment. Hence, many more girls (most of whom were in white-collar occupations) managed to make their initial job their permanent one, at least until marriage or pregnancy forced them to leave. On the other hand, the boys, with their poorer educational background and jobs in manual occupations, had a much higher number of jobs per person and much greater periods of unemployment.

One can only speculate on the nature of the strains which this situation imposes on the courtship and dating relationships at this time in their lives. The boys, in occupational terms, are going through a period marked by instability of employment and uncertainty of income while the girls hold down white-collar jobs marked by stability and secure in the knowledge of continued employment. Indeed, these strains may well be carried on later into family life, for as Burgess and Cottrell[1] showed as early as the 1930's, stability of employment is a strong predictor of marriage satisfaction in the United States.

Two-thirds of the girls with working-class social origins interviewed in this study found work in white-collar occupations, while only one-third of the boys with similar origins did so. Hence it would appear that available marriage partners, as well as dates, for most of these girls, who will be working for a few years in an essentially middle-class atmosphere, will be men whose working environment has been predominantly one wherein working-class values and norms prevail. There is already much evidence in the literature on the family and marriage to indicate the nature of the problems of marital adjustment which might arise under these circumstances. Most of these studies, however, have been concerned with the differing values and attitudes of the marriage partners due primarily to differing social-class origins and ethnicity rather than with different socialization of the marriage partners in the world of work.[5]

The three major sources of assistance for the boys in finding their first job were: (1) personal contacts, that is, through family and friends; (2) self-help, by finding the job on their own initiative; and (3) part-time work, that is, part-time after-school jobs became full-time jobs after leaving school. Finding one's own job appears to be the manner in which the largest proportion of girls made their initial entry into business and industry; although personal contacts and "schools and teachers" assistance combined provided the means of entry for approximately two-fifths of the girls.

The study began as an exploration of the transition from the life of a secondary-school pupil to the life of a gainfully employed person. Initially, the school world was viewed as a fundamentally coeducational world, offering roughly identical services to boys and girls. In addition, the work world was seen as one organized by men for men, with women invading it at various points. Before the end of the study these notions were all called into question.

The secondary-school world of Paulend turns out to be, fundamentally, a feminine world. It provides an academic atmosphere in which girls thrive and boys fail. The girls manage it with marked success at a relatively early age. The boys linger in it, showing conspicuously higher failure rates. It is a world to which girls adapt with relative ease. Boys appear to reject it, and eventually it rejects them.

The school is also a feminine world in the vocational sense. It prepares the girls admirably for their careers in the work world. The skills learned by girls in school seem ideally adapted for transfer to the job with little time delay. This is particularly true of that large contingent who enter clerical occupations, particularly stenographers and typists.

For the boys, it is otherwise. Those who drag along to matriculation are in many cases really unfitted for university work. If they choose to enter a teachers training college they find themselves in what is essentially a girl's milieu. When they head for the strictly masculine side of industry, into the skilled trades, they find that their prior schooling is deemed by employers to have little bearing on their jobs, and they are asked to spend from three to five years serving an apprenticeship. There seem to be few places where skills learned by boys in school, even in vocational school, can be applied to a specific job. This is, of course, in marked contrast to the position of the girls. The graduate of a stenography course at high school can start work immediately as a full-fledged stenographer; the male graduate of a four-year course in mechanics starts as an apprentice. Even the girl who, for whatever the reason, dropped out of high school as early as the beginning of the second year can enroll in a commercial course at a private business college and after six months or so can easily find employment in a business office. The business school cushions her fall from the academic world; boys have no such advantage. There appear to be no facilities which can help a boy step from half-completed schooling into the enjoyment of a well-established job.

In this context, it is worthy of note that Canadian society provides much more in the way of specialized training facilities for girls than for boys. The two outstanding examples are the nursing schools and the teachers training colleges, although males are beginning to invade these two areas. Both nursing and teaching represent what are essentially short-term careers for girls. This means that in any one generation several recruits are trained for each available position. Indeed, schoolteachers themselves recognize this state of affairs by referring to the emergence of the "trousseau teacher," implying that a teaching certificate is the modern equivalent of the dowry. Canadian society provides a costly scheme for training nurses and teachers. One is hard put to discover comparable outlays for boys embarking on long-term work careers of a comparable level of complexity. It might well be that more boys will have to be guided into these two essentially feminine areas of work.

The foregoing then provides a background against which the vocational guidance officer or teacher has to offer his or her services. The specific formal guidance services of the schools, as far as our respondents are concerned, have left only a vague imprint on the vast majority of students passing through the secondary schools, and the "Occupations and Work" or "Careers" course offered in the schools appears to have made little or no impression on our respondents. Those boys and girls who left school early had little or no remembrance of the classes, and in any case most of them had rejected the whole school system of which the classes were an integral part. Hence, the few statements which they did make concerning the course and its value were generally negative. The girls who followed the commercial course at school found these lectures of little value because as one of them, now a Nursing Assistant, pointed out, "Everyone at the school assumed we were going to work in a bank anyway." The basic criticism of these classes, so far as the commercial-course girls were concerned, was the limited scope of the teachers' knowledge about the newer types of work open to girls in the office milieu. A number of the girls who were business-machine operators or working with electronic data-processing equipment commented on the difficulty they had encountered in finding out about this type of work while still in school.

Some of the more articulate students who followed the academic course to the point where decisions had to be made concerning the selection of a university course or some other postsecondary training had particularly caustic remarks to make concerning these lectures and the efficacy of the personal interviews they had with the guidance officers. Most of them felt that the guidance teachers knew little about the real world of the university today, and as some of them noted the guidance people thought that there were only two professions for girls who matriculated, nursing and teaching, and one for boys, teaching.

Very few of the students had any awareness of the facilities offered by the National Employment Service for guiding the school-leaver into an appropriate niche in the work world. Hence, the people in the community most qualified to advise the would-be school-leaver and other students about the world of work—the nature and duties of a job, physical conditions of work, qualifications demanded by employers, relative stability of type of employment, and so on—are not likely to meet the school-leaver until he or she has had at least one job and comes before them when in search of another post. By and large, then, the formal facilities for bridging the transition from school to work are ignored; students use their own initiative and/or flounder in moving from school to work.

References

1. BURGESS, E. W., and L. S. COTTRELL. *Predicting Success and Failure in Marriage.* New York: Prentice-Hall, 1939.
2. FLOUD, J., and A. H. HALSEY. "Intelligence Tests, Social Class, and Selection for Secondary Schools," *British Journal of Sociology,* VIII, No. 8 (1957), 33–39.
3. HALL, O., and B. McFARLANE. *Transition from School to Work.* Ottawa: The Queen's Printer, 1965.
4. PORTER, J. *The Vertical Mosaic: An Analysis of Social Class and Power in Canada.* Toronto: University of Toronto Press, 1965, esp. pp. 165–198.
5. In discussions with colleagues Dr. Peter C. Pineo, David Chandler, and Constance McFarlane, the question has been raised whether these girls completely accept the norms and values of the middle classes due to their working environment or only play the game while at work and on their return home to the working-class milieu become "themselves" again. Some insight into the nature of the problem may be gained from M. GOLD and C. SINGER, "Office, Factory, Store—and Family: A Study of Integration Setting," *American Sociological Review,* XXIII (1958), 64–74, and from R. D. MILLER and G. E. SWANSON, *The Changing American Parent.* New York: Wiley, 1958.

Eating Problems

EDITORS' INTRODUCTION   It is fitting that we open this section with a consideration of eating problems, because of all psychiatric disorders these appear to have the most differentiated relationship to adolescence. As John A. Sours points out, anorexia nervosa has been described both in small children and in adults, but it is most common in adolescents; and Hilde Bruch emphasizes, too, the particular significance of obesity in this period, characterized as adolescence is by a sudden spurt in physical growth and development and by the special meaning of bodily size and configuration to an adolescent struggling to achieve his "grown-up" identity.

It is paradoxical that in our modern world, in which problems of overpopulation, poverty, and hunger are so widespread and so pressing, our Western culture should place so much emphasis on the dangers of overeating and obesity. This is probably only in small part based on recent medical theories which link arteriosclerosis and heart disease with cholesterol metabolism and seems more related to aesthetic values and to an ideal image of the maintenance of youthful athletic vigor in an aging population. Whatever their origin, these cultural attitudes form the backdrop for the development in many adolescents, especially girls, of a special concern about obesity and dieting. Such concerns not infrequently become exaggerated into problems that come to the attention of psychiatrists and pediatricians. Apart from reactions to the values and pressures of society and their representation inside the family circle, adolescents are also influenced by oral needs, which like other instinctual drives increase their pressure during this

181

period and manifest themselves in ways that have been influenced by fixations and patterns of gratification of earlier development with consequent pathogenic potential.

Although our two chapters deal explicitly with contrasting clinical pictures—anorexia nervosa and obesity—they have many themes in common. Sours comes to the conclusion that despite the characteristic features of anorexia nervosa described by many authors, this is not a definable nosological entity, but rather a syndrome or behavior constellation of variable pattern and mixed causation which manifests idiosyncratic features from case to case. Bruch emphasizes the varied clinical picture and the multifactorial causation of obesity and warns against the oversimplification of dealing with it as an "entity." Both writers conceptualize overeating or undereating as one element, often particularly meaningful, in a disorder of varied pathological intensity and prognosis during the crucial personality developmental process of adolescence and very much influenced by interpersonal as well as intrapersonal psychological and physical factors.

Sours, in reviewing the literature on anorexia nervosa, traces the historical development of ideas about this condition, which appears to be increasing in incidence in our food-rich Western culture, which makes noneating a behavior pattern that arouses public concern. Although it is still comparatively rare, with an estimated prevalence of 50 to 75 per 100,000, it is attracting much international interest partly because it may offer a key to an understanding of crucial reverberating links between bodily processes and ego development and partly because it is one of the few psychiatric conditions that involve a direct threat to life: the mortality rate is as high as 7 to 15 per cent of diagnosed cases.

Sours differentiates secondary anorexia nervosa, which is one of the possible manifestations of a wide range of neurotic and psychotic conditions, from primary or "true" anorexia nervosa, which is usually characterized by gross disturbance in body image and in the accuracy of enteroceptive perception and cognition, as well as by lowered effectiveness of behavior. The behavior of those who suffer from this condition, as described particularly in a series of papers by Bruch, is usually not autonomous, but a passive compliance or a negativistic response to interpersonal and social stimulation.

The pathophysiological disturbances of true anorexia nervosa are often dramatic and may lead to death because of circulatory collapse. Sours discusses the historical development from early views of the condition as primarily an endocrine disturbance to many of the recent writings which conceive of the organic changes as a consequence of elective restriction of food intake, but which in their turn may progress to metabolic and cortical depression with psychological consequences.

The development of anorexia nervosa is regarded by some psychiatrists as a manifestation of a long-standing ego weakness complicated by the increased instinctual pressures of adolescence and the renewal of oedipal

strivings, which lead to regression of drives and ego functions and an analization of behavior. Other writers emphasize the conceptual and perceptual
disturbances. Sours integrates these complementary ideas by postulating
that a basic feature of the condition is a deep sense of personal ineffectiveness and a compensatory drive for cognitive and perceptual control by restricting the focus of life interest onto food intake and by using noneating as
a means of gaining absolute power over the body, the self, parents, and
significant others.

In her chapter, Bruch points out that some of the confusion regarding
obesity results not only from the wide variations in a syndrome which may
occur in various degrees of intensity on its own and associated with every
conceivable psychiatric disorder as well as in basically healthy personalities,
but also from the need to differentiate among the psychological problems
that influence the development of obesity: those which complicate the
obese state, especially in view of current negative social attitudes to overeating, and those that are precipitated by efforts at weight reduction which
may attack defenses necessary to the person's psychological equilibrium.

She centers her main discussion on the phenomenology of the obese person's inability to regulate his food intake in accordance with his physiological needs. Many such individuals appear to react indiscriminately to any
discomfort as though it signaled a desire for food and do not appear to be
able to perceive or conceptualize correctly enteroceptive bodily stimuli.
This leads her to question how an individual normally achieves a sense of
ownership of his own body and how this relates to the development of his
"biological identity."

In discussing this theme, Bruch postulates a simple model which differentiates individual behavior as (a) initiated within the individual and (b)
responding to outside stimuli. In regard to the latter, she classifies environmental influence as *stimulating* or *responsive, appropriate* or inappropriate.
She then suggests that if parental behavior toward a child is inappropriate
and not differentiated in response to the child's needs and behavioral cues,
he is likely to fail to develop an autonomous ego, and his diffuse ego boundaries will lead him to feel helpless in reacting effectively to the forces of the
outside world. There is likely to be lack of reinforcement or contradictory
and inconsistent reinforcement of the necessary sequence of felt discomfort,
signal, appropriate response, and felt satisfaction. Without this regularly
repeated experience, a profound deficit in essential learning develops, resulting in the disordered awareness of bodily functioning and a disturbed
body concept.

Bruch describes two cases of obese adolescents to illustrate her thesis.
She focuses not on the traditional psychoanalytic interpretive approach of
asking *why* the disorder developed, but on the fact-finding approach needed
to discover *how* the pathology unfolded. In both cases parental responses to
child-initiated cues were inappropriate. In particular, food was used as an
all-purpose pacifier without reference to the nature of the child's current

discomfort. This undifferentiated response to his needs influenced a recipro-cal lack of differentiation in the child's perceptions and concepts of his internal bodily states.

Bruch ends her chapter with a brief discussion of the implications of her thesis for the therapy of cases of obesity which develop along such lines. She points out that promoting the patient's insight into emotional conflicts and unconscious fantasies is valuable, but not sufficient. In addition, the therapist must evoke the patient's awareness of those feelings that originate inside him and help him learn to recognize, utilize, and satisfy them in a *discriminating* way.

It is of interest to realize the similarity between Bruch's views and those of Anthony, Redl, Lidz, and Shapiro, all of whom emphasized in their chapters the connection between insensitive, inconsistent, constricted, or distorted reactions of parents to the behavioral cues and other expressions of needs of a child and disordered development of his ego autonomy. The question arises as to why in certain cases the pathological development should take the path described by Bruch and result in an eating disturbance. The elucidation of this must await further research, such as comparative studies of obese adolescents and groups like those investigated by Shapiro. It seems plausible that one significant factor might be that which was so obtrusive in Bruch's two case examples, namely, the use by the parents specifically of feeding as a major mode of "shutting the child's mouth" and stifling his demands, rather than some other mode, such as verbalization or isolation, as described by the other authors.

15

Anorexia Nervosa: Nosology, Diagnosis, Developmental Patterns, and Power-Control Dynamics

John A. Sours

I. INTRODUCTION AND HISTORY

The need for further psychiatric research in anorexia nervosa is evident on several grounds. First of all, the disorder is one of the few psychiatric illnesses that can result in death. Follow-up studies suggest a mortality rate of 7 to 15 per cent and a morbidity rate of 34 to 65 per cent in terms of chronic psychopathology and sexual dysfunction.[65, 66] In addition to being a therapeutic challenge, [8, 36, 38, 52, 66, 77, 84, 89, 113] research in anorexia nervosa has stimulated new concepts of nosology[19, 69, 103, 106] and pathogenesis,[9, 10, 17, 18, 28, 101] as well as over-all contributions to the knowledge of drive theory, ego functions and mechanisms, family psychopathology, dynamics, and metacommunication patterns.

The conceptual history of anorexia nervosa is outlined in Table 15–1. Curiously, there are no references to this disorder in antiquity or the Middle Ages. Perhaps its recorded history commenced with the apocryphal story of Lora, daughter of Miles Standish, who pined away for Henry Winslow. Later in the seventeenth century, Norton referred to anorexia nervosa as "nervous consumption." But it was not until 1868 that Gull described the self-induced aspects of anorexia nervosa and indicated that it could also occur in young men.[52] Simmonds' description of pituitary deficiency in 1914, however, led clinicians to search for endocrine disturbances in anorexia nervosa, until Ryle's reminder in 1936 that psychic trauma could often be found in the histories of these patients.[60] The view that anorexia nervosa was directly related to pituitary dysfunction persisted in some quarters, even though there was much evidence to the contrary.[11, 95] As an alternative thesis, Reifenstein's concept of "hypothalamic amenorrhea" offered a psychophysiological approach to the study of menstrual-endocrine disturbances in anorexia nervosa.[91, 95, 104]

Table 15–1. History of the Anorexia Nervosa Syndrome

1694	NORTON	Nervous consumption.
1868–1874	GULL	"Morbid mental state." Hysterical disorder.
1874	LASEGUE	Hysteria.
1903	JANET	Psychasthenia.
1907	GEE	Melancholy.
1914	SIMMONDS	Defined pituitary cachexia; syndrome seen as endocrine deficiency.
1936	RYLE	Psychic trauma distinguishes anorexia nervosa from pituitary cachexia.
1939	RAHMAN	Compulsive features.
1939	BRILL	Simple schizophrenia.
1940	WALLER et al.	Rejection of wish to be pregnant.
1943	ROSE	Resistance to stages of human development.
1945	BERLIN et al.	Oral-sadistic tendencies and reaction formation against incorporation wishes.
1949	DU BOIS	Compulsive neurosis with cachexia.
1950	KEYS et al.	Biological and psychological effects of human starvation.
1952	KAY AND LEIGH	No neurosis specific to anorexia nervosa; no specific anorexia nervosa.
1956	FALSTEIN	Male patients: feminine identification, wish to remove fat associated with female form.
1957	MEYER AND WEINROTH	Attempt to re-establish mother-child unity.
1958	WILLIAMS	Primary somatic disorder.
1958	BINSWANGER	Existential analysis of a case of "anorexia nervosa": role of shame and secrecy.
1960	BLISS AND BRANCH	Criterion of 25 lbs. weight loss for psychological reasons only necessary for diagnosis.
1960	LESSER et al.	Not a disease, but a constellation of symptoms.
1960	JESSNER AND ABSE	Regressive forces in anorexia nervosa.
1961	THOMA	Drive disturbance with oral ambivalence. Age significant factor; atypical case after age 18.
1962	BRUCH	Perceptual and conceptual disorders.

Table 15–1 (*continued*).

1963	S E L V I N I	Effort to escape passivity and gain independence.
1963	K I N G	Primary anorexia nervosa a distinct nosological entity.
1965	G Ö T T I N G E N S Y M P O S I U M	Multidisciplinary studies on anorexia nervosa.
1965	R U S S E L L *et al.*	Hypothalamic defects postulated.
1965	C R I S P	Avoidance response to postpubertal emotional conflicts.
1966	F A R Q U H A R - S O N *et al.*	Good prognosis for some patients.

In the last twenty years there has been increasing international interest in this disorder. The studies of Bliss and Branch,[10] Bruch,[18] Thoma,[107] and Selvini [101] represent contemporary research efforts and approaches. In 1965, a multidisciplinary conference on anorexia nervosa was held at Göttingen University.[81] The renewed interest is at least partly a reflection of an increase in incidence of anorexia nervosa. Apparently, a food-rich culture is essential for anorexia nervosa as well as for politically coercive noneating, if these eating behaviors are to have meaning to other people. Since World War II the increased incidence of anorexia nervosa has been noted not only in Western cultures but also in Japan, most strikingly there in professional families who have adopted Western cultural values and practices.[59] The increased incidence notwithstanding, anorexia nervosa remains an uncommon malady, principally affecting girls in the second decade, at a risk, according to sociological studies by Pflanz, of 50 to 75 per 100,000.[86] Undetected mild cases of pubescent girls who reject their sexual role by altering their body by food fads and diets are probably common.

II. NOSOLOGY AND DIAGNOSIS

The psychiatric criteria for diagnosis of anorexia nervosa are controversial.[5, 10, 43, 61, 65, 69, 71, 79, 80, 81, 101, 106, 108] Differentiation, however, from panhypopituitarism is no longer difficult since body wasting and preservation of adrenocortical and thyroid function do not occur in panhypopituitarism.[95] Bliss and Branch's criterion of loss of 25 pounds or more due to psychological reasons[10] does not discriminate between primary and secondary psychogenic anorexias.[19, 69, 71, 103] "Nervous malnutrition," they believe, is a more apt generic designation for anorexic symptoms in any psychiatric disorder. King's categorization of anorexia nervosa into primary and secondary forms attempts to establish anorexia nervosa as a specific nosological entity, "an obscure organic disease, a primary disorder of appetite regulation." [69] Bruch also distinguishes between two groups of psychogenic anorexics. Relentless pursuit of thinness in a struggle for control, definition of identity, and sense of effectiveness are, according to Bruch, the core issues of "true anorexia nervosa." Refusal to eat because of neurotic and schizophrenic conflicts, symbolic in the eating function, marks the "pseudoanorexia nervosa" patients. Furthermore, the latter group of patients is said not to have the characteristic developmental history of the "true anorexia nervosa," which, according to Bruch, is marked by gross body-image disturbances, defects in accuracy of enteroceptive perception and cognition, and a sense of ineffectiveness.[8, 16, 17, 19]

The trend toward establishing anorexia nervosa as a specific entity is reminiscent of past attempts to find a symptomatic focus for anorexia nervosa, which from time to time has been hysteria, obsessional neurosis, as well as variants and *forme fruste* of manic-depressive or schizophrenic psychosis (Table 15–1). Kay and Leigh's conclusions—there is no specific neurosis in anorexia nervosa and no specific anorexia nervosa—have been articulated by others.[44, 60, 71, 72, 99, 103, 106] As in obesity,[10] no distinctive personality configuration has been found. But still the nosological flotsam and jetsam from the past keep returning.

In general, the predominant tendency today is to view anorexia nervosa, not in terms of traditional nosological groups, but along the lines of either a syndrome with primary and secondary clinical features[103] or a typical behavioral-dynamic pattern and constellation with a range of nosological subgroups.* [66, 70, 71, 72, 82, 106, 108] Both views of anorexia nervosa complement each other. In the medical tradition, anorexia nervosa is a syndrome: a symptom-complex of a disease, with X_1, X_2, X_3, X_n component parts related without a specific reciprocal cause Y.[31] As a behavior-dynamic pattern, anorexia nervosa is given a motivational meaning, a maladaptive attempt to resolve a conflict along symptomatic and characterological lines.

Anorexia nervosa as a syndrome is phenomenologically defined along the lines of its component signs and symptoms, which are presented in Table 15–2. Voluntary restriction of food, avoidance of eating, and pursuit of thinness are observable phenomena, usually associated with apparent pleasure and pride over the demonstrable control exercised by the patient. Rarely is anorexia a first symptom. Overactivity and increased energy output without fatigue are often prodromal, but may not be clinically recognizable, hidden in sports, schoolwork, and subtle ritualistic activities. Amenorrhea and decreased libido can occur as a prodromal sign and symptom in that they may precede the onset of food refusal.[94, 95] Secondary features are present in varying degrees, depending in large part on the basic character structure of the patient and the style of the latter's transactions within the family matrix. Thus a prolixity of psychiatric symptomatology can coexist with the essential signs and symptoms of anorexia nervosa. And, like Bin-

---

* The APA *Manual on Psychiatric Nomenclature* categorizes anorexia nervosa as a psychophysiological disorder—gastrointestinal type.

Table 15–2.   Phenomenology of Anorexia Nervosa Syndrome

A. PRIMARY SIGNS AND SYMPTOMS	B. SECONDARY SIGNS AND SYMPTOMS
1. Elective restriction of food. 2. Pursuit of thinness as pleasure in itself. 3. Frantic efforts with establishing control over the body and its functions. 4. Food avoidance and preoccupation. 5. Hyperactivity and increased energy output. } Can be prodromal 6. Amenorrhea. }	1. Manipulation of environment around food and diet. 2. Distrustful attitude to significant objects. 3. Sadness and guilt, but no clinical depression. 4. Occasional bulimia.

swanger's famous patient, Ellen West, many anorexia nervosa patients are borderline psychotics and difficult nosologically to categorize.[9]

III. PATHOPHYSIOLOGICAL FINDINGS

The physical signs and symptoms of anorexia nervosa are, it appears, results of elective restriction of food (Table 15–3). Even when severely ill, these patients reluctantly take to their beds. A number of these findings and their pathophysiology have been well described.[6, 68, 81] Less common findings[46] are carotenemia,[32] leukopenia, and relative lymphocytosis.[24]

Table 15–3.   Pathophysiological Disturbances in the Anorexia Nervosa Syndrome[10, 65, 68, 71]

1. Emaciation	11. Anemia—decreased RBC Volume
2. Lanugo hair	12. Leukopenia—decreased polys[24]
3. Hypothermia	13. Relative lymphocytosis[24]
4. Hypotension	14. Endocrine studies in normal range or after refeeding. ?Insulin response. ?Gonadotrophins
5. Bradycardia	
6. Amenorrhea or delayed menarche	
7. Decreased libido	15. High turnover of N_{15} glycine during refeeding[35, 63]
8. Dehydration	
9. Carotenemia. Vitamin A deficiency[32]	16. Possible circulatory collapse and death
10. Hypoproteinemia	17. ?Dystrophic cerebral damage[40]

In advanced starvation hypokalemia[7, 112] and circulatory collapse[68] can occur. The possibility of long-standing undernutrition leading to a chronic brain syndrome in anorexia nervosa patients has been suggested.[40, 75] If this is true, chronic brain syndrome may be one factor that contributes to ego disorganization in adult anorexia nervosa patients who have starved themselves for years.

Metabolic findings in anorexia nervosa are outlined in Table 15–4.

Table 15–4. Metabolic Findings of the Anorexia Nervosa Syndrome[11, 28, 29, 30, 35, 63, 76, 77, 85, 93, 94, 95]

1. Delta glucose values normal after refeeding.	6. Follicle stimulating hormone (FSH) secretion in some cases low.
2. Glucose tolerance restored to normal after refeeding.	7. Human pituitary gonadotrophins show no consistent rise to normal after refeeding.
3. Insulin response abnormally sustained even after feeding.	8. Thyroid function normal.
4. Water balance normal after refeeding.	9. Metopirone (SU 4885) test for pituitary = adrenal function normal.
5. Total estrogen output approaches normal after refeeding.	

Delta glucose values, glucose tolerance, and water balance are restored to normal after refeeding.[29, 93, 94, 95] Likewise, evidence of gonadal failure disappears with usually total fractions of estrogens returning to normal. There is, however, no consistent rise of human pituitary gonodotrophin to normal range after feeding.[95] A persistent absence of cyclical ovulatory activity can remain for years after the anorexic female has commenced eating.[94, 95] For this reason Russell suggests the possibility of a hypothalamic disorder in anorexia nervosa.[95] Patterns of amenorrhea in concentration-camp victims substantiate the fact that malnutrition is not necessarily the prime cause of amenorrhea.[104]

A host of clinical curiosities has been found in anorexia nervosa patients.[6, 7, 12, 46, 56, 112] For reasons not clear, insulin response may be abnormally sustained even after refeeding and correction of carbohydrate deprivation. Crisp has discussed this finding at some length.[29] Balance studies and N_{15} glycine studies of protein synthesis during refeeding in anorexia nervosa bear on the relationships of caloric and nitrogen intake.[35, 63]

IV. HUNGER AND APPETITE

Anorexia nervosa has been dubbed a disturbance in appetite regulation.[10, 16, 18, 69, 81] There is much in the psychiatric literature on the subject of hunger.* Neurophysiological and neuropsychological mechanisms have

---

* In the psychiatric literature the semantics of "hunger" are confusing. Hunger can mean, for instance, awareness of gastric contractions, affective loss, dissatisfaction, greed, feelings of emptiness, or "love made hungry in the schizoid position." [42, 53]

been postulated, either singly or in combination, to explain the eating disturbance. Their proponents frequently ignore the fact that the neurophysiology and psychology of hunger and satiety are hardly delineated, even though a great deal of research has been done.[14] The glucostatic mechanism and ventromedial hypothalamic glucoreceptors are integral parts of the mechanisms regulating short-term food intake. Important also are affective states, eating habits, and adipose tissue which may "serve as the basic 'memory' for this mechanism of correcting errors of day-by-day regulation." [78] Recognition of hunger signals entails learning throughout development of a variety of sensations. Likewise, signals of satiety must also be learned, a developmental process which involves both operant preverbal and verbal and identificatory learning within the family matrix. Although there is a correlation between glucose utilization and hunger feelings and gastric hunger contractions,[74] the use of mininaturized intragastric electronic and pressure equipment has demonstrated a low correlation between gastric and hunger contractions.[25, 26, 27, 29]Furthermore, in regard to anorexia nervosa patients, both intragastric pressures and gastric peristaltic activity have been shown to be unremarkable in those patients thus far studied.[29]

Table 15–5 summarizes various facets of the phenomenology of eating and hunger in the anorexia nervosa patient. What is often clinically over-

Table 15–5.   Hunger Disturbance in the Anorexia Nervosa Syndrome

---

1. Gross denial of hunger.
2. Hunger variable during course of illness:

(a) Attention directed to feeding others.	(d) Affective state diminishes hunger.
(b) Hunger assuaged by high fluid intake.	(e) Sexual feelings with anxiety reduce hunger.
(c) Hunger relieved by bulimia and vomiting.	(f) Hunger present only in evening or middle of night.

---

looked is that the anorexia nervosa patient varies in her recognition and perception of hunger.[101, 102] Appetite can wax and wane during starvation. She may have no desire for food, feel nauseated at the thought of eating, be made acutely uncomfortable by "hunger pangs," and assuage her distress by drinking water. Or she can experience hunger only at night. She can use any number of maneuvers to displace and redirect her desire for food: preparing recipes for the family, taking over the kitchen duties from the mother, feeding other patients during the hospitalization, and perusing popular food-illustrated magazines. And after months or years of starvation hunger can practically cease.[68] Hunger may also wane during purges when the patient initiates vomiting and excessively uses cathartics and thereby produces a disturbance in electrolyte balance.

The patient who alternately starves and binges for hours or days tends to be either a preschooler or postpubertal, as well as atypical in other ways.[107] Ego organization is often borderline with massive defense mechanisms, particularly reaction formations, which do not hold up against strong oral-aggressive needs. Falstein *et al.* suggest that phasic food refusal and bulimia are more common in male anorexics.[43] Theilgaard found that bulimic patients use more primitive defense mechanisms, particularly introjection and projection.[106] Such patients may surreptitiously avoid all carbohydrate foods and then in a frenzy plunge themselves into a carbohydrate binge, followed by frenetic self-induced vomiting. Bruch refers to this form of compulsive behavior as "nutritional disorganization," marked by dichotomous parallel phases: starvation and binge eating, and control and dyscontrol.[8] She believes that this behavioral pattern is typical of "true anorexia nervosa."

V. PSYCHODYNAMIC FORMULATIONS

Innumerable psychodynamic formulations have been made for anorexia nervosa (Table 15–6). In a sense, each formulation can be correct for certain patients with this disorder. Rejection through starvation of a wish to be pregnant and fantasies of oral impregnation are clinically encountered, but do not seem as common in anorexia nervosa patients as once suggested in the literature.* [8, 92, 102, 109] Oral impregnation fantasies are most commonly found in young adolescent girls, especially those with hysterical personality structure, whose illness first presented with amenorrhea. For them food intake is apt to be sexualized. In general, however, anorexia nervosa patients are loath to report fantasies, as well as dreams. Once trust is established in the psychotherapeutic relationship, a few fantasies may be revealed; and this may mark the turning point in therapy. Usually the fantasies involve markedly naïve, even primitive, concepts of genital anatomy and intercourse, as well as notions of sexual assault and violence. Eating can be symbolized in terms of sexual, anal, and aggressive meaning.[43]

Other frequently observed dynamic patterns in anorexia nervosa are: guilt over aggression to an ambivalently regarded mother, dependent seductive relationship with a warm but passive father, fear and avoidance of pubertal and adult sexuality and responsibilities, and, often concomitantly, desire for control, autonomy, and self-initiated behavior. Anorexia nervosa patients can present a kaleidoscopic array of both psychopathology and dynamics.[18, 19,]

The dynamics in anorexia nervosa are determined in part by the developmental stage of the patient. Perhaps the youngest reported case of anorexia

---

* Following the Klein-Fairbairn tradition, Selvini believes that the anorexic's fear of pregnancy is "not a sexual fear" but instead "a sexual symbol of a more primitive experience, that of being invaded by the object" (mother).[102]

Table 15–6. Psychodynamic Constellations Reported for the Anorexia Nervosa Syndrome[8, 29, 43, 45, 51, 71, 72, 77, 109]

---

1. Guilt over aggression to mother vis-à-vis oedipal conflict.
2. Apathetic depression resulting from object loss.
3. Compliant attempt to get close to mother through a regressive identification.
4. Death wish to mother via incorporative destructive impulses.
5. Overdependent seductive relationship with father.
6. Avoidance response to overwhelming postpubertal conflict.
7. Attempt to establish autonomy and self-initiated behavior.
8. Rejection of wish to be pregnant through starvation.
9. Oral-sadistic tendencies and reaction formation against incorporative destructive impulses.
10. Passive hostile control of family which has overinvested eating with cultural symbolism.
11. Feminine identification of male patients; wish to remove fat associated with female form.
12. Attempt to control sexuality by self-starvation which leads to shutdown of sexual metabolism and hence sexual arousal.
13. Inability to differentiate sensations indicating nutritional needs from other body states and emotional feelings due to developmental functioning under influence and in the service of someone else.
14. Disturbances in body-image accuracy of perception or recognition of bodily states and an all-pervading sense of ineffectiveness.

---

nervosa is that of Sylvester,[105] who treated a 4-year-old with alternating food refusal and bulimia. Depression and oral-sadistic mechanisms were conspicuous in this case. Analization of the oedipal conflict had not occurred. In older patients with anorexia nervosa, preoedipal material is abundant. It has long been recognized that pubescent girls, fearful of sexuality, may resort to anorexia[50] and regress to a preoedipal level of development. Oral-sadistic fantasies and reaction-formation against incorporative impulses, as well as hidden anal fantasies of food as destructive and poisonous,[8] are seen in clinical[60] and projective material of anorexia nervosa patients.[106] Thus, a preoedipal developmental "stamp" is deep, even in the late adolescent and adult patients.

Jessner and Abse emphasize in their developmental model for anorexia nervosa "early oral deprivation followed by a period of closeness and gratification" and later ambivalence and displacement of anal defiance.[60] Oedipal rivalry, marked sibling jealousy, and prolonged separations augment the ambivalence. Developmentally, oral deprivation and overprotection block individualization and body-image and self-concept differentiation. With pubescence and genitality, the tie to the mother is threatened when the girl strives to work out an identity with sufficient autonomy for heterosexual object relationships. Unable now to retain the mother or find a substitute, preoedipal restitutive regressive forces push the patient back to an oral-anal mode of drive discharge and ego functioning.* This dynamic formulation is historically a popular one for anorexia nervosa, found in various forms and combinations in the literature.[8, 43, 45, 60, 71, 72, 77, 80, 105, 113]

In the last decade, however, dynamic formulations of anorexia nervosa have not been so widely based on drive theory and traditional psychoanalytic concepts. (Thoma's studies in 1961, however, are the exception in that he focused principally on the eating function and its drive disturbance).[107] Selvini has avoided the eating function, asserting that hunger can persist in the starving patient until the terminal phase.[102] She doubts whether the anorexic is afraid of food; instead, it is "the feeling that the nourished body is threatening, gnawing and indestructible," which frightens the patient. This is in keeping with her subscribing to Fairbairn's concept that the goal of the libido is not pleasure, but the object itself. "The body is felt as the threatening entity which must not be brutally destroyed, but must merely be held in check." This is, for Selvini, the central phenomenon of anorexia nervosa that distinguishes it from any other form of anorexia.[102]

She has elaborated a developmental theory embodying these concepts. The mother is overprotective and unable to see her daughter as separate. The mother overcontrols the child and goes against the latter's efforts to derive pleasure from her body. Compliance is rewarded. The child's learning experiences are inseparable from the mother's signals and operations, leading to a sense of ineffectiveness in thought and action. Prodromally, the anorexic develops "a depression of the ego, faced by tasks it cannot overcome." It is the helplessness of the ego, rather than only oral-aggressive needs, that is central to the depression. Furthermore, the patient views "her body as a whole incorporated object that disparages her and forces a passive role onto her." According to Selvini, the anorexic patient distinguishes oral incorporation and identification. From the experience of oral helplessness the ego incorporates and represses the bad object. In latency, identification with the real mother is attained by compliant surrender, and in puberty there is splitting between the incorporating ego and the identifying ego.

Selvini's theorizing is partly along the lines of Klein and Fairbairn's formulations.[42, 53] Repression of the bad object is central to her theory. "The real mental anorexic therefore makes use of a formidable repressive mechanism that leads to a splitting of the ego." [9] The splitting gives rise to "coenaesthetic diffidence" which, she feels, is akin to Bruch's concepts of conceptual and perceptual disturbances in anorexia nervosa. She also subscribes to a similar theory involving the mother's failure in allowing the child to recognize his own signals and needs. Body-image disturbances for the anorexic patient are related to two factors: equation of the body with

---

* Dynamically, Jessner and Abse view anorexia nervosa as a final common pathway, "involving a complex succession of pathological and restitutional mechanisms." [60]

the bad object and failure in recognition of body needs and signals. She likewise supports Bruch by subscribing to the position that the anorexia nervosa patient is burdened with "a special psychosis." Specifically, the psychosis is for Selvini "mid-way between the schizo-paranoid position and depression," whereas Bruch views the ego disorganization along the lines of schizophrenic despair.[19]

No other dynamic formulation of anorexia nervosa is as well conceived and articulated as that of Hilde Bruch, who over the last quarter of a century has devoted herself to research on eating disorders.[16, 22] After making contributions to our knowledge of the psychodynamics and symbolism of food and eating, Bruch turned to the study of conceptual-perceptual processes in patients with eating disorders and schizophrenic reactions. Her basic interest has been the modes by which eating functions are transformed maladaptively in the service of nonnutritional needs. Thus her focus shifted to a neurophysiology and neuropsychology of enteroexteroceptive learning, the underpinnings of which, she thought, could not then be found in extant analytic theory. She turned instead to neurophysiology and developmental psychology.[20, 54, 55, 87] She rejected the notion of utter helplessness in narcissism; the infant is capable of emitting signals and clues of his needs, to which his significant objects may respond, dutifully or negligently, inhibiting or permissive, appropriately or inappropriately, and stimulate interaction. These infantile transactions are regarded as precursors to later interpersonal relations.[16] The processes of emitted and elicited behavior, operative and respondent learning, and assimilation and accommodation constitute the various levels of interaction between the environment and infant. From this synthetic developmental learning theory,[47, 67] starting with the Piagetian sequence of presymbolic conceptualization, Bruch has constructed a pathogenesis of falsified learning experiences (neural codifications of incorrect learning experiences attained at various levels of maturation). She has aptly used Harlow's primate research as a paradigm for this developmental learning theory.

It is with this developmental theory and approach that she views anorexia nervosa, as well as varieties of developmental obesity. Unless a child is taught by the mother to recognize hunger as distinct from other internal needs and perception, he is at a loss to respond specifically and appropriately to his nutritional needs.* Similarly, the same kind of mother generally "programs" her child to her own needs and impulses. The child learns to respond exclusively to his mother's bodily needs and emotions, culminating eventually in blurring and diffuseness of his ego boundaries, core identity, and body-image. His leitmotiv is based on responses to others, either with overcompliance or with rigid negativism.

From this model of a developmental matrix, Bruch has derived concepts

---

* Bruch suggests that the psychobiology of appetite and hunger is largely a matter of various modes of learning: from the infant dependent on his mother to the gourmet attached to his *Larousse Gastronomique*.

of personality development and psychopathology for anorexia nervosa[18] as well as for schizophrenia and developmental obesity.[17, 20, 88] She maintains that for anorexia nervosa there is a triad of disturbances: disturbances of body-image, perception, and effectiveness. Pathognomic of anorexia nervosa is the distortion of body-image:* denial of emaciation concomitant with a long-standing fear of ugliness and fatness which is regarded by Bruch as tantamount to a delusional disturbance in body-image and self-concept. Otherwise, reality testing is at least grossly intact until later in the illness, when, according to Bruch, disordered thinking and transient breaks in reality occur. Disturbances in perception and cognitive interpretation of bodily stimuli (both denial and nonrecognition) involve hunger and appetite, as well as fatigue, weakness, and cold. In extreme emaciation the anorexia can be secondary to nutritional deficiency.[15] Laxatives, enemas, and self-induced vomiting, presumably for control of weight, express disturbances in awareness of integration and regulation. Absence of sexual feelings and responsiveness and inability to conceptualize emotional states can fall into the same category of disturbance, according to Bruch. The third disturbance, a sense of ineffectiveness, which is developmentally related to the other disturbances, may be shrouded by defiance and negativism.

Bruch believes that these developmental disturbances and associated pathology are distinctive enough to warrant establishment of a specific nosological entity. Although she wants to avoid setting up nosological subgroups and instead employ concepts of deviant adaptational patterns, she finds that her model of "true anorexia nervosa" closely resembles those that have been described for schizophrenic development.[19] Thus, anorexia nervosa, for Bruch, becomes a distinct variety of schizophrenia.

She views the need for autonomy and effectiveness, maladaptively sought through control over the body, as a key diagnostic factor in "true anorexia nervosa." The same criteria, along with several others, are employed in the differentiation of hysterical noneating disorders (Table 15–7).

Bruch does not restrict the diagnosis of anorexia nervosa to female patients. Other workers, however, have excluded males by making amenorrhea an essential diagnostic criterion.[43] Selvini does not believe that her three male anorexics meet her diagnostic standards because of two atypical signs: desire for food and exhibitionistic display of fasting behavior.[102] Kay and Leigh do not exclude male patients; they attributed the low frequency in males to the importance of the hysterical and phobic mechanisms that equate pregnancy with fat.[65] In a study of four prepubescent male anorexics, Falstein *et al.*[43] noted that the male patients were inordinately tied to their mother, with whom they identified and by whom they were overfed. En-

---

* Bruch's concept of body-image differs appreciably from traditional neurological formulations. She not only includes perceptions coming from body surface and musculoskeletal systems, via afferent tracts to the temporoparietal cortex, but also, as Kolb suggests, all modalities of enteroceptive sensations—an inflated notion of body-image which might be better called "body concept." [70]

Table 15–7. Differential Diagnosis of True and Pseudo Anorexia Nervosa (after H. Bruch)[18, 19]

A. TRUE ANOREXIA NERVOSA

1. Food refusal and pursuit of thinness with singular goal of achieving autonomy and effectiveness through bizarre control over the body and its functions.

2. Over-all psychopathology can be neurotic or borderline schizophrenic (mainly cognitive disturbances). Depressive features, if presents are related to the despair of the schizophrenic reaction.

3. Triadic Disturbances:

(*a*) Disturbance in body-image and body concept of delusional proportion, fundamentally expressed via lack of concern over emaciation.

(*b*) Disturbances in the accuracy of perception or cognitive interpretation of stimuli arising within the body: failure to interpret enteroceptive signals indicating nutritional needs, absent awareness of hunger and appetite, nutritional disorganization with bizarre food preferences and cravings and often alternating food refusal and bulimia, overactivity and denial of fatigue, and inability to recognize internal affects and emotional reactions, often within a religious-ethnic subculture that supports food ideologies.

(*c*) Paralyzing sense of ineffectiveness: actions only in response to demands from others, and compliance camouflaged by negativism and stubborn defiance.

B. PSEUDO ANOREXIA NERVOSA

1. Hysterical Noneaters:

(*a*) Food refusal not based on goal of achieving autonomy and effectiveness.

(*b*) Complaints about loss of weight and thinness.

(*c*) Awareness of hunger and weakness.

(*d*) Eating functions used in symbolic ways.

(*e*) Few episodes of bulimia.

2. Schizophrenic Noneaters:

(*a*) Food refusal not based on goal of achieving autonomy and effectiveness.

(*b*) Acknowledgment made regarding hunger and weakness, if not too indifferent or withdrawn to respond.

(*c*) Body-image disturbances do not encompass weight and appearance.

(*d*) Ritualistic and bizarrely symbolic meaning attached to eating and food.

(*e*) Few episodes of bulimia.

---

couragement by the mother to diet in latency—often given to the son with a guilty exhortation to assume a more masculine role—precipitates the boy into self-initiated starvation to which the mother responds by forced feedings. A struggle for mastery and control ensues between mother and son.

Through starvation the male anorexic attempts to kill the incorporated mother and reduce the fat which he associates with the female body.

Food refusal and peculiar ideologies about eating, without overt psychosis, are found in males. Often the male anorexia nervosa patient, however, is otherwise clinically different from the female. Kay and Leigh made this distinction: "Fear of becoming fat is not expressed, and hysterical *'la belle indifférence'* and apparent self-satisfaction are uncommon. On the other hand, hypochondriacal anxieties or preoccupations are more often found." [65] The prognosis for the male anorexic is considered more guarded, especially in terms of later exfoliation of the anorexia nervosa symptoms into frank paranoid psychosis. Bruch implies that overt schizophrenia is more apt to be masked by anorexia nervosa in the male patient.[19]

In the male, anorexic traumatic homosexual experiences are frequently reported, especially ones connected with seduction by a father.[103] Interestingly, in 1893 Breuer described a 12-year-old boy who had been urged by a man to perform active fellatio.[18] Fleeing from the scene, the lad developed hysterical symptoms of anorexia and vomiting, which persisted for some weeks until he confessed the incident to his mother. Breuer postulated that the sexual trauma had excited passive feminine wishes in the boy. Much the same dynamics have been postulated for the male anorexia nervosa patient.

VI. DEVELOPMENTAL PATTERNS

Collaborative psychiatric and medical studies at the Columbia-Presbyterian Medical Center have revealed a spectrum of deviations in the developmental histories of anorexia nervosa patients.[18, 19, 71, 103] Table 15–8 shows some essential features of, and differences between, anorexics admitted to Babies Hospital and the N.Y.S. Psychiatric Institute. Obviously, demographic factors and hospital policy affected case selection. Nevertheless, a dichotomy by age, sex, socioeconomic status, duration of illness, and hospitalization is possible. Patients admitted to Babies Hospital mainly came from materially comfortable suburban or rural families, were mostly female, and were either in late latency or pubescence. On the other hand, those admitted to N.Y.S. Psychiatric Institute were urban, of mixed sex, pubescent to late adolescent or young adult, had a longer duration of illness, and required lengthy hospitalizations. This group tended to display more psychopathology, especially of dysintegrative variety and particularly those disturbances in cognition and perception delineated by Bruch.*

Developmentally, quantitative and qualitative differences between the groups were visible. As Bruch has indicated elsewhere, the state hospital

---

* A number of investigators have stressed that both adult age and male sex are associated with the "atypical anorexia nervosa patient." But this designation can mean: not truly anorexic, grossly schizophrenic, vastly different in dynamics from female anorexics, or, in connection with projective testing, less productive and possibly intellectually compromised by prolonged starvation.[66, 101, 102, 106, 107]

Table 15–8. Comparison of Anorexia Nervosa Patients Admitted to a Pediatric and Psychiatric Hospital

Item	Babies Hospital	N.Y.S. Psychiatric Hospital
1. Residence	Suburban	Urban
2. Sex	Mostly female	One-third male
3. Age of onset	10–12 years old	11–21 years old
4. Duration of illness	6 months	3–6.5 years
5. Hospitalization	15 weeks	1–3 years
6. Infant behavior	"Perfect" infant	"Pride and joy" of parents
7. Oppositional behavior	None	None
8. Autonomy	Not encouraged	Not encouraged
9. Gratification needs	Delay and control	Delay and control
10. Dietary preoccupation in family	Frequent	Frequent
11. Ego-function style	Control and mastery	Control and mastery
12. Body-image	Minimal disturbance	Gross disturbance
13. Thought disorder	Rare	Frequent
14. Diagnosis	Character neurosis	Schizophrenia
15. Prognosis	Fair	Poor

patients as children had been well nurtured. They had been exposed to and stimulated by athletic and cultural contacts and events; they were the pride and joy of their parents, often born to fulfill the mission of improving the family status or replacing a dead or disappointing sibling. Neonatal and infant histories indicated that the patients had been healthy and vigorous, well fed and cared for. There was no history of food finickiness or food allergies. Some mothers reported that the infants had been less motorically active than their siblings. Over and above this, there was a tendency for the parents to view the child as a "perfect model," which was even operative during the child's infancy.* Preschool oppositionalism had been minimal, if present at all. The patients seemed reluctant to experiment with muscular activity and motility. Their compliance in the early years was striking. Toilet training for these parents was no problem. Encouragement toward self-expression was grossly lacking in these families. The children were taught that their feelings should reflect those of the mother. Exemplary performance in school was inculcated by the parents and usually at-

---

*Crisp's findings, in his series, that anorexic females weighed more than their sisters at birth and were overnourished throughout childhood suggested to him a hypothesis: the child's good nutritional status may lead to relatively early pubescent growth spurt and menarche and consequently, both developmentally and maturationally, an early confrontation with adolescent sexuality. Control over the developmental crisis is initiated by food refusal which "leads to a selective shutdown of sexual metabolism and hence its attendant arousal." [29]

tained, but with little sense of personal achievement, gain, or pleasure. The mothers tended to be ambitious, joyless women, often proud of their own accomplishments. Although reasonably successful, the fathers felt inferior. At home the fathers were apt to be warm but retiring. Characteristic of both parents was the intense interest in physical appearance, proper decorum, successful performance, and stellar accomplishments. Thinness and an appealing physical appearance were overvalued by the parents. The parents emphasized family values which they believed were culturally accepted, but with adolescence the child's conformity was frequently transmuted into an age-excessive rebellion.

The developmental histories of the younger patients revealed not only many similarities but also significant differences. As children they were also compliant. Oppositionalism was seldom apparent, at times detectable in the form of passive defiance and provocation, and expressed with considerable trepidation toward the mother. The form of discipline used by the parents of anorexia nervosa patients was difficult to categorize. The two dimensions of maternal behavior—Love versus Hostility and Control versus Autonomy —used in Schaefer's circumplex model of maternal behavior can be best applied to these mothers, who tended to be hostile and overcontrolling.[4]

In late latency the children were infantile and dependent on the mother, slavishly conforming to the mother's ambitions and expectations. Yet these children, compared to the other group, were given comparatively more freedom to express their needs, even if later nullified by authoritarian parental responses. As preschoolers, these children separated reluctantly from the mother; the first day at school was recalled with still vivid narratives of mother-child anguish over separation, and in adolescence, vestiges of separation anxiety persisted, often even after resolution of the eating disorder.*
The family constellation was greatly similar to that of the older group: again emphasis on performance, achievement, form, fitness, good health, and vigor through diet and a sense of "normality." On psychological testing (MMPI), they were detected as dissimulators of pathology, individuals who wished to conceal personal inadequacy and low self-esteem.[57, 58] Likewise, delay and control of gratification patterns and mastery of the body and its functions were vital to the humorless parents. Their capacity for pleasure was minimal. In their peer group they were awkward socially and frequently rejected for their intellectual precocity. Physically, they were more mature. Pubescence had occurred early for them. Often the girls were ashamed of their early breast development and pubic hair. These children were not comfortable with younger children, with whom they could identify, and with middle-aged adults, most notably strict perfectionistic spinster schoolteachers.

With the onset of pubescence, the child's defensive posture was chal-

---

* King has also observed the high degree of separation anxiety in anorexic patients.[69]

lenged. Unlike many adolescent girls, they did not romanticize men; instead, they fantasied assault and violence. They perceived men as rascals who accost innocent little girls. The girls manifested defensive use of denial, intellectualization, ascetism, and reaction formation. In the face of puberty with its multiple meanings* (for instance, sexuality, freedom, push to separation from the mother, need for self-reliance without a sense of autonomy, and crisis in identity[62]), the children experienced severe anxiety and frustration.[39] Identity diffusion, so common in puberty, was heightened in these children.[41] With avoidance of the female sexual role, eating functions became overdetermined. Elective food refusal was the child's attempt to regain the mother and regressively sidestep the female sexual role. Frequently, increasing closeness to the father had become intolerable. In addition, the diet was an effort at establishing autonomy based on an identification model provided by the mother. In the male anorexia patient, however, the dynamic configuration, beyond basic sexual differences, varied considerably, as elaborated previously.

The classical formula for neurosis[49] is applicable to these children: regression to pregenital fixation points with heightened ambivalence and sexual-aggressive impulses, wishes, and fantasies. The resultant anxiety and guilt attendant on the drive regression result in defensive operations of the ego under the influence of the superego. Characterological or symptomatic compromise formation results, with exaggerations under stress of earlier personality modes, which for these children tend to be anywhere along the hysterical-obsessive characterological axis. (The hysterical children were often dependent, unreflective, and less perfectionistic and came from families where the oedipal conflict was more patent.) The gamut of hysterical and obsessive defenses is displaced in such abundance as to suggest to some investigators a panneurosis.[106]

Along with drive regression there is a concomitant functional regression of the ego[96] that overshadows the oral mechanisms found in anorexia nervosa. The pleasure from ego control and mastery, learned during the anal-muscular stage, is heightened. The ego turns against drive satisfaction; ego pleasure is now derived from control and mastery of the body, bodily movements, sensations and perceptions of bodily states. The highly analized ego functions are most clearly seen in perceptual and cognitive functions. Magical-omnipotent thinking is paramount. In short, cognitive and perceptual control becomes the leitmotiv of these children. Their style of

---

* It is possible that a pubescent girl can experience gastric distress (from changes in gastric motility) with increase in sexual metabolism. (A proportion of women taking estrogenic oral contraceptives report nausea and pregnancy "sensations" during the initial rise in estrogen levels.) Such physiological responses may well be the nidus for oral pregnancy fantasies, as well as a signal for avoidance-response between food and sexual arousal. Moulton's studies of a patient with cyclical vomiting demonstrated a correlation between vomiting and estrogenic activity.[83] Further psychophysiological research is needed along these lines.

thinking becomes more rigid, and their focal attention is markedly restricted to the task of limiting food intake. They seem unwilling to consider anything outside of eating and weight; they appear oblivious to their hostility, competitiveness, and power motives and attempt to hide behind innocence and suffering.[2, 98]

The ego pressure for control seems to outweigh oral drive gratification. In this light many of the signs and symptoms of anorexia nervosa can be dynamically understood. The goal of the anorexia nervosa patient is attainment of absolute power—of the body, self, parents, and other significant object relations.[100] The narcissistic pressure of attaining supreme thinness as modes of defiance and protest outweighs the realistic ugliness of cachexia and the gnawing of hunger; the pleasure from control dissociates bodily feelings from their visual impressions of their body; the pleasure from limitless energy and activity nullifies the ennui of fatigue; the pressure to attain "perfect performance" outdistances the high ego ideals of the parents; and the masochistic delight of suffering attenuates the pain of superego strain. Negativism preserves pride, restores control, repairs a precarious self-esteem, and gives pleasure in mastery. As a result, a diffuse personal identity with inadequate coping devices available is created.[90]

In the anorexia nervosa syndrome, power and control motives are apparent. Crisp referred to food refusal as control in the service of shutting down sexual metabolism.[29] Lesser pointed out the anorexic's "reversion to an infantile method of passive-hostile control in a family setting." [72] Theilgaard found control blatantly represented in the anorexic's psychological test protocols.[106] Selvini observed the dynamism of control and mastery vis-à-vis hunger and the body. She in fact referred to anorexia nervosa as "intrapersonal paranoia," "the search for power—[which] is experienced as impossible in interpersonal relationships and is carried out in the intrapersonal structures, in the fight against the body." [102] Bruch viewed the fatiguing power struggles which anorexic patients create as compensatory to their sense of ineffectiveness.[18] The pleasure components of food abstinence are recognized by King.[69] He pointed to the delight these patients take in inspecting their thin bodies and recording their daily weight loss. So impressed was King with the phenomenon of pleasure from food refusal that he used this criterion to distinguish anorexia nervosa from other psychogenic anorexias.[69]

The studies of Bruch, Selvini, and others have clearly demonstrated the role and importance of ego psychology in the understanding of anorexia nervosa. Nevertheless, the question remains: What are the ego disturbances in this disorder? A recent study, reported elsewhere,[103] of four anorexia nervosa patients (and nuclear families), diagnosed by generally accepted clinical criteria, but of different ages and of mixed sexes and psychiatric diagnoses, demonstrated, both in terms of clinical and psychological test results, that there is a wide range of conceptual and perceptual disturbances in anorexia nervosa. No distinctive psychophysiological dysfunction of appetite regulation was apparent. Neurotic and borderline anorexics varied markedly in regard to ego functions and defects.

What was common to the group of patients, as well as their families, was the exaggerated modes of ego function typical of the anal-muscular phase of development. At the toddler age these patients had been taught to conform to parental models of behavior, which stressed performance, achievement, fitness, and "perfect normality"—at the expense of self-esteem and a sense of competence.[111] With the approach of pubescence and renewed oedipal strivings, a drive regression and parallel ego-functional regression resulted, with increased analization of behavioral modes. Their cognitive and perceptual processes were more geared to control and mastery, which became more pleasurable than drive gratification. This style of ego-functional regression seems typical of patients with anorexia nervosa. Nevertheless, our findings do not explain individual differences in perceptual and cognitive function, between either patients or their families.[114] An intensive study of one family, with five daughters, two of whom have had anorexia nervosa, may provide some information in this direction.[78]

VII. TREATMENT

The natural history of anorexia nervosa is so variable—from a brief abortive anorexic episode of a chubby sexually frightened pubescent girl to a lifelong recurrent starvation in an amenorrheic, frigid, psychotic woman —that there can be no specific psychotherapeutic approach (just as there is no specific anorexia nervosa entity).[10, 65, 84, 107] Reports of treatment in anorexia nervosa indicate a failure rate of 25 to 50 per cent. The treatments vary from psychoanalytic[107] to psychosurgical,[97] from milieu ("substitute-parents")[51] to behavior therapy.[1, 64]

Significant weight loss and continuing determination to starve oneself are indications for inpatient treatment. What medical regimen and psychiatric therapy to employ is another matter. The literature abounds in therapeutic platitudes and clichés. Personally favored treatment methods are often passionately recommended. Insight therapy, once generally recommended, has been disparaged more recently by former enthusiasts.* [77] Kay and Leigh, in their 1942 study, concluded that psychotherapy was not the treatment of choice unless the patient was not seriously ill and chose to co-operate with her physician. They strongly recommended for resistive cachexic patients tube feeding, ECT, and even leucotomy. Since the late 1950's, however, bed confinement, regular feedings, either voluntary or forced, and Chlorpromazine have become the popular physical regimen for anorexia nervosa. Reduction of anxiety, stimulation of appetite, and an acceleration of metabolism are the goals of this regimen.[30, 34, 97]

---

* At one point it was suggested by several workers that the principal focus of psychotherapy should be on unconscious material involving oral impregnation.[109]

Reminiscent of the polemics over medical-surgical versus psychotherapeutic treatments of ulcerative colitis, Williams' study was a stark reminder
that anorexia nervosa is a wasting disease with a significant mortality.[113]
In pointing out the value of intubation as a lifesaving measure, however, implications arose that anorexia nervosa is a somatic disease, treatable by
somatic methods only. This debatable position precipitated a flurry of irate
letters to the editor of the *British Medical Journal* and obfuscated the main
point of the study. Regardless of its psychological import and symbolism,
intubation is a vitally necessary measure for the extremely cachexic patient
whose physical status suggests impending circulatory collapse.

Langford and Dunton have recommended an inpatient regimen for anorexia nervosa.[71] At the time of admission the patient should be told that
although the illness is not fundamentally caused by lack of appetite and by
starvation she will be expected to drink a high-protein substance (Sustagen),* 250 cc four times a day. She is told that the Sustagen for her is a
medicine as well as a food. Otherwise, the topics of appetite and eating are
generally avoided by the therapist in order to enhance a therapeutic alliance. The patient is also told that a period of two to three months of hospitalization is often required for treatment. She is told that discharge from the
hospital is not dependent on how much weight is gained. She is told that
both she and the therapist will know when the patient should go home.

Food-eating manipulations by the patient, as well as staff allegiances and
power tactics, can be avoided only through a concerted effort on the part of
the nursing and ancillary staffs. The nursing staff is instructed that regular
meals with some margin of personal selection should be given the patient,
but without cajoling, threats, pleas, or rewards. If the nursing staff is not
familiar with the power stratagems of the anorexia nervosa patient, the
therapist should regularly meet with the head nurse and staff.

After admission to the hospital and orientation, an exploratory-relation-
ship period with the patient is useful as a forerunner to future psychotherapy. Issues of mistrust and autonomy soon emerge in therapy. In following
his etiologic hypothesis of anorexia nervosa, Crisp indicates that an explanation of the patient's dieting behavior—a metabolic method for reducing
frightening sexual feelings and strengthening her tie with her mother—be
made with an invitation for further discussion.[30] Bruch recommends, especially in the early phase of therapy, active participation of the therapist with
key emphasis on the patient's recognition of needs, feelings, and impulses,
instead of motivational analyses and insight.[21] This technique is most helpful with anorexic patients with borderline ego integration. Structure and
meaning are given to the patient's experience, an approach also espoused by
DesLaurier for the treatment of child schizophrenia.[37] In instances where
the basic disturbance is neurotic, a motivational analytic technique is applicable after a relationship is established. In short, many anorexia nervosa

---

* Meade Johnson.

patients are accessible to psychotherapy, but the psychotherapeutic approach, of course, must be fashioned to the individual patient. As therapy unfolds, the specific meanings of the ego-functional regression (the pleasure from control and mastery) and the need to deny feelings of helplessness are understood and worked through. The patient must learn to substitute self-sufficiency for perverted power. Frequently, conjoint family therapy is useful in giving the patient greater self-awareness and initiative, and for the neurotic pubescent girl, more awareness of sexual fears and oedipal conflicts.

VIII. FOLLOW-UP STUDIES

Because of the wide quantitative and qualitative spectrum of the anorexia nervosa syndrome, statements about natural history are difficult to make and even harder to evaluate. Follow-up reports are not always meaningful. (Follow-up criteria may include any combination of factors: eating behavior, weight change, sexual function, menstrual history, mortality, and morbidity.)

Follow-up claims from the literature are given in Table 15-9. It is obvious that the findings, among other things, represent differences in diagnostic criteria and patient population.[115] On the basis of their study, Kay and Schapira indicate that scrutiny of three factors—(1) patient's relationship with parents, (2) type and severity of personality deviation, and (3) depth and direction of actual conflict over food—can provide prognostic information for the individual patient.[66] No reference is made to the efficacy of various therapeutic approaches.

From the follow-up information, one must conclude that for most facets of this syndrome, each anorexia nervosa patient must be individualized. There are few axioms or statistical truisms that apply absolutely to this variegated syndrome. But patients with hysterical personality traits have a better prognosis than those with compulsive and schizoid traits.[72] And in general, about one-third of the patients recover spontaneously.

IX. SUMMARY

The need for psychiatric research in anorexia nervosa is apparent on several grounds. First of all, it is one of the few psychiatric illnesses that can result in death. In terms of chronic psychopathology and sexual dysfunction, the disorder has a relatively high morbidity rate.

Besides being a therapeutic challenge, anorexia nervosa has stimulated much thinking and speculation in regard to its pathogenesis and nosology. Research in anorexia nervosa has also contributed to our knowledge of drive theory, ego functions and mechanisms, family psychopathology, dynamics, and metacommunication patterns.

In this review, the history of the concept of anorexia nervosa is pre-

Table 15–9.   Follow-Up Results for the Anorexia Nervosa Syndrome

---

1. Variable in mortality and morbidity. From a short-term single illness to a persistent disorder resulting in death.[72]
2. Development of disorder in an adolescent, despite its apparent severity, does not necessarily imply a deep-rooted psychoneurosis or psychotic tendency.[44]
3. High frequency of relapse and of partial recoveries. Menstrual irregularities, disturbances in appetite, and low or fluctuating weight common. Sexual adjustment seldom achieved. Fifteen per cent die from the illness or its complications.[65]
4. Outcome depends on the nature of the conflict and the type of personality. Predominantly "hysterical" personality traits augur a better prognosis than predominantly schizoid or compulsive traits.[72]
5. Patients developing the disorder after 18 years of age are "atypical," with symptoms and course distinctly different from the puberty group.[107]
6. Two-thirds of the patients recover or improve; one-quarter relapse; and 7 per cent die.[3]
7. Neurotic symptoms or personality defects are found at follow-up, and social and sexual adjustment is impaired. Schizophrenia is an uncommon development unless characteristic symptoms are present at an early stage.[66]
8. Nearly 50 per cent of the patients married; only one-third still report health problems, and most of them are minor.[115]

---

sented. The studies of Bliss and Branch, Bruch, Thoma, Selvini, and others are discussed. The criteria for a phenomenological definition of anorexia nervosa are examined. Primary and secondary signs and symptoms, as well as resultant signs and symptoms of anorexia nervosa, are presented. Recent metabolic studies are reviewed. Differential diagnostic aspects are examined, and the concept of primary and secondary anorexia is analyzed. Psychodynamic formulations, often found in anorexia nervosa patients, are given; and typical developmental histories of anorexia nervosa patients are delineated. Treatment and follow-up studies are reviewed.

Research on the conceptual and perceptual disturbances in anorexia nervosa demonstrates a variety of disturbances in these patients. Dysfunction in appetite regulation, primary defects in body-image, and enteroceptive perceptual and conceptual disturbances are not uniformly found in anorexia nervosa.

It is concluded that although anorexia nervosa is a syndrome with a distinctive phenomenology, there is little clinically to justify its classification as a specific nosological entity. The anorexia nervosa syndrome is found in a wide range of psychopathology. In pubescent and pubertal girls, anorexia nervosa is usually a neurotic disorder; in older females and in male patients, it is often part of a borderline to blatant psychosis.

There are, however, some similarities for all anorexia nervosa patients in developmental and family dynamics. In particular, a style of ego-functional regression is characteristic of patients with anorexia nervosa, but it does not explain individual differences in cognitive and perceptual function.

References

1. BACHRACH, A. J., W. J. ERWIN, and J. P. MAHR. "The Control of Eating Behavior in an Anorexic by Operant Conditioning Techniques," in L. P. ULLMAN and L. KRAMER, eds., *Case Studies in Behavior Modification*. New York: Holt, Rinehart, and Winston, 1965.
2. BARNETT, J. "On Cognitive Disorders in the Obsessional," *Contemporary Psychoanalysis*, II (1966), 121.
3. BECK, J. C., and K. BROCKNER-MORTENSEN. "Observations on the Prognosis in Anorexia Nervosa," *Acta. Med. Scan.*, CXLIX (1954), 409.
4. BECKER, W. C. "Consequences of Different Kinds of Parental Discipline," in N. L. HOFFMAN and L. W. HOFFMAN, eds., *Review of Child Development Research*. New York: Russell Sage Foundation, 1964, I, 169.
5. BERGEN, L. VAN, et al. "Anorexia Nervosa: A Study of 38 Patients," *Ned. T. Geneesk.*, CV (1961), 464.
6. BERKMANN, J. M. "Anorexia Nervosa: The Diagnosis and Treatment of Inanition Resulting from Functional Disorders," *Annals of Internal Medicine*, XXII (1945), 679.
7. BERKMANN, J. M., C. A. OWEN, JR., and T. B. MAGATH. "Physiological Aspects of Anorexia Nervosa," *Postgraduate Medicine*, II (1952), 407.
8. BERLIN, I. N., et al. "Adolescent Alternation of Anorexia and Obesity. Workshop," *American Journal of Orthopsychiatry*, XV (1945), 65.
9. BINSWANGER, L. "The Case of Ellen West," in R. MAY, E. ANGEL, and H. ELLENBERGER, eds., *Existence*. New York: Basic Books, 1958, pp. 237–364.
10. BLISS, E. L., and C. BRANCH. *Anorexia Nervosa*. New York: Hoeber, 1960.
11. BLISS, E. L., and C. J. MIGEM. "Endocrinology of Anorexia Nervosa," *Journal of Clinical Endocrinology*, XVII (1957), 766.
12. BLITZER, J. R., N. ROLLINGS, and A. BLACKWELL. "Children Who Starve Themselves: Anorexia Nervosa," *Psychosomatic Medicine*, XXIII (1961), 369.
13. BREUER, J., and S. FREUD. *Studies on Hysteria 1893*, trans. A. A. BRILL. New York: Nervous and Mental Disease Publishing Co., 1937.
14. BROBECK, J. R. "Regulation of Feeding and Drinking," in J. FIELD, ed., *Handbook of Physiology*, Section I: Neurophysiology. Washington, D.C.: American Physiological Society, 1960, p. 1197.
15. BRUCH, H. "Psychopathology of Hunger and Appetite," in G. E. DANIELS and S. RADO, eds., *Changing Concepts of Psychoanalytic Medicine*. New York: Grune and Stratton, 1956.
16. BRUCH, H. "Transformation of Oral Impulses in Eating Disorders," *Psychiatry Quarterly*, XXXV (1961), 458.
17. BRUCH, H. "Falsification of Bodily Needs and Body Concept in Schizophrenia," *Archives of General Psychiatry*, VI (1962), 18.

18. BRUCH, H. "Perceptual and Conceptual Disturbances in Anorexia Nervosa," *Psychosomatic Medicine,* XXIV (1962), 187.
19. BRUCH, H. "Anorexia Nervosa and Its Differential Diagnosis," *Journal of Nervous and Mental Disease,* CXLI (1966), 555.
20. BRUCH, H., personal communication, 1966.
21. BRUCH, H. "Psychotherapy with Schizophrenia," *A.M.A. Archives of General Psychiatry,* XIV (1966), 346.
22. BRUCH, H., *et al.* "Adipositas: Panel Discussion on the Theory of Hilde Bruch," *Acta Psychiat. et Neurol. Scandinavica,* XXXIII (1958), 151, Fasc. 2.
23. CAPLAN, G., and S. LEBOVICI, eds. *Psychiatric Approaches to Adolescence.* Amsterdam: Excerpta Medica Foundation, 1966.
24. CARRYER, H. M., J. M. BERKMANN, and H. L. MASON. "Relative Lymphocytosis in Anorexia Nervosa," *Proceedings of Staff Meeting of the Mayo Clinic,* XXXIV (1959), 425.
25. CODDINGTON, R. D., H. BRUCH, and J. KELLER. "Gastric Perceptivity in Normal, Obese and Schizophrenic Subjects," paper presented at the Annual Meeting of the American Psychosomatic Society, 1963.
26. CODDINGTON, R. D., and W. KOHLER. "The Relation between Maternal Affect and Gastric Secretion in Twin Infants," paper presented at the Annual Meeting of the American Psychosomatic Society, 1966.
27. CODDINGTON, R. D., J. A. SOURS, and H. BRUCH. "Electrogastrographic Findings Associated with Affective Changes," *American Journal of Psychiatry,* CXXI (1964), 41.
28. CRISP, A. H. "Clinical and Therapeutic Aspects of Anorexia Nervosa. A Study of 30 Cases," *Journal of Psychosomatic Research,* IX (1965), 67.
29. CRISP, A. H. "Some Aspects of the Evolution, Presentation and Follow-Up of Anorexia Nervosa," *Proceedings of the Royal Society of Medicine,* LVIII (1965), 814.
30. CRISP, A. H. "A Treatment Regime for Anorexia Nervosa," *British Journal of Psychiatry,* CXII (1965), 505.
31. DALBIEZ, R. *The Psychoanalytic Method and the Doctrine of Freud.* London: Longmans, Green, 1941, I, 295.
32. DALLY, P. J. "Carotenaemia Occurring in a Case of Anorexia Nervosa," *British Medical Journal,* I (1959), 1333.
33. DALLY, P., and W. SARGENT. "A New Treatment for Anorexia Nervosa," *British Medical Journal,* I (1960), 1770.
34. DALLY, P., and W. SARGENT, "Treatment and Outcome of Anorexia Nervosa," *British Medical Journal,* II (1966), 793.
35. DEGRAEFF, J., A. KASSENAAR, and M. A. M. SCHUURS. "Balance Studies during Refeeding in Anorexia Nervosa," *Metabolism,* IX (1960), 814.
36. DEJERINE, J., and E. GANCKLER. *The Neuroses and Their Treatment by Psychotherapy.* London: 1915.
37. DESLAURIER, A. M. *The Experience of Reality in Childhood Schizophrenia.* New York: International Universities Press, 1962.
38. DUBOIS, F. S. "Compulsion Neurosis with Cachexia (Anorexia Nervosa)," *American Journal of Psychiatry,* CVI (1949), 107.

39. DUCHE, D. J., W. A. SCHONFELD, and S. TOMKIEWICZ. "Physical Aspects of Adolescent Development," in CAPLAN and LEBOVICI, op. cit.

40. EITINGER, L. "Der Parallelismus zwischen dem KZ-Syndrom und der Chronischen Anorecia Nervosa," in J. E. MEYER and H. FELDMANN, eds., Anorexia Nervosa, Symposium am 24./25. April 1965 in Göttingen. Stuttgart: Georg Thieme Verlag, 1965.

41. ERIKSON, E. "The Problem of Ego Identity," Journal of the American Psychoanalysis Association, IV (1956), 56.

42. FAIRBAIRN, W. R. D. "A Revised Psychopathology of the Psychoses and Psychoneuroses," International Journal of Psychoanalysis, London, XXII (1941), 250.

43. FALSTEIN, E. I., S. C. FEINSTEIN, and I. JUDAS. "Anorexia Nervosa in the Male Child," American Journal of Orthopsychiatry, XXVI (1956), 751.

44. FARQUHARSON, R. F., and H. H. HYLAND. "Anorexia Nervosa: The Course of 15 Patients Treated from 20 to 30 Years Previously," Canadian Medical Association Journal, XCIV (1966), 411.

45. FENICHEL, O. The Psychoanalytic Theory of Neurosis. New York: Norton, 1945, p. 175.

46. FERRARA, A., and V. J. FONTANA. "Celiac Disease and Anorexia Nervosa," New York State Journal of Medicine, LXVI (1966), 1000.

47. FINCH, J. R. "Scientific Models and Their Application in Psychiatric Models," A.M.A. Archives of General Psychiatry, XV (1966), 1.

48. FINCH, S. M. Fundamentals of Child Psychiatry. New York: Norton, 1960.

49. FREUD, A. Normality and Pathology in Childhood. New York: International Universities Press, 1965.

50. FREUD, S. "From the History of an Infantile Neurosis," in Standard Edition of the Complete Psychological Works, Vol. 17. London: Hogarth, 1957.

51. GROEN, J. J., and Z. FELDMAN-TOLEDANO. "Educative Treatment of Patients and Parents in Anorexia Nervosa," British Journal of Psychiatry, CXII (1966), 671.

52. GULL, W. W. "Anorexia Nervosa (Apepsia Hysterica, Anorexia Hysteria)," Transactions of the Clinical Society of London, VII (1874), 22.

53. Guntrip, H. "A Study of Fairbairn's Theory of Schizoid Reactions," British Journal of Medicine and Psychology, XXV (1952), 86.

54. HARLOW, H. F., and M. K. HARLOW. "Social Deprivation in Monkeys," Scientific American, CCVII (1962), 136.

55. HEBB, D. O. The Organization of Behavior. New York: Wiley, 1949.

56. HULTGREN, H. N. "Clinical and Laboratory Observations in Severe Starvation," Stanford Medical Bulletin, IX (1951), 175.

57. HUNT, H. F. "The Effective of Deliberate Deception on Minnesota Multiphasic Personality Inventory Performance," Journal of Consulting Psychology, XII (1948), 396.

58. HUNT, H. F. "The Differentiation of Malingering Dissimulation, and Pathology," in press.

59. ISHIKAWA, K. Über die Eltern von Anorexia-nervosa-Kranken," in MEYER and FELDMANN, op. cit., p. 154.

60. JESSNER, L., and D. W. ABSE. "Regressive Forces in Anorexia Nervosa," British Journal of Medicine and Psychology, XXXIII (1960), 301.

61. JORES, A., and E. THEIREMANN. "Experiences from the Treatment of Thirty Cases of Anorexia Nervosa," Third European Conference on Psychosomatic Research, Copenhagen, 1957.

62. KAGAN, J. "Acquisition and Significance of Sex Typing and Sex Role Identity," in HOFFMAN and HOFFMANN, *op. cit.*, I, 137.

63. KASSENAAR, A., J. DEGRAEFF, and A. T. KOUWENHOVEN. "N$_{15}$-Glycine Studies of Protein Synthesis during Refeeding in Anorexia Nervosa," *Metabolism*, IX (1960), 831.

64. KAUFER, F. H., and J. S. PHILLIPS. "Behavior Therapy," *A.M.A. Archives of General Psychiatry*, XV (1966), 114.

65. KAY, D. W. K., and D. LEIGH. "Natural History, Treatment and Prognosis of Anorexia Nervosa, Based on a Study of 38 Patients," *Journal of Mental Science*, C (1952), 411.

66. KAY, D. W. K., and K. SCHAPIRA. "The Prognosis in Anorexia Nervosa," in MEYER and FELDMANN, *op. cit.*

67. KESSEN, W. "Research in the Psychological Development of Infants: An Overview," *Merrill-Palmer Quarterly*, IX (1963), 83.

68 KEYS, A., *et al.* The Biology of Human Starvation, Vol. I. Minneapolis: University of Minnesota Press, 1950.

69. KING, A. "Primary and Secondary Anorexia Nervosa Syndromes," *British Journal of Psychiatry*, CIX (1963), 470.

70. KOLB, L. C. "The Body Image in the Schizophrenic Reaction," in A. AUERBACH, ed., *Schizophrenia*. New York: Ronald, 1959.

71. LANGFORD, W. S., and H. D. DUNTON. "Psychodynamic Study of Pubescent Girls with Anorexia Nervosa," in preparation.

72. LESSER, L. I., *et al.* "Anorexia Nervosa in Children," *American Journal of Orthopsychiatry*, XXX (1960), 572.

73. McKNEW, D. H., and J. A. SOURS. "The Psychiatric Ecology and Dynamics of an Anorexia Nervosa Family," in press.

74. MAIER, H. W. Three Theories of Child Development. New York: Harper and Row, 1965.

75. MALLER, O. "The Late Psychopathology of Former Concentration Camp Inmates," *Psychiatry and Neurology, Basel*, CXLVIII (1964), 140.

76. MARKS, V., and R. G. BANNISTER. "Pituitary and Adrenal Function in Undernutrition with Mental Illness (Including Anorexia Nervosa)," *British Journal of Psychiatry*, CIX (1963), 480.

77. MEYER, B. C., and L. A. WEINROTH. "Observations on Psychological Aspects of Anorexia Nervosa: Report of a Case," *Psychosomatic Medicine*, XIX (1957), 389.

78. MEYER, J. "Why People Get Hungry," *Nutrition Today*, I (1966), 1.

79. MEYER, J. E. "Diagnostische Einseilungen und Diagnosen in die Psychiatrie," in H. W. GRUKLE *et al.*, eds., *Psychiatrie der Gegenwart*. Berlin: Springer, 1960.

80. MEYER, J. E. "Des Syndrom der Anorexia Nervosa," *Archiv für Psychiatrie, Berlin*, CCII (1961), 31.

81. MEYER, J. E., and FELDMANN, eds., *op. cit.*

82. MOULTON, R. "Psychosomatic Implications of Pseudocyesis," *Psychosomatic Medicine*, IV (1942), 376.

83. MOULTON, R. "A Psychosomatic Study of Anorexia Nervosa, Including the Uses of Vaginal Smears," *Psychosomatic Medicine*, IV (1942), 62.

84. NEMIAH, J. C. "Anorexia Nervosa: Clinical Psychiatric Study," *Medicine*, XXIX (1950), 225.

85. OBERDISSE, L., G. SOLBACH, and H. ZIMMERMAN. "Die endokrinologischen Aspekte der Anorexia nervosa," in MEYER and FELDMANN, *op. cit.*

86. PFLANZ, M. "Sozialanthropologische Aspekte der Anorexia Nervosa," in MEYER and FELDMANN, *op. cit.*, p. 146.

87. PIAGET, J. *The Construction of Reality in the Child*. New York: Basic Books, 1954.

88. QUAADE, F. *Obese Children. Anthropology and Environment*. Copenhagen: Dansk Videnskabs Forlag A/S, 1955.

89. RAHMAN, L., H. B. RICHARDSON, and H. S. RIPLEY. "Anorexia Nervosa with Psychiatric Observations," *Psychosomatic Medicine*, I (1939), 335.

90. RAPAPORT, D. "Cognitive Structure," in *Contemporary Approaches to Cognition*. Cambridge, Mass.: Harvard University Press, 1957, p. 157.

91. REIFENSTEIN, E. C. "Psychogenic or 'Hypothalamic' Amenorrhea," *Medical Clinic of North America* (1946), p. 1103.

92. ROLLINS, N., and A. BLACKWELL. "Anorexia Nervosa," paper presented at the Sixth International Child Psychiatry Congress, Edinburgh, July 1966.

93. RUSSELL, G. F. M. "Dietetic Treatment of Patients with Anorexia Nervosa," *Nutrition*, XIV (1960), 1.

94. RUSSELL, G. F. M. "Metabolic Aspects of Anorexia Nervosa," *Proceedings of the Royal Society of Medicine*, LVIII (1965), 811.

95. RUSSELL, G. F. M., *et al.* "Gonadotrophin and Oestrogen Excretion in Patients with Anorexia Nervosa," *Journal of Psychosomatic Research*, IX (1965), 79.

96. SANDLER, J., and W. G. JOFFE. "Notes on Obsessional Manifestations in Children," *Psychoanalytic Study of the Child*, XX (1965), 425.

97. SARGENT, W., E. SLATER, and P. DALLY. *Physical Methods of Treatment in Psychiatry*, 4th ed. London: Livingstone, 1963.

98. SCHACHTEL, E. G. *Metamorphosis*. New York: Basic Books, 1959, p. 251.

99. SCHIELE, B. C., and J. BROZEK. "Experimental Neurosis Resulting from Semistarvation in Man," *Psychosomatic Medicine*, X (1948), 31.

100. SEARLES, H. F. "The Effort to Drive the Other Person Crazy," *British Journal of Medical Psychology*, XXXII (1959), 1.

101. SELVINI, M. P. *L'Anoressia Mentale*. Milan: Feltrinelli, 1963.

102. SELVINI, M. P. "Interpretation of Mental Anorexia," in MEYER and FELDMANN, *op. cit.*

103. SOURS, J. A. "Conceptual and Perceptual Disturbances in Anorexia Nervosa," in press.

104. SYDENHAM, A. "Amenorrhea at Stanley Camp, Hong Kong, during Internment," *British Medical Journal*, II (1946), 159.

105. SYLVESTER, E. "Analysis of Psychogenic Anorexia and Vomiting in a Four-Year-Old Child," *Psychoanalytic Study of the Child*, I (1945), 167.

106. THEILGAARD, A. "Psychological Testing of Patients with Anorexia Nervosa," in MEYER and FELDMANN, *op. cit.*

107. THOMA, H. *Anorexia Nervosa*. Bern-Stuttgart: Huber-Klett, 1961.

108. TOLSTRUP, K. "Die Charakteristika der jungeren Falle van Anorexia Nervosa," in MEYER and FELDMANN, *op. cit.*, p. 51.

109. WALLER, J. F., M. R. KAUFMAN, and F. DEUTSCH. "Anorexia Nervosa," *Psychosomatic Medicine,* II (1940), 3.

110. WEINBERG, N., M. MENDELSON, and A. STUNKARD. "A Failure to Find Distinctive Personality Features in a Group of Obese Men," *American Journal of Psychiatry,* CXVII (1961), 1035.

111. WHITE, R. W. *Ego and Reality in Psychoanalytic Theory,* Psychological Issues, Monograph II, Vol. 3. New York: International Universities Press, 1963.

112. WIGLEY, R. D. "Potassium Deficiency in Anorexia Nervosa, with References to Renal Tubular Vacuolation," *British Medical Journal,* II (1960), 110.

113. WILLIAMS, E. "Anorexia Nervosa: Somatic Disorder," *British Medical Journal,* I (1958), 190.

114. WITKIN, H. A. "The Problem of Individuality in Development," in B. KAPLAN and S. WAPNER, eds., *Perspectives in Psychological Theory*. New York: International Universities Press, 1960, p. 335.

115. ZIEGLER, R., and J. A. Sours. "Follow-Up Studies in Anorexia Nervosa," in press.

16

Obesity in Adolescence

Hilde Bruch

Obesity (enlarged body size due to excessive accumulation of fat tissue) is a complex, far from uniform clinical condition with disturbances in many areas. There is evidence of genetic factors, of disordered regulatory mechanisms, of differences in the endowment with fat cells, of disturbances in the deposition and release of fatty acids, and of other metabolic or endocrine malfunctioning. This diversity holds true for any age group, but it is particularly apparent during adolescence. Excess weight may be a sign of a temporary imbalance during this active period of growth, or, at the other extreme, a symptom of long-standing and ominous maldevelopment with obesity as the most visible manifestation, or in extremely rare cases, of organic brain disease.[9]

It looks as if clinical interest and obesity research have gone through definite cycles. During the thirties concepts of endocrine malfunctioning dominated the field.[2] Early psychiatric studies were as much preoccupied with proving the irrelevance of the endocrine factors as with establishing definite psychodynamic syndromes. Now, during the sixties, there is renewed emphasis on constitutional factors, on various patterns of interaction between neuroendocrine regulation and metabolic disorder, on the importance of inactivity as well as overnutrition, and a much more open-minded approach to what constitutes psychiatric problems and how they are interrelated with the physiological factors.[20] Characteristically modern investigators acknowledge the existence of different types of obesity. It remains a puzzle why so many then proceed to describe the topic of their particular interest as being relevant for all obese patients. It appears to be quite difficult to maintain a truly multidimensional position and to integrate various factors into one's own considerations.

Obesity may be associated with every conceivable psychiatric disorder, with neurosis as well as psychosis; and it may occur in otherwise healthy

213

individuals. The degree of involvement with the apparent psychiatric condition varies widely. Serious mental illness may occur in obese people without a relevant relationship between the two conditions, and, at the other extreme, obesity and paralyzing inactivity and excessive food intake, which contribute to its development and maintenance, may be core problems in serious maldevelopment of the total personality.

It is also necessary to differentiate between the psychological problems that play a role in the development of obesity, those that are created by the obese state, and finally, the problems that are precipitated by efforts at reducing. Furthermore, the problems during the active progressive phase of obesity, with its dramatic increase in weight, need to be differentiated from those encountered in people who have arrived at the stationary stage of obesity, with stable weight. To differentiate between stages of illness is of utmost importance in anorexia nervosa, where the refusal to eat provoked a complete change in the patterns of intrafamilial interaction.[6, 16]

Western culture is so hostile and derogatory to even mild degrees of overweight that every obese person faces some problems in his social relations, adolescents in particular, all of whom are struggling for self-respect and a respected identity in the adult world. However, some recent studies have overstressed this factor, as if it were the chief cause for the psychological difficulties of obese adolescents.[21, 22] In my own experience, based on the longitudinal study of a large group of fat children, this condemning cultural attitude is most damaging for those who arrive at puberty, due to confusing early experiences, with low self-esteem and poor body-image.[7, 9]

In evaluating the influence of social factors, the importance of cultural attitudes and socioeconomic class needs to be considered.[10] Observations derived from the midtown study in Manhattan documented the powerful influence of social class on the prevalence of obesity in an urban population, showing, for example, that only 5 per cent of upper-class women were obese, as compared to 30 per cent of lower-class women.[23] It has been claimed that prevailing concepts on the psychopathology of obesity have been derived, to a large extent, from intensive psychotherapy of upper-class patients and that they do not apply to lower-class people.

My own observations are based on several quite distinct population groups. The earliest observations were made in the pediatric outpatient department of a large hospital in New York City during the depression years. Most patients were of lower middle-class or lower-class status. A large percentage were children of recent immigrants. Many had been referred to the obesity clinic by a school physician or some other clinic in the Medical Center. Conspicuous was the bewilderment of the mothers, who could not understand why anybody should object to a child's being big and plump. This group was followed into early adulthood. The figures are incomplete and represent only approximate percentages of the outcome.[7, 8] Less than one-third "outgrew" the condition during adolescence, with the encouragement of friends or by separating from their homes without too much difficulty. More than half of the group had remained obese. A few had made a good general adjustment, though moderately overweight. In these cases the parents had not been anxiously preoccupied with the obese state of their children, who had been exposed to the least amount of treatment. The majority of those who had remained fat or had grown superobese showed evidence of serious emotional and mental disease; quite a few were frankly psychotic.

It appears that a generalized statement that obesity in lower-class individuals is not associated with serious maladjustment is not justified, and certainly not in relation to children and adolescents. The concept of developmental obesity as a preschizophrenic state was formulated on the basis of observation in this lower-class group. This concept was found to be relevant for the upper-class patients who were studied during intensive psychotherapy later.[10, 11]

It is also not justified to consider all cases of "juvenile obesity" as representing a uniform group.[21] The erroneous impression that early obesity is always a sign of serious maladjustment may be gained if one considers only individuals who have become fat adults. By evaluating psychological factors and the dynamics of the family interaction, it is possible to differentiate between children and adolescents who have a good prognosis and those who are emotionally disturbed.[7, 9] In retrospective evaluation the Draw-a-Person test was found to be of greatest prognostic significance. Most children who had done well on the Draw-a-Person test had "outgrown" their obesity or had turned into competent, though overweight, adults. Those with poor performance on the Draw-a-Person test were poorly adjusted, had severe personality problems, or had even become psychotic; many had become progressively more obese.[11]

The understanding not only of obesity but of adolescence itself has suffered from the tendency to draw generalized conclusions from so-called "age norms"; this criticism applies to the study of its physical as well as its psychological aspects. Adolescence is the period in man's life that bridges the gap between childhood and adult maturity. It is a time of rapid changes in physical size and bodily functions, in personality development, and in a subject's role in society. The specific biologic event of the adolescent years is puberty, the maturing of the sex organs and the development of secondary sexual characteristics. This point has been emphasized so much that often it is not stressed enough that it is also the time when an individual attains his mature size and stature.

Human growth follows a specific human pattern, rigid in its sequence, but varying considerably from one individual to another in intimate details. Growth curves based on average figures tend to conceal the magnitude of the events that take place in an individual child. Puberty is related to other processes of growth. Stature growth precedes a gain in weight, which also takes place before and at puberty. This gain in weight, the filling-out process, is greater in girls than in boys. Of the various factors involved in this

complex process of growth, nutrition appears to be the one most determined by external conditions and seemingly most under the influence of the
voluntary action of an individual.

In the psychological study of adolescence, psychoanalytic theory has
dominated the field to such an extent that many of its assumptions are just
repeated as if they were facts. There is a feeling that since we "know" the
schedule of psychosexual development during childhood, we are prepared
to see the various stages through which the child supposedly has progressed
repeated and re-enacted at puberty.

These concepts of psychic determinism and repetition stand in contrast
to modern, dynamic concepts of growth and development.[1] The organism
has no time to waste on repetition, and the functional problems to be dealt
with at each period are determined by the demands of the new situation and
the organism's inherited or acquired ability to deal with them. Challenging
the concept of "repetition" implies no denial of the importance of childhood experiences. However, they are here conceived of as precursors, as the
developmental phases during which the necessary tools are acquired that
will make it possible to deal with new demands. To the extent that an individual is properly equipped he will succeed and grow up healthy; if he has
developed defects or deficiencies in his physiologic regulation and psychologic orientation, he will suffer from symptoms of varying severity in his
sense of self-regulation and efficacy.

I shall focus here on a question that has found little attention in psychiatric and psychoanalytic literature, namely, how does an individual achieve
a sense of ownership of his own body, the awareness of being a self-directed
separate organism, with the ability to identify bodily urges, to define his
needs, and to present them to himself or to the environment in such a way
that they can find appropriate satisfying responses? Psychological studies of
adolescence have focused on the achievement of "identity" in a psychological sense and on attaining adaptive maturity for sexual and interpersonal
intimacy.

The neglect of how we develop the feeling of being at ease with our adult
body and its functions, of how biological identity is established, might suggest that it usually develops so smoothly that we take it for granted. Observations on many patients with severe emotional problems who had grown
obese during childhood or adolescence revealed one common feature: the
feeling of not being in control of their sensations and actions. They lacked
discriminating awareness of the signals of bodily urges and also the sense of
emotional and interpersonal effectiveness. Specifically, they were unable to
recognize hunger and satiation or to discriminate between bodily discomfort and psychological tension, suffering from a basic misconception of not
being an independent self and a conviction of being the misshapen and
wrong product of somebody else's action.

The question of ownership of the body has not been entirely overlooked
in psychoanalytic writings. It has been dealt with in characteristic over-

generalized fashion, such as "until puberty the child's body is the mother's property." Such a statement contains a basic error, namely, that of not differentiating between external action and inner experience. True, until adolescence it is part of a mother's function to provide or supervise her child's hygienic care. But becoming aware of one's own sensations and needs and learning to define and express them in a distinct way are part of a development that begins in earliest infancy and progresses throughout childhood. Self-awareness of functional separateness does not suddenly spring into existence during adolescence, though there may be a daring testing out of the limits of one's strength and ability and a reckless struggle to have one's independence recognized in every area.

Applied to food, to eat what one wants is considered an adult privilege, and the adolescent, in this transition, is rudely outspoken about refusing or demanding certain foods. In spite of his extravagant food fads the healthy adolescent "knows" and is sure of what and how much he wants to eat. His self-regulation is in harmony with his physiological requirements, though there may be a temporary imbalance with a mild degree of thinness or plumpness during the period of most active growth.

This self-regulation appears grossly disturbed in adolescents who grow fat or become cachetic not on the basis of an organic defect, but on account of a deficit in their awareness of and control over bodily needs. It appears now that the old reproach of obese people as having "no will power" describes an important deficit in their functioning related, in part at least, to their inability to recognize their bodily needs. Not being clearly aware of bodily sensations, they cannot exercise control over their functions. The frustrating clinical experience that many fat people do well when their lives and habits are regulated from the outside, only to relapse when left to their own devices, is in good agreement with these considerations.

The idea of "hunger" as a learned experience may sound debatable, even farfetched. Yet it was a physiologist, Hebb, who first demonstrated that eating behavior contains important learned features, that even in a rat certain learning must be acquired for appropriate food-seeking behavior, and that cognitive factors must be considered when "hunger" and "satiation" are studied in the mature animal. In humans, with their much more complex brain organization, the ways of learning are also more complex.[18]

Hebb feels that this learning aspect has been overlooked because it does not fit into the concept of hunger as an innate drive, or of an alternative sensation to the physiological signs of food deprivation, conceptions that are taken for granted in clinical medicine. Psychoanalysis bases its whole theoretical structure on the assumption that the organism is inhabited by certain "drives" or "instincts" which, during various stages of psychosexual development, progress and mature, or, through vicissitudes in the life experiences, become "fixated," or "regress" at times of emotional crisis. Obesity is considered the result of some disturbances during the "oral stage" when an infant's drives are supposedly centered around his mouth.

Psychoanalytic studies have played an important role in the understanding of obesity. They helped to recognize that food could be symbolically equated with an insatiable desire for unobtainable love, but also with inhibited destructive impulses. It may stand for self-indulgence or substitute for sexual gratification and the wish to be pregnant, and also for punishment of forbidden impulses. Preoccupation with food may appear as helpless, dependent clinging to the parents or as hostile rejection of them. One could easily enlarge this list. If I do not do so it is not because I underestimate the value of clarifying the underlying meaning of a patient's disturbed behavior, but because in the course of my work it has become gradually apparent that this interpretive mode of inquiry fails to deal with some other, probably more basic, problems, namely, the question of *how* bodily functions become symbolically represented in the brain and thus available for accurate use, or, as in the anorexic and obese, for indiscriminate misuse.[12, 13] Abnormal eating habits do not occur in isolation, but are associated with other difficulties in the area of active or passive self-awareness and in the sense of identity. Conspicuous in the young obese is the failure to develop muscular skills and to derive pleasure from sports and athletics.

In an effort to understand how early learning could be influenced by the environment and how faulty parental attitudes may be transmitted to a child, I felt it necessary to construct a simplified conceptual model of the transactions in human development. I have come to assume that there are two basic forms of behavior that need to be differentiated, namely, behavior that is initiated in the individual and behavior in response to stimuli from the outside. This distinction applies to both the biologic and the social-emotional field and also to pleasure- or pain-producing states. Behavior in relation to the child can be classified as stimulating and responsive. The interaction between the environment and the infant can be rated as appropriate or inappropriate, depending on whether it serves the survival and development of the organism or disregards it. These elementary distinctions permit the dynamic analysis, irrespective of the specific area or content of the problem, of an amazingly large variety of clinical situations.

Appropriate responses to clues coming from the infant, initially in the biological field and subsequently in the social and emotional field, are significant building stones for the development of self-awareness and self-effectiveness. If confirmation and reinforcement of his own initially rather undifferentiated needs and impulses has been absent or has been contradictory or inaccurate, a child will grow up perplexed when trying to differentiate between disturbances in his biological field and emotional and interpersonal experiences, and he will be apt to misinterpret deformities in his self-body concept as externally induced. Thus he will become an individual deficient in his sense of separateness, with "diffuse ego boundaries," and will feel helpless under the influence of external forces.

Detailed reconstruction of early life experiences as they were revealed in the accounts and transference behavior of my obese patients, and in the transactional patterns in their families, suggested that something along this line had actually taken place. It could be demonstrated in individual cases that responses to child-initiated clues, indicating various stages of discomfort, had been continuously inappropriate.

For healthy development, experiences in both modalities are essential: confirmation of clues originating in the child, and a child responding to outside stimuli. It must be assumed that this applies to all areas of development. How it operates can be observed in the eating function. When a mother offers food in response to signals indicating nutritional need, the infant will gradually develop the engram of "hunger" as a sensation distinct from other tensions or needs. If, on the other hand, a mother's reaction is continuously inappropriate, be it neglectful, oversolicitous, inhibiting, or indiscriminately permissive, the outcome for the child will be a perplexing confusion. When he is older he will not be able to discriminate between being hungry and being sated, or suffering from some other discomfort. At the extremes of eating disorders, one finds the grotesquely obese person who is haunted by the fear of starvation and the emaciated anorexic who is oblivious to the pangs of hunger and the weakness, fatigue, and other symptoms characteristic of chronic undernutrition. Rarely, if ever, is nutrition the only function that is falsified in this way. The learning process is not restricted to infancy, but is continuous through childhood. The content of this learning relates to the whole range of experiences that characterize human life.

Robotlike conformity to environmental demands may convey a façade of adequate functioning. The gross deficit in initiative and active self-expression will become manifest when the child is confronted with new situations and demands for which misleading routines of his early life have left him unprepared. Such an adolescent, not having developed an integrated body concept, will feel helpless under the impact of his bodily urges, or feel as if controlled from the outside, like "not owning" his own sensations and his own body.

This theoretical frame goes beyond, or avoids, the traditional dichotomy of somatic and psychological aspects of development. An infant handicapped by genetic factors or suffering from unrecognized paranatal injuries, or confusing earliest experiences, is apt to give clues to his needs that are weak, indistinct, and contradictory. It would be difficult for any mother to satisfy them appropriately and will be completely confusing to a mother who herself is emotionally disturbed, preoccupied with her own problems, and thus impervious to the various expressions of a child's needs.

In extreme situations when a mother in a one-sided way superimposes on the child only what corresponds to her own emotional or bodily state, completely disregarding the impulses originating in the child, he will grow up without a sense of identity, living almost exclusively by responding to others, be it with overcompliance or rigid negativism, without the experience that his thoughts, feelings, or actions could be effective, except by being evil and destructive. Such disturbances in body concept, including the falsified awareness of proprioceptor impulses, seem to represent the link to schizophrenia, which is a not uncommon occurrence in severe eating disorders.[13]

I wish to illustrate the difference between an interpretive and fact-finding approach through the history of a 14-year-old boy who weighed nearly 300 pounds when I saw him in consultation. He was inert and inactive, seriously handicapped by being so conspicuously fat and also by lacking in ordinary skills of social behavior. His way of relating was that of playing the clown.

He was the youngest of three children, with two apparently healthy sisters. The mother had not wanted this pregnancy and had only reluctantly consented to having a third child under pressure from her husband and father-in-law. She developed a severe backache which made it impossible for her to lean over the crib or to pick up the baby.

The original information had been that he had "always" been an insatiable eater; later it was said that from about ten months on, his desire for food had been without limit. During his first eight months, the family had lived in the grandfather's house and the baby had slept in the room of his parents. When they moved to their own apartment, he slept in a separate room. He had weighed only five pounds at birth and was difficult to feed at first, with spitting up and slow feeding for several months. The father was more patient than the mother and would get up during the night and sit as long as two hours holding the baby and feeding him. During the daytime, the grandfather would help out and carry the baby around when he cried.

The clinical summary contained an interpretive statement that the excessive desire for food had developed in infancy as a response to the rejecting attitude of the mother, in particular to the loss of love and emotional support when he was removed from his parents' bedroom. Correspondingly, therapy had been conducted under the principle of not frustrating him, in order to compensate for this early loss of love. There was no supervision of his food intake, with the result that this giant boy grew still fatter while in the hospital.

There is another way of looking at his development. From about seven months on, he was able to sit in a high chair and was entirely in the care of his mother; his weight was normal at that time. Since the mother could not lift him, he sat for long stretches and would become restless and cry. She discovered that she could keep him quiet by putting a cooky in his mouth. This would not pacify him for very long, and the mother complained that no amount of food would silence him. As the rate of feeding him increased, so did his weight; by ten months he appeared chubby, and by two years he was so heavy that he was taken to the Mayo Clinic. He was placed on a 500-calorie diet and lost some weight, but this restriction was not adhered to for long. As he grew older, he would go to the home of his grandfather, who would cook for him all day long. His father died suddenly when the boy was 10 years old, and his eating habits became completely uncontrolled.

The detailed but factual history reveals a highly inappropriate feeding situation after his seventh month, but no change in the emotional climate of the home. "Food" was offered as the great pacifier, with complete disregard of the true reason for the child's discomfort. Little attention was paid to him except for stuffing him with food. This early "programing" of his regulatory centers, as well as that of higher brain function, left him without capacity for control. All this took place at a time when an infant shows a beginning of differentiated perception, cognition, and outward-directed explorative behavior, to all of which his mother failed to respond in an encouraging way.

Another line of recent investigation needs to be considered in this context, namely, that a relationship exists between disorders of the internal metabolism and early feeding experiences. When infant rats were allowed access to unlimited food for only two hours out of twenty-four hours each day, they lost weight for three or four days and then began to gain in excess of their litter mates, due to voracious eating and increased lipid synthesis. This excess gain in weight persisted even after the eating situation was returned to normal.[19] It is always debatable whether to apply animal observations directly to the human situation. However, it is conceivable that a child who is exposed to such continuous inappropriate feeding not only develops faulty regulatory mechanisms but will also develop metabolic disturbances, such as increased lipogenesis and a decrease in the amount of available fatty acids. Thus there may be a continuous tissue need for more nutrient in spite of the large fat depots.

This type of development without distinct awareness of bodily needs may also be encountered without weight disturbances during childhood. Parents of anorexia nervosa patients stress how normal, "on schedule," the early development had progressed until the illness began, maybe after some adolescent plumpness. Outstanding are the complete disregard of hunger and fatigue and the frantic denial that the skeletonlike appearance is abnormal. Underlying an all-pervasive negativism is a sense of utter helplessness, the fear that all will be lost if control of the body and its needs is relaxed just for one moment. These starving adolescents are afraid to eat because they fear that with one bite too much they may lose control completely and will not be able to stop eating.[16]

This same sense of helpless uncontrol can also be observed in some obese adolescents who have been slim as children. The *second example* is that of a young girl who had been "perfect" in her parents' opinion until age 14, when she became plump.

The father, a self-made man, was extremely proud of his success and was obsessively concerned with appearance and position. He made it a fetish that his wife and daughter should be slim. The mother used to be somewhat plump. She and the patient, when 15 years old, went on a diet, with the mother maintaining the low weight. For the girl there began a period of continuous preoccupation with her weight, which fluctuated between 105 and 170 pounds. She was unable to stay at college and returned to her parents' home. Until then she had been quite athletic, but now gave up all exercise. At first there was a tendency for her to sleep constantly and desire to be left severely alone. After a course of ECT, she became extremely antagonistic to her father and very suspicious and threatening toward both parents. Finally she locked herself in her room and gained weight progressively. When 21 years old she was admitted to a psychiatric hospital after she had not moved out of her parents' home for over a year.

As an only child, with two grandmothers in the picture, she was raised with extreme indulgence, and every need was anticipated. She was considered "extremely reasonable" as a child, who adjusted well to whatever the parents planned and would not object to disappointments. She was the pride and joy of the family, with enormous emphasis on prettiness. The parents showed off their pretty child in spite of her shyness. She dreaded this, but was afraid to oppose them.

In the hospital she made friends on a superficial level. Outstanding was her conformity, her complete inability to say "No" to any request, complaining of "emptiness" when no one told her what to do. She described her past as "Mother always knew what I was thinking."

Speaking about food, she said that she felt it had human characteristics, except that it was better. "It is always there. People are not comfortable, but with food you don't have to make excuses; you just take it. With people you have to be polite all the time, and you can't say 'No.' " An effort was made to help her to become specific about her sensations. She related that she ate without awareness of hunger; she felt only an undifferentiated, uncomfortable feeling. "I feel so empty, I do not know who I am."

She suffered several anxiety attacks with the feeling of floating, of having no body, or would wake up from sleep, intensely anxious: "I feel pulled down on my bed, my face and muscles are pulled back, all my muscles are pulled back. It is a horrible experience that I cannot move." Usually she was afraid during sleep of "fading away." Even her movements felt different. She had always been athletic, but now she felt like just gliding along. After a temper outburst and argument with another patient, she explained: "It was not me doing it; it happened to me."

Often she felt befuddled, unaware whether she was asleep or awake. At times she was confused about temperature sensations, not knowing whether she felt warm or chilly. As treatment progressed she gradually learned to differentiate between feeling anxious and relaxed.

This girl, who had been raised as an exhibit for her vain parents, seemed to function adequately until she was separated from them. Yet this "normalcy" was a façade performance, without autonomy or self-reliance and without barrier to protect herself against demands by anyone she met. This deficit was expressed in her inability to control her weight, and "obesity" was the leading complaint, the first defect in being a slim and beautiful showpiece.

I have no figures to indicate the frequency of such serious disturbances among the countless adolescents who are dissatisfied with their weight. However, numerous or not, these are the ones who will come to the attention of the psychiatrist, not only because they are unable to stabilize at a normal weight but also because they have problems and difficulties in many areas of living. A reducing regime should be the last step in an effort to help such a disturbed youngster to lead a more effective life.

This recommendation to postpone reducing effort, or not to make it at all, runs contrary to the prevailing medical and popular attitude. With all the progress in physiological knowledge and psychological understanding, a fat person is attacked with the time-honored prescription to reduce his food intake and to increase his activities; maybe these recommendations are given today in a more individualized form than in the past, or, recently, in the radical form of complete starvation. The patient's response, too, has remained the same: an indignant feeling of being deprived of something he feels is necessary for his well-being, however much he may deplore his fatness.

Psychotherapy, too, needs to be geared to the special needs of these disturbed fat youngsters. The traditional psychoanalytic interpretive approach has been disappointing. Becoming aware of unconscious conflicts and motivations is still an important aspect of therapy, but only one step. The essential therapeutic task is evoking awareness of feelings and impulses that originate in themselves and which they can learn to recognize, satisfy, or use in a discriminating way.[14] Such awareness may first appear in a different body area than the eating function. Becoming aware and capable of controlling their body function is an important step to feeling effective in interpersonal relations and in becoming independent of their families, who seem to have exercised such a damaging overcontrol.

Problems are entirely different for basically normal overweight adolescents who have well-established regulatory awareness. Once the active growth spurt is passed, they can take advantage of the endless stream of reducing aids that are advertised, or they can benefit from new habit patterns acquired during a supervised reducing regime. Increasingly it is recognized that new activity and exercise habits are as important as dietary restrictions. Emphasis on slimness is so forceful in our society that there is danger for many adolescents of overreducing, of trying to be thinner than their optimal weight. Anorexia nervosa in the rare extreme, but there are many young people obsessively preoccupied with their weight. Though they look normal, they remain basically "thin-fat people." [9]

The important task for the health profession would be to influence the hostile cultural attitude which hammers it into every American child day in, day out, that the goal of life is to be thin and beautiful, that this is the road to popularity and happiness, and that he is excluded from what life has to offer if he is sloppy and fat. Health education often proceeds on a similar refrain, promising longevity as reward for slimness. If we want to be of help to obese youngsters, the least we can do is to develop a realistic and respectful attitude toward their problems.

References

1. BLECHSCHMIDT, E. "Das genetische Grundgesetz," *Stimmen der Zeit*, I (1964/65), 40.
2. BRUCH, H. "The Froehlich Syndrome," *American Journal of Diseases of Children*, LVIII (1939), 1282.
3. BRUCH, H. "Energy Expenditure of Obese Children," *American Journal of Diseases of Children*, LX (1940), 1082.
4. BRUCH, H., "Physiologic and Psychologic Aspects of the Food Intake of Obese Children," *American Journal of Diseases of Children*, LXIX (1940), 739.
5. BRUCH, H. "Obesity in Childhood and Personality Development," *American Journal of Orthopsychiatry*, XI (1941), 467.
6. BRUCH, H. "Psychological Aspects of Reducing," *Psychosomatic Medicine*, XIV (1952) 337.
7. BRUCH, H. "Fat Children Grown Up," *American Journal of Diseases of Children*, XC (1955), 201.
8. BRUCH, H. "The Emotional Significance of the Preferred Weight," *American Journal of Clinical Nutrition*, V (1957) 192.
9. BRUCH, H. *The Importance of Overweight*. New York: Norton, 1957.
10. BRUCH, H. "Adipositas: Panel Discussion on the Theory of Hilde Bruch," *Acta Psych. et Neurol. Scand.*, XXXIII (1958), 151, Fasc. 2.
11. BRUCH, H. "Developmental Obesity and Schizophrenia," *Psychiatry*, XXI (1958), 65.
12. BRUCH, H. "Transformation of Oral Impulses in Eating Disorders," *Psychiatric Quarterly*, XXXV (1961), 458.
13. BRUCH, H. "Falsification of Bodily Needs and Body Concept in Schizophrenia," *Archives of General Psychiatry*, VI (1962), 18.
14. BRUCH, H. "Effectiveness in Psychotherapy," *Psychiatric Quarterly*, XXXVII (1963), 332.
15. BRUCH, H. "Prognosis and Treatment of Obesity from a Psychiatrist's Point of View" in *L'Obésité*. Paris: Expansion Scientifique, 1963, p. 176.
16. BRUCH, H. "Anorexia Nervosa and Its Differential Diagnosis," *Journal of Nervous and Mental Disease*, CXLI (1966), 555.
17. BRUCH, H., and G. TOURAINE. "The Family Frame of Obese Children," *Psychosomatic Medicine*, II (1940), 141.
18. HEBB, D. O. *The Organization of Behavior*. New York: Wiley, 1949.
19. HOLLIFIELD, G., and W. PARSON. "Metabolic Adaptations to a 'Stuff and Starve' Feeding Program," *Journal of Clinical Investigation*, XLI (1962), 245.
20. MAYER, J. "Some Aspects of the Problems of Regulation of Food Intake and Obesity," *New England Journal of Medicine*, CCLXXIV (1966), 610, 662, 722.

21. MENDELSOHN, M. "Psychological Aspects of Obesity," *International Journal of Psychiatry*, II (1966), 599.

22. MONELLO, L. F., and J. MAYER. "Obese Adolescent Girls: Unrecognized Minority Group?", *American Journal of Clinical Nutrition*, XIII (1963), 35.

23. MOORE, M. E., *et al.* "Obesity, Social Class and Mental Illness," *Journal of the American Medical Association*, CLXXXI (1962), 962.

24. STUNKARD, A. J., and M. MENDELSON. "Disturbances in Body Image of Some Obese Persons," *Journal of the American Dietary Association*, XXXVIII (1961), 328.

Depression and Suicide

EDITORS' INTRODUCTION Suicide and attempted suicide among adolescents have lately been attracting increasing attention among psychiatrists, as we have begun to realize how common they are. Moreover, in some countries, such as the United States, the suicide rates, especially among adolescent males, have been rising: the rate per 100,000 among white males aged 15 to 19 has risen from 3.7 in 1951 to 6.4 in 1963, and among nonwhite males from 1.7 in 1951 to 3.7 in 1963.* When we take into account that below the age of 19 it appears that the ratio of suicidal attempts to successful suicides is 33 to 1† and that all such figures are probably substantial underestimates because of obvious difficulties in obtaining valid data on these issues, it becomes clear that we are dealing with a major community problem that may be increasing in severity, at least in certain countries.

It is difficult to obtain reliable statistics that compare the rates of suicide and attempted suicide among different age groups in various countries at successive periods, and therefore we are pleased to open this section with a chapter by Tsung-yi Lin, of the World Health Organization. He has studied the epidemiological and vital statistics prepared by his organization in order to investigate changes over recent years in the suicide rates of

---

* Vital Statistics of the United States, National Center for Health Statistics, Washington, D.C.

† Statistics from State of Hawaii quoted by Michael L. Peck, of Los Angeles Suicide Prevention Center, in personal communication May 5, 1967.

young people in Japan and to compare these with the rates in other countries and age groups.

Lin reports that young people in Japan had a uniquely higher suicide rate in the years following World War II in comparison with similar age groups in other countries and with older people in their own country. The rates rose until about 1958 and then fell, although even in 1963 they were still comparatively high, being exceeded only by those in Hungary, Austria, and Switzerland.

Lin suggests that this postwar rise and then fall in the suicide rate of Japanese adolescents can be explained as their reaction to concurrent changes in the sociocultural and socioeconomic situation in their country. In the years following the war, Japanese youth were much more exposed than in the past to Western values which exaggerated the usual conflict of Japanese middle and late adolescence between personal inclinations and social directives, particularly with respect to the family choice of marriage partner and career. By the 1960's both the family traditional system and the adolescents had become adjusted to the new era, and this conflict had become less intense. Over the same period there was a major shift in the economic situation of the country from the postwar depression to a progressively improving economy, which has provided more attractive and varied job opportunities and also expectations of a more secure life. Such societal changes have also occurred in other countries, and Lin suggests that the reason they are more marked in their effect on suicide rates in Japan may be related to the particular personality propensities of the Japanese and the romantic tradition of suicide in that country. It would be of great interest someday to have a study, or at least some clinical impressions, by our Japanese colleagues as to whether they have noticed similar changes over the same time period in the incidence and severity of other psychiatric conditions and whether, therefore, the rise and fall of suicide rates is a specific manifestation or is one criterion of a general psychopathological trend.

The following chapter, by Ulf Otto, of Sweden, reports his investigation of 1,727 children and adolescent patients who attempted suicide during the period 1955–1959 and were treated in hospitals and clinics throughout his country. He points out that although four times more girls than boys attempted suicide, twice as many boys as girls succeeded in killing themselves. The reason appears to be that boys more often utilize active and aggressive methods, such as hanging, jumping from heights, and shooting, whereas girls more often use passive and less dangerous methods, such as taking pills. Boys who attempt suicide usually suffer from more serious mental disturbances, whereas girls who attempt suicide often do so impulsively when they are frustrated, for example, by disappointment in love, and do not appear to be seriously seeking death by their act.

The suicidal attempts were associated with many types of personality disorder—infantile, psychopathic, and hysterical—as well as neuroses, mental subnormality, depressions, and schizophrenia. The precipitating factors were also manifold, including difficulties with parents; school problems, especially fear of or failure in exams; frustration in love; pregnancy; difficulties in adjusting to compulsory military service; and so on.

Otto attempts to define a syndrome of presuicidal behavior that might be used as a criterion for preventive intervention. But his analysis of the data forces him to the conclusion that this is not feasible, apart from recognizing that in the period immediately preceding a suicide attempt the adolescent often shows a depressive or neurotic reaction with signs of increased tension, such as restlessness, anxiety, sleep disturbance, nail-biting, increased irritability, and oversensitivity. Some of the cases also showed deterioration in social behavior, such as lack of conformity in school or at work, truancy, disregard of hygiene, and alcoholism. None of these symptoms are sufficiently specific to be particularly useful in predicting a suicide attempt, and the only lesson we can draw from this investigation is that those who take care of adolescents, such as teachers, doctors, foremen, and army officers, should pay more attention to signs of their maladjustment to social, educational, and occupational demands and should provide increased support and supervision when they identify a recent exacerbation of symptoms of strain.

The next chapter, by Don A. Winn, reports on an investigation of the phenomenology and significance of hallucinations among a group of severely ill adolescents in a state hospital in New York who were admitted following a suicide attempt. The patients came from congested poverty-stricken neighborhoods of New York City. Half of them were Negroes, one-quarter Puerto Rican, and the remainder from Caucasian families. Most of them were psychotic, the primary diagnosis being schizophrenia in two-thirds of the cases.

The study focuses on 30 male and 30 female cases, aged 11½ to 15 years, arbitrarily selected from successive patients admitted to hospitals following a suicide attempt. Of these, 40 per cent had auditory hallucinations of voices which told them to kill themselves, and another 43 per cent had other types of auditory hallucinations during the preceding twelve months.

The author describes, with examples, the regularly occurring patterns of voices which seemed to play an active part in the symptoms associated with the suicide attempt. In many cases the adolescent heard a bad voice, often a harsh malevolent-sounding man, which told him to kill himself or do something very bad, and a good voice, often a woman, which comforted or tried to rescue him. Winn associates the malevolent male voice and the rescuing female voice with the deprived background of these youngsters, 80 per cent of whom had no father in the home, and an equal proportion of whom were separated from their mother for periods of one to eight years during their early childhood.

Of considerable interest is Winn's report that the majority of these cases from such poor backgrounds and with such florid psychotic symptoms have a remarkably good prognosis, the majority having spontaneous remissions or responding to supportive psychotherapy, medication, or electroshock within a few weeks. This raises the question of the psychopathological meaning of their breakdown and its dramatic manifestations in the light of their sociocultural environments. Moreover, cultural factors, such as a widespread primitive belief in the supernatural, were probably of considerable significance in facilitating and molding the hallucinations. It would be valuable if Winn would discuss these issues in a future paper and if we could have a comparable investigation of the frequency and role of hallucinations in psychotic adolescents from other cultures and social classes who attempt suicide.

The last chapter in this section, by James M. Toolan, presents the thesis that, contrary to popular clinical impressions, depressive illness is not infrequent during adolescence. Toolan agrees that the traditional adult clinical picture of depression with psychomotor retardation, insomnia, suicidal preoccupation, and feelings of depression, worthlessness, and apathy is rare in adolescence, although he has seen some such cases in adolescents over the age of 15. He also quotes other authors who agree that manic-depressive reactions are exceedingly rare below the age of 16. But he believes that young adolescents do suffer quite frequently from "depression equivalents," the main symptoms being boredom, restlessness, seeking of constant stimulation, fatigue, poor concentration, hypochondriasis, and bodily preoccupation. He points out that acting out and denial are common in adolescents, and they often literally run away from their problems in trying to run away from their horrible and devalued image of self. He believes that the frenetic sexual acting out which is often seen in adolescents is often an attempt to escape from an underlying depression.

Toolan explains the transition from the "depressive equivalents" of early adolescence to the increasingly frank depressions of middle and late adolescence by the normal psychological developmental changes of this period. He ascribes depression to the loss of a desired love object or of one's valued previous self, and he postulates that in latency and early adolescence, depression is evaded and denied in order to protect the good image of the parents. As the child matures, his improved reality testing makes this denial difficult, and he begins to blame his parents for his loss. The anger is then turned in onto the introjects of the parents in the adolescent's superego, which has by now developed its mature structure, and this produces the clinical picture of depression as typically seen in adults.

The chapter ends with a plea for the more adequate recognition and management of depressive reactions in adolescence, not only to prevent suicide but also because these reactions lower effectiveness at crucial periods of career development. This is in line with the message of the previous chapters, which strongly suggests that child psychiatrists should focus more attention on this subject. We need more epidemiological and clinical studies of the phenomena of depression and suicide among adolescents in different cultures and classes, and we very much need to devote greater efforts to developing methods and services of prevention and control.

17

Some Epidemiological Findings on Suicides in Youth

Tsung-yi Lin

Since the available information is insufficient to permit a fruitful review of suicide among youth in general, it would seem appropriate for me to present a few interesting epidemiological findings on juvenile suicide in Japan, not only because of the availability of fairly detailed data but also because of my own personal acquaintance with the Japanese situation. The comparison of suicide in Japan with that in other countries would seem to reveal a few clues for understanding the psychosocial dynamics of the phenomenon of suicide.

CHARACTERISTICS OF SUICIDE IN JAPAN

It has been customary in the past to regard Japan as having one of the highest suicide rates in the world, comparable with that of Austria, Denmark, Switzerland, and Sweden, although Table 17–1, which compares the rates for Japan with those for Italy, France, Sweden, Switzerland, and the United States, suggests that this has not always been the case. In fact, the high rates for Japan seem to have been a phenomenon of the period since 1940, and the over-all rate, which reached a peak of 25.7 per 100,000 in 1958, has since been decreasing. Not only in Japan but in the European countries shown in Table 17–2, there were increases in the over-all suicide rates after the postwar low rates; these reached their peak values at

All the tables of this chapter are based on information contained in the *Annual Epidemiological and Vital Statistics* for years 1953–1963, published by World Health Organization, Geneva. Grateful acknowledgment is due to Miss Eileen Brooke, Consultant Statistician, WHO Headquarters, for her assistance in bringing the statistical data on suicide up to date.

various times during the decade 1953–1963. By the early 1960's, the over-all suicide rate for Japan had fallen to tenth of 45 countries, the ranking order being as follows:

1. Hungary	26.8	6. Germany Fed. Rep.	19.3
2. Austria	22.3	7. Sweden	18.9
3. Czechoslovakia	20.9	8. China-Taiwan	18.5
4. Finland	20.4	9. Switzerland	17.6
5. Denmark	19.7	10. Japan	16.3

Suicide rates in Japan have the following characteristics:

A. One of the Highest Suicide Rates among Youth

Table 17–1 makes it clear that the Japanese rates for both males and females aged 20–39 declined from a relatively high prewar rate to a much lower rate after the war, and then in the early 1950's increased sharply, whereas in the other countries there had been either a continuing decrease or else a small increase in the early 1950's. Table 17–3 analyzes the rates for four 5-year age groups in 1953, 1958, and 1963 and shows that in particular people aged 15–29 in 1958 were subject to exceptionally high rates; this applies to both males and females.

Table 17–1. Incidence of Suicide and Its Evolution Since the Beginning of the Century at Various Periods in Selected Countries and by Large Age Groups

(Death rates per 100,000)

Period	Japan	Italy	France	Sweden	Switzerland	U.S.A.
	AGE GROUP 20–39. MALES					
Beginning of century	26.8	13.1	—	25.2	39.3	—
Before World War I	30.7	18.1	—	32.3	42.6	—
After World War I	32.7	14.8	22.1	24.8	32.0	19.1
Between World Wars	—	15.5	23.9	22.6	36.2	20.2
Before World War II	38.0	12.5	25.3	20.9	39.5	19.9
After World War II	22.1	9.0	13.0	20.1	30.2	13.8
Early 1950's	40.9	7.6	12.7	23.0	31.4	13.0
	AGE GROUP 20–39. FEMALES					
Beginning of century	17.0	3.8	—	5.4	9.3	—
Before World War I	18.9	7.2	—	6.4	11.1	—
After World War I	22.3	6.7	7.8	6.2	12.2	7.5
Between World Wars	—	6.4	7.4	6.4	11.7	8.9
Before World War II	23.2	5.4	7.8	7.1	11.3	8.2
After World War II	16.8	4.0	4.8	7.3	12.0	5.3
Early 1950's	23.7	3.8	4.0	7.6	10.7	4.5

Table 17–1 (*continued*).

(Death rates per 100,000)

Period	Japan	Italy	France	Sweden	Switzerland	U.S.A.
	AGE	GROUP	40–59.	MALES		
Beginning of century	40.5	17.9	—	52.4	84.6	—
Before World War I	36.0	21.3	—	62.6	72.4	—
After World War I	41.3	18.0	47.9	48.6	68.1	38.6
Between World Wars	—	31.7	49.4	52.6	71.3	49.5
Before World War II	39.5	22.2	50.7	48.2	64.2	43.6
After World War II	32.1	17.2	32.4	37.8	57.1	31.5
Early 1950's	29.5	18.6	43.0	44.7	51.1	27.6
	AGE	GROUP	40–59.	FEMALES		
Beginning of century	16.5	3.9	—	9.1	15.8	—
Before World War I	17.2	5.5	—	11.3	15.8	—
After World War I	19.0	4.7	13.6	11.6	18.3	10.4
Between World Wars	—	6.9	14.3	11.4	20.6	12.6
Before World War II	19.8	6.4	13.6	12.8	19.4	12.7
After World War II	16.4	5.0	10.2	13.3	21.7	9.8
Early 1950's	18.0	5.9	11.1	13.4	16.0	8.2
	AGE	GROUP	60 AND	OVER.	MALES	
Beginning of century	70.9	20.5	—	58.3	104.5	—
Before World War I	71.1	25.5	—	72.7	114.1	—
After World War I	83.9	23.3	90.0	55.6	95.0	54.0
Between World Wars	—	36.2	89.7	54.4	100.0	73.5
Before World War II	85.4	31.9	90.6	54.4	97.3	60.1
After World War II	85.8	23.0	62.3	48.5	83.2	48.9
Early 1950's	71.0	26.0	65.7	55.4	77.8	45.9
	AGE	GROUP	60 AND	OVER.	FEMALES	
Beginning of century	41.1	4.1	—	9.9	12.0	—
Before World War I	39.8	5.4	—	16.1	15.8	—
After World War I	42.0	4.8	20.6	12.3	23.1	10.1
Between World Wars	—	7.3	19.6	10.4	21.1	12.1
Before World War II	36.0	6.5	19.0	10.6	19.9	11.1
After World War II	52.7	5.6	14.9	11.0	19.5	9.4
Early 1950's	47.4	6.8	16.7	12.2	21.2	8.2

Just as dramatic as the increase in the Japanese rates was their subsequent decline by 1963. The male rate for the age group 15–19 declined from 31.4 to 11.0 and was exceeded by the rates in several other countries, for example, Austria, Switzerland, and Hungary, while the rates at ages 20–24 and 25–29 were exceeded by those for Hungary and, in the latter age group, for Finland. Among females, however, the rates for Japan in 1963 were still highest of those in 26 countries at ages 20–29.

Table 17–2. Trends in Suicide Rates, 1925–1964, in Seven Selected
Countries

(Rates per 100,000)

	United States			Japan			Italy		
	P	M	F	P	M	F	P	M	F
1925	12.0	18.0	5.8	20.6	25.2	16.0	9.4	14.0	4.9
1930	15.6	24.1	6.9	21.8	27.4	16.1	9.6	14.7	4.7
1935	14.3	21.7	6.8	20.5	25.1	15.8	7.7	11.5	4.1
1940	14.4	21.9	6.8	13.8	16.3	11.3	5.9	8.9	3.1
1945	11.2	17.2	5.8	—	—	—	4.8	6.9	2.7
1950	11.4	17.8	5.1	19.6	24.1	15.3	6.5	9.5	3.6
1955	10.2	16.0	4.6	25.2	31.5	19.0	6.6	9.6	3.7
1960	10.6	16.5	4.9	21.6	25.1	18.2	6.1	8.6	3.7
1963	11.0	16.5	5.8	16.1	18.9	13.4	5.3	7.4	3.2
1964	10.8	—	—	15.1	—	—	5.4	—	—

PEAK YEARS IN THE PERIOD 1953–1963

1963		11.0	1958		25.7	1956			6.7

At any time there are some stresses acting on people which are normal to
their particular age group, for example, those involved in starting work, in
courtship and the early days of marriage, in success or failure in work, and
in bereavement and old age. When suicide rates in different age groups are
considered over time it is not always remembered that different groups of
people are being discussed at each stage. An increase in the rates in particular age groups may indicate that the stresses common to people who happen
to be of that age at the time are being reinforced by some other pressures. If
the latter applied generally, a rise in the suicide rates at all ages might be
expected. The factors which caused the high suicide rates in young people
in 1958 as compared with 1953 did not apply to the middle-age groups,
and although the rates in older people aged 60 and over were higher in
1958, the rise was not as great as among the young people. Particularly
noticeable is the decrease in the rates between 1958 and 1963, which applied to all age groups but was more striking among the younger and older
people than among the middle-aged.

Table 17–4 shows the suicide rates in later years of the groups of people
who were aged 10–29 in 1953. For example, people aged 10–14 in 1953
were aged 15–19 in 1958 and 20–24 in 1963. When the suicide rates are
looked at in this way, the Japanese rates are very interesting in comparison
with those for some of the other countries. Both males and females who
were aged 10–14 in 1953 had much higher rates in 1958 when they were
aged 15–19 (males 31.4; females 26.4), but five years later, when they

Table 17-2 (*continued*).

(Rates per 100,000)

France			Sweden			Switzerland			Austria		
P	M	F	P	M	F	P	M	F	P	M	F
19.3	30.4	8.9	13.5	21.8	5.6	21.9	35.6	9.1	32.3	—	—
19.0	29.8	9.0	15.8	25.8	6.2	26.1	40.8	12.4	38.3	53.2	24.4
20.1	32.1	8.9	15.5	24.9	6.4	26.4	42.5	11.3	37.1	—	—
18.7	28.4	10.3	17.1	27.2	7.1	23.6	36.8	11.2	35.7	48.2	24.0
12.3	19.3	6.3	15.3	23.1	7.7	27.8	39.1	17.3	—	—	—
15.2	23.8	7.2	14.9	22.8	6.9	23.5	34.8	12.9	23.8	34.2	14.7
15.9	24.7	7.8	17.8	27.2	8.5	21.6	31.4	12.4	23.4	33.0	15.0
15.9	24.0	8.2	17.4	26.3	8.6	19.0	27.7	10.8	23.1	32.4	14.8
15.5	23.8	7.7	18.5	27.1	9.9	17.1	24.9	9.6	21.7	31.0	13.4
14.9	—	—	19.8	—	—	17.0	—	—	22.8	—	—

PEAK YEARS IN THE PERIOD 1953–1963

| 1956 | | 17.4 | 1956 | | 20.1 | 1954 | | 22.6 | 1959 | | 24.8 |

were 20–24, their rates had not increased any further. The rates for both sexes aged 15–19 in 1953 had more than tripled when they were aged 20–24 (males 78.2; females 53.0 in 1958), but by the time they reached ages 25–29, their rates dropped to 30.9 for men and 17.8 for women. It is also clear that the rates for people aged 25–29 in 1953 drop as they enter the middle-age group.

The generally low rates in Italy show little variation as the groups reach higher ages, except that the rate for males aged 15–19 in 1958 doubles five years later when they are aged 20–24. In Sweden and the United States, on the other hand, each of the 1953 age groups has an increasing suicide rate as it moves into the higher age groups. Compared with the decrease in the Japanese rates in 1963, the increase in the male rates for Hungary is very striking.

B. A Very High Rate of Suicide among the Aged

Apart from the high rate among youth, Japan has low rates for the middle-aged and high rates among elderly persons. Compared with 1953 and 1963, 1958 was a peak year for suicide rates for both men and women aged 60 and over. The decrease in rates by 1963 is especially marked for men (Table 17–5), so that of the countries being considered, the Japanese rates at ages 60–79 are lower than for France and considerably lower than

Table 17–3.   Suicide Rates among Young People Aged 10–29 in Selected Countries in 1953, 1958, and 1963

(Per 100,000 population in sex-age groups)

Country and Year		Males				Females			
		10–14	15–19	20–24	25–29	10–14	15–19	20–24	25–29
Japan	1953	0.8	25.1	58.8	41.4	0.5	17.7	35.9	22.3
	1958	1.1	31.4	78.2	54.2	0.8	26.4	53.0	31.1
	1963	1.3	11.0	31.4	30.9	0.4	9.3	26.1	17.8
Italy	1954*	0.5	3.1	6.0	7.2	0.3	3.3	4.0	3.0
	1958	0.5	2.4	5.4	5.8	0.2	3.8	3.5	2.9
	1963	0.5	2.7	4.8	4.4	0.5	2.6	2.3	2.2
France	1953	0.6	3.6	7.2	10.2	—	2.4	3.2	3.8
	1958	0.7	4.4	7.2	14.8	0.1	3.6	4.5	5.3
	1963	0.4	4.5	9.4	15.7	0.0	2.8	5.3	5.4
Austria	1953	—	13.0	24.5	29.9	0.3	6.7	17.7	14.1
	1958	1.6	13.9	27.0	33.9	0.8	4.4	7.7	13.1
	1963	2.4	16.9	27.2	26.8	1.7	6.5	8.0	13.3
Switzerland	1953	1.7	17.1	34.6	32.6	0.6	8.7	7.6	12.1
	1958	1.8	13.6	38.2	25.2	0.5	5.1	10.0	8.1
	1963	1.0	15.8	20.6	24.4	0.5	5.7	7.6	11.0
Sweden	1953	0.4	4.2	15.8	15.2	—	3.8	9.0	7.7
	1958	—	3.9	6.8	20.2	—	3.2	5.1	4.9
	1963	0.3	7.3	18.1	26.8	—	5.1	9.0	12.4
United States	1953	0.8	3.8	9.5	12.7	0.2	1.7	2.8	4.4
	1958	0.8	4.3	10.8	13.3	0.2	1.7	3.0	5.2
	1963	0.9	6.0	12.8	15.8	0.2	1.9	4.4	6.4
Hungary	1958	2.1	16.4	36.9	29.9	2.9	11.6	11.4	13.8
	1963	5.0	21.1	40.9	35.2	0.9	12.7	15.4	12.3

* Figures for 1953 not available.

for Hungary. The female rates remain higher than in the other countries, although less than in the peak year of 1958.

When one considers the rates at 5-year intervals for people aged 60–79 in 1953, elderly people show the same pattern as the young (Table 17–6). In 1958, when the 1953 group is five years older, their rates show a substantial increase, both for males and females, but by 1963, when the survivors are another five years older, the rates have greatly decreased for men and to some extent for women also. However, this pattern does not appear uniformly in the other countries. In particular in French males there is a continuous increase in the rates as these groups age, while in Hungary men

Table 17–4. Suicide Rates in Cohorts of Young People in Selected Countries

(Per 100,000 population in sex-age groups)

Country and Year		Males				Females			
		10–14	15–19	20–24	25–29	10–14	15–19	20–24	25–29
Japan	1953	0.8	25.1	58.8	41.4	0.5	17.7	35.9	22.3
	1958	31.4	78.2	54.2	27.2	26.4	53.0	31.1	18.4
	1963	31.4	30.9	20.3	16.8	26.1	17.8	13.1	11.0
Italy	1954*	0.5	3.1	6.0	7.2	0.3	3.3	4.0	3.0
	1958	2.4	5.4	5.8	6.2	3.8	3.5	2.9	2.6
	1963	4.8	4.4	5.4	6.2	2.3	2.2	2.7	2.9
France	1953	0.6	3.6	7.2	10.2	—	2.4	3.2	3.8
	1958	4.4	7.2	4.8	17.5	3.6	4.5	5.3	5.2
	1963	9.4	15.7	18.7	22.7	5.3	5.4	6.2	5.8
Austria	1953	—	13.0	24.5	29.9	0.3	6.7	17.7	14.1
	1958	13.9	27.0	33.9	35.5	4.4	7.7	13.1	14.7
	1963	27.2	26.8	32.5	30.7	8.0	13.3	10.0	19.0
Switzerland	1953	1.7	17.1	34.6	32.6	0.6	8.7	7.6	12.1
	1958	13.6	38.2	25.2	24.4	5.1	10.0	8.1	12.7
	1963	20.6	24.4	20.5	26.1	7.6	11.0	13.2	8.9
Sweden	1953	0.4	4.2	15.8	15.2	—	3.8	9.0	7.7
	1958	3.9	6.8	20.2	26.7	3.2	5.1	4.9	6.9
	1963	18.1	26.8	32.5	30.7	9.0	12.4	13.3	11.0
United States	1953	0.8	3.8	9.5	12.7	0.2	1.7	2.8	4.4
	1958	4.3	10.8	13.3	15.0	1.7	3.0	5.2	6.0
	1963	12.8	15.8	17.5	21.2	4.4	6.4	8.0	9.9
Hungary	1958*	16.4	36.9	29.9	31.8	11.6	11.4	13.8	12.7
	1963	40.9	35.2	44.3	48.6	15.4	12.3	14.7	13.5

AGE GROUP IN 1953

* Data for 1953 not available.

who were 60–79 in 1953 show a dramatic increase in the rates between the time they reach 65–84 and when they are 70–89.

C. A Relatively High Suicide Rate among Females

This is another feature observed in Japan. While in Western countries the over-all suicide rate for females amounts to about 30 to 40 per cent of the male rate, in Japan it reaches 65 to 70 per cent of the male rate. Table 17–7 shows that not only is the ratio for Japan higher than in the other

Table 17–5. Suicide Rates among Elderly People Aged 60–79 in Selected Countries

(Per 100,000 population in sex-age groups)

Country and Year		Males				Females			
		60–64	65–69	70–74	75–79	60–64	65–69	70–74	75–79
Japan	1953	51.4	61.7	81.8	108.0	29.2	40.7	59.8	74.6
	1958	52.2	71.4	84.6	116.6	33.1	44.9	64.4	67.7
	1963	42.6	48.6	57.6	76.2	23.5	34.0	46.7	57.3
Italy	1958	21.9	22.7	28.1	27.7	6.8	7.0	6.4	8.3
	1963	18.8	19.7	20.7	26.4	5.7	8.0	6.2	6.5
France	1958	58.9	58.4	65.1	79.3	18.8	22.3	22.4	21.7
	1963	57.5	55.6	58.2	76.8	15.0	17.9	19.1	18.2
Austria	1958	47.8	59.1	65.9	60.3	24.2	25.7	20.5	30.0
	1963	53.5	52.5	46.6	71.8	18.9	19.5	26.5	24.3
Switzerland	1958	59.1	63.6	82.3	92.2	24.3	11.9	16.5	15.1
	1963	43.2	44.2	46.2	70.6	13.0	14.9	16.5	16.2
Sweden	1958	50.4	51.6	53.2	56.0	15.3	17.7	14.5	8.0
	1963	53.5	52.5	46.6	71.8	15.7	14.9	7.0	10.8
United States	1958	41.7	44.1	49.4	51.5	9.2	10.0	9.3	7.1
	1963	35.8	35.6	41.6	48.0	10.2	9.6	8.5	7.8
Hungary	1958	63.9	71.6	80.9	84.8	25.5	24.5	31.1	44.1
	1963	56.3	59.9	80.4	113.2	27.6	33.6	34.3	36.8

countries discussed but by 1963 the female to male ratio has increased to 70.9 per cent, so that the gap between the male and female rates has decreased still further. In 1963 this percentage ratio of female to male rates is highest in the age groups 15–19 and 20–24 (85 and 83 per cent, respectively) and lower in the succeeding age groups up to 65, then at ages 65–69, 70–74, and 75–79 the ratios are 70, 81, and 75 per cent, respectively.

D. No Significant Urban-Rural Difference

Contrary to the universal observation that suicide is more or less an urban phenomenon, the suicide rates show very little difference between the urban and rural populations in Japan, for example, 19.7 per 100,000 versus 17.9 per 100,000. This phenomenon is observed in all age groups. It should also be noted that the male-female ratio shows almost no difference between the urban and rural populations, which is not usually the case in Western countries.

Table 17–6. Suicide Rates in Cohorts of Older People in Selected Countries

(Per 100,000 population in sex-age groups)

Country and Year		Males 60–64	65–69	70–74	75–79	Females 60–64	65–69	70–74	75–79
		AGE GROUP IN 1953							
Japan	1953	51.4	61.7	81.8	108.0	29.2	40.7	59.8	74.6
	1958	71.4	84.6	116.6	122.8	44.9	64.4	67.7	75.7
	1963	57.6	76.2	115.5	90.9	46.7	57.3	72.4	63.4
Italy	1953	18.6	23.7	22.5	25.8	6.1	8.0	7.1	6.1
	1958	22.7	28.1	27.7	29.5	7.0	6.4	8.3	5.3
	1963	20.7	26.4	38.0	21.6	6.2	6.5	8.4	5.2
France	1953	49.9	56.7	66.1	81.7	15.5	15.8	16.0	17.5
	1958	58.4	65.1	79.3	100.6	22.3	22.4	21.7	15.8
	1963	58.2	76.8	88.2	130.8	19.1	18.2	13.6	19.2
Austria	1953	69.4	55.1	62.4	82.6	26.4	20.0	21.2	16.2
	1958	59.1	65.9	60.3	38.8	25.7	20.5	30.0	27.7
	1963	46.6	71.8	66.9	57.1	26.5	24.3	31.8	35.3
Switzerland	1953	80.3	62.3	78.3	97.1	23.2	19.0	16.4	16.6
	1958	63.6	82.3	92.2	72.5	11.9	16.5	15.1	12.2
	1963	46.2	70.6	66.5		16.5	16.2	13.8	
Sweden	1953	62.1	63.1	70.6	55.9	14.0	11.8	15.7	9.0
	1958	51.6	53.2	56.0	64.6	17.7	14.5	8.0	4.1
	1963	46.6	71.8	66.9	57.1	7.0	10.8	3.6	—
United States	1953	40.5	44.5	47.3	51.4	8.8	8.2	7.7	7.9
	1958	44.1	49.4	51.5	64.6	10.0	9.3	7.1	5.0
	1963	41.6	48.0	52.2	55.8	8.5	7.8	6.6	5.0
Hungary	1958	71.6	80.9	84.8	166.7	24.5	31.1	44.1	48.7
	1963	80.4	113.2	149.7	251.9	34.3	36.8	20.6	96.3

DISCUSSION

It is clear from the findings above that youth in Japan has a uniquely high suicide rate not only in comparison to youth in other countries but also to the middle-age groups of their own country and that the postwar increase of suicide rates in Japan is most markedly observed in the youth. One cannot explain this fact simply by the common notion that "suicide—Harakiri" is an age-old honored practice in Japan. Such a cultural practice alone should not be held responsible for the selective vulnerability of modern

Table 17–7. Percentage Ratio of Female to Male Suicide Rates for All Ages, 1958 and 1963

Year	Japan	Italy	France	Austria	Swit-zerland	Sweden	United States	Hungary
1958	67.8	40.9	35.3	43.4	35.4	33.6	28.0	43.4
1963	70.9	45.9	32.4	43.2	38.6	36.5	35.2	44.8

youth to suicide, since modern youth in Japan is relatively less influenced by such a cultural tradition. The fact that middle-age groups show lower suicide rates than youth makes it difficult to accept such an explanation, because the middle-aged have been more exposed to this cultural practice.

Although one cannot point to a few definite factors with certainty to explain this phenomenon, one may try to relate this to the effect of social and culturally determined disruptions and crises in the life cycle. Youth in Japan, for both boys and girls, represents a critical period of conflict between their own personal inclinations and social directives which require them to be submissive in respect of a family choice for a marriage partner or a professional career. In the postwar era, when Japanese youth was more and more exposed to the Western value system that contributed to the exaggerations of their conflict, both real and imaginary, the suicide rate increased accordingly. Of course, one cannot entirely ignore actual social factors, such as a lack of opportunity for employment and schooling, which may be partly responsible for the increased suicide rate. The groups of people aged 15–29 in 1953 who show exceptionally high rates of suicides belong to those who passed through the war (1940–1945) between the average ages of 7 and 17, which may be an indication of the vulnerability of young people to the conditions of war.

Although these features of crises in youth are found in most modern societies to some degree, it is the particular personality propensities of the Japanese and the available romantic tradition of suicide that make youth particularly vulnerable to resolving their dilemmas through suicide. The relatively high rate of female suicide in Japanese youth may be a reflection of the difficult social position which women and girls held and still hold.

The lower suicide rate of the middle-age groups may be partially explained by the paternalistic and protective network of obligation in Japanese society when an occupational or marital commitment is made. The middle-aged continue to be taken care of by a company or an organization or by their family, to which they remain loyal. On the other hand, the old-age group which has undergone the stress of war and social and economic crises after the war maintains a high suicide rate.

The decrease of suicide rates in Japanese youth in the early 1960's may be interpreted as a sign of their adaptation to the changing conditions of life. This decline may also be related to rapidly improving social-economic conditions in Japan which gave youth a brighter prospect for future opportunities of jobs as well as a sense of security. In contrast to Japan a significant increase of suicide rates in youth was observed in Hungary and other European countries in the late 1950's and early 1960's. A careful epidemiological and sociological study of this phenomenon may provide interesting clues which will lead to a better understanding of the relationship between social factors and suicide and give indications for possible preventive measures.

18

Suicide Attempts among Swedish Children and Adolescents

Ulf Otto

Only a few investigations on the frequency of suicide and suicidal attempts among children and adolescents have been published. It is reasonable to assume that the frequency of suicides among children varies from country to country, just as is the case among adults. Hence we have found it to be of interest to investigate the situation among Swedish children and adolescents. There is reason to question the real circumstances behind the given statistics from various countries because of the difficulties in rendering an objective account of them. The method applied in this chapter probably comes close to the truth in gaining a real understanding of the frequency of suicide attempts among children and adolescents. However, it can elucidate only a minimum of cases. To gain an exact knowledge of the number of suicide attempts is probably impossible.

The records of all children and adolescents under 21 who were hospitalized for suicide attempts during the years between 1955 and 1959 were gathered from all the hospitals and clinics in Sweden. The sample consists of 1,727 patients from all over the country. There is an obvious advantage in the fact that the material is not taken from merely one hospital or one clinic. In such cases there is the risk of drawing too sweeping conclusions from specific and limited material. The disadvantage is that the records are prepared differently by different doctors.

There are many reasons why it is so difficult to get at the exact number of suicide attempts and suicides. For example, relatives and others may wish to conceal the fact that an attempt has taken place. In many cases there is no contact with a physician, or the patient may try to explain the suicide attempt as an accident which befell him. Also a great many suicide attempts take the form of consuming an overdose of pills before retiring at night. It is plausible that in many cases of this type where a spontaneous awakening occurs the following morning, the family does not interpret it as a suicide attempt and no action is taken. The border line between an accidental over-consumption of sedatives and a planned suicide attempt is in many cases indistinct.

One-fifth of the suicide attempts recorded are made by boys. But among the actual suicides there are twice as many boys as girls. The number of suicide attempts increases with age. There is a quick acceleration related to puberty.

Fluctuation in the frequency of suicide during different seasons of the year has been observed. In Sweden the lowest number occurs during June and July, and the highest in November, followed by February and March. According to investigations made in the United States, there is a high tide of suicide attempts among children and adolescents during the spring and early summer resulting from increased pressure at school the previous months. In our investigation this would seem less conclusive since 70 per cent of our sample of adolescents had already finished school. Why Swedish children and adolescents show an increased tendency to suicidal acts during the darker seasons of the year cannot be proved by any scientifi-cally acceptable measures.

It is impossible to conclude from this sample if constitutional or exoge-nous factors are the more important to children who try to commit suicide. The variation of the frequency of attempts between different countries is greater for children than for adults, which signifies that external factors are more crucial in the earlier years than at mature ages. The suggestion has been made that there is a specific hereditary factor which conduces toward suicide. However, this has been contradicted among others, for instance, by Kallman in his study of twins. That the environment does play an important role is proved by the fact, among others, that there is a relatively higher frequency of suicide attempts among youngsters in big cities than in smaller communities and in rural areas.

In an attempt to study the causes and motives behind the suicide at-tempts one runs into a great many obstacles. For example, motives men-tioned immediately after the attempt often differ from those given a few days later.

Children as well as adults use the suicidal act as a means of punishing their family, to gain attention and secure love from their close relations. The decisive moment is often trivial and of slight importance compared to the conglomeration of predisposing factors that move the patient to the point where the suicidal act seems to be the only way out.

Problems in love are the most commonly given cause (39.2 per cent); that is, disturbances in relationships with the opposite sex. Second, prob-lems within the family (32.1 per cent). Other causes are school difficulties (6.2 per cent), military service (1.7 per cent), pregnancy (3.4 per cent), and mental illness (17.5 per cent).

Passive methods, like taking pills, are employed to a higher degree by women than by men. This seems to be in accord with the fact that men predominate among those who complete the act of suicide because they employ more active methods. This tendency among men to use more active, aggressive means, like hanging, strangling, weapons, and so on can be observed also among children and adolescents. However, passive methods predominate in these age groups. The most common means is by taking pills (86.9 per cent), while all other methods together make up the remaining 13.1 per cent (Table 18–1). Suicide by pills would be judged as an

Table 18–1. Methods of Suicidal Attempts

Method of suicidal attempt	SEX ♂	SEX ♀	TOTAL Number	TOTAL %
Narcotic drugs	269	1232	1501	86.9
Hanging and strangulation	24	17	41	
Shooting	4	1	5	
Gas poisoning	14	18	32	
Leaping from height	8	10	18	
Throwing self before vehicle	1	6	7	13.1
Drowning	5	13	18	
Cutting self	15	51	66	
Swallowing sharp object	6	1	7	
Other methods	5	27	32	

unsatisfactory method by contemporary medical opinion if death were the real aim of the act.

It seems reasonable to regard suicide attempts among boys as more serious than those among girls, and probably they are the result of graver mental disturbances. The frequency of recurrent attempts is also somewhat higher among boys. Among most girls it would appear that the attempts at suicide were impulsive acts born out of comparatively moderate, even banal acute traumata, like romantic troubles.

Many studies have been published which have tried to account for the mental state or the personality type of those who commit suicidal acts. It can be mentioned, for instance, that the frequency of psychoses in different samples ranges from 3 to 66 per cent. This results from difficulties inherent in defining stages of psychic illnesses and also the fact that the samples are too limited and not representative enough.

Concerning the constitutional aspects which are expressed as variables of personality in this investigation, we have found that among children and adolescents more than one-third (35.7 per cent) are labeled as hysteroid, and about the same number (32.7 per cent) as infantile, while the asthenics register only 12.9 per cent (Table 18–2). The infantile and hysteroid per-

Table 18–2. Distribution of Personality Variables

Personality variables	Number	%
Hysteroid type	177	35.7
Infantile type	162	32.7
Oligophrenia	72	14.5
Asthenic type	64	12.9
Schizoid type	18	3.6
Cycloid type	3	0.6
Total	496	100.0

sonalities thus predominate among children and adolescents who commit suicidal acts; that is, they are immature, naïve, extrovert, impulsive, playacting personalities.

Neurotics predominate among mental conditions (53.0 per cent). Psychotics absorb only 16.5 per cent, with two-thirds schizophrenics (11.8 per cent) and one-third manic-depressives (4.7 per cent) (Table 18–3). These

Table 18–3. Distribution of Psychiatric States of Illness

Psychiatric states of illness	Number	%
Neurotic-depressive reaction	144	29.8
Neurosis	112	23.2
Psychosis		
Schizophrenia	57 ⎫ 80	11.8 ⎫ 16.5
Manic-depressive psychosis	23 ⎭	4.7 ⎭
Psychopathy	64	13.2
Adolescent adjustment reaction	52	10.7
Brain damage	32	6.6
Total	484	100.0

statistics coincide with the results of other investigations. American scientists especially, however, have stressed the importance of the schizophrenic state in suicidal acts.

Different methods are employed in different mental states. It was mentioned above that boys commonly use active methods. Active methods are mostly used by schizophrenics (24.6 per cent) and those with a primary character disorder (25.0 per cent), that is, mental states that often are characterized by explosive, impulsive actions and reactions. The use of active methods is more unusual in neurotics (14.3 per cent) and reactive neurotic depression (12.4 per cent). If we accept the active method as more serious than the passive, this difference in frequency supports the thesis that the vast majority of children and adolescents who commit suicidal acts choose a less dangerous method—a method that does not entail death. The conscious or unconscious motivation of the suicidal act is thus something other than attaining death.

Prophylactic activity is receiving more and more attention from medical and social authorities. It is, of course, of the greatest importance to be able to predict and thereby prevent a suicidal act, but, since this has a most polymorphic background and is a comparatively rare state which can occur in several different types of personality and in completely different psychic illnesses, it seems to be impossible to find a specific psychic frame that foretells a suicidal act. There have been many attempts to outline a presuicidal picture, but none of them has been successful. It is common to stress the importance of the depressive state in suicidal acts. However, the schizophrenic state as particularly predisposing has also been suggested.

Several scholars have pointed out that suicide candidates often warn their families and friends in different ways during the period before the suicidal act. The difficulty of predicting a suicidal act in spite of this is underscored by the fact, among others, that a comparatively large per cent of those who commit suicidal acts are already under medical observation.

But this point has not been given special attention in research concerning children and adolescents. Starting with our discussion and observations, one would guess that a specific presuicidal syndrome among children and adolescents does not exist. In order to investigate this problem the three-month period before the suicidal act occurred was examined to find out if a change of behavior had taken place. In 38.3 per cent a depression had set in which corresponds to the observations made on adults. Then follow a group of behavior changes (30.1 per cent), encompassing such neurotic symptoms as sleep disturbances, psychosomatic symptoms, anxiety conditions, nail-biting, and the like. In 16.2 per cent of the cases symptoms of increased irritability, aggressiveness, oversensitivity, and so forth have been reported. Changes of social behavior, such as difficulties in adapting at school or at work, disregard for hygiene, truancy, alcoholism, misuse of pills, were observed in 12.1 per cent. In short, it can be concluded that a specific presuicidal syndrome does not exist among children and adolescents. The most common presuicidal change is of a depressive kind where symptoms of a neurotic type manifest signs of increased tension.

In the youngest group of children, those under 14, there is a balance between the sexes, while among the older ones, as has been pointed out, girls predominate in suicide attempts and boys in completed suicides. The youngest cases studied were 10 years of age. Much younger cases are reported in the literature. Problems of home life and problems involving parents are naturally in the majority for this group (69.0 per cent), followed by school problems (16.7 per cent). This is in contrast to the sample as a whole, where love problems predominate. It seems to be true, as has been said, that those who had the responsibility of giving the children security and safety—the parents—were unsuccessful and have betrayed their children. This is the most important cause among the younger children.

In contrast to some investigators, we have not found that active methods of suicide are particularly common in the youngest group. In this sample the active and the passive methods are distributed evenly through all the age groups, with a pronounced preference for the passive methods.

Children have a view of death which differs from that of adults. It is more realistic, and yet they do not believe that they themselves can die. That is for old people. They often believe, too, that death is a reversible stage and that is why they can talk about it in a manner so casual that it may shock adults.

One of the greatest and most important changes occurs in life when a child starts school. The mental problems to which children and adolescents are exposed in school have become the focus of increasing interest and a growing concern not only with the school's importance in educating and communicating knowledge but also with its importance for the development of personality. Problems of discipline have gained more and more significance and have now at last become the center of attention. Hence the Swedish school has increased its staff of psychiatric, psychological, and sociological experts. Children can show symptoms of insufficiency as a result of difficulties in school: anxiety, sleep disturbances, stomach-aches and headaches, vomiting, stuttering, bed-wetting, for example. The suicidal act is one of the more dramatic examples of the difficulties of adjustment. The role of the school in these cases has not yet been sufficiently studied except by child psychiatrists. A comparatively common form of conflict which may lead to a suicide attempt crops up when the pupil is exposed to overly strong demands from the school and becomes anxious and bored by the whole thing. The parents are disappointed and ask for improvement and are unable to abandon the idea that the child's studies should lead to a high-school diploma. This conflict could lead to an acutely difficult situation where the pupil feels abandoned and tired and in despair commits a suicidal act. Less than one-fifth (18.8 per cent) of those who were in school in this sample mentioned school as the reason for their suicide attempt. In other words, it seems that school provides a comparatively insignificant factor in suicidal acts.

The distribution through the months of the year for the school group does not coincide with the sample as a whole, but relates directly to those months which bring final tests, entrance tests, and exams, that is, periods of increased pressure. In Sweden this means the end of spring term and the period just before the beginning of fall term. Bad results on tests were the cause of the suicide attempts in the school group in almost half of the cases (46.7 per cent). In 11.3 per cent of the cases the pupil had wished to quit school, but the family had opposed the idea. This then provoked the suicide attempt. In our sample we found a significant predominance of high-school forms (*realskola* and *gymnasium*). It would appear that in this group we are dealing with children and adolescents who are forced by their parents to continue school without being interested on their own and who are exposed to too much pressure while lacking the capacity to absorb the education offered.

Among the girls who were pregnant, 11.8 per cent of the sample made a suicide attempt after being denied an abortion. An investigation preceding authorization of an abortion in Sweden is a complicated affair with medical, gynecological, psychiatric, and social examinations being undertaken first at the local level. Then the local report is sent to a central institution (Kungliga Medicinalstyrelsen) to be evaluated. From the standpoint of suicide risk, the second and third month of pregnancy are the most critical (18.6 and 23.3 per cent). This is the period when pregnancy is usually discovered. The most common reason given by the pregnant girls for attempting suicide is their pregnancy (43.6 per cent), followed by problems in love and difficulties in communication (37.2 per cent). It is not easy to distinguish among these reasons since love problems often conceal a conflict with the male partner that may have arisen in connection with the pregnancy. It has also been proved that single and abandoned women more often threaten to commit suicide than women who continue to be in touch with their male partners.

The frequency of serious mental illness is less among the pregnant women than for the rest of the sample. The difference can at least be partially accounted for in this manner: the provoking momentum—the pregnancy—is such a forceful factor that vulnerable personalities react with suicidal acts without suffering from any mental disturbances. To support this argument, there is also the fact that the neurotic states and the reactions of insufficiency dominate strongly (82.1 per cent) and that not a single case of psychosis was observed among the pregnant girls.

Among the boys in the investigation who were in military service, 59 per cent pointed to that as the reason for their suicide attempt. It is interesting to note that in this group the greatest number of suicide attempts happen in connection with leave and usually toward the end of it. Hence it is *before* the return to the regiment after a stay in private life with its different atmosphere that vulnerable personalities react with suicide attempts. I have previously pointed out that asthenic personalities seem to have especially great difficulty in adjusting to military life. Among the boys in military service who commit suicidal acts, the asthenic types predominate (44.0 per cent). This is in contrast to the sample as a whole where the hysteroids and those with infantile personality traits predominate. It should be noted that 46 per cent of the boys had gone to the military doctor during the month preceding the suicide attempt complaining about nervous symptoms, and 54 per cent had seen the doctor in the week just preceding the attempt. At that time two-thirds complained about symptoms of nervousness, and one-third referred to somatic symptoms. The tension which triggered the suicide attempt had probably been building up for some time and had taken different forms, but the conflicts behind the symptoms had not been revealed and therefore adequate countermeasures could not be taken.

SUMMARY

An account is presented of the conditions surrounding suicide attempts by children and adolescents under 21 years of age in Sweden covering the five-year period 1955 to 1959. Girls are in the majority. Neurotic states and hysterical and infantile personality variables are predominant. The existence of a presuicidal syndrome is discussed as well as the background of suicide attempts within certain groups as, for instance, boys in military service, pregnant girls, children with school problems, and the very youngest group of the sample.

References

1. BERGSTRAND, C. G., and U. OTTO. "Suicidal Attempts in Adolescence and Childhood," *Acta Paediat. Scand.*, LI (1962), 17–26.
2. OTTO, U. "Suicidal Attempts Made during Compulsory Service," *Acta Psychiat. Scand.*, XXXIX (1963), 298.
3. OTTO, U. "Changes in the Behaviour of Children and Adolescents Preceding Suicidal Attempts," *Acta Psychiat. Scand.*, XL (1964), 386.
4. OTTO, U. "Suicidal Attempts in Adolescence and Childhood-States of Mental Illness and Personality Variables," *Acta Paedopsychiat.*, XXXI (1964), 397.
5. OTTO, U. "Suicidal Attempts Made by Pregnant Women under 21 Years," *Acta Paedopsychiat.*, XXXII (1965), 276.
6. OTTO, U. "Suicidal Attempts Made by Children and Adolescents because of School Problems," *Acta Paediat. Scand.*, LV (1966), 348.
7. OTTO, U. "Suicidal Attempts Made by Psychotic Children," *Acta Paediat. Scand.*, Vol. LVI (1967).

19

Adolescent Suicidal Behavior
and Hallucinations

Don A. Winn

This study concerns adolescents in the Children's Unit of Creedmoor State Hospital who have threatened to kill themselves. The Children's Service, under the direction of Lauretta Bender, M.D., is a residential treatment center for 400 emotionally disturbed children and adolescents. We admit yearly about 250 adolescents, approximately one-third of whom have made a suicidal threat. Though we admit nearly the same number of adolescent boys and girls, the incidence of suicidal threats by girls is nearly 45 per cent, whereas it is only 20 per cent among the boys. Our adolescents come predominantly from heavily populated neighborhoods of New York City, and most of their families are in the low to lowest socioeconomic groups. Approximately half of our adolescents are Negro, a fourth are white, and a fourth are Puerto Rican. Nearly all of our adolescents who have threatened to kill themselves are "very disturbed," and three-fourths are regarded as psychotic. Schizophrenia is the most frequent diagnosis, being considered the primary diagnosis in two-thirds of the cases.

Most of our suicidal adolescent girls, who are often histrionic and manifestly manipulative, are hospitalized primarily because of their suicidal threats. The boys are more often admitted primarily as a result of serious antisocial behavior or aggressive threats toward others, such that the suicidal threat may seem incidental or of secondary importance. Typically, both the boys and the girls are acutely psychotic at the time of the threat, but psychotic depression, as may be seen in adults with grossly altered affect and psychomotor retardation, is quite infrequent. Depression, which is in itself a most elusive symptom in adolescents, is often the least persistent symptom, and adolescents who persist long in appearing sad or forlorn are more often showing schizophrenic withdrawal. Once they are in the

252

hospital, further suicidal threats are seldom made. The frequent evaluation of our adolescents as having psychosis implies a grave disturbance, but it does not necessarily imply a grave prognosis. On the contrary, the overt manifestations of psychosis are relatively quick to go into abeyance. Many adolescents go into remission spontaneously, and the majority with supportive psychotherapy, adjunctive medication, or electric convulsive therapy in some cases lose the more obvious manifestations of their illness in a matter of weeks. It is only about 10 per cent of our suicidal adolescents who follow a protracted overtly psychotic course over several months. The majority of the girls are able to return home in two to four months. The average duration of hospitalization for the boys is somewhat longer. However, approximately one-third of the girls return to the hospital in the next few months because of further suicidal threats, sexual acting out, or running away. And the boys have a somewhat higher readmission rate, usually returning because of antisocial behavior in the community. They seldom return as a result of further threats of suicide. In the ten years that the Children's Unit has been open, none of the suicidal adolescents once treated here are known subsequently to have killed themselves, though one boy and one girl are known subsequently as young adults to have committed murder by the same means with which they had once threatened suicide.

This study is a descriptive one, the purpose of which is to emphasize hallucinations as frequently influencing the suicidal behavior of our adolescents. Sixty adolescents were initially selected for this study without regard for the presence or absence of hallucinations. The cases were selected arbitrarily from two wards of adolescent boys and two wards of adolescent girls until there were thirty boys and thirty girls. The only requirements were that the adolescents had threatened to kill themselves and that they be neither grossly brain-damaged, epileptic, nor grossly retarded intellectually. Mildly disturbed adolescents are circumstantially absent due to the fact that we generally receive more seriously disturbed adolescents by referral from other hospitals or guidance centers. The adolescents in this study ranged in age from 11½ to 15½ years at the time of the threat. The three most frequent means by which the boys had threatened to kill themselves were to jump from a height, stab themselves, or hang themselves; whereas the girls most frequently had threatened to take poison, stab themselves, or jump from a height. The girls were more prone to have made multiple threats. The adolescents averaged 3½ years retardation in their school function, and their average I.Q. upon testing by the WISC gave a full-scale I.Q. of 84, with an average verbal of 81 and a performance of 89.

Twenty-five, or 40 per cent, of the 60 adolescents had experienced hallucinations telling them to kill themselves. Eleven of these were boys and 14 were girls. There were an additional 5 boys whose voices did not tell them to kill themselves, but they threatened suicide in part because of anticipated guilt occasioned by voices directing them toward external aggression. Thus 50 per cent of the original 60 adolescents felt that their threat was influenced by hallucinations. Many of the 25 adolescents whose voices were suicidal in content had also, at one time or another, had other voices, or even the same voice with different content. Moreover, when hallucinations of any kind were considered, 50 out of 60, or 83 per cent, of the adolescents examined for this study had experienced hallucinations within the year preceding their admission. The hallucinations that were specifically suicidal in content may be better understood by first giving some description of all the various hallucinations as they occurred in the broader group of 50 adolescents and by giving at the same time some brief comparison to similar experiences that may occur in younger children.

Generally the auditory hallucinations of our prepubertal children are of a simple order with a good and a bad voice that tell the child to do something or not to do it, such that they are action-oriented voices. The voices may be relatively benign, as when the bad voice may tell the child to run away or not to do his homework, or when the good voice may tell him to do his homework or not to run away. The voices are more malignant when they direct the child to do such things as kill himself or set a fire, or when they are more bizarre in content, as for example, in the child who hears the sky crack. When there are both a good and a bad voice the good counterpart will usually follow the bad voice and contradict it. The good voice could better be called the "rescue" voice, for that seems largely to be its function. The voices are usually personified as coming from God or the devil, but the good voice may also be personified as that of the mother, or an angel which is feminine, or occasionally Jesus, and the bad voice may be said to come from a monster, an animal, or a witch. Children usually perceive the voice as coming from inside their body, and especially from their own head, though the good voice may localize to the right ear and the bad voice to the left ear. Young children often describe the voice as coming from an incorporated object.

In contrast to the voices that are encountered in younger children, none of the adolescents in this study experienced voices as coming from an incorporated object, and 75 per cent of them perceived the voices as coming not from their own bodies or heads, but from some source external to themselves. The good and bad voice pattern was retained, but in contrast to younger children there was a tendency away from personifying the voices. About the only bad voice personification retained was that of the devil in 40 per cent of the 50 adolescents. The bad voice had more often become one of an indefinite male or rarely an indefinite female. The good voice was personified in about 45 per cent as coming from their own mother, the Virgin, or another religious figure, but most were thought to come from indefinite females. Twenty per cent of the adolescents also heard voices which they felt came from the dead, and these might be good or bad. The good voice continued on the whole to have a rescue function. Only one boy in the study had a rescue voice described as being that of his father. In view of the absence of father rescue voices, it is of interest to note that 80 per cent of the adolescents in this study had never known or were long separated from their fathers. It may also be noted that many of the adolescents described the hallucinations as arising in association to real or threatened separation from the mother or mother surrogate, and the first vague hallucinations they remember having were often of their mother calling their names. It is of interest to observe that 80 per cent of our adolescents had as children experienced prolonged separation from the mother or mother surrogate for as much as one to eight years.

Like the voices of younger children, the voices of our adolescents were still predominantly action voices with the bad voice telling them to fight, run away, steal, kill someone, or, as is important for this study, kill themselves. Action voices were present in 85 per cent of the 50 adolescents with voices. In the other 15 per cent the hallucinations were either so vague or so benign in content as to seem insignificant. The voices were accompanied in 40 per cent by visual hallucinations as well, and these became important in several instances of adolescents with suicidal voices, because to them the voices emanated from the visions. The visions would also often occur with good and bad counterparts and were often personified in the same way as the voices, but they were also often left indefinite, being typically called a bad black man or a nice lady in white, or they were described as partial representations with eyes, faces, and shadows having been perceived. The action voices were accompanied in four adolescents by accusatory voices which told them they were bad or called them bad names. One girl would hear the voice of the Virgin telling her she would have painful menses after she acted out sexually, and several adolescents had action voices that would also threaten worse consequences if not obeyed; but on the whole, accusatory and threatening voices, which are common in disturbed adults, were more conspicuous by their absence.

Thus the suicidal voices were typically externally projected, action-oriented voices, felt often to come from unpersonified malevolent males. The bad voices were often followed and contradicted by feminine rescue voices, which some of the adolescents accredited with putting an end to the suicidal behavior. These observations of phenomena so much on the surface merit description because the adolescents with voices of suicidal content seemed often to have acted out their threats the more extremely, and they were themselves very distressed by the voices. In this study compelling hallucinations seemed particularly operative among adolescents who had most seriously endangered their lives, as in the instance of a girl who jumped off a roof four floors up, or of a boy who rode his bicycle head on into a moving car, or of a girl who cut deeply into her arms. Our prepubertal children are usually less distressed by hallucinations than the adolescents. The children with suicidal voices often do not understand or appreciate the significance of death, so that they are no more disturbed by a voice telling them to die than by one that tells them to steal. By contrast, the adolescents are fully appreciative of the consequences of death and are very distressed by a voice that tells them to harm either themselves or another person. Equally or more distressing to the adolescents is the fact that having voices or visions implies to them that they are "crazy" and thereby different.

In their developmental history, broader ideation, or general behavior there was nothing remarkable to distinguish the adolescents with suicidal hallucinations from those in this study who did not have such hallucinations. For example, corollary projective defenses, such as ideas of reference or of influence, which had been present among half of the 60 adolescents, were just as frequent among those with suicidal hallucinations as among those without. With respect to their conscious motivations all 60 of the adolescents focused their attention on the precipitating events as leading to suicidal behavior. They did not always do so directly since some would initially deny their behavior by calling it accidental, some would minimize it by treating it facetiously, and many of those with voices telling them to kill themselves would initially regard the voices as literally causative. The voices, however, had always arisen in situations of mounting anxiety occasioned by one or more precipitating events, and the adolescents would come soon enough to discuss the precipitating events as bearing more significantly on their behavior. Schneer and Kay,[1] in a study of suicidal adolescents in Kings County Hospital, described the same kinds of precipitating circumstances as those of which all 60 of our adolescents complained. In their study the manifest events were: separation (from parents or other significant persons or objects), disclosure of forbidden activity (such as drinking beer at school), defiance (of parental or other authorities), restriction (by parents), criticism (for example, for obesity by a friend), and exclusion (as, from home or school to an institution). The conscious ideation surrounding these events consisted of thoughts about punishment, being separated from parents, being beaten by parents, hurting and killing parents or siblings, jealousy of siblings, rape, defective sexual identity, coercive or dramatized bids for attention, and getting rid of auditory hallucinations.

Impulsivity was prominently a part of the suicidal behavior of most of the 60 adolescents in this study. The presence of hallucinations did not necessarily make the threats less impulsive since the voices would often occur suddenly or unexpectedly, and there were some adolescents with recurring hallucinations who felt they had impulsively obeyed voices that they had previously been able to resist. Teicher and Jacobs,[2] in a recent study of the conscious deliberations of suicidal adolescents, tend to discredit the importance of impulsivity when the suicidal threat is viewed in the context of the life history. For at least two-thirds of our adolescents impulsivity had in fact been a very real problem for them through much of their life history, dating often to descriptions of hyperactivity and poor impulse control in the preschool years. We would suggest that impulsivity, in combination with unconscious motivating factors and the pressure put on the adolescents to explain their threat, resulted in the adolescents' being burdened with describing their motivations in more concrete terms and with a greater semblance of logic than was in fact merited. Compelling hallucinations, however distressing they may have been, were not necessarily so disadvantageous after the suicidal threat had passed, for the adolescents could retrospectively make of them a concrete and internally logical justification for their behavior that could temporarily ward off further feelings of guilt or recrimination.

The following eight abbreviated case histories are given primarily to illustrate the suicidal hallucinations that had influenced the behavior of half of the adolescents in the study. The cases are secondarily arranged in a manner to allow for brief comment on a few disturbances that were frequently encountered in the total group of 60 adolescents, these being disturbances in aggressive impulses, disturbances in sexual impulses, and disturbances of body-image.

The first two cases are of a boy and a girl with compelling hallucinations in which poor control of aggressive impulses was a major problem.

Case 1

Walter was an enormously large 14-year-old boy who had always been oversize. At age 9 he had begun to feel that other boys could read his mind and he theirs. Thereafter he had been largely seclusive. At age 14 he was mannerly and not unfriendly, but he liked animals only and did not like people. He was a pacifist, and during an episode of depersonalization he felt transported to a world where there was no war or fighting. He was hospitalized because of several sudden rage reactions in which he had once threatened to kill a teacher and once a construction worker and because he had threatened to stab himself to death. The incidents were triggered by minor rebukes or criticism. He described hearing the voice of an unidentified man telling him to kill himself and fight. He also had comforting visions of God, dead people, and animals, none of whom disturbed him by talking. He was of average intelligence and came from an intact family.

Case 2

Geraldine was a 13-year-old girl who had been having hysterical "spells" since age 12, in which she would thrash about and roll her eyes. At age 13 she began to feel that other girls watched her and talked about her. Her acute disturbance was precipitated by truancy and aggressive behavior at school followed by restrictions at home. She was hospitalized when she threatened to jump from a window and stab her father with a kitchen knife. She was told to do both by the devil, whom she saw and heard. Her parents were fanatically religious, and her mother was hallucinatory as well. Since the age of 9 Geraldine had been communicating with God and Jesus and speaking in tongues, which the mother encouraged. Since she had the "touch of God" she was used for faith healing at her parents' church. Her parents only became concerned about her when she became possessed by the devil. She was of low average intelligence.

Walter had a typically externalized unpersonified male action voice telling him to fight or kill himself. He had comforting hallucinations that would often follow the bad voice and rescue him, but these curiously were only visual and did not talk. He was one of the few adolescents who came from an intact family, but interestingly he had long been distressed by his parents' frequent verbal battles. Geraldine's bad voice was personified as that of the devil. As often occurred, the bad voice had a double component in which she was told to kill another person and herself. Her good voices did not follow the bad and did not have a rescue function. Geraldine was one of four adolescents in this study whose family, for reasons of religion or black magic, encouraged hallucinations. She was also one of eight adolescents to have had hallucinations as a child.

Walter and Geraldine both had difficulty in controlling externalized aggressive impulses. Walter was typical of the many boys who were hospitalized as much or more because of external aggression as for suicidal behavior. Among the 60 patients in the study, 85 per cent of the boys had shown delinquent behavior, including such things as burglary or extortion, and 60 per cent of them had threatened to kill another person. The girls were less externally aggressive, but 35 per cent of them had also threatened to kill another person. The other persons whom the adolescents had threatened to kill were members of their own family in 70 per cent of these instances. Both the boys and the girls could very facilely shift from internalized to externalized aggression.

The next two cases are of a girl and a boy in whom the control of sexual impulses was a major problem.

Case 3

Josephine was a vivacious and charming 13-year-old girl with a long history of disruptive school behavior. Two years earlier she had appeared in court for sexual misconduct, and sexual acting out with men and boys was recurrent thereafter. She became more acutely disturbed when a boy friend lost interest in her and heavier restrictions were imposed on her by her mother. She began to feel that people made fun of her and that her brother wanted to kill her. She thought a neighbor was trying to make her crazy. She began to hear the devil telling her to kill herself, but she was usually stopped by the rescue voices of God and angels. She was eventually hospitalized because she threatened serially to jump out of a window, hang herself, and stab her mother and herself. On admission she was delusionally pregnant and had fantasies bordering on the delusional, telling that she had tried to castrate an impertinent boy and that she had had an illegitimate baby. She was of low average intelligence. She herself was illegitimate and had never known her father, though she had had a series of common-law stepfathers.

Case 4

William was a 15-year-old boy who had begun at age 14 to sleepwalk, to feel that people watched him, and to refuse to bathe. He began to carry knives and once threatened to kill his uncle. He became increasingly hypo-chondriacal, and his insect phobia became more marked. He began to play with children's toys and became preoccupied with magic to the extent that he tried to sew his fingers together because he thought he was magically protected. Six months before admission he became recurrently plagued by a male voice telling him to steal and rape. He would try to suppress it by playing basketball. He was hospitalized after he had attempted to rape a 5-year-old girl and his 7-year-old half sister. He was stopped at the point of violent penetration in both instances by getting a sudden feeling that eyes were watching him. Because of disclosure of the rape attempts, his own guilt, and his fear that the voice would someday drive him to rape, he threatened to leap from a suspension bridge. He was of average intelligence. He had been illegitimately born to a 13-year-old mother. He was reared by his grandmother. His mother reappeared periodically and in later years would go on double dates with him. The mother had had a *post partum* psychosis after the birth of her second child.

Josephine made several suicidal threats that were rather directly influenced by her hallucinations. William had never heard a voice telling him to kill himself. He was one of the five boys in the study who did not have suicidal voices, but were suicidally influenced by guilt-provoking voices telling them to harm someone else. William's voice told him to commit rape, and the other four boys had voices telling them to kill other persons.

Josephine and William both had difficulty in controlling sexual impulses. Among the 60 patients in this study overt sexual problems were especially frequent among the girls, with 60 per cent of them having acted out sexually. Fantasies of rape and of prostitution were often present even among the girls who had not acted out. Six girls in the study had had sexual play with stepfathers, and two girls had been seduced by their real fathers at a younger age. Their suicidal threats were often precipitated by separations from boy friends. Only 37 per cent of the boys had overt sexual disturbances either in their behavior or in their conscious ideation. Two boys had made rape attempts, and two had exhibited themselves in public, but the more frequent problem was one of confusion in sexual identification. A few boys with confused identity showed exaggerated masculinity, but worried about homosexuality. Five boys were blatantly homosexual or had shown transvestism. Sexual disturbances are not, of course, sharply separate from aggressive disturbances, and the one may stand for the other. This was particularly evident among many of the promiscuous girls and the overtly homosexual boys, for their sexual experiences were often empty and the boy friends, over whom they may ostensibly have threatened to kill themselves, were of no real importance. Their sexual behavior seemed more to be used as an indirectly aggressive means of provoking or outraging their families and especially their mothers. Spitefulness was prominent in their ideation and was often accompanied by charges of hypocrisy against promiscuous mothers.

The next two cases are of a boy and a girl with compelling hallucinations in which disturbances of body-image were a major problem.

Case 5

Clark was a 14-year-old boy long preoccupied with death, who was hypochondriacal and feared closed rooms. He fantasied flying to the moon and when younger had thought he could be Superman because his first name was the same as Superman's alias, Clark Kent. His admission was precipitated by threatening boys at school with a knife and by recurrent episodes of depersonalization in which he believed he had died in a car accident. He would see himself as an angel with other angels, or his body would be floating in the air and he would hear his own voice coming from a distance. He also had visions of a man dying with a knife in his back. His suicidal threat, however, occurred after he improved and was to be sent home. As the day passed and it was obvious his uninterested mother would not come, the environment again became unreal to him and he heard a man's voice telling him to kill himself. He ran from the hospital and stopped traffic by lying down in the street. He was of low borderline intelligence. His father was an alcoholic whom he had never known, and his mother had once threatened suicide with sleeping pills.

Case 6

Michele was a 15-year-old who had shown seclusiveness and neurotic traits since age 9. Fear of the dark and of school became a problem at age 11. With menarche at age 12 she became afraid of crowds, busses, and the odors of matches, cigarettes, and gasoline, progressing finally to the fear that her vagina smelled of feces. She thought people could smell the vaginal odor, and if they denied it, they had a cold. Menstruation would wash away the odor, but between periods she coated her vagina with Mennen's Deodorant for Men and Ice Blue Secret. Over the next three years she had repeated episodes of depersonalization accompanied by hallucinations of the devil telling her to kill herself or her mother. Serially she attempted suicide by swallowing cologne; she next burned herself badly on a radiator and finally swallowed an overdose of Bufferin. Repeatedly, she would think of herself as raped, as a prostitute, or as pregnant, though she was in fact virginal. On her final admission she thought her saliva was poisonous, and she was grossly paranoid, thinking among other things that electronic rays were being sent into her body. She was of average intelligence. Her great-grandfather and grandfather had committed suicide, and her father had tried. Her father was a chronic schizophrenic who had not been home since attacking his wife with a hammer when Michele was six years old. He had been skilled in electronics.

The hallucinatory voice in Clark's case is particularly illustrative of one that arose rather suddenly and unexpectedly in a situation of mounting anxiety and led to an impulsive suicidal threat. The boy was intensely disappointed by his mother's failure to come for him, and he later spoke of feeling angry and vengeful toward her, but in the immediate period following the threat the voice for him had been literally causative. Michele had very often heard a voice telling her to kill herself and had usually been able to resist the voice. Her decision to obey the voice on three occasions was to some extent impulsive and would follow a superficially trivial quarrel with her mother or brother. She, however, was more deliberate in her suicidal behavior than were most of the adolescents in this study, and she was one of a few adolescents who felt that they had really wanted to die.

Clark and Michele had both experienced severe disturbances of body-image. Among all 60 of the adolescents depersonalization as a more extreme distortion of body-image had been present in 30 per cent of the girls and 15 per cent of the boys. Though relatively infrequent as a manifest symptom, fantasies or fears that could be associated with depersonalization were quite frequent and appeared to be an integral part of the adolescents' often long-standing preoccupation with death. Hypochondriasis as a lesser disturbance of body-image was frequent among the 60 adolescents, and sexual confusion as another aspect of body-image disturbance has already been noted.

The final two illustrative cases in the study are of a boy and a girl with compelling suicidal hallucinations which arose in association with pathological or unresolved mourning over the loss of the mother by death.

Case 7

Kenneth was a 12-year-old whose hypertensive mother died when he was 8 years old. The father had earlier abandoned the family. The boy was asthmatic, but had no problem otherwise before his mother's death. His mother's last gift to him had been a dog, which his sister later made him give away. He showed little reaction to his mother's death and did not cry, but his school performance fell; he became truant, defied his family, and was in trouble for extorting money from peers. Two years later he sobbed uncontrollably and was depressed following the death of a nephew. When he was 9 he had acquired a large imaginary dog companion named King. At age 12, King became hallucinatory, and he would go with King to a special spot in a vacant lot during the full moon where his mother would talk to him. Her voice protected him from the voice of a man which told him to be bad. In his own room his mother would send him a leprechaun through the keyhole. His acute disturbance was heralded in by a dream in which the surgeon replaced his heart with that of his dead mother. He was hospitalized after threatening to hang himself with a belt, having been told to do so by his mother, who wanted him to join her. As a postscript to his leaving the hospital he was arrested for burglarizing a house, but the only thing he stole was the woman's pet dog. He was of average intelligence.

Case 8

Brenda was 13½ when she threatened suicide. When pregnant with Brenda her mother developed carcinoma of the breast. She would not allow the pregnancy to be interrupted despite her husband's protest. Brenda was 7 when her mother died. She did not react to her mother's death, but her school performance declined, and she became a "loner." In latency she acquired an imaginary companion named Gloria, and she became very attached to a sister who was six years older than she. At age 11 she was frightened by the onset of menstruation. She resented the acquiring of a stepmother and two stepsisters, and her favorite sister left the home to marry. Shortly after the marriage, Brenda was caught having intercourse at school. She threatened to kill a teacher, and she pulled a knife on some schoolmates. About this time she began to hear and see a comforting angel. She maintained a seclusive uneasy adjustment until she was overwhelmed at age 13 when her favorite sister died of an overdose of heroin. She began to feel followed by girls and government agents and thought heroin was being put in her Ovaltine. She threatened to kill and dismember her father and stepmother. She feared underworld revenge because she thought she had murdered six people, including her psychopathic brother-in-law. A month later, and six years after her mother's death, she was acutely depressed and obsessively ruminated about the death of her mother. She stopped eating and would rock in a frenzy. Her angel became six angels, and she saw them standing about her casket at her own funeral. When they called to her she slashed her wrists and tried to take poison. She was of average intelligence.

Kenneth and Brenda were representative of five adolescents in this study with a variant kind of hallucinatory experience who were of specific interest because their cases lend vivid clinical evidence to the proposition that death may represent reunion with the lost mother. As already noted, most of the adolescents with suicidal hallucinations regarded them as bad voices coming from the devil or unspecified malevolent males. Good feminine rescue voices would often follow and redirect or comfort the adolescents. For these five adolescents what had been a good or comforting rescue voice became reversed in role and was endangering. The adolescents still regarded the voice as benevolent, even though it called upon them to die. For Kenneth and two others the voice was directly personified as that of their dead mother. For one girl it was a vision of the Holy Mother which told her to die. The vision was described as resembling photographs of the girl's dead mother. Brenda's multiple angel was probably representative of both the dead mother and the older sister, the sister herself having served as a mother surrogate until she too died. The five adolescents whose mothers had in fact died were the only ones to give good personifications to voices calling them to their death. An additional three adolescents in the study lost their mothers by death, but they did not develop voices of this kind. Several more adolescents had living mothers who were effectively just as lost to them, and some of them experienced hearing or seeing an absent mother, but the voices could remain comforting without telling them to die. In their conscious fantasies they would often cling to the hope of being reunited with their mothers, and a few of them suggested that their suicidal threat was in part motivated by spiteful feelings against authoritative figures or institutions who they felt kept them from their mothers.

SUMMARY

From a group of 60 seriously disturbed adolescents who had threatened suicide, 30 adolescents alluded to their suicidal behavior as being influenced by hallucinations. Such experiences were very distressing to the adolescents, and they often regarded the hallucinations as being literally responsible for their behavior. The hallucinations telling them to kill themselves arose in situations of mounting anxiety occasioned by one or several precipitating events. The precipitating circumstances were largely the same for all 60 adolescents, whether or not they had compelling hallucinations. Fifty of the adolescents had experienced hallucinations of some kind. The suicidal hallucinations were typically action-oriented and differed only in content from the hallucinations as they occurred more broadly in the other adolescents. The usually masculine malevolent voices were often followed by usually feminine good or rescue voices. Eight abbreviated illustrative case histories were given primarily to describe the influencing hallucinations. The first six cases were secondarily arranged to allow brief comment on a few of the major problems for all 60 of the adolescents, these being poor control of aggressive impulses, poor control of sexual impulses, and gross disturbance of body-image. The past two cases were representative of compelling hallucinations which arose during the final crisis occasioned by unresolved mourning over the loss of the dead mother.

References

1. SCHNEER, H., and P. KAY. "Suicidal Behavior in Adolescents," *Psychiatric Quarterly*, XXXV (1961), 507.
2. TEICHER, J., and J. JACOBS. "Adolescents Who Attempt Suicide: Preliminary Findings," *American Journal of Psychiatry*, CXXII (1966), 1248.

20

Depression in Children
and Adolescents

James M. Toolan

Depression is a common problem in adult psychiatry. Similar clinical pictures are rarely encountered in children and adolescents, at least until 14 or 15 years of age. In fact, the absence of the usual clinical picture has led most psychiatrists to the erroneous conclusion that depression does not occur in younger people.[7] I shall attempt to show in this study that depression is a most important problem in childhood and in adolescence and one which is unfortunately often overlooked. We have to cease thinking in terms of adult psychiatry and instead become accustomed to recognizing the various manifestations by which depression may be represented in younger people.

In infants depression is often evidenced by eating and sleeping disturbances, colic, crying, and head-banging. It is of interest that the mothers of such infants are frequently depressed and/or anxious. These complaints come usually to the attention of the pediatrician, seldom to that of the psychiatrist. At a somewhat later age, withdrawal, apathy, and regression may be evidence of the same difficulty. These symptoms may often be encountered in emotionally deprived infants.[9] In severe cases emotional deprivation may lead to permanent emotional and intellectual impairment and even to death. As the child grows somewhat older, behavioral problems begin to displace depressive feelings: temper tantrums, disobedience, truancy, running away from home, accident proneness; masochism, as indicated by the child who manages to get beaten up by the other children; self-destructive behavior. The youngster is convinced that he is bad, evil, unacceptable. Such feelings lead him into antisocial behavior, which in turn only further reinforces his belief that he is no good. The youngster will often feel that he is inferior to other children, ugly, and stupid.

In the latency child and especially in the adolescent we seldom see a clear picture of depression. Boys especially have a need to hide their true feelings, particularly any soft, tender, weak sentiments. Denial is one of the most characteristic mechanisms used by the adolescent, and this mechanism on both a conscious and an unconscious level is of great assistance in the avoidance of depressive feelings. At times the teen-ager may deliberately mask his true feelings by a pretense of happiness and exhibit the picture of a smiling depression.

Rather than the usual clinical picture of depression in the adolescent, we encounter a set of symptoms which I prefer to call "depressive equivalents." Boredom and restlessness are exhibited by the adolescent to a remarkable degree. He appears uninterested in anything one moment, then is preoccupied with trivia the next. He loses interest quickly even in his most prized activities and then frenetically seeks something new to entertain him. He must be constantly busy; otherwise he is bored to distraction. He cannot stand being alone, even for a short period of time. He seeks constant stimulation.

Hand in hand with boredom, the teen-ager frequently complains of fatigue. He alternates between overwhelming fatigue and inexhaustible energy. Undoubtedly some of this fatigue is physiological, being the result of the very rapid growth processes taking place at this time. We should always be suspicious, however, when the fatigue in a physically healthy youngster appears out of proportion to his activity and when it interferes with his normal activity. It is also noteworthy when the adolescent complains of being excessively tired upon awakening in the morning after an adequate amount of sleep. We are all accustomed to observing this symptom in adult patients suffering from depression. Hypochondriasis and bodily preoccupation have also frequently to be considered as evidence of depression, as is also the case in many involutional depressions.

Many depressed youngsters complain of difficulty in concentration. In fact, this is one of the chief presenting complaints to the school physician and should always be taken seriously, else within a very short time an otherwise capable student may fail and leave school, to the amazement of parents and faculty alike. Confronted with such a problem, the conscientious student will often spend long hours on his studies with little benefit. He will see others achieving better grades with much less effort and will soon become convinced that he is not capable of mastering his work. Discouraged, he will then cease trying.

Anyone who has worked with adolescents is well aware of their propensity for acting out. This, plus denial, is their main method of handling problems. Rather than face a problem, they will run away from it. This can be a most distressing obstacle to therapy, but is met even more frequently in the daily activity of adolescents. The acting out of some adolescents may lead to serious delinquent behavior. The work of Kaufman[6] has shown that many a delinquent youngster is literally running away from himself. Anyone who has successfully treated delinquents has been struck by the very severe underlying depression which often frightens the patient away from therapy. These delinquents suffer from a severely impoverished self-image and a profound emptiness of ego comparable to the emptiness of the schizophrenic ego. Any activity, no matter how dangerous or destructive, is better than facing this horrible image of oneself.

In many adolescents and adults we encounter sexual acting out as a method of relieving their depressive feelings. Such a person frenetically seeks contact with another human being by means of sexual intercourse, the only method of relating that he knows. Quite often, as in the case of the alcoholic, this activity produces only further depression and guilt, which once again he attempts to relieve by further sexual acting out.

Some children and adolescents who feel neglected and unloved by their parents may turn to animals as love objects. These youngsters are able to love and care for animals and in turn feel needed by the animal. They do not fear rejection by the animal, as they do by human beings.

Psychological data can be of great assistance also in the recognition of depressive reactions in children and adolescents, provided we realize that the data are different than in most cases of adult depression. The record at first glance often appears to be immersed in nondepressive data. There is a close relationship between anger and depression, more so than in most adult records. The anger often tends to be expressed overtly at the expense of the depressive feelings, whereas in the adult the relationship between the two appears often to be reversed. The Wechsler scale will often show a higher performance than a verbal score, the opposite of the situation with adult depressive reactions. This may be related to the tendency toward acting out. In addition they may show a psychopathic pattern, as seen in the fact that the object assembly plus picture arrangement is greater than the block design plus picture completion. On the Rorschach, acting-out and angry content are interspersed with depressive content. There may be a diminution in the color response, with the substitution of black as a color and the figure drawings often heavily black. Rorschach protocol often reveals percepts of emptiness, with many aggressive, sadistic images such as biting and tearing apart. Explosive acts are not uncommonly depicted.*

It should be mentioned at this point that manic-depressive reactions are seldom if ever seen in children. Kanner[4] states that they are exceedingly rare before 15 or 16 years of age. Kasanin and Kaufman,[5] in a series of 6,000 admissions, described only four affecting psychoses before 16 years of age. All four had their initial onset after 14 years of age.

Over the past several years further observations have shown that actual clinical depression is not so uncommon as was formerly thought,[12] particularly in adolescents over 15 years of age. I have had the opportunity to

---

* The section on psychological data was prepared with the assistance of Joan Bardach, Ph.D., of the New York University Rehabilitation Unit.

work with several adolescents who exhibited the classical signs of adult depression: retardation in physical and mental activity, feelings of depression, worthlessness, nihilism, apathy, and insomnia as well as suicidal preoccupation.

Sandler and Joffe, in a recent discussion on childhood depression, make the significant point that depression "can be best viewed as a basic psychobiological affective reaction which, like anxiety, becomes abnormal when it occurs in inappropriate circumstances, when it persists for an undue length of time and when the child is unable to make a developmentally-appropriate adaptation to it." [8] This author has previously noted that the common denominator in all depressive reactions is the loss of the desired love object, whether it be in fact or in fantasy. Sandler and Joffe, influenced by Bibring,[1] modify this concept insofar that although what is lost may be an object, it may equally be the loss of the previous state of the self, a feeling of having been deprived of an ideal state. They note that as the child grows older the object loss becomes more important than the loss of the state of well-being embodied in the relationship to the object.

If one accepts the thesis that depression is a reaction to loss, it enables us to understand better the vicissitudes of depressive reaction at various ages. It is true, of course, that not every child reacts to loss with a depressive reaction. But certainly we are aware that individuals vary considerably in their ability to tolerate pain or discomfort of any sort, whether it be physical or mental. In general, the initial reaction to loss is anger. In some children, especially younger ones, this is quickly followed by a feeling of helplessness and resignation leading to a state of apathy. Where the loss arises during the latency and early adolescent periods it will lead the child to hate the lost object, who, he feels, has deserted and betrayed him.[2] The child will often exhibit this anger directly through behavioral symptoms or may inhibit it out of a fear of superego punishment or in the hope that his parents may once again love him if he is good. He often turns the hostility against himself, feeling that he is evil and has been deserted for that reason. As previously described, an evil self-image can only lead the child to evil acts, the frequent acting out so characteristic of depressed children. This, of course, only compounds the difficulty. It drives the parents further away and makes them more punitive. It also reinforces the child's image of himself as an evil, horrible person, and this in turn increases his depressive feelings.

The child attempts many defensive operations to ward off the recognition of the depressive feelings. In younger children regression is often utilized. At a somewhat older age denial and repression are most commonly employed. In adolescence displacement onto somatic symptoms is often attempted. Occasionally, we may encounter youngsters who utilize a reversal of affect.

As the child approaches middle adolescence his reality testing improves with his advancing age. He then finds it increasingly difficult to utilize denial as a defense against depressive feelings. He begins to recognize the role of his parents in the object loss, and as a result his hostility toward them increases, but so, too, do his guilt feelings. The hostility previously directed toward the parents is now directed toward their introjects within the child. As previously described by the author, the superego does not reach maximum development until middle or late adolescence. This, plus the further realization that reality will not change, reinforces his feelings of helplessness and leads to the clinical picture of depression described. We must not overlook another important factor in the production of depression in adolescence. The reactivation of the oedipal complex and its resolution at this period causes a definite sense of loss leading to depressive feelings. This may often reinforce feelings of loss from an earlier age.

I have mentioned the preponderance of females and first children. A previous study of suicide attempts in children and adolescents[11] also emphasized the preponderance of first children. The loss of the unique relationship to the parents is undoubtedly experienced with greater discomfort in first children who have never had to share their parents' love, as do other siblings.

The therapy of depressed patients at any age is a difficult task. There is the always present danger of suicide plus the tendency of depressed persons to believe that they are unable to change, but are helpless. In addition, they wish to avoid facing the pain of recognizing their profound sense of loss and helplessness. Antidepressant medication and ECT are often very effective in reducing these feelings in adults, especially those suffering from psychotic depressions. In adolecents, unfortunately, these tools offer little assistance. For whatever reason, adolescents do not usually react favorably to either drugs or ECT. Thus we must rely entirely on psychotherapy. In one respect, at least, the task is easier than with the younger child who is manifesting depression by behavioral symptoms. The depressed adolescent recognizes that he is troubled and ordinarily is eager to obtain help.

The recognition and proper management of depressive reactions is of the utmost importance. The suicide rate of the 15–19 age group in the United States has doubled over the past ten years. Far more important, however, is the deleterious effect that depression has on the functioning of the adolescent, especially in his schoolwork. Many youngsters troubled by difficulty in concentration do poorly academically and drop out of school, altering their entire future. We have, as yet, little information as to the effect of depression during the adolescent years on psychic functioning. While some might spontaneously overcome these feelings it is likely that many continue as depressed adults. One can only wonder what influence depressive feelings during the adolescent years have on the psychotic depressions of the involutional years.

CONCLUSION

The clinical picture of depression as seen in adults is extremely rare in children and younger adolescents. In younger individuals depression is manifested by a constellation of symptoms which can best be labeled as "depressive equivalents." In middle adolescence, however, frank depressive reactions become evident and are fairly common in older adolescents. Such a change in the clinical picture is due to normal psychological changes occurring during this period.

The common denominator of depression is the loss of the desired love object and the resultant feeling of helplessness. The younger child reacts against such a state by anger toward the lost love object. The latency child inhibits this anger to some extent and turns it against himself, feeling responsible for the loss. As the child matures his improved reality testing makes it difficult for him to utilize the mechanisms of denial and repression. He more clearly recognizes the parents' role as the cause of his loss. The anger tends to be directed, at this stage of development, toward the introjects of the parents in the superego, producing the clinical picture of depression similar to that seen in adults.

References

1. BIBRING, E. "The Mechanism of Depression," in P. GREENACRE, ed., *Affective Disorders.* New York: International Universities Press, 1953.
2. BOWLBY, J. "Processes of Mourning," *International Journal of Psychoanalysis,* Vol. XLII (1961).
3. JACOBZINER, H. "Attempted Suicides in Adolescence," *Journal of the American Medical Association,* CXCI (1965), 101.
4. KANNER, L. *Child Psychiatry.* Springfield, Ill. Charles C Thomas, 1946.
5. KASANIN, J., and M. R. KAUFMAN. "A Study of the Functional Psychoses in Childhood," *American Journal of Psychiatry,* IX (1929), 307–384.
6. KAUFMAN, I., and L. HEIMS. "The Body Image of the Juvenile Delinquent," *American Journal of Orthopsychiatry,* XXVIII (1958), 146–159.
7. ROCHLIN, G. "The Loss Complex," *Journal of the American Psychoanalytic Association,* VII (1959), 299–316.
8. SANDLER, J., and W. G. JOFFE. "Notes on Childhood Depression," *International Journal of Psychoanalysis,* XLVI (January 1965), 88–96.
9. SPITZ, R. "An Inquiry into the Genesis of Psychiatric Conditions in Early Childhood," in *Psychoanalytic Study of the Child.* New York: International Universities Press, 1945, I, 53–74.
10. TOOLAN, J. M. "Changes in Personality Structure During Adolescence," in J. H. MASSERMAN, ed., *Science and Psychoanalysis.* New York: Grune and Stratton, 1960, Vol. III.

11. TOOLAN, J. M. "Depression in Children and Adolescents," *American Journal of Orthopsychiatry*, XXXII (April 1962), 404–415.

12. TOOLAN, J. M. "Suicide and Suicidal Attempts in Children and Adolescents," *American Journal of Psychiatry*, CXVIII (February 1962), 719–724.

Other Conditions

EDITORS' INTRODUCTION This section deals with two examples of psychiatric conditions, endogenous psychoses and drug abuse, which
are commonly encountered in adolescents. These conditions also occur in
adults, and the question arises as to whether they have any specific characteristics when they originate in adolescence. We believe that they do not,
apart from being colored by the typical psychosocial manifestations of this
developmental phase. It is likely that the upheavals of the adolescent crisis
play a significant role in the precipitation of some disorders, but probably
no more so than other developmental crises, such as pregnancy, childbirth,
climacterium, and old age. It also appears that many conditions occur
within a context of other signs of psychological disorder and do not appear,
as it were, in pure culture. This raises interesting differential diagnostic
questions, the most difficult usually being to determine whether the presenting disorder in behavior is simply a particular temporary manifestation of a
commonly occurring expectable adolescent upset, or whether it signals the
emergence of a clinical syndrome with long-term pathological implications.

These questions are discussed in the chapter on endogenous psychoses by
Robert J. Corboz. He devotes most of his attention to a discussion of schizophrenia in adolescence, and he reports that this disorder is nowadays believed by many authorities to originate not only in adults but also in childhood and frequently in adolescence and to occur at these ages in all degrees
of severity and prognosis.

When the illness starts in adolescence it is hard to diagnose because the

271

usual ego changes of this period resemble those of early schizophrenia. Corboz feels that often only prolonged observation of the unfolding of the disorder allows us to differentiate an evanescent and benign adolescent upset from schizophrenia. However, since he also affirms that some cases of schizophrenia in adolescence are short-lived and of good prognosis, it is clear that even this approach will not entirely resolve our diagnostic doubts in difficult cases. In some instances it is possible to rely on the fact that a normal adolescent retains contact with reality and that his behavior is usually only disturbed selectively in certain settings, such as at home or in school, whereas elsewhere he adjusts well, in contrast to the schizophrenic, whose behavior Corboz feels is relatively uninfluenced by his current environment. The author believes that a nonpsychotic's behavior, however deviant, is always comprehensible to adults, again in contrast to the behavior of a schizophrenic. Both these points may be helpful in making a differential diagnosis, but we doubt whether they are completely reliable, nor are projective tests, which Corboz also advocates as a diagnostic aid.

In this issue, as elsewhere in the clinical field of adolescent disorder, it appears that the advice of experts, such as Corboz, can afford a diagnostician only general guidance and that his diagnostic decision must fundamentally be based on a complicated subjective judgment of the multitudinous factors in the history and manifestations of the patient and his family in their cultural setting.

In briefly dealing with problems of treatment of adolescent schizophrenics, Corboz emphasizes the importance of attention to schooling and vocational training in addition to utilizing the methods of treatment that are of value in adults. He concludes his study by mentioning that the depressed type of manic-depressive psychosis is increasingly being recognized in adolescence, and here he is in some disagreement with the views expressed by Toolan in the previous chapter. Perhaps, as psychiatrists are beginning to have more contact with adolescents and to become more familiar with their characteristic patterns of upset, we are able to identify more illnesses which previously we encountered only in our adult patients and to penetrate the adolescent coloring so that we are able to uncover and diagnose the basic syndromes.

The next chapter on drug taking in Great Britain, by P. H. Connell, discusses a problem which, although it also occurs in adults, appears to be particularly troublesome in adolescence and seems to be increasing at an alarming rate in many countries at the present time. Connell reports a sevenfold increase in the prevalence of heroin taking in his country over the last three years, based on governmental statistics. He believes that not only are these figures an underestimate, for obvious reasons, but in addition they are only part of a much bigger problem involving the taking of "softer" drugs, such as marihuana, amphetamines, barbiturates, and hallucinogens like LSD. The last of these is just appearing in Great Britain, but its use, especially by adolescents, has reached major proportions in recent years in the United States.

Connell describes the clinical picture in adolescents who are sent to a psychiatric hospital because of the toxic effects of taking an amphetamine-barbiturate combination, which not infrequently precipitates psychotic episodes with alternations of consciousness and hallucinations. In fact, some of these effects are sought by the adolescents who take drugs for the thrill of temporarily "expanding consciousness" or "taking a trip" away from their current identity. The psychiatrist usually only sees the few cases which get out of hand.

Connell recognizes that the medical aspect is only one facet of the situation, and he spends much of his chapter discussing the larger sociocultural dimensions and implications of adolescent drug taking in Britain. He describes the current vogue for adolescents to congregate in coffee clubs in London, especially on week ends, and to take drugs as one form of "hippie" behavior, which is also characterized by other types of disturbance and rebellion against the norms of the adult world. He points to the danger of more serious types of delinquency and addictions because these coffee clubs are also frequented by prostitutes, perverts, and heroin takers. On the other hand, he cautions against an overreaction to this danger, as well as against going to the other extreme of unduly belittling or denying it; and he calls for a balanced approach: social control of the supply of drugs and improved services for the identification and treatment of drug takers who are becoming addicted. Diagnosis is difficult because the drug taking is so likely to be only one aspect of a generalized adolescent disturbance complicated by all types of additional pathology and social maladjustment; the author strongly advocates routine urine testing to detect the presence of excreted drugs. Treatment of these cases encounters the same problems as with other disorders of adolescence. We shall discuss these in the next sections.

The major question is how the community should deal with the sociocultural problems by legislation and other means of social control. Connell describes briefly the steps being taken in this regard in Britain, which has a history of enlightened legal and social management of "hard" drug addiction as a platform from which to operate. The author does not deal with the issue of how governmental and community action, and especially the maintenance of the attitudinal balance which he so rightly advocates, can be facilitated by psychiatrists and their mental health colleagues. Clearly this is an arena in which we should be active and in which many of us have been for some years. It is one in which the borders of our professional domain are vague and in which we cannot claim more than partial competence, since most of us cover only some of the psychological, social, cultural, legal, and ethical factors involved. If we restrict our professional activities to the areas we control and in which we are the relatively undisputed competent authorities, all kinds of far-reaching decisions will be taken by community leaders and other professionals which we shall not have the chance to influence and which will modify the type and flow of disordered adolescents whom eventually we shall be asked to handle.

From this it follows that perhaps we should pay more attention to collaborating with the other community leaders and professionals in fields such as the control of drug taking and that we should formalize these endeavors by reporting and analyzing them in our journals and giving them a more central place in our professional discussions. This is already happening to some extent, but perhaps the process should be accelerated in view of the salience of this issue at the present time.

21

Endogenous Psychoses of the Adolescent

Robert J. Corboz

It is a matter of conjecture whether there are psychiatric syndromes specific to adolescence or whether the syndromes encountered in other phases of life take on a characteristic aspect when they present themselves in an individual in the process of pubertal transformation. One essential argument pleads in favor of the second alternative: there are hardly any psychic disturbances found exclusively during adolescence. At most, there is only one exception to this thesis: the crises of puberty. These have a special character in that they are profound, rapid, and deep mental transformations, taking at times a pathological turn, which lead the child to the threshold of adulthood. But if one compares the crises of puberty to the psychic upheavals found at other decisive turning points of life, such as the phase of opposition and the first affirmation of the ego, or the biopsychic transformation of the seventh year, or the disturbances of the menopause, they lose their singularity.

In this study we shall describe briefly the characteristics of the major psychiatric syndromes during adolescence. We shall limit ourselves to the endogenous psychoses, deliberately omitting the psychoses of organic origin such as endocrinopathic disorders and psychoreactive and psychosomatic disorders, even if the severity of their clinical picture places them in a nosological framework close to that of the psychoses. This is the case with anorexia nervosa as well as with attempts at suicide.[9] Neither shall we discuss here puberty in the mentally retarded child or in individuals presenting an asynchronism of their biopsychical maturation. By the term "endogenous psychoses" we understand the schizophrenic group[3] as well as the manic-depressive or cyclothymic disorders.

The endogenous psychoses are rare during childhood. Before the work of

Lutz[11] even the existence of childhood schizophrenia was doubted. Its manifestations during childhood are now generally admitted, although its definition is yet to be agreed on.[2, 15, 16] Its most important symptom is a loss of affective relations with the environment. The affected child or adolescent withdraws into an ivory tower, a phenomenon called autism. This primary manifestation of the psychosis is accompanied by a discordance of affectivity which leads to the well-known contrasts: on the one hand, indifference, inactivity, and reveries; on the other, hypersensitivity, emotional outbreaks, and manifestations of anxiety, panic, and profound depression that may even lead to suicide.[13]

On the intellectual level parallel phenomena are found, for example, dissociation of thought, and obviously, the younger the child, the more difficult this is to disclose. The so-called secondary symptoms such as hallucinations and delusions are rare in childhood and play only a negligible role at the diagnostic level. However, it is admitted that any real childhood schizophrenia may lead to a loss of previously acquired mental functions, or at least may seriously impair the further development of the personality, resulting in eccentricity or the uselessness of mental functions.

At a time when even the existence of childhood schizophrenia was doubted, an unfavorable decline in a patient leading to dementia, in the absence of organic, that is, encephalitic, signs, was irrefutable proof. Thus, the prognosis seemed to be very poor. Today the existence of less severe forms is generally admitted—forms susceptible of remission or even of cure.[1]

Faced with an adolescent schizophrenic disorder, one wonders first of all whether the illness is in its initial stages or goes back to a preceding stage of development. In general one has to deal with the first alternative, for only 1 per cent of all schizophrenics manifest the illness before the age of 10[11] and 4 per cent before the age of 14.[3]

However, whether it is a question of the onset of a new psychosis or of the reactivation of an earlier schizophrenic disorder brought out by puberty, one almost always comes up against serious difficulties in the matter of diagnosis, unless the psychosis is of a severe nature from the beginning and calls for hospitalization. Often, however, the beginning is insidious. The clinical picture can hardly be differentiated from a crisis of puberty. When an adolescent becomes more and more seclusive, when he presents a disconcerting lability of mood, when his nerves are on edge, when he is sometimes lost in fantasy, sometimes aggressive with his siblings and impertinent to his parents, when he oscillates between depression and dysphoric exaltation, it is usual to think of the onset of schizophrenia. Suspicion of this is reinforced by silly, infantile, and inadequate reactions on the part of the adolescent and by his inclination toward extremes; for instance, a need for the absolute that is hardly compatible with reality. It is hard to know whether time spent in front of the mirror contributes to the recognition of the new personality of the adolescent or represents an attempt to defend himself against the process of pathological depersonalization.

In fact, there are astonishing psychological parallels between the phenomena of the transformation of the personality during the first phase of puberty and the beginning of a schizophrenic psychosis. In both cases the ego suffers a weakening, if not even a partial disintegration, which is accompanied by regressive phenomena. In both cases there is a fluctuation of the affective equilibrium, with a heightened tendency to dysphoric and depressive reactions as well as anxiety phenomena. In both cases, finally, there is a more or less brusque rupture of the affective ties with the environment and an exaggerated affirmation of egocentric tendencies accompanied by opposition: in the healthy adolescent there is independence and a sometimes clumsy affirmation of the growing personality; in the schizophrenic adolescent, there are autism and negativism.

The differential diagnosis, therefore, is a hard task. Often only prolonged observation allows one to make a decision one way or the other. Certain signs, however, may lead one to the right diagnosis from the start. Thus, the nonpsychotic adolescent will maintain, even at the height of his crisis, an adequate contact with reality. His behavior, seemingly pathological at first sight, will be limited to his home and family, whereas elsewhere (in the workshop, at school, or among young people) he will appear quite normal. It is not the same with the young schizophrenic, whose strange behavior and inability to adapt will scarcely be influenced by his environment. Moreover, the tendency to forced originality, the normal adolescent's need to "show people," should not be confused with the phenomenon of discordance of the young schizophrenic.

As a matter of fact, the attitude of the young person in revolt, full of feelings of inferiority and anxiety, remains comprehensible even to those who have had no special training in psychology. This is not the case for the young schizophrenic, whose behavior immediately appears chaotic and without any real purpose. As soon as such symptoms as real hallucinations and delusions appear, there can no longer be any dispute about a diagnosis of psychosis.

In cases where clinical examination itself does not lead to a diagnosis, tests, especially drawing, painting, modeling, and Rohrschach tests, may add important information. What the young patient cannot express verbally or in his behavior he can often represent in a symbolic form that is most interesting.[12]

Once the diagnosis of psychosis is made, it is important to eliminate the possibility of an organic disorder that resembles schizophrenia. The trouble could well be encephalitis or an extracerebral disorder, possibly of infectious origin, which might cause a so-called schizophrenic reaction. The latter is distinguished from true schizophrenia by its transient nature and its tendency to complete remission.

On the clinical level, adolescent schizophrenia can manifest itself either with a hebephrenic aspect or in a catatonic form, or as "schizophrenia simplex"—that is, a psychosis evolving without much disturbance and without secondary symptoms tending toward insanity. The seriousness of schizophrenic psychoses is variable; there are mild forms which permit the adolescent to remain in his family and even in school. Other more severe forms require the institutionalization of the adolescent in a child guidance clinic or hospital. This solution is considered most often when the psychosis is accompanied by hypochondriac complaints. Finally, in the most severe cases, treatment in a psychiatric hospital is necessary. Often this cannot be in an adolescent unit, and the result is association with adult patients, which has known disadvantages.

Because adolescent schizophrenia is different from the forms found in children and in adults, its treatment also demands special measures. During the acute phase medicinal treatment, especially the prescription of neuroleptic drugs, together with psychotherapy is of prime importance. Nevertheless, whether the adolescent can remain with his family or must be placed in a home or clinic, the educational element should not be neglected. The educator plays a significant role, and his collaboration with the doctor deserves attention.

During convalescence other pedagogical problems specific to adolescence present themselves: the completion of schooling and a professional orientation. The adolescent thus finds himself in a situation that is infinitely more difficult than that of the adult. Often and fortunately the adult can begin his life again where he left off when he became ill, but the adolescent finds himself confronted with the very difficult task of planning for his future without a great deal of strength.

What has just been said about schizophrenia can in principle be applied as well to a manic-depressive psychosis. Its frequency during childhood is still the subject of controversy. However, there is a growing tendency to admit that fluctuations of mood of endogenous origin are more frequent before puberty than was once believed. They are manifested by disturbances in the child's behavior that do not, however, require hospital treatment. But with puberty, circular symptoms set in progressively, with a span between the different phases that often is still brief. In young girls these symptoms are often correlated with the menstrual cycle. Manic or hypomanic phases are often not very marked during adolescence and are sometimes confused with a sudden overflowing of instinctive impulses, especially on the sexual level. Depressive phases are difficult to distinguish from the morose attitude of the young adolescent, from a physiological lowering of vitality and performance, and from a tendency to lethargy, symbolically represented in the Sleeping Beauty fairy tale. As for psychotic oscillations of mood, they have their counterpart in the affective lability of the adolescent. To the basic disorder is often added a psychoreactive structure, evoked in part by failures at school or in professional training, in part by conflicts within the family.

The psychic maturation of the adolescent is frequently hampered by psychosis, especially by its depressive phase. Parents who feel that their child is ill have a tendency to keep him in a state of dependence which is hardly compatible with his evolution toward independent adulthood.

References

1. ANNELL, A. L. "The Prognosis of Psychiatic Syndromes in Children," *Acta Psychiat. Scand.*, XXXIX (1963), 235–297.
2. ASPERGER, H. *Heilpädagogik*. Vienna: Springer, 1956.
3. BLEULER, M. *Lehrbuch des Psychiatrie*. Berlin: Springer, 1949.
4. CORBOZ, R. J. "Conceptions actuelles de la schizophrénie infantile," *Criança Portuguesa*, XIV (1955), 71–112.
5. CORBOZ, R. J. "Reaktive Störungen bei Kinder schizophrener Eltern." Zurich: Second International Congress for Psychiatry, 1957, III, 457, 462.
6. CORBOZ, R. J. "Gibt es Geisteskrankheiten im Kindesalter?" *Schweiz. med. Wschr.*, LXXXVIII (1958), 703.
7. CORBOZ, R. J. *Die berufliche Eingliederung geistig Abnormer in "Die Eingliederung des behinderten Menschen in Kulturgemeinschaft."* Freiburg, Switzerland: Universitäts Verlag (1959).
8. CORBOZ, R. J. "Klinische Erfahrungen mit Psychopharmaca im Kindesalter," *Acta Paedopsychiat.* Suppl. I, XXXII (1965), 24–39.
9. DUCHÉ, D. J. "Les tentatives de suicide chez l'enfant et l'adolescent," *Psychiat. Enfant*, VII (1964), 1–114.
10. KUHN, R. "Ueber kindliche Depressionen und ihre Behandlung," *Schweiz. med. Wschr.*, XCIII (1963), 86–90.
11. LUTZ, J. *Kinderpsychiatrie*. Zurich: Ratopfel, 1964.
12. MUELLER, F. "Kunstlerische Ausdrucksmöglichkeiten bei einem schizophrenen Mädchen in der Pubertät." Thèse de Zurich (in preparation).
13. ROBIN, G. *Précis de neuropsychiatrie infantile*. Paris: Doin, 1950.
14. SPIEL, W. *Die endogenen Psychosen des Kindes und Jugendalters*. Basel: Karger, 1961.
15. STUTTE, H. *Kinder und Jugendpsychiatrie in Psychiatrie der Gegenwart*. Berlin: Springer, 1960, II, 952–1087.
16. TRAMER, M. *Lehrbuch der allgemeinen Kinderpsychiatrie*. Basel: Schwabe, 1965.

22

Adolescent Drug Taking
in Great Britain

P. H. Connell

The problem of drug taking among the adolescent population has not been of concern in Great Britain until recently, though other countries, notably the United States (which has this problem in cities such as New York) and Japan (such as the city of Kurume), after the war, have had to face this problem.

The statistics relating to addiction to Dangerous Drugs (defined in the Act relating to Dangerous Drugs) were reported in the Second Report of the Interdepartmental Committee on Drug Addiction in November 1965. These figures were obtained not by an official registration policy, but by the vigilance of Home Office staff and police who scrutinize all prescriptions of dangerous drugs and therefore are able to discover persons who are dependent on regular prescriptions of dangerous drugs, such as morphine, heroin, and cocaine, from doctors. These figures do not include, of course, individuals who may be taking dangerous drugs and obtaining them from illegal sources, though the number of these is thought to be very small. It should also be stated that every registered medical practitioner in Britain at the moment has the power to prescribe dangerous drugs or any drugs to an addict if such treatment is considered to be of value to the patient, so that there may not be the motivation or need to obtain drugs from illegal sources.

The figures for addiction to dangerous drugs, quoted in the Second Report of the Interdepartmental Committee,[7] are shown in Table 22–1.

Since this report was published figures for heroin taking in the under-20 age group in 1965 were double the figures for 1964 (see table 22–1). From these figures it will be seen that although the figures for narcotic addiction in the under-20 population, so far as official sources are concerned, are still

Table 22–1.

	1959	1960	1961	1962	1963	1964	1965
Age under 20	—	—	—	3	17	40	145
Taking heroin	—	1	2	3	17	40	134
Age 20–34	50	62	94	132	184	256	347
Taking heroin	35	52	87	126	162	219	319

small, there has been a very significant increase between 1962 and 1965, and the rate of incidence per year of heroin taking in the under 20's is increasing at an alarming rate.

However, round about 1962–1963, a pattern of adolescent behavior began to emerge, mainly in the West End of London, which has been reported in detail elsewhere.[2, 3, 4, 5, 6, 8, 10]

Briefly, this pattern, which appears to be socioculturally determined, consists of adolescents who leave their homes either on Friday evening or on Saturday and spend the whole week end in the West End of London, moving from one basement club (where coffee, tea, and soft drinks are sold) to another, while taking, at regular intervals, amphetamine drugs or amphetamine barbiturate mixtures.

An analysis of some of these individuals, who were finally referred to a psychiatric outpatient evening clinic at the Maudsley Hospital,[5, 6] suggested that they had taken the drugs for "kicks," had tried a number of drugs, including marihuana, Dexedrine, Benzedrine, amyl nitrite sniffing, and so on, but had found that Drinamyl—an amphetamine barbiturate mixture containing 5 mg dexamphetamine and 32 mgm amylobarbitone—was best; had taken up to 120 5-mg tablets over the week end, and all, without exception, had problems of adolescent adjustment, the majority showing these problems in overt disturbances of behavior before taking the drugs.

On high doses of these drugs many had experienced short-lived psychotic states in which paranoid ideas, delusions, and hallucinations (visual and auditory) took place. This psychotic state was identical with that previously described in adults[1] who had been taking amphetamine alone, but in the case of the adolescents taking amphetamine barbiturate mixtures (Drinamyl) it only lasted a short period of time, up to an hour in duration. This was presumably due to the fact that the barbiturate modified the action of the amphetamine and cut down the duration of the psychosis.

Since this form of adolescent behavior began there has been a quick spread among the adolescent population in London; many adolescents come from the suburbs and from provincial cities to the West End of London and spend their week ends there. During the past two years, however, it has been clear that these drugs have become readily available in more peripheral areas so that the adolescent no longer has to go up to the West End to obtain them. The individuals who sell the drugs usually haunt the coffee-bar clubs where adolescents foregather whether or not they are looking for drugs. Recently there have been reports of LSD taking, but this is a rarity.

A further point, made first by Sharpley[10] in 1964 and confirmed in my own studies of individual cases, shows that in the West End, at any rate, the clubs frequented by teen-agers who take Drinamyl are also frequented by a small fringe population of prostitutes, sexual perverts, and addicts to hard drugs such as heroin and cocaine. Thus most of the adolescents are well aware of how to get hard drugs if they wish to do so.

The significance of the development of this kind of drug taking in the British population remains to be evaluated. Nevertheless, there is just as much danger in understressing the dangers as in becoming too vociferous about them and encouraging panic measures. In this respect one wonders whether the popular press, television programs, and the like, which are meant to be informative and instructive, may unwittingly add glamour and attraction to the very form of behavior they are warning against.

So far as the medical profession is concerned, there are several levels of involvement in the drug-taking problem:

(1) The problem of diagnosis of drug taking.

(2) The problem of treatment of the addict.

(3) The problem of assessment of the wider issues concerning drug taking and advising the appropriate authorities and social agencies, and so on, what needs to be done in the light of present knowledge.

(4) The undertaking of research into the problem both by clinical examinations, treatment, and follow-up and by co-operating in research with such bodies as social agencies, psychopharmacologists, sociologists, and all who are concerned with the problem and have something to contribute to the further evaluation of it.

The problem of the diagnosis of drug taking is, perhaps, one of the most difficult a doctor has to face, and although the expert may spot most cases by a careful psychiatric examination, some will evade detection. The physical signs, for instance, of amphetamine taking are not pathognomonic.[1, 5] This means that there should be easy availability of laboratory services so that tests of urine or blood can be carried out in order to demonstrate the presence or absence of a suspected drug.

The problem of the treatment of the adolescent addict raises considerable issues, such as whether treatment in mental hospitals is suitable, whether this is desirable, and what methods should be used.

In my experience, the problem of the treatment of the adolescent drug taker is the same as the problem of the treatment of any adolescent psychiatric disturbance in that the patient needs to be assessed in terms of his past development, his progress along the developmental scale, his family background, the relationships he has with the individuals in his family, the methods of child rearing used, the approach of the parents to his adolescent maturation, and the particular stresses he may suffer from in relation to his school or work situation and in his particular subculture.

It is my practice, therefore, since I find no special common denominators in the patients I see and have to treat them as individual unique patients, to use a flexible approach in which the basis is supportive psychotherapy combined with regular analysis of the urine for drugs. This may be, and often is, amplified by work with the parents in order to help them to understand the problems of their child in growing through adolescence and their own problems in this respect, and sometimes direct treatment of a parent who may have a psychiatric illness. Occasionally, psychotherapy including the patient and his girl friend (or vice versa) may be used. In some cases the basis of supportive psychotherapy is converted into psychotherapy at greater depth.

It is my view that there is a need for some inpatient treatment facilities for young drug takers and that it may be necessary to differentiate those who are taking "soft" drugs from those who are taking "hard" drugs. It does not seem to me to be appropriate in general to admit to mental hospital such cases where they may be mixed with older confirmed addicts and alcoholics or older patients suffering from psychiatric disorders, though, of course, in some cases there may be no harm. Furthermore, a full evaluation of the individual case may well lead to the conclusion that the type of personality disorder present is best dealt with in such residential establishments as approved schools or Borstal institutions. In this respect it has recently been found by Scott and Willcox[9] that at least 16 to 18 per cent of a sample of boys and girls admitted to remand homes contained amphetamine in their urine and that there were no basic differences between this population and a control population in the remand home who had not taken drugs, with regard to numbers of previous offences, seriousness of offences, ethnic group, illegitimacy, broken homes, parent with criminal record, long-standing marital disharmony, and so on. Thus, the drug taking itself did not seem to play an etiological role in the actual antisocial behavior which led to the placement, through the juvenile courts, in a remand home.

The social implications of the development of drug taking in adolescence are well known. Social measures to deal with the situation have been, in many countries, punitive rather than therapeutic, and these terms have been used as though they are alternatives. Thus, this country is often referred to as the one that allows free access to drugs and adopts a therapeutic orientation, and it is then sometimes stated that this is why our drug problem has been so small.

Since, however, this adolescent culturally determined behavior has sprung up, social measures have had to be taken, and the Drugs (Prevention of Misuse) Act of 1964 came into being, directed at drugs of the amphetamine type. It began operation on October 31, 1964, and gave some powers for the control of distribution, export, and import; powers to bring individuals before the court who were shown to be in possession of drugs which they could not establish were prescribed by a medical practitioner; and powers to search clubs and cafés. The amphetamines, however, are on a schedule which merely restricts them to prescription by doctors. No obligation is placed on doctors or pharmacists for the accounting of every single tablet or for the placement of these drugs under maximum security (as is the case with morphine, heroin, and so on).

It is early to be able to state what effect the Drugs (Prevention of Misuse) Act has had, but impressions would suggest that the effect has been less than hoped for and that the powers given in the act do not go far enough.

The drug problem in this country is developing, but even now it would appear to be small compared with that in other countries. Nevertheless, we know by the experience of other countries that a serious social evil can develop and get out of hand, and we are therefore in the somewhat unique position of being theoretically able to nip the "infection" in the bud, as it were. Whether or not we shall succeed in doing so will depend on how far these two aspects—the one of social measures to control the supply of drugs and discover those taking the drugs, and the other, the appropriate treatment (using this term in the wide sense of placement in penal institutions or hospitals, psychotherapy, or social measures of support)—can be provided in large enough measure to deal with the problem.

In this respect the recommendations of the Interdepartmental Committee (1965) can be welcomed, including notification of addicts to dangerous drugs (drugs covered by the Dangerous Drugs Act) to a central authority, special treatment centers for the treatment of addicts; powers for compulsory detention of addicts in these centers, restriction of the powers to prescribe heroin and cocaine to addicts to those doctors on the staff of treatment centers, and the setting up of an advisory committee to keep under review the whole problem of drug addiction.

This latter recommendation, which is particularly welcome, is phrased in terms which make it clear that not only dangerous drugs but other drugs likely to produce dependence would come within the ambit of the advisory committee.

ADDENDUM

Since completing this chapter the recommendations of the Interdepartmental Committee (1965) have been accepted by the government with the exception of the recommendation concerning powers of compulsory detention of an addict. The government has considered that the evidence warranting such a step is not strong enough, but will keep this aspect under review.

The government has set up a Standing Advisory Committee on Drug Dependency which has already met several times, and plans are being prepared to establish treatment centers. A bill is before Parliament which contains provisions to implement the other recommendations, including the restriction of the right to prescribe heroin and cocaine to addicts to doctors working at treatment centers. Research is to be encouraged. The Institute of Psychiatry (London University) is setting up an Addiction Research Unit which, in the first instance, is to study sociological and epidemiological aspects, while the Maudsley Hospital and Bethlem Royal Hospital (the hospitals associated with the Institute of Psychiatry) are setting up a Clinical Research and Treatment Addiction Unit which will include an inpatient unit of twenty-two beds: ten beds for narcotic addicts and twelve for nonnarcotic addicts. These two groups will be separate. The institute unit and the hospital unit will work closely together.

References

1. CONNELL, P. H. *Amphetamine Psychosis*. Maudsley Monograph No. 5. London: Oxford University Press, 1958.
2. CONNELL, P. H. "Amphetamine Misuse," *British Journal of Addiction*, LX (1964), 9–27.
3. CONNELL, P. H. "Adolescent Drug Taking," *Proceedings of the Royal Society of Medicine*, LVIII (1965), 409–412.
4. CONNELL, P. H. "The Assessment and Treatment of Adolescent Drug Taking with Special Reference to Amphetamines," *Proceedings of the Leeds Symposium on Behaviour Disorders*. Dagenham: May and Baker, 1965, pp. 10–17.
5. CONNELL, P. H. "Clinical Manifestations and Treatment of Amphetamine Type of Dependence," *Journal of the American Medical Association*, CXCVI (1966), 718–723.
6. CONNELL, P. H. "What to Do about Pep Pills," in T. RAISON, ed., *Youth in New Society*. London: Rupert Hart-Davis, 1966.
7. Interdepartmental Committee on Drug Addiction (Second) Report. London. (Ministry of Health and Department of Health for Scotland). London: Her Majesty's Stationary Office, 1965.
8. LINKEN, A. *Sunday Times*, January 27, 1963, p. 24.
9. SCOTT, P. D., and T. WILLCOX. "Delinquency and the Amphetamines," *British Journal of Psychiatry* (1965), 865–875.
10. SHARPLEY, A. *Evening Standard*, February 3–6, May 1, 1964.

Problems in Communication

EDITORS' INTRODUCTION The four chapters in this section deal with problems in communication which complicate the process of treatment of disturbed adolescents and with individual and group methods which are being developed in order to solve them.

The first chapter, by Albert Bryt, focuses on failure in communication between patient and psychotherapist which may lead to therapeutic disappointment or to premature termination by dropout. This is a not uncommon phenomenon with adolescents in general and is very frequent when middle-class therapists treat patients of lower-socioeconomic class, as is happening increasingly in the United States as part of the antipoverty program. Bryt points out that a shared semantic framework is a prerequisite for the verbal communication that is the traditional basis for psychotherapy. This shared semantic framework is often nonexistent when there are significant socio-cultural differences between patient and therapist, despite the fact that both ostensibly speak the same language. He illustrates his thesis by describing two cases of psychotherapy with adolescents from culturally deprived backgrounds. Analysis of these examples emphasizes the importance of the therapist's understanding the nonverbal meaning of speaking, irrespective of the ostensible symbolic content of the words used by the patient. Bryt feels that children of lower socioeconomic class often use words not in order to communicate information about themselves, but as a defensive barrier against an invasion of privacy; and he believes that nowadays even among middle-class people words about the self are ceasing to be the accepted means of

287

establishing interpersonal intimacy. He therefore suggests that therapists who treat adolescents, particularly from culturally deprived backgrounds, should focus their initial efforts on identifying and then remedying the absence of a shared semantic framework. The remedy lies in building a relationship of trust by "action language," that is, by behavioral signs rather than by verbal symbolic communication. On the basis of this relationship, the therapist may then develop a shared verbal code, which increases the communication ability of the patient and enables him to use what he learns as a bridge to the adult world.

The next chapter, by James B. McWhinnie, continues the discussion of this theme by focusing on the author's experience with adolescent delinquents. McWhinnie contrasts delinquents and neurotic patients he has treated in regard to their capacity for abstract conceptualization. He does not tell us whether there was a major difference in socioeconomic class between the two groups, but he provides enough details about the family background of his delinquent patients to indicate that they came from poverty-stricken and culturally deprived homes, where they had little opportunity to learn verbal communication, especially in relation to abstract concepts. He points out that a reduced capacity for abstract verbal expression increases the likelihood of antisocial acting-out behavior. He quotes Skinner, who maintains that the superego is a verbal structure, and Piaget, who traces the development in the child and adolescent from egocentric speech to socialized speech linked with the progression from conformity to norms because of concrete constraints toward conformity because of moral judgment and social co-operation.

McWhinnie then points out that traditional methods of rehabilitating delinquents reinforce their fixation on concrete constraints by exposing them to disciplinary training, often coercive or buttressed by concrete rewards and punishments; and he feels that such methods, which seem to be based on the hope that good behavior established under such conditions will be subsequently maintained, are often unsuccessful. In their place, he suggests psychodynamic treatment which attempts to influence the delinquents to appreciate abstract values, such as morality and social responsibility, by means of appropriate communication. This approach, however, must overcome the initial technical obstacle that the delinquents have little or no capacity for abstract verbal communication, on the basis of which they can be influenced. This brings him to the same point as that previously raised by Bryt.

McWhinnie's remedy is a group and community analogue of the individual method advocated by Bryt. He recommends that the delinquents be exposed to group and milieu therapy in a therapeutic community, where they will identify with the dominant social values, including the importance of verbal communication. The chapter continues with a description of the method which McWhinnie has worked out in a correctional institution in Scotland for delinquents sentenced by the courts. A central aspect of the method is reliance on daily discussion groups led by child-care workers who have themselves been trained by the experience of attending a short residential course, where they learned "leaderless" group techniques. These workers are given regular supervision by a visiting psychiatrist. McWhinnie describes the regularly occurring sequential phases of such discussion groups, and from the point of view of our present interest, what emerges is that on the basis of identifications with the expressed values of the institution, the delinquents gradually learn to think and communicate in abstract words; and this moves them from a morality of constraint to a morality of social cooperation. This process is consolidated by organizing similar discussion groups for their parents, so that when the delinquents go home they will share with their families their newly learned capacity for meaningful verbal communication.

Further light is thrown on this last issue by Alex H. Kaplan, who in the following chapter discusses the importance of involving parents in the treatment of their adolescent children. He describes his method of conducting joint parent-adolescent interviews during the introductory phase, and also intermittently in response to need, during the course of psychotherapy with younger adolescent patients. His main objectives are not those of family therapy—the resolution of intrafamilial conflicts—but to diminish the opposition of adolescent or parents to therapy, to reduce countertransference in the therapist, and to supply realistic information about the relationships inside the family and the general environment of the adolescent.

Kaplan criticizes the traditional practice of collaborative therapy, such as occurs in many child guidance clinics where different workers treat the adolescent and one or both parents. Communication is supposed to be maintained in this system by contacts among the therapists. In reality they usually have inadequate time for this, and what often happens is an isolation of the communications of family members in separate streams. Separation inside the family is thus reinforced.

The author also discusses the difficulty of maintaining his patient's confidentiality if there is separate contact between the therapist and the parents. On the other hand, if the therapist denies the parents access to him and to some information about their child, they often become frustrated and interrupt the treatment. Joint interviews handle this difficulty very effectively.

Another major benefit of joint interviews is that they allow the therapist to identify and remedy inadequate or distorted communications between parents and adolescent. The method advocated by Kaplan, consisting as it does of a relatively small number of sessions apparently geared to a fairly superficial plane, may not suffice to handle deeply based distortions of communication such as those discussed earlier in this book by Lidz and by Shapiro. For the remedy of these, full-scale family therapy would probably be necessary. But there are many instances of more superficial disorders of communication, in which vicious circles based on misunderstandings or discrepant expectations lead to blocks and confusions which can relatively easily be reduced in intensity by the opportunity for a free and open discussion in the presence of a therapeutic mediator and communication bridge. In the past, many psychiatrists have been prejudiced against such joint interviews because they have felt that the adolescents would oppose them, particularly if they were preoccupied by rebellious and rejecting feelings toward their parents, from whom they were seeking independence. Kaplan reports that such opposition on the part of his adolescent patients was not a serious obstacle. This is in line with what one would expect from our discussion in Section II of this book. An adolescent who loudly proclaims his rejection of his parents is also very much in need of the continuation of his relationship with them. He expects the therapist not only to listen to his complaints but also to reinforce his positive attachment and to safeguard a constructive balance, on the basis of which he can develop the identifications necessary for his adult personality. Joint interviews provide an excellent opportunity for the therapist to demonstrate such a balanced approach to the parents, while making it clear that he is working for the good of the adolescent.

Kaplan does not deal with the issue of cultural deprivation, which was discussed in the previous chapters. It appears that his patients were mostly drawn from the usual middle-class clientele, or at least from those who share our semantic framework, so that he does not mention problems of building up a valid verbal basis for communication between therapist and the adolescent and his parents. His method, however, clearly provides such an opportunity where this is called for and is an interesting alternative to the separate group meetings of adolescents and parents advocated by McWhinnie.

The last chapter in this section, by W. H. Allchin, discusses the problem of communication within the therapeutic community of a residential institution for disturbed adolescents. The author enumerates some of the possible divisive boundaries to communication in such an institution based on differences in age between the groups of patients and staff, contrasting roles of patients and staff, and instinctual drives demanding expression among patients and the controls which staff feel called upon to institute, all of which easily lead to a polarization between the two groups that may result in authoritarianism and an antitherapeutic system. He contrasts this with the therapeutic goal of promoting the emergence of a joint consciousness and a shared story within the institutional population, which engenders the identification of the patients with the social system that supports and strengthens their weakened egos.

Allchin discusses the concept of myth as "collective thinking" and as a shared record of the life of the institution, which exerts a powerful effect on the values and expectations of its members, and defines the acceptable limits of their speech and behavior. He describes his work in an institution for neurotic and borderline psychotic adolescent boys and girls and particularly his organization of a daily meeting for patients and staff which has the primary function of molding the development of the myth or chronicle of the institution. This meeting has a somewhat different format from the group sessions described previously by McWhinnie. It does not focus explicitly on developing a vocabulary and a shared communication about abstract concepts of values and social co-operation, although such communication undoubtedly must take place, at least on the implicit level. Instead, the focus is on discussing and recording, if only in the memory of the participants, the daily happenings of the institution as they are in process of passing into its history or myth. In such discussions, the different versions of the same happening by various individuals are compared, and distortions corrected. Allchin reports that certain patients and staff members are particularly active as informal chroniclers and that some of their accounts are particularly colored by individual needs and biases. When discrepant reports are given at these meetings, distortions can be corrected by consensual validation.

In the myth of the institution that gradually unfolds, its life history, with the superimposition of the life histories in the institution of individual patients and staff, begins to take shape and to embody ideas and values and orientation in time and place, which become integrated into a common culture that acts as a "home base" for the identity of the members. The family as a psychic and social system normally fulfills this role of providing a framework for identity formation in its members. For the sick adolescents this has usually broken down, and the institution is a replacement. The daily meetings provide some control over the process, which is especially needed in order to ensure that issues of authority and communication with adults, which are sensitive areas for adolescents, can be therapeutically and constructively handled.

Allchin ends by referring briefly to the point which was raised by Bryt and by McWhinnie; namely, that some of the most significant messages concerning values and norms of conduct cannot be delivered through the symbolic communication of verbal content, but must be conveyed by other means. He feels that the institutional myth is a major communication modality in accomplishing this.

23

Dropout of Adolescents
from Psychotherapy:
Failure in Communication

Albert Bryt

THE PROBLEM

Dropout from psychotherapy of adolescent outpatients, where they are free to do so, is an old problem. Reasons for premature termination of treatment have been explored, and remedies have been suggested. An understanding of sociocultural factors and of the vicissitudes of interpersonal relationships proves helpful in this respect.[15]

In recent years the issue has become more important in the United States. There is greater awareness of the role of emotional factors in atypical behavior. Also, there has been a remarkable increase in mental health facilities where treatment is available to a broader section of the population than heretofore: this means to patients with little "psychologic literacy," as Slavson terms it.[13]

Therapy with these patients, largely from the lower socioeconomic strata, has been disappointing. Their dropout rate has been reported as exceeding 50 per cent.[10] The suggestion has been advanced that they are untreatable.[2] Hence the search for procedures that will assure a more economic use of therapeutic time.[4] This search is especially relevant to adolescents whose "prodigious richness" and "groping efforts" [9] one should wish to harness for psychotherapy.

There is an interesting parallel to a debate of many years about the suitability of adolescents for psychoanalysis. Here it has come to be recognized that psychoanalytic technique had to be modified in the treatment of adolescents.[1]

In the search for a better working definition of psychotherapy with ado-

293

lescents attention has been focused on criteria for acceptance and on limitations of goals. Criteria for acceptance of patients, underprivileged or not, need to be established. They should be in line with the facilities available in a given clinical setting, appropriate to the patients' psychopathology. Flexibility of services offered is important. Probably no one type of treatment is appropriate all the time, even for one single patient. Therapeutic goals may have to be limited for a variety of reasons. However, this should not be done on theoretical grounds or because of the pessimism of those in charge of therapy.

In this study I shall concern myself with one aspect of the dropout problem which has received but scant attention. This is the nature of the process of communication between patient and therapist. Hunt's emphasis, in this regard, is too restrictive that "successful psychotherapy requires as a prerequisite a linguistic and semantic framework, the basic components of which are shared by patient and therapist." [5] Rather, it should be clearly recognized whether such a semantic framework is operative. When it is not, the facilitation of the communicative process by the therapist and the elaboration of a shared semantic framework are therapeutically effective in themselves.

It is true enough that ethnic differences between patient and therapist may foreclose linguistic correspondence. Under such circumstances both participants may accept, perhaps too readily, that they cannot communicate. Therapy then often fails, not primarily because of language difficulties, but because of the shared negative expectations. [7]

In any event, the assumption that one shares a semantic framework because he speaks the same language as the other person may be erroneous. Such a supposition may easily lead to the conclusion that certain patients are untreatable. There is more to language than the use of words. The sociocultural, and especially the familial, backgrounds add affective flavoring. Thus distinct personal idioms come into existence in any language, occasionally only remotely related to commonly accepted semantic symbolizations.

Failure to recognize personal connotations in the use of language or to explore them may lead to unexpected consequences. The following cases may help to illustrate this point.

PRESENTATION OF CASE MATERIAL

Robert was a 14-year-old boy from a racial minority group, the older of two children, the product of a broken home, socioeconomically deprived. He was referred because of chronic truancy. Of average intellectual endowment, he had an academic performance that had been below par for years. He was severely retarded in reading and arithmetic. A diagnosis of passive-aggressive personality was made.

He wanted treatment because he did "not want to be sent away" * for truanting, he said. He expected that the psychiatrist would help him find out why he could not go to school. He did not know why, and he said that this worried him. He thought that he needed a good education to get a job. However, he did not appear concerned.

Accepted for treatment, he kept most appointments. Sometimes he failed because his mother sent him on an errand or because he became embroiled in arguments with her, refusing to obey. Without being talkative, he seemed co-operative. He readily accepted psychodynamic explanations, though they did not seem to stick with him. He knew "nothing" about his feelings and never contradicted a suggestion that he must be angry or sad.

In the course of treatment the issue of school attendance was raised repeatedly in an attempt at uncovering the secondary gains from his truanting. He seemed stuck in a mutually dependent relationship with his mother. Seemingly he was also afraid that he could not, all at once, make up for lost work and keep up with current assignments. Therefore, with Robert's foreknowledge, a modified school program was arranged for him. Still he did not go to school.

He concurred with the view that if he could but once master his fear he would then be able to control it and return to school. Therefore, it was decided that the doctor would accompany him; he had refused to let his mother do so. He missed the first appointment arranged to this end. He came for the subsequent one with the help of his mother. On the way to school the conversation was about his fear to go. But, as if belying what had been said, he entered the school building eagerly, leading the doctor. He agreed that he would be able to go the next day, and he went.

He failed his appointment on the day after that. The mother reported that he had returned from school enraged, refusing to speak to anyone. He declined to return for his sessions, even to discuss why he did not want to continue. Collateral information obtained from the school failed to reveal an apparent reason for this reaction. Four days later he stopped attending school for the second time.

It had been impossible, up to then, to involve the mother in any form in the treatment program, despite her declared eagerness. It now seemed imperative to enlist her help. She concurred enthusiastically. She kept two appointments. Thereafter, she was too busy trying to find better living quarters for her family.

Obviously, something had gone wrong in treatment. Somewhere, the wires had become crossed. It was thought that this could be explained by the mother's subtle, albeit unconscious, interference with her boy's strivings for independence.

---

* This refers to possible placement, by court order, in a supervised residence for boys.

By contrast to Robert's case the circumstances seemed much less auspicious with another boy, and yet . . .

John was 15 years old when he was referred by the school for truancy. He was the only child of his widowed mother and came from a socioeconomically deprived home. Of average intellectual potential, he functioned at a lower level of over-all intelligence. He was retarded in reading and arithmetic. He was diagnosed as a schizoid personality.

He had repeatedly broken his promise to go to school. Leaving the house in the morning as if going, he never made it to class. He did not account for how he spent his time. Outside of school hours he was mostly at home watching television. He was generally unco-operative. When he went out he reportedly associated with undesirable companions. He had threatened his mother with violence. She felt that she could no longer control him and wanted him placed away from home. He voiced no objection to this. He was only opposed to being told what to do.

In a conjoint interview the doctor suggested that John might be unhappy. The mother disagreed emphatically. John merely shrugged his shoulders in reply. The doctor explained at some length that the boy's hardened appearance undoubtedly meant that he wanted to be left alone. But he ventured that it might also hide a longing to be cared for, loved, and taken seriously for what he wanted. He went on to say that matters seemingly had reached the point where John no longer cared for either his welfare or his satisfaction. The mother had never known him to be different. She recalled violent arguments between him and his father. Most of her comments seemed negative, the doctor remarked. Yet, the youth also seemed bright and able to assert himself; this was in his favor. At this the boy became tearful and did not reply when spoken to. This prompted the mother to heap further invective on him.

Alone in the interview, John was taciturn. He denied knowing or caring why he was sent to the clinic. He was unconcerned about being "sent away"; he just did not want to go to school. He planned to get a job and did not think that his education mattered. Though he wanted to be left alone and declared that he needed no help, he agreed to keep his appointments, since he had to. His mother was emphatic in her refusal to co-operate and dismissed out of hand the suggestion of appointments for herself. She declared that, regrettably, only placement away from home could make her feel more accepting of her son.

At one of the early appointments the doctor suggested that he and John go for a walk. The boy acquiesced with a shrug. Later they went on many walks. They spoke about a variety of things, that is, the doctor did, mostly. John was interested in automobiles and always spoke of them with enthusiasm. Topics of interest to him always led to lively discussion. On the rare occasion when his obvious problems were brought up, it was a vain effort trying to engage him. Following a silent session he always arrived early, but seemed less friendly then. The therapist frequently stressed John's choice in how the sessions were to be spent. He also speculated on the possibility that the patient might feel isolated when he had nothing to talk about.

Eventually John spoke of his mother and father. They had always "bossed him around." They never were bound by their own good rules, which he was supposed to follow. Several weeks after he had begun to attend school again, he mentioned it casually to the therapist. The doctor had known about it from school. He had not brought it up, thinking that the patient would do so in his own time. He reminded him that they had agreed to use the sessions trying to understand what troubled John and what gave him satisfaction. Since John now had raised the issue, the therapist suggested some adjustment in curriculum. They agreed that the doctor should try to make appropriate arrangements.

At about the same time the mother requested an appointment. She reported that John was more communicative at home. He was eager to share with her his progress in school. She now wanted guidance in how to help her child to "get back on his feet."

There was consistent progress. Several weeks later the psychiatrist suggested, tentatively, that they discuss termination of treatment, since the ostensible problem seemed solved. The mother concurred that John seemed to be "doing all right." He agreed, too readily perhaps, that it was time to end. At first he could see no purpose in discussing the matter. Eventually he revealed that he felt that his therapist did not want to see him any longer. He was reassured on that count. Treatment, with mother's active co-operation, continued for another six months. Then, by seemingly valid mutual agreement, it was stopped.

COMMENT

Both cases present striking contradictions between stated intent and eventual outcome.

Robert said that he wanted treatment and that he wanted an education. His mother eagerly expressed co-operation. Yet, after having mastered his initial fear, after having, presumably, derived noticeable benefit from treatment, he dropped out of therapy and out of school. His mother, after fleetingly lending her active support, became unavailable for further help. Even with added pressure this could not be changed.

John, on the other hand, was explicitly set against therapy and against going to school. At the beginning of treatment he let it be known that he "could be made to come, but not to talk." His mother was unwilling to give him any support or even to be less outspoken in her antagonism to him. Yet, eventually she accepted regular appointments for herself; John became engaged in treatment and returned to school spontaneously. Despite his denial, he responded to pressure; otherwise he would not have kept his appointments, and he would not have accepted, so readily, the first suggestion that therapy be concluded.

The most important difference in these two cases may be found in the approaches used by the two therapists. Robert's doctor accepted at face value what the boy said. One might speculate that he did so because it fitted his favorable expectations for a good therapeutic result. The possibility was not considered, as undoubtedly it should have been, that verbal language had no potential communicative meaning to this adolescent. Nor was the thought entertained, as well it might have been, that Robert's use of words was but a means of action, a way of maintaining distance by building a wall of words. Quite likely, exploration of the mother's role might have revealed a double bind built into her messages. Robert was not helped to emancipate himself. Therapy was ineffective because it failed to replace his self-centered "verbal action" by not establishing the means for verbal communication.

John's therapist proceeded from a different conceptual framework. He assumed, rightly, that the patient's words were not meant to inform. Rather, both his language and his attitudes bespoke John's distrust in authority figures. Therefore it was important, at first, to establish that any assistance to the boy would be for his sake and not for the sake of what he should do. The doctor did not *speak* of collaboration; he *acted* it, since "action language" seemed to be John's personal idiom. He looked for and found areas of common interest: automobiles, for example. He demonstrated his respect for the patient by letting him set his own speed.

Robert's return to school was the treatment goal and the measure of its success. John's truancy was looked upon as sort of fortuitous; it had brought him to treatment, though transiently it was mistaken for his nuclear problem, as at the time of the first thought of termination of treatment. Robert's language was evaluated for what it seemed to be in terms of verbal expressions, rather than for its functional significance. To the contrary, with John, the content of what he said was largely disregarded. He was seen as using language as the equivalent of action in his search for self-assertion. Robert found himself trapped in therapy as he had been trapped in other life situations, especially with his mother. She had made no allowances for his needs, except when they were "right" needs, though with obvious ambivalence. Therefore, he had to drop out of treatment, because there, as well, the concern was only with what was "right." John's mother unequivocally made no allowances for his needs. The doctor, on the other hand, unambiguously did make provisions for them. His major emphasis was not on the "right." John, therefore, could remain in treatment. His mother could be motivated to be more accepting of him, since she was less conflicted over her disapproval of him.

Sufficient developmental and familial data are not available to hypothesize on the evolution of the semantic framework within which each of these two patients operated. However, it is apparent that their individual semantic symbolizations are not clarified through the literal meaning of the words used.

DISCUSSION

It is not uncommon to see consistently good results, in psychotherapy of adolescents from the lower-income groups, randomly assigned to a given therapist. Similar assignments to another therapist, apparently with equal qualifications, have been seen to end in premature termination with comparable consistency.

Here is an area where systematic research may help to establish criteria for selective assignments in accordance with therapeutic style. Judicial alterations in style, also, might become possible to accommodate the needs or potentials of a given patient. Undoubtedly appropriate adaptations have to be reckoned with in the patient's milieu, in his school, and in the opportunities for recreation and for remedial help. Nor can sources of strength and of support be neglected which from within the familial setting may lend impetus to treatment. These also can be used, albeit with discrimination, to satisfy an adolescent's specific needs. The mobilization and utilization of these ancillary means is greatly enhanced when *meaningful* communication has been established in the dyadic relationship between doctor and patient—the object of this study.

At this point an interpolation seems permissible. The incidence of psychiatric disturbances and their recognition in the developing countries may be expected to increase. Therefore, the number of professionals seeking psychiatric training outside their own country is likely to rise, as will the demand for psychiatric teachers from foreign lands. Such contingencies warrant great caution on our part, lest we forget that present data and psychotherapeutic assumptions are derived from findings in and are applicable to intervention with members of the middle class in our Western civilization. Here, no less than in our work with the underprivileged of our own society, in order to function constructively, we must be prepared to accept and initiate substantial modifications of what heretofore we have taken for granted.

Psychiatrists working with adolescents from deprived backgrounds may have to re-examine the validity of time-honored technical principles of psychotherapy. Since it is impossible to embark on any therapeutic venture without preconceptions, these might be the product of observable phenomena rather than of metapsychological speculations. Thus an unbiased exploration of the doctor-patient relationship, here and now, may take precedence over the presumed genetic interpretation of its vicissitudes. Patients' apparent resistance to therapy may then become a reliable indicator of garbled communications in the dyad.

It seems fairly well established that culturally deprived children use action for self-expression—"action-language," even in using words, rather than verbal language—despite the use of verbal symbols. So long as a con-

sensus has not been established between the two participants on the semantic framework within which therapeutic operations are carried out, it may
be appropriate to take communicative cues from the patient's actions, verbal as well as nonverbal. In recent years much attention has been paid to
these nonverbal cues. To this it may be appropriate to add the operational
meaning of the spoken language itself, irrespective of content.

In this context it seems worth mentioning that verbal communication for
the establishment of interpersonal intimacy seems to be out of fashion.
With increasing frequency, even with middle-class patients, there can be
found a diminishing reliance on the spoken word as a means to tell about
oneself. In our society a sense of alienation is suffered not only by those in
the out-group but by those in the in-group as well.

In any event, as regards the underprivileged, the phenomenon of non-
communication which interferes with therapeutic progress can be elucidated
with the help of certain research findings. Working-class mothers, so Sears,
Maccoby, and Levin have shown,[11] are emotionally cold. They demand
achievements from their children for which there is no prototype in their
immediate subculture. They are also intolerant and punitive when it comes
to sexual behavior, to expressions of anger, and to the satisfaction of emotional needs. Children, therefore, fail to experience helpful parental permissiveness. They live in a state which Murphy compares to sensory deprivation where "lack of stimulus, lack of sensory richness and lack of social
opportunity" [8] interfere with proper differentiation of self and with adequate relatedness to others. These children have to contend with physical
and emotional inconsistencies. They cannot rely on verbal communication
for the purpose of role definition. Since verbal, interpersonal transactions
abound with negative attitudes, prohibitions, and reprimands, "postural and
behavioral Gestalten" predominate, as Spitz has shown.[14]

Under these circumstances the internalization of action behavior (in
Piaget's terms) as an expression of intellectual and perceptual adaptation
fails to occur. It remains directed toward immature, egocentric satisfaction
without communicative purpose. Speech itself is not used with the listener
in mind, but remains unsocialized.[3] Semantic symbolizations are almost
irrelevant. Their evolution and patterning, therefore, remain rudimentary.
Hence, with adolescents, they have not progressed to the expected age level
of hypotheticodeductive reasoning.[6] This, incidentally, seems to contribute
to the reading disabilities so often encountered among these adolescents.
Their foresightful behavior is severely truncated, limited to avoidance of
immediate anxiety and displeasure, rather than being geared to long-range
efforts of constructive planning.

However, as I have said elsewhere,[1] there arises with adolescence an
exquisite ability to repair some of the earlier damage. This may occur in a
new social setting when the use of language is geared to convey needs and
to share feelings. The therapeutic situation can be such a setting. However,

it is probably unrealistic to expect that psychotherapy alone can suffice in even a majority of cases. The patient's milieu must contain the ingredients favorable to the pursuit of these goals, once their personal appropriateness has been discovered in the course of treatment. Therapy can provide only the impetus for the change. It can be structured to facilitate the socialization of language. This is what happened in the work with John, the second of our patients. He achieved, as Sherif[12] would formulate it, a consistency in his perception of himself and of others based on his interaction with his therapist. There John learned of the potentials built into communicable language. His therapist reduced the complexity of the reciprocal relationship between them by refraining from imposing his own system of values. On the contrary, in the case of Robert, the first patient, such caution was deemed unnecessary. The form and content of his language did not reveal his alienation from cultural values. These seemed to be close to those of the therapist, who failed to be mindful of the fact that deprived adolescents do not "function conceptually and cannot relate in consistent fashion to persons, groups, events and goals not immediately present in their environment." [12] It is easy to understand how one might have accepted what Robert said for its seeming communicative quality without finding it necessary to validate its communicative meaning.

Robert and John derived their immediate sense of self-consistency from the values of their "membership group" [12]—in our instance, those of the "lower class." Their frame of reference was the use of language not primarily for the purpose of communication, but mostly for the purpose of egocentric avoidance of anxiety. Both can be seen as having been damaged in their self-concept as a result of their aspirations to the values of the "reference group," [12] in our instance the "middle class," white, Protestant American. The treatment situation provided for both the first real opportunity to relate in a personal way to a representative of that group, namely, the doctor.

In Robert's instance the outcome was unfortunate, not only because therapy was ineffective. The therapist's failure to understand him probably contributed also an increased sense of isolation. This in turn may account for his rage and his unwillingness to participate in any further exploration of his reactions. It is likely, also, that his potentials for collaboration were heavily mortgaged by this unrewarding experience.

The therapist is the only member of the dyad capable of the necessary effort to establish a meaningful semantic framework. Of course, the odds against his success are great. He must overcome the patient's usual style of self-expression, which lends itself easily to misunderstanding because it is not tailored to be communicative. Thus, the patient's explicit request for help is not a reliable indicator that he knows what help means. Nor is his protest against such offered help unfailingly indicative that he cannot be helped. This may be but an indication that he has been severely disappointed whenever he was in need of help.

It used to be axiomatic that psychotherapy, which is "talking treatment," was directed toward and could be helpful in stimulating personality growth, provided the patient *really wanted* to change. This can no longer be accepted as the only, nor the most telling, criterion. We may well have to be more circumspect. We may be able to learn from our therapeutic failures if we can dispense with labeling every dropout a resistance against treatment. Our lack of success may be a function of the maladapted use of an imperfect tool, namely, the spoken language. The promise of success may lie in our communicative skill. Not only must we be able to make ourselves understood by others; we must strive to perceive and to decode garbled communications as well.

References

1. BRYT, A. "Modifications of Psychoanalysis in the Treatment of Adolescents," in J. H. MASSERMAN, ed., *Science and Psychoanalysis*. New York: Grune and Stratton, 1966, IX, 80.
2. FIERMAN, L. B. "Myths in the Practice of Psychotherapy," *Archives of General Psychiatry*, XII (1965), 408.
3. FLAVELL, J. H. *The Developmental Psychology of Jean Piaget*. Princeton: Van Nostrand, 1963, p. 271.
4. GOULD, R. E. "Dr. Strangeclase: Treating the Blue-Collar Worker," *American Journal of Orthopsychiatry*, XXXVII (1967), 78.
5. HUNT, R. G. "Social Class and Mental Illness," *American Journal of Psychiatry*, CXVI (1960), 1065.
6. INHELDER, B., and JEAN PIAGET. *The Growth of Logical Thinking*. New York: Basic Books, 1958, pp. 334–350.
7. KARNO, M. "The Enigma of Ethnicity in a Psychiatric Clinic," *Archives of General Psychiatry*, XIV (1966), 516.
8. MURPHY, G. "Communication and Mental Health," *Psychiatry*, XXVII (1964), 102.
9. OSTERRIETH, P. A. "Psychological Aspects of Adolescence," in G. CAPLAN and S. LEBOVICI, eds., *Psychiatric Approaches to Adolescence*, Sixth International Congress of Child Psychiatry, Pre-Congress Publication. Amsterdam: Excerpta Medica Foundation, 1966, p. 32.
10. OVERALL, B., and H. ARONSON. "Expectations of Psychotherapy in Patients of Lower Socio-Economic Class," *American Journal of Orthopsychiatry*, XXXIII (1963), 421.
11. SEARS, R. R., E. E. MACCOBY, and H. LEVIN. *Patterns of Child Rearing*. White Plains, N.Y.: Row, Peterson, 1957, p. 480.
12. SHERIF, M. "The Self and Reference Groups," in E. HARMS, ed., *Fundamentals of Psychology*. Annals of the New York Academy of Sciences, XCVI, No. 3 (1962), 797.
13. SLAVSON, S. R. *A Textbook in Analytic Group Psychotherapy*. New York: International Universities Press, 1964, p. 119.

14. Spitz, R. *The First Year of Life.* New York: International Universities Press, 1965, p. 142.
15. Thomas, A. "Pseudo Transference Reactions Due to Cultural Stereotyping," *American Journal of Orthopsychiatry,* XXXII (1962), 894.

24

Forms of Language Usage in Adolescence and Their Relation to Disturbed Behavior and Its Treatment

James B. McWhinnie

The observations and conclusions in this study are based on psychiatric work over the past six years, largely with adolescent delinquents. Such work has been compared and contrasted with current and previous experience of a hospital child psychiatric clinic and of an inpatient psychiatric unit for adolescents. In individual interviews and therapeutic discussion groups with delinquent adolescents, an impressive contrast was found in the quality of their language usage compared with adolescents with psychoneurotic disorders. The interrelationships between linguistic expression and psychotic and organic conditions are not being considered in this study. Accepting the descriptions of concreteness of thinking by Inhelder and Piaget[11] as being concerned with the facts of reality in the immediate situation, and by Goldstein[8] as being determined by and being unable to proceed beyond some immediate experience, object, or stimulus, it was found that the form and content of the language used by young delinquents, in giving communication to their thinking, were predominantly concrete and that they showed only a very limited capacity for the formulation and communication of abstract concepts. Abstract conceptualization, as described by the same authors, involves relative detachment from the immediate perceptual experience, and communication would be concerned with more generalized concepts, where situations and experiences are classified and interrelated, with discernment of the relations of the parts to the whole, with capacity for

304

deductive and inductive associations and for creative imaginative symbolization and planning ahead ideationally.

The delinquent in general appears to lack linguistic apparatus to formulate and to communicate understandingly about such abstract concepts as personal morality, social responsibility, and awareness of guilt or indeed of retribution, such as can be so evident, if not exaggerated, in some neurotic patients. The delinquent, however, can describe feelings of shame or of being discomfited, but this consists of a much more concrete appreciation of overtly expressed disapproval of his actions by others. His criteria for the moral appropriateness of any potentially delinquent act are determined more by expediency and by what would be its immediate concrete results. He tends typically to talk about whether or not to behave in a delinquent way, not so much in relation to any abstract concept of this possibly being morally wrong, but with regard to the concrete factors of possibly being detected, being physically punished, being apprehended by the police and sentenced by a court.

It is, of course, true that the cultural delinquent who is a member of an antisocial gang may describe feelings of loyalty to the gang. This again, however, is referred to in terms of adhering to a concrete code of gang behavior and of either being physically approved and accepted or being rejected and possibly physically abused.

Such concrete communication by the delinquent clearly contrasts with the capacity for verbalization by the neurotic patient about such feelings as guilt, inadequacy, and hopelessness and about particular attitudes to such concepts as immorality, responsibility, and overconscientiousness, which are all much more personal individuated abstract formulations.

Such conclusions were reinforced by the comparative analysis of tape recordings of group discussions and individual interviews. There were, of course, exceptions to such general observations in that a small proportion of the adolescents studied showed delinquency denoting neurotic motivation, expressing the conflict of highly abstract conceptualizations. On the other hand, although immature attention-seeking behavior was not uncommon, specific hysterical symptoms were, as found also by Friedlander,[6] Gibbens,[7] and in other studies quoted by the latter. Such symptomatology would clearly be a manifestation of abstractly conceived motivation.

To express such observations most simply, one could say that the emotionally insecure or socially frustrated delinquent youth, who is unable adequately to express his feelings by releasing them in an abstractly conceived manner, may, in a self-proving or self-comforting way, tend to act out his personal conflicts in concrete delinquent behavior involving property or physical assaults. On the other hand, the young person capable of abstract verbalization tends less to need to act out, but may express his difficulties by the abstract formulation of concepts which may be expressed in neurotic symptoms.

Such findings appear to be largely unrelated to innate intellectual capacity (again excluding the effects of organic or functional disorders affecting speech) or to attainment in basic educational subjects, although, of course, young people of very dull intelligence, whether delinquent or not, do tend to limit their verbal communication only to concrete language. The use of a predominantly concrete mode of language or one capable of abstract expression is independent also of the subcultural usage of slang or jargon and of participation by the adolescent in any such current fashion of slang usage by his peer group.

Whether linguistic communication is restricted to concrete formulation and expression, or whether it is capable of more abstract conceptualizations, such as those of ethics, morality, and social responsibility, appears from the study of the family history of adolescent patients to be related to the pattern of verbal communication within the family setting and in the social group. Concrete or abstract appreciation might also be related to aesthetics, and, as suggested by Hoggart,[10] this may account for the differences between our so-called "pop" culture, which could be considered to be essentially concrete, and our more sophisticated and classical artistic expression, which has more inherently abstract qualities. As found in individual and group work with the families of delinquent adolescents, and especially in the parents' counseling groups to be described later, the delinquent whose language is restricted and concrete can be observed to have grown up in a family where the pattern of communication has been essentially limited and concrete, often allowing no opportunities for elaborated verbal learning. The normal curious questionings of a child in such a family may tend to receive simple concrete "Yes" and "No" answers, with little or no opportunity for fuller abstract explanations. Such a restricted pattern of parent-child verbal communication inhibits the development of abstract expression. In such a family behavior in a child which is antisocial or potentially dangerous would tend to be handled by concrete constraints, and not controlled by more elaborative explanations. The latter would involve more continuing verbal communication, which would afford opportunities for the verbal learning and expression of abstract concepts.

In his descriptive appraisal of verbal behavior, Skinner[21] affirms that the Freudian superego of Judaeo-Christian conscience is essentially verbal. In his discussion of personal controls, he illustrates how with each other young children can be verbally more tolerant and co-operative than adults.

Although psycholinguistic studies appear largely to have been neglected by psychotherapists, James Burnett, Lord Monboddo, a Judge of the Court of Session in Edinburgh, as early as 1773 wrote "that there must have been in the progress of language two kinds of it, the one rude and barbarous, and the other succeeding to it, a language of art." [18] In 1932, Hughlings Jackson[12] distinguished between *well-organized* and *now-organizing* speech, the former restricting and the latter more readily permitting analytical and abstract thought processes. It is particularly relevant, however, in child psychotherapy and in the treatment of delinquents to consider Piaget's observations on the development in children of language, of thought, and of moral judgment. Piaget with Inhelder[11] describes thinking as developing from an infantile sensorimotor stage, through a symbolic and preconceptual stage (up to about 4 years), an intuitive stage (from about 4 to 7 years), and then concrete operational stages up to the age of about 11 years, after which the child can become capable of abstract operational thinking. In his description of language behavior, Piaget[19] does not similarly distinguish between a concrete mode of language and abstract language usage, but describes how the child first uses *egocentric speech* and more gradually develops *socialized speech*. With regard to moral judgment, Piaget[20] explains that the child's development of moral awareness up to the age of about puberty tends to be that of a morality based on concrete constraints, whereas after puberty maturation allows development of moral judgment to be that based on the more abstract appreciation of social co-operation. Luria, in his study of the role of speech in the regulation of behavior,[15] discusses how such individual control develops when external speech forms become displaced by internal speech affording a capacity for abstract conceptualization and social rules, this occurring at an earlier age than in Piaget's observations. Spitz,[23] in his discussion of the child's use of the words "No" and "Yes," also shows that the social co-operation can be learned earlier than Piaget would suggest. Piaget, however, emphasizes that his findings are applicable only to the cultural groups he studied. More recent workers, notably Bernstein[1, 2, 3] and Hess and Shipman,[9] would dispute the sequential order of cognitive development as described by Piaget, arguing that the form of communication and language within the family and in the social setting decides the mode of thought and the nature of social controls. Bernstein[3] distinguishes two forms of linguistic codes, restricted and elaborated, and Hess and Shipman[9] associate these with person-oriented and with status-oriented control systems of communication within the family. A variety of modes of communication and of control can thus occur in different families in different cultural groups, but in therapeutic work with young delinquents Piaget's distinction between a morality of constraint and a morality of co-operation provides an invaluable concept. It is very similar to Makarenko's description[16] of the constraining value of *routine* within the family compared with the need for children to learn co-operative *discipline*.

It is suggested that for many adolescent delinquents the nature of their family and social upbringing has retarded their development of thought and of moral judgment at the level of the concrete and of constraint. Traditional approaches to the reformative rehabilitation of delinquents have, however, tended to be based on the reinforcement of concrete constraints. Conventionally this has been conceived and described as training. By training appears to be implied the superimposition upon the individual offender from outside himself of a concrete regime of discipline, education, and usually work training, reinforced by concrete incentives, rewards, and punishments. The apparent supposition is that such an externally imposed concrete program of discipline will continue as a learned pattern. There is little evidence, however, that this is in fact so. It is considered that professional workers with delinquents have had no significant basic philosophy, rationale, or body of knowledge to clarify the objectives of their work. Indeed, it is felt to be generally true of all youth workers, particularly those concerned in the leisure activities of young people, that they lack a basic philosophy or understanding about what they are really trying to achieve.

Such a traditional concept of youth training by concrete measures externally imposed can be contrasted with the concept suggested by psychodynamic treatment. The latter is designed to promote a situation in which the individual, using his own internal resources, can grow in his inner life and mature in his social life. In such a way he can be capable of responding to communication about and developing an awareness of such abstract values as personal morality and social responsibility. Such growth from within the individual toward a capacity for abstract conceptualization and communication must inevitably be more effective than a concrete regime imposed from without.

Such treatment, by both individual and group methods, has much to offer the neurotic patient. Offering such individual treatment to the delinquent, however, is much less likely to be helpful. For a delinquent who has grown up in a family and social situation that has afforded him little opportunity to learn to think and communicate in other than concrete language, clearly individual treatment to promote an awareness of more mature abstract concepts would have to be based on the most intensive and long-lasting personal transference relationships. Nonetheless, in most countries of the world, society's management of the problem of its delinquents tends to be conceived in terms of individual moral exhortation and personal and social moral example. Such an approach, based on abstract linguistic communication, is manifestly not meaningful to delinquents limited in their capacity for this. Such methods are commonly reinforced by concrete punishments and constraints. Punitive measures, whether effected by deprivation of liberty or by material sanctions, must always remain an expression of society's need to defend itself against intolerable behavior. To be effective, however, such punishment must be not merely a concrete expression of retribution but a measure the social necessity for which must be abstractly understood by the offender. In this way social punishment becomes a part of treatment; but for this to be accepted as such requires, again, verbal communication capable of abstract appreciation.

In the treatment of delinquents, communication about and the formulation of abstract concepts, such as those of social morality and responsibility, can be achieved only by living and learning experiences and identifications within the setting of group and milieu therapy. In a program of frequent regular therapeutic discussion groups, delinquents can begin to experience and develop and learn through group communication and identification the abstract concepts of morality and responsibility which they have lacked in their previous linguistic experience. Such group learning affords the opportunity to develop a morality based on social co-operation developing from within and must inevitably be more effective than the traditional methods of reinforcing a morality of concrete constraint imposed from without.

Such conclusions are derived from and supported by the author's experience over the past five years of participating, through teamwork and discussion with all the staff concerned, in effecting in several Approved Schools, visited weekly, a transition from traditional training methods to a more therapeutic approach based on group structures. Approved Schools in the United Kingdom are residential correctional institutions for adolescents sentenced by the courts. Length of stay ranges from about one to two years. As most of such schools in Scotland originated in the voluntary Industrial, Reformatory, and Ragged Schools of the early Victorian period, with an emphasis on industrial training, the tradition of the rehabilitative program has been that of a training approach.

As discussed by Miller,[17] following the work of Slavson[22] and his colleagues in the United States, the descriptions by Jones[13, 14] of the functions of the therapeutic community, and the influence of the Tavistock group in London,[4] the use of group processes has become hopefully fashionable in the past ten years or so as a possible way of improving "success rates" in British correctional institutions. In one Approved School it was thus suggested that one or two discussion or counseling groups be started, by then untrained staff, with a view to evaluating the effectiveness of such methods. It had been the experience of the author, however, in penal institutions for older youths, that such a gradual introduction of group counseling, by staff ill-prepared for this, created more problems than were solved, since the two existing major groups—of the staff and inmates—now became four groups —of staff and inmates involved in counseling groups and those who were not—thus further handicapping the development of constructive communication. In the Approved School it was thus decided that the introduction of group counseling be delayed until sufficient staff were adequately trained for all the pupils to be simultaneously involved in the group process.

In the author's view, the only effective way to obtain adequate training in group work and understanding of group dynamics is by personal participation in a group learning experience. A week's residential course was thus arranged for senior Approved School staff, part of which consisted of the learning experience of unstructured, nondirective leaderless group discussion. A similar course of weekly meetings was provided for all staff self-selected to undertake group counseling. After several months it then became possible to offer participation in a weekly discussion group, of some eight to twelve members, lasting about one and a half hours, to all the one hundred pupils within this school. This developed into a situation in which there were open reception groups lasting two or three months, closed groups continuing for most of the period of stay within the school, and open prerelease groups lasting a few weeks. Each group was taken by one member of staff, who became a permanent member of that group. Weekly meetings were as regular as possible, but might sometimes be interrupted by periods of leave for pupils and staff, by school camps, and by specific work projects. In addition to the initial training for such group work described above, the staff member experienced continuing training in group methods at regular weekly meetings of all the staff members undertaking group counseling, attended by the deputy headmaster, who has become very experienced in group work, and by the visiting psychiatrist or clinical psychologist.

The group discussions are intended to be unstructured, nondirective, confidential, and virtually "leaderless" with maximal horizontal group communication; but with immature youths, often with limited educational attainment and verbal capacity, the staff member may sometimes have to assume a more directive role, especially in the early stages of group development. The groups can be observed to progress through five main stages, usually but not necessarily successive, and commonly repeated; first a phase of catharsis, of "letting off steam," of ventilating complaints and grievances, with some indirect "testing-out" of the staff member, especially in relation to his more authoritarian role outside the group; second, a phase of more directly testing out the staff member, usually with particular regard to his respect for the confidentiality of the group, and the subsequent gradual development of more secure individual and group relationships with him; third, a phase of greater interaction between individual members of the group, with testing out of each other and the adoption and interplay of group roles; fourth, a phase of resistance and defensiveness, often with prolonged silences, which could be difficult to understand and accept by the staff member, unless appreciated as being preparatory for the fifth stage, that of orientation and task formulation, leading to voluntary discussion of such topics as personal and family problems, rehabilitation, future employment, sexual relationships, and future responsibilities. Within the group there is now a developed awareness of integration, identity, and loyalty. Following this a group may reach a sixth and final stage of "plateau," where further progress is no longer possible for it.

Such groups have come to be known as "counseling groups," this term having been inherited from Fenton.[5] This description is unfortunate, since counseling as such by a staff member is not implicit in the group process. It is more intended that group members should learn by counseling each other, and, as already mentioned, Skinner[21] has shown that young people's groups can show greater verbal tolerance and co-operation than adults.

Such experience does not support the views of Miller[17] that for group work with young delinquents to be of value, this must be carried out by an experienced psychotherapist. As found also by Fenton,[5] group work by institution staff can be effective, provided that they themselves have had adequate prior training by participation in a learning group experience, and provided that they have the continuing training and support of regular weekly meetings with their fellow group workers in which an experienced psychotherapist can participate, to release more dynamic understanding and to interpret. In the view of the author, it is in this area that a visiting child psychiatrist to a large institution for adolescent delinquents can make his major contribution.

Where participation in group counseling is an established routine program involving all the pupils of an Approved School, it is found that even quite seriously emotionally disturbed individuals can be integrated into a constructive group process, provided that it is recognized by them and by the group that individual psychotherapeutic help is regularly available to them and provided adequate support is available from the psychotherapist to the staff member of the group. Group selection should also ascertain that not more than one, or two at the most, disturbed acting-out psychoneurotic individuals are included in any one group, since the problems for the group of integrating a higher proportion into a group of eight to twelve members would inhibit the constructive progress of the group as a whole. In general, however, groups as they progress through the stages described do not formulate tasks which they recognize that they themselves are unable to resolve, and for this reason it is found that group membership of emotionally disturbed pupils simultaneously receiving individual psychotherapy presents a problem, if any, of only short duration.

Furthermore, apart from the potentialities for learning offered to individual group members, comprehensive group counseling in a large institution undoubtedly breaks down the "us/them" inmate/staff barriers of communication. This would not occur if group work were carried out by outside visiting therapists.

Some further developments of group communication methods within Approved Schools progressing toward the concept of a therapeutic community have been the introduction of regular unstructured school meetings with senior staff, dormitory meetings with house staff to discuss domestic matters, and regular meetings of all staff attended by the visiting psychiatrist and psychologist to discuss matters of school policy and the problems and progress of individual pupils and their families.

It has been argued, of course, that no matter how intensive and comprehensive diagnostic and treatment methods might become in correctional institutions, these could have only a minimal lasting effect if the individual were simply, at the end of his stay, to return to exactly the same unmodified family and environmental situation from which he came. For this reason, in several Approved Schools, developing from the group counseling program and carried out by the staff trained and experienced in such work, similar group counseling methods have been extended voluntarily by invitation to parents and families. Such parental counseling, in groups of up to twelve couples, held in the evenings, and planned to continue to meet for at least twelve sessions, has proved to be very acceptable and in fact popular with most parents. In some families, only one parent may be able to attend meetings, because the other may have to stay at home to look after younger children or may be employed on evening work, but sometimes father and mother may alternate in coming to meetings. Difficulties which would have arisen from the problem of having some distance to travel to the school have been met by arranging group meetings in various local centers throughout Scotland. For more disturbed, suspicious, antiauthoritarian or socially inadequate parents, who decline invitations to participate in such meetings, individual family case work is, of course, required, and this frequently has the result that such parents later volunteer to attend parents' group meetings.

Other permutations of the application of group methods to the family situation are at present being introduced when suggested by particular situations, as, for example, mixed groups of parents and their children where communication within the family is nonexistent, inadequate, or strained.

In all such group situations, both for pupils and for parents, when the fifth described stage of group development is reached, opportunities are afforded in a way often not possible in any other setting for experiencing and formulating verbal modes of communicating about such abstract concepts as co-operative morality and personal and social responsibility. In Piaget's terminology,[20] such groups can progress from a purely concrete awareness of a morality of constraint to abstract conceptualization and potentialities for social application of a morality of co-operation. Applying Bernstein's dimensions,[3] communication limited to restricted language codes may develop to the expression of a more elaborated usage. As Hess and Shipman[9] would evaluate the process, status-oriented controls may change to those which are person-oriented.

Although nonverbal factors, of course, play a part in a therapeutic process, and even silence has its own special significance in individual and group relationships, the main vehicle for the experiencing, learning, and development of more mature, stable, and responsible moral and social attitudes is linguistic communication. The study of linguistic usage suggests that, as the predominant language mode of delinquents is concrete and their pattern of moral control is based on constraint, traditional methods of training based on concrete constraints must be replaced by a transition to the concept of a therapeutic community, in which all aspects of group living and communication can become opportunities for the learning and verbalization of abstract concepts of morality and responsibility. As exemplified by the part which can be played in the work of residential schools for adolescent delinquents as described above, it is concluded that the role of the psychiatrist or psychologist working in such a setting is to be catalytic in facilitating this transition.

References

1. BERNSTEIN, B. "Social Class and Linguistic Development: A Theory of Social Learning," in A. H. HALSEY, J. FLOUD, and C. A. ANDERSON, eds., *Education, Economy and Society*. Glencoe, Ill.: The Free Press, 1961.
2. BERNSTEIN, B. "Family Rôle Systems, Communication and Socialisation," paper presented at the Conference on the Development of Cross-Cultural Research on the Education of Children and Adolescents, University of Chicago, 1964.
3. BERNSTEIN, B. "A Socio-Linguistic Approach to Social Learning," in J. GOULD, ed., *Social Science Survey*. Harmondsworth, Middlesex, England: Penguin Books, 1965.
4. BION, W. R. *Experiences in Groups and Other Papers*. London: Tavistock, 1960; New York: Basic Books.
5. FENTON, N. *An Introduction to Group Counselling in Correctional Service*. New York: The American Correctional Association, 1957.
6. FRIEDLANDER, K. *The Psycho-Analytical Approach to Juvenile Delinquency*. London: Routledge and Kegan Paul, 1947.
7. GIBBENS, T. C. N. *Psychiatric Studies of Borstal Lads*. London: Oxford University Press, 1963.
8. GOLDSTEIN, K. "Methodological Approach to the Study of Schizophrenic Thought Disorder," in J. S. KASANIN, ed., *Language and Thought in Schizophrenia*. Berkeley: University of California Press, 1944.
9. HESS, R. D., and V. C. SHIPMAN. "Early Experience and the Socialization of Cognitive Modes in Children," *Child Development*, XXXVI, No. 4 (December 1965), 869.
10. HOGGART, R. *The Uses of Literacy*. London: Chatto and Windus, 1957.
11. INHELDER, B., and J. PIAGET. *The Growth of Logical Thinking from Childhood to Adolescence*, trans. A. PARSONS and S. MILGRAM. London: Routledge and Kegan Paul, 1958; New York: Basic Books.
12. JACKSON, J. H. *Selected Writings*, Vol. II. London: Hodder and Stoughton, 1932.
13. JONES, M. *Social Psychiatry*. London: Tavistock, 1952, as *The Therapeutic Community*. New York: Basic Books, 1953.
14. JONES, M. *Social Psychiatry*. Springfield, Ill.: Charles C Thomas, 1962.
15. LURIA, A. R. *The Role of Speech in the Regulation of Normal and Abnormal Behaviour*. London: Pergamon, 1961.
16. MAKARENKO, A. S. *A Book for Parents*. Moscow: Goslitizdat, 1937.
17. MILLER, D. *Growth to Freedom: The Psychosocial Treatment of Delinquent Youth*. London: Tavistock, 1964.
18. MONBODDO, JAMES BURNETT, LORD. *Of the Origin and Progress of Language*. 6 vols. Edinburgh: Kincaid and Creech, 1773.
19. PIAGET, J. *The Language and Thought of the Child*, trans. M. WARDEN. London: Routledge and Kegan Paul, 1926; New York: Harcourt, Brace.

20. PIAGET, J. *The Moral Judgment of the Child,* trans. M. GABAIN. London: Routledge and Kegan Paul, 1932.
21. SKINNER, B. F. *Verbal Behaviour.* London: Methuen, 1957.
22. SLAVSON, S. R. *Introduction to Group Therapy.* New York: The Commonwealth Fund, 1943.
23. SPITZ, R. A. *No and Yes; On the Genesis of Human Communication.* New York: International Universities Press, 1957.

25

Joint Parent-Adolescent Interviews in the Psychotherapy of the Younger Adolescent

Alex H. Kaplan

When the younger adolescent (12–16) is seen for psychotherapy, some involvement with the parents seems to be mandatory if the psychotherapy is to show any degree of success. This is also true to some extent in the psychotherapy of the late adolescent (17–20), although in such situations psychotherapy may be adversely affected by a too close relationship of the parents with the therapist. Parents insist on participating, and their interests and needs must be met. On the other hand, parental involvement needs to be carefully evaluated so that it does not create too much resistance in the therapist-adolescent relationship and destroy the collaborative efforts made by the therapist. The purpose of this presentation is to discuss the usefulness of joint parent-adolescent interviews in the psychotherapy of the younger adolescent. This special technique, employed mainly in the introductory diagnostic phase but continued throughout psychotherapy as needed, has proved to be a valuable adjunct to the treatment process by encouraging the therapeutic alliance and facilitating the therapeutic contract by diminishing parental and adolescent resistances to therapy, reducing countertransference reactions in the therapist, and supplying valuable information concerning the intrafamily neurosis and the outside world of the adolescent, all essential for successful treatment.

I have not been able to find any reference in the psychoanalytic literature describing techniques of handling the parents of adolescents in analysis. The book edited by Balser[2] does discuss the need for maintaining contact with the parents, sometimes by interviews with the therapist, at other times

315

by referral of them to another therapist, more specifically, a social worker. Welsch[8] feels that involvement with the adolescent's parents is necessary within every therapeutic problem as in the therapy with children. Attempts at collaborative therapy,[6] where parents are seen by one therapist and the patient by another, are fraught with considerable difficulties. Counterreactions frequently develop in each therapist toward the other's therapy, and few psychotherapists are comfortable enough to be free to discuss their therapeutic activities with peers. Grotjahn[4] has recommended collaborative therapy for marital and family problems, but has expressed the feeling that unless he has personal confidence in the other therapist, such therapy does not succeed. My own experience with collaborative therapy in private practice or in hospitals with the therapeutic community concept of patient care has been disappointing. In child guidance clinics where in the classical sense the psychiatrist may see the patient and the social worker the parents, what theoretically starts out as a collaborative therapeutic program, on a practical level, becomes two isolated therapeutic endeavors with little collaboration and much resistance developing between therapists.

More recently the practice in psychotherapy of combining treatment of child and parent, oriented more pointedly to the reality of the family, has markedly increased. However, many psychotherapists and psychoanalysts still refuse to interview other family members on the premise that this would interfere with the conduct of the patient's psychotherapy or psychoanalysis. Ackerman[1] has discussed the isolation of the psychoanalyst in such situations, who is solely dependent for information concerning family experience on the emotional, biased interviews of his individual patient. He felt that the traditional custom of the psychoanalyst as well as the psychotherapist of avoiding interviewing other family members, unless this complicates his relationship with his patient, needs to be re-examined for its dynamic implications. Hammer and Holterman[5] studied families of 54 adolescents with behavior problems six months to three years after completion of their initial work-up in order to determine how many of them had followed clinic recommendations. Besides other factors for the discontinuation of treatment, they found that communication between parents and therapists was poor and often parents felt uninformed or excluded from their children's treatment.

Anna Freud emphasized the specific difficulties in the analyses of adolescents, "namely the urgency of their needs, their intolerance for frustration and their tendency to treat whatever relationship evolves as a vehicle for wish fulfillment and not a source of insight and enlightenment."[3] She also spoke of the need of the parents of the normal adolescent for help and guidance to be able to bear with him until he works out his own solution. This need on the part of parents is exaggerated when the adolescent is in need of treatment.

The young adolescent is rarely mature enough to initiate the primary contact with the therapist. This contact is ordinarily carried out by the mother. Earlier in my experience with the younger adolescent in private practice, I would see the mother or both parents for the initial complete psychosocial history. However, in specific cases the adolescent might be seen first. As might be expected, the adolescent came to see the therapist with greater or lesser reluctance, and often there was a considerable denial of personal problems (more true of adolescents with ego-syntonic rather than ego-alien symptomatology). Subsequently, after further study, including additional interviews with the child or psychological studies, a diagnostic session was held with one or both parents and a separate one with the child at which time recommendations were made as to subsequent treatment. While there were always parental resistances to overcome, there was frequently the task of overcoming the continued denial by the adolescent of his need for treatment. Separate interviews added to the complexity of developing a therapeutic alliance with the adolescent and encouraging a therapeutic contract with the parents. Often at this point in the study, contact was broken by the parents or the adolescent.

Although there were considerable efforts on my part during the diagnostic phase to advise and encourage the parents as to their role in the treatment of their adolescent, when therapy started parents frequently called and often insisted on being seen. When such requests were refused, treatment was frequently adversely affected or broken off. These phone calls and visits with the parents, among other items, also involved some discussion of material obtained from the therapeutic hours, albeit carefully selected to preserve confidentiality. Subsequently, information from the parental interview was relayed to the adolescent, although frequently some material was omitted, either consciously to protect the patient or unconsciously because of countertransference attitudes primarily involved with the parents. The problem of maintaining a therapeutic relationship with the patient and some contact with the parents increased the problem of confidentiality, since the therapist was interposed between the needs of the parents and those of the patient, adding to the complexity of the treatment. Moreover, the lack of complete awareness of the outside reality when the parents were rarely or never seen adversely affected the treatment situation. The problem of the therapist's overidentifying either with the adolescent or with the parents, and the increased resistance exhibited by the parents to behavioral changes in the patient as a result of treatment, were not easily worked through because of what I began to recognize as a faulty system of communication between the therapist, the patient, and his family. All the above would not apply to those infrequently seen, highly motivated adolescents in treatment with ego-alien symptoms whose parents have been in therapy or have been psychoanalyzed or who are unusually flexible in their response to changes in intrafamily personality dynamics resulting from the treatment. Such treatment experiences can be carried on with almost no communication with parents, as is true in the psychotherapy of adults.

In an attempt to solve this problem of inadequate communication, after some experimentation with various techniques of solving the problem of faulty intrafamily communication, I began to employ joint parent-adolescent interviews. Such quadrangular conferences are felt to be of benefit to the treatment situation. They are designed not only to gain an insight into the family neurosis, with its complicated interactions between the adolescent and his parents, but to facilitate the therapeutic process. Knowledge gained during these interviews is used in therapy like any other material gained during the course of the therapy with the adolescent. However, the therapist must retain enough detachment during such joint interviews to avoid complicating countertransference difficulties. Essentially he remains a participating observer and should not be an actor in the family drama.[4] These interviews, used mainly in the introductory diagnostic phase, but repeated as needed throughout the therapeutic process, eliminate the need for more frequent parent-therapist contacts, focus on the presenting intrafamily pathology, give a better picture of the adolescent's reality, improve the intrafamily communications, facilitate the therapeutic alliance and contract, and eliminate the need for any guarded confidentiality on the part of the therapist.

My diagnostic studies at this time routinely include in the initial contact a joint interview with parents and adolescent. Pursuing the same objectives in my original contact with the parents as I did separately with the parents and adolescent, I obtain the reasons for the referral, the background of the adolescent, and the personal history of the parents themselves. The interplay between the members of the family in a joint interview, with the unfolding backgrounds of both parents and their adolescent child, gives one the unique opportunity of evaluating the family interactions which may have been responsible for the adolescent pathology presented by the patient. Although originally I had expected that the adolescent would vigorously oppose this group meeting, I was surprised to discover that he generally felt more comfortable when his first approach to the therapist was with his parents very much like his past experience with the pediatrician or family physician. Often, such a joint interview gave the adolescent his first awareness of his parents' conflicts and their effect on his behavior. Of course, there are exceptions to this general rule, especially when the adolescent is so antagonistic toward his parents that he will not participate in a group interview. At some point during the first contact with the parents and their child, I leave enough time to see the adolescent alone to ally myself with the patient and also give him the opportunity of reacting to the group confrontation that sometimes may be painful because of the hostile parental attitudes.

Following succeeding individual contacts with the adolescent and/or other studies such as a psychological examination, unless there is some specific contraindication, final recommendations for both the adolescent and his parents are again made in a joint postdiagnostic conference. This again has many advantages, for it does not facilitate the many distortions which frequently occur when members of the family are seen separately. The adolescent and his parents are not allowed the luxury of denial of their problems, especially if everyone is available for rebuttal and reaffirmation of the problems. On the other hand, such a conference encourages a therapeutic alliance with the patient and helps to develop a constructive therapeutic contact with the parents. In such an interview the patient can contrast the behavior of his parents with that of the therapist and gain the hope that he can solve his own conflicts and relieve his suffering through treatment.

Should the parents become involved in psychotherapy or psychoanalysis, I usually maintain no contact with the parents' therapists, but continue to maintain whatever contact becomes necessary through joint quadrangular interviews. Financial arrangements, setting up the hours for therapy, preparing the parents for their own therapy or for the treatment of the adolescent, and other administrative problems are routinely discussed in these joint meetings prior to the beginning of treatment. When treatment is begun, no further personal contact is maintained with the parents by telephone or individual personal contacts outside of a joint conference. Such a prohibition by itself limits the tendency of the parents to communicate with the therapist. Requests from the parents for contact with the therapist are routinely taken up with the patient, and only when the problems cannot be resolved within the treatment situation, a joint quadrangular conference is set up.

DISCUSSION

The basic reason for using joint interviews is their use as an effective technique to facilitate the treatment process. Its purpose is not to treat the parents, although positive therapeutic results may accrue from such meetings. Parents that need more intensive help are referred for treatment to other therapists. The information and insight gained from such joint meetings is useful as therapeutic material to be treated as such in the psychotherapy of the adolescent.

Although there is no doubt that such joint interviews affect the transference relationship with the patient, even occasional telephone calls and infrequent personal contacts with parents affect the basic therapist-patient relationship. Frequently the lack of adequate controls for parent-therapist communications results in increased patient resistance and a breakdown of the therapeutic contract. The important issue that needs to be examined is the effect such joint interviews have on the therapeutic alliance, the therapeutic contract, and the therapist's position as a transference figure. Certainly, if the therapist's position is negatively affected, such technique destroys the possibility of any treatment and should be avoided. However, if the transference relationship is positively benefited, essentially unaltered or only temporarily influenced but modifiable by interpretation, then such a technique may be a very helpful adjunct to the treatment of the adolescent.[4] If such techniques prove to be successful, the need for continued joint interviews will disappear and the treatment will continue with little or no further contact with the parents. It is my growing conviction that such joint interview techniques are successful in facilitating the therapeutic contract and alliance, have a positive effect on the treatment situation, and do not interfere adversely with the developing transference and resolution of conflicts.

In addition, these quadrangular joint interviews help to bring into group consciousness the family complementary neurotic patterns responsible for the continuation of family pathology and adolescent symptoms; parental and adolescent inconsistent behavior, parental seductiveness, parental encouragement of regressive and symptomatic adolescent behavior; adolescent acting-out behavior; a better evaluation of the external reality; and the manipulative behavior of parents and adolescents.

Obviously much depends on the problem for which the adolescent has been referred. For some children a continuing period of conjoint family therapy is indicated when the family conflict or family neurosis is more pressing than the individual difficulty in the child. For those neurotic, depressed, or well-stabilized personality disorders, individual therapy with the adolescent is indicated, with occasional quadrangular interviews as needed to initiate and maintain the course of therapy. These contacts with the parents usually drop out at the point where the adolescent gives up trying to solve his own emotional conflicts by attempts to modify his parents' behavior or their reactions to him.

Joint parent-adolescent interviews as part of the psychotherapy of the younger adolescent are also used as needed for the older adolescent and occasionally for adults. All treatment disrupts the basic family equilibrium, and techniques must be developed to cope with the ensuing transference problems of the untreated family members.[7] This happens more vividly in adolescent psychotherapy, and joint parent-adolescent interviews can help to overcome the family disequilibrium.

References

1. ACKERMAN, N. W. *The Psychodynamics of Family Life*. New York: Basic Books, 1958, p. 31.
2. BALSER, B. H., ed. *Psychotherapy of the Adolescent*. New York: International Universities Press, 1959.
3. FREUD, A. "Adolescence," in *Psychoanalytic Study of the Child*. New York: International Universities Press, 1958, VIII, 255–278.
4. GROTJAHN, M. *Psychoanalysis and the Family Neurosis*. New York: Norton, 1960.
5. HAMMER, T. and J. HOLTERMAN, "Referring Adolescents for Psychotherapy, *Clinical Pediatrics*, IV (1965), 462–467.

6. JOHNSON, A. M. "Collaborative Psychotherapy: Team Setting," in H. MAR-CEL, ed., *Psychoanalysis and Social Work*. New York: International Universities Press, 1953, pp. 79–108.
7. ROSEN, V. H. "Changes in Family Equilibrium through Psychoanalytic Treatment," in V. W. EISENSTEIN, ed., *Neurotic Interaction in Marriage*. New York: Basic Books, 1956.
8. WELSCH, E. E. "Discussion," in Balser, *op. cit.*, pp. 144–152.

26

A Living Myth: The Problem of Communication within a Community

W. H. Allchin

I. INTRODUCTION

In recent years much work has been done on the characteristics of institutions and on the effects which residence has on both staff and inmates. Any institution or "setup" inevitably gives tangible expression to a series of organized ideas, feelings, value judgments, and concepts. This underlying idea system or ideology is not often made explicit. In fact, British psychiatry, with its stress on eclecticism and pragmatism, has been slow to study these matters, and hospitals and special institutions seem to have remained largely unconscious of the importance of ideology. However, the work of Russell Barton[1] on institutional neurosis and the development of the concept of the therapeutic community under the hand of Maxwell Jones[5] have clarified matters, and Rapoport's book *Community as Doctor*[7] has laid bare the ideology expressed by a setup such as the Henderson Hospital.

It is now clear that an institution must be positively good if it is to avoid adding to a patient's illness a further layer of difficulty.

Such considerations are of great importance in the case of psychiatric hospitals specializing in the residential care of children and adolescents, for by reason of age and illness these patients are vulnerable to institutional pressures in a high degree. Burdened by neurotic or psychotic illness, the young patient has to sustain a separation from home and to struggle with his relationship to a new peer group and to the strange adults who form the staff.

Certain divisive factors are inevitable in such a community. There is the barrier of age, and the sometimes sharply contrasting roles of staff member and patient. Then, again, the characteristic theme of adolescent develop-

322

ment adds to the problems. Thus, the patient group may become identified with the instinctual drives, so that staff members feel under constant strain as they try to represent the realities of ego control and social conscience. Yet life in the institution soon makes it clear that the division into staff/patient groups by no means corresponds with the apparent divisions between sane/ mad, or between good/bad.

Observation shows that it is all too easy for a polarization to occur, and this is most clearly seen in the case of penal institutions which deal with young people. P. D. Scott writes:

> As soon as offenders or the antisocially inclined are segregated there is a tendency for staff and inmates to consolidate at opposite poles; a hierarchy tends to develop among the offenders; a threat is thus offered to the staff which calls out a repressive authoritarian regime and the possibility of a vicious circle of resentment and counterresentment.[8]

Such polarization, which tends to occur in the psychiatric as well as the penal institution, leads to the exposure of individuals to strong peer-group pressures, and positive identifications with staff members may be hampered or even prevented.

A therapeutic community is one in which these divisions have been healed or at least minimized. Efforts to establish free and informal communication are at the same time efforts to link the two groups within the institution together. This entails bringing together the history and "life story" of each group, its past and its present experience. The aim is to create a joint consciousness, to write together, as it were, a shared story, which itself has a vitalizing and unifying effect on the social processes of the community as a whole.

At this point it is necessary to turn to the consideration of myths, for here we shall find evidence of just these socially shared stories of the lives of communities. The equation of the word "myth" with fable has fortunately waned, and furthermore modern writing has already blurred what looked like a clear-cut distinction by the introduction of concepts such as the "factual novel" or the "fictional documentary." Mircea Eliade, in his book *Myths, Dreams and Mysteries,* speaks of the myth as "collective thinking," or as the expression of a mode of being in the world. He writes:

> A myth always narrates something as having really happened, as an event that took place, in the plain sense of the term—whether it deals with the creation of the world, or of the most insignificant animal or vegetable species or of an institution.[2]

An account of the life of the institution is the record of how the present is experienced and, recorded, passes into the history of the place, and lives on from one generation of patients and staff to another. Such information is, of course, by no means academic, for it has a powerful effect on people in the institution, conveying ideas of values, suggesting expectations, and defining the unspoken limits of speech, behavior, and acting out. Newcomers, relinquishing the values of their homes, are initiated into the new system. A critical account of such processes is given by E. Goffman in his book *Asylums*.[4]

II. THE SHARED STORY OF THE COMMUNITY

These reflections and observations have arisen out of the experience of working in a psychiatric unit dealing with neurotic and near-psychotic boys and girls whose ages range from 12 to 18. The unit has 28 beds and is situated in southern England. It stands on its own, an isolated workhouse of the Victorian era, which up till 1961 was used as a tuberculosis sanatorium. Administered as part of a general hospital group, there has been neither the support nor the hindrance of a parent hospital.

One of the chief instruments in the work of drawing together the two worlds within the community has been a daily meeting of staff and patients for half an hour. It represents the effort of the community to become conscious of its actual life together—who is present, and what is happening.

Thus, the meeting, taking place in a room, rather bare, and just large enough to contain the circle of chairs, begins with seeing who is present and who is absent. This itself requires conscious effort and demonstrates the way in which individuals may exist for the community with varying modes of intensity. Silences are frequent and stressful and often broken by defensive words by staff or patients. Incidents or happenings come under discussion, and it soon appears how a particular incident is beginning to pass into the history of the community with various degrees of distortion. At times the meeting can correct some of these distortions and a more generally acceptable version can be adopted. Highly charged happenings which may have occurred the day before will already have developed into special accounts of what was seen or thought to have been seen. Various versions will have passed from one staff member to another and from one patient to another. Patients and staff members will already have discussed it together. Some people may have heard nothing until the daily meeting. They may have been off duty, or on leave, or unconnected to any branch of the official or informal lines of communication. The paper by C. G. Jung called "A Contribution to the Psychology of Rumour"[6] gives a fascinating account of the spread of a story in a girls' school. It opens up interesting speculation on the informal modes of communication, part of the collective feeling and thinking, of the community which pass under the title of the "grapevine" or the "bush telegraph." Certain people turn out to be much more active as collectors and dispensers of information than others, and distortions may occur in line with their own emotional needs and systems of projection. The way events are perceived, communicated, and recorded is itself influenced by the myths already operative, and they go to add to the story themselves. And, as always, expectations precede observations. Patients have to explain to themselves how they come to be in the institution and how a particular experience makes sense to them. It is much harder to explain the need to be having treatment in a psychiatric unit than to accept that, following a court appearance, you have been "put away" for three years.

However, there may be hints of what the living myth is, even though those who are immersed in the life of the community are unlikely to get a very clear view of it. Even the shortest story has a basic structure: a beginning, a middle, and an end. The starting of a new venture catalyzes a whole series of attitudes and expectations and may help to unify the different groups within the community. If there is pioneering to be done, a high level of spirit may be manifested. A group of boys with their staff march off from one institution to start another from scratch. So, too, with our unit. Its early years have, in discussion, been likened to those of the newly born infant or small child. In this way the fragility of a new setup is recognized, and exceptional effort may be made by members to nurse it along. Similarly, in the first period, staff members are themselves making a new start and endeavoring to realize potentialities which have hitherto been unused. So there will be change and turmoil and trial and many errors. The institution in this stage remains highly sensitive and reactive, but nevertheless prepared to accept experimentation. As confidence grows and there seems to be increasing stability, it will be all the more important for staff to be open to communication from the patients. It is unlikely that many patients will become fully aware of the ideas implicit in the unit or hospital in which they find themselves. But they may be able to perceive things in such a way as to realize that, although staff preferences go to quiet, reasonable, and sensible behavior, yet bad behavior is also tolerated, and the idea becomes accepted that people may behave in certain ways because they feel depressed or anxious. Inevitably, those who are most ill (or, frequently, those who behave in more difficult ways) will get the most attention, and this will often make it seem that little value is placed on getting well. Further, it may appear as if the identity question can be solved by developing a unique pattern of symptoms. There is also much fruitful uncertainty in a system where there is no set scale of punishment or reward. When the community meeting has been dealing with a problem of stealing, there is always a straightforward call from some members for punishment. It is also difficult, in a community which offers no special series of privileges and rewards, for people to discover that work may be rewarding in itself and is not just another way of notching up a few more points on the rat-race ladder.

Every patient's own admission is itself a story with a beginning, a middle, and an end. After discharge the patient still exists, and some remain in the community's memory although no one in the current group of patients ever knew them. Sometimes this is the result of their having made a particular impact on staff members. Then the name will be mentioned and a new patient told that they will be a second so-and-so, or that the same thing will probably happen to them.

The danger here is that a patient, craving an identity in the unit, will take up this hint and make it into something for himself. An example of this is given by J. Genet, describing life in a children's reformatory in France. He writes:

> . . . but the gravest comment was that of the heads of families and other colonists who told me . . . that I resembled Divers. Physically, it seems. And when I wanted to know who Divers was, everyone agreed that he was a tough customer, a thug, an 18 year old big shot, and immediately, without knowing any more about him, I cherished him. . . . And so he galloped in and took possession of the world, that is of me. And he dwelt within me.[3]

When the ideology of a community comes under discussion, it is not easy to get a clear picture, for the life of a community is a continually evolving process, and its myth or story describes the actual happenings which are expressive of the underlying ideas.

In the adolescent unit trying to develop along therapeutic community lines, great value is placed on communication which is as free and honest as possible. There is emphasis on the rights of the individual within the community and on his or her claim to special attention when it is needed. It is recognized that everyone cannot be treated in the same way, and the problems caused by accepting this are also susceptible to discussion and resolution. It is not always easy to accord full individual rights to children; adolescents are able to be more self-assertive. Parents sometimes cease to hit their children when adolescence is reached, not because of a sudden conversion to the idea of an individual's right to physical integrity, but on account of the fear of physical retaliation. Thus the young person learns to accept physical force as a validating element.

In the therapeutic community sharing, participation, and informality are all valued and the solution of problems by discussion is preferred to the arbitrary exercise of force or authority, however covert this may be. Value is also placed on self-control and self-understanding. Bad or violent behavior tends to be seen as evidence of emotional disturbance. Verbal aggression is on the whole tolerated better than physical forms. Bullying and gossiping both occur and spread a vague but perceptible aura of unease. These have also been discussed by the community and understood as efforts to get rid of one's own unhappiness. Toleration of others and concern for them is also talked about. It is seen, but with difficulty, that to tell the staff that someone has tablets or is intending to run away is not necessarily an infringement of peer-group loyalty, but may be important in helping a fellow patient.

The community not only expresses ideas. It also provides members with an orientation in time and place and gives the rudiments of an identity.

Ideally, the family as a psychic and social system performs these tasks, but mostly such systems have been functioning badly for patients or have broken down altogether. The family story should include a solid but interesting past and provide, with a reasonably secure present, a foothold from which to project oneself into the future. Where this has failed, the school or hospital, or even the peer group or the armed services, are pressed into operation to supply these needs.

As with the family, so the community has its own special contacts, objects, photograph albums, stories and jokes, and even private words and phrases. Thus the quality of community life is of a special importance for the child or young person. Genet, with no home connections, gives a vivid description of this, for his whole life at this stage was the institution, the reformatory at Mettray. According to him, it lived its own myth in the shadow of an adult prison nearby. Thus for Genet the identity with evil and criminality is inevitable.

CONCLUSION

It seems, then, that at two key points the problems of institutions and those of adolescence come into sharper focus. These points are authority and communication.

With respect to authority, we have taken into account the age range of our patients and have aimed at a lesser diffusion of authority in a democratic way than would be possible with an older age group. But we have tried to develop a flexible mode which can take account of the state of the community at any particular time. Thus in more creative, constructive, or less turbulent phases, the staff can withdraw and allow the vacuum to be filled from the patient group. At other times, the emphasis must shift back toward the staff. Ideally, this very mixed group of adults and boys and girls should evolve their own specific pattern of living in which the locus of authority finds its own natural "center of gravity." For the first two years, the community meeting reflected this, being thought of as the doctors meeting. Authority was exercised in establishing the pattern of daily meeting, and it was necessary to point to this meeting as an essential part of the treatment program of the unit. Absence was allowed only with the permission of the patient's own doctor or therapist. Staff absences were taken up informally by the director. A step from this pattern eventually became possible when it was agreed that the chairmanship of the meeting should be decided each morning, and the pattern then emerged of alternating a staff member one day and a patient on the next. The group decided on a restricted task for the chairman, an almost ritual opening and closing of the meeting. It was felt that it was not the chairman's job to bring up topics for discussion or to fill the gaps of silences too prolonged or anxiety-filled. But varied assessments are made by staff or patients as to the place of authority in the unit, some staff members feeling that the patients have too much say and can get away with anything. Some patients, for their part, still feel that staff tend to dominate excessively.

Flexibility and experimentation in modes of authority and responsibility are of obvious importance for the adolescent who is engaged in trying to resolve his problem of dependence/independence and in finding out what his personal identity is to be as he or she moves steadily away from the comparative safety of childhood. Such an attitude is equally important for staff members, who usually have real fears that the patient group may get out of control. Where patients are staying in the institution for comparatively long periods, these continual adjustments and developments are necessary to ensure for all members the absence of "institutionalization."

It is notorious that during adolescence communication with grownups becomes increasingly difficult. This seems especially to relate to the parents and to radiate out to those with similar roles in schools, clubs, hospitals, and the like.

If a number of disturbed adolescents are to be treated in the same place, this question is one which cannot be side-stepped, for patients can be absorbed into the peer group and become increasingly inaccessible to the adults. And this peer-group influence can have a strong effect both on the individual's attitude to his illness and its treatment and on the kind of restraints which he will try to exercise on his social behavior. In our unit, where each patient has individual therapeutic sessions, there is always the possibility that some adult influence may percolate through to the patient group. Where a close doctor-patient relationship exists there are likely to be increased communication difficulties. For other staff members, the patient's therapist becomes very present, even in his absence, and staff may feel and complain about the fact that a particular patient has a sort of magical protection and has to be allowed to do just what he or she pleases.

The aim of free communication in all directions, without formality, is one thing. Its achievement is a function of the total living atmosphere of the community. It is this living atmosphere, this elusive tissue of thought and feeling, which I have characterized by the idea of the myth or story of what has happened and what is happening in the present.

In the space of a few years, and within the context of the administrative setting of a national service, with its inevitable rigidities, there is a limit to what can be done. Small, independent units, often schools, have pioneered much of this development. We hope to achieve some greater interpenetration between the staff and patient groups. Much goes on within each group separately and at the interface. But insofar as some of the life together can be shared, there can develop a common consciousness and concern and a vehicle which facilitates communication. Where this concept of the myth seems to me to be of additional importance is in the purveying of values. These cannot easily be communicated verbally or in a didactic fashion. The appreciation of them comes out of the experience of living situations which actually embody them. Thus much of the disdain with which young people face those in authority comes from their all-too-ready understanding of the verbal assent to values which the adults give out and the obvious discrepancies in their actual behavior.

To suppose that the treatment of psychological disorders was solely a matter of techniques correctly applied would be to fall into the great and menacing tendency of our age, to depersonalize and to objectify that which is personal and subjective.

A community can lay claim to be therapeutic only if it actually embodies the values and ideas which are healing to the human mind and spirit.

References

1. BARTON, R. *Institutional Neurosis.* Bristol: J. Wright, 1959.
2. ELIADE, M. *Myths, Dreams and Mysteries.* London: Harvill, 1962, p. 24.
3. GENET, J. *Miracle of the Rose.* London: A. Blond, 1965, p. 70.
4. GOFFMAN, E. *Asylums.* New York: Anchor Books, 1961.
5. JONES, M. *Social Psychiatry.* London: Tavistock, 1952.
6. JUNG, C. G. *The Psychology of Rumour,* in *Collected Works.* London: Routledge and Kegan Paul, 1961, IV, 35.
7. RAPOPORT, R. N. *Community as Doctor.* London: Tavistock, 1961.
8. SCOTT, P. D. "The Treatment of Psychopathy," *British Medical Journal* (1960), p. 1644.

Philosophies of Treatment

EDITORS' INTRODUCTION During recent years developments in the planning and organization of health, mental health, and welfare services in the community, the increased availability of child psychiatrists and their colleagues in psychology, social work, nursing, and special education, as well as the emergence of the new ideal of the right of all citizens and their families to high-quality care, have significantly widened the classes of the population from which patients come for psychiatric treatment. In addition, the increased demand for services has led to a variety of attempts to find ways of more efficiently utilizing our available professional resources and particularly of maximizing the collaboration of specialists in adjoining fields. Such developments have led to our recognition of the need to supplement our traditional doctor-patient-treatment-in-relative-isolation model and our concept of psychotherapy as a long-term personality repair operation with additional models and concepts which may guide our exploration of new methods of service.

In this section we include two examples of these new philosophies of treatment, each of which is enjoying increasing popularity in the United States as well as in some other countries, but which it is still too early to evaluate in comparison with the traditional approaches that have stood the test of time and with whose benefits and drawbacks we are by now familiar.

The first conceptual framework, which is discussed by Milton F. Shore and Joseph L. Massimo, on the basis of their work with adolescent chronic delinquents, is the "crisis model." This is a set of ideas concerned with the development of personality through successive phases ushered in by periods of psychological upset, or crises, in which the focus of attention is on the changes in the person during the crisis, which are thought to have a significant effect on his subsequent adjustment. It appears that during the relatively short period of crisis upset the individual is more open and susceptible to outside influence than during his regular stable psychological state. This provides a leverage point, so that minimal intervention may lead to a significant and lasting effect on the trajectory of subsequent psychological maturation. This model has mainly been used as a basis for efforts at mental health promotion and the primary prevention of mental disorder. Shore and Massimo use it, as it has also been used by others, in guiding their treatment and rehabilitation of chronically disordered patients.

The authors base their treatment program on the expectation that the chronic delinquents, like all adolescents, will experience a series of crisis upsets. As in other developmental transition phases, such as pregnancy, climacterium, and old age, these upsets are related not only to the unfolding of inner psychobiological forces but to frequently occurring significant events in the outside world which face the individual with stresses and challenges involving novel demands for which he has no ready response based on past experience. Shore and Massimo, instead of focusing on recapitulative problems from past pathological conflicts which hamper their patients' attempts to grapple with such current adaptive demands, place their emphasis on support in the here and now for their patients' emerging relatively conflict-free ego functions. As a strategic platform they base their program of interventive support on the adolescents' early attempts to enter the employment field. Getting a job is a reality task that confronts most adolescents of lower socioeconomic class, whether or not they have a history of chronic delinquency or personality disorder; and it is a particularly difficult task in the present-day urban United States for those who are inadequately educated, as are many of the culturally deprived.

Shore and Massimo accordingly do not wait for cases to be referred to them when they have broken down and have been defined as mentally disordered, but they systematically reach out and contact their patients with an offer of practical help in finding a job within twenty-four hours of the adolescents' leaving school. Subsequently, they make themselves readily available to help deal with any of the crises that emerge, whether in the area of job training or in adjusting to the demands of the work situation. Although the authors are often aware of the deep psychological implications of the predicaments into which their patients fall, they maintain their explicit focus on assisting them with the reality tasks of getting and keeping a job. This not only provides the adolescent with an opportunity for successive corrective emotional experiences but, as with the work described by Bryt, also leads to the building up of a relationship of trust with the therapist and probably to a consequent identification and a learning of verbal communicative skill, which expand opportunities for abstract conceptual control.

The authors conclude their chapter with a brief report on an evaluative study of their method. They compared a group of treated boys with a matched group of delinquents who were not treated. They found profound changes in ego functioning in the treated group as contrasted with the controls, and these changes continued two to three years following a ten-month treatment period. Such results justify a further trial of their approach by other therapists grappling with the problems of similar difficult groups of chronically disturbed adolescents and testify to the apparent value in this instance of the crisis model.

The second chapter, by Edgar H. Auerswald, deals with another treatment philosophy, based on "general or ecological systems theory." This is a larger conceptual framework, of which the crisis model is one particular subunit. It is an ambitious behavioral science attempt to develop a holistic theory to conceptualize the reverberating relationships between an individual and the series of subsystems and suprasystems in which he is involved over time in his ecological field.

The author discusses the practical implications of the new philosophy by describing the way a 13-year-old Puerto Rican boy in New York City, suffering from restlessness, poor concentration, temper outbursts, and aggressive behavior, would be treated, based on the traditional model of defining him as suffering from an illness which demands treatment by a psychiatrist and his assistants in an outpatient clinic and a psychiatric hospital. He contrasts this with how the problems of the boy and his family would be handled if the boy's disordered behavior were conceptualized as one specific manifestation of a disequilibrium in an ecological field involving a variety of relevant systems and subsystems in the family and community, and reacted to by a variety of care-giving health, mental health, welfare, educational, police, correctional, and vocational systems, of which the psychiatrist and his medical facilities were one significant set of units within a comprehensive human services program.

Auerswald uses his example of the details of professional strategy which emerges from the ecological systems model to develop some ideas for new ways of thinking about residential treatment centers. Instead of planning them as asylums or hospitals in which patients are sheltered or treated in relative isolation from their families and community, he sees them as performing certain specialized tasks within an integrated system of local delivery of comprehensive care for members who remain linked to many of their community systems, even though for certain periods they may temporarily reside in the institution. The specialized tasks include alleviation of danger to the individual and others; cognitive training, as discussed in the chapters by McWhinnie and Allchin; extended nursing care for those with severe physical problems; and research.

Many of the issues raised by Auerswald will be taken up again in the next section by Buckle and by Caplan in their discussions of problems of planning community services for adolescents. It is valuable to see in Auerswald's case description how the larger community policy decisions lead to specific action implications for the detailed management of a patient and his family and the degree to which our fundamental theoretical approach can influence both policy and individual treatment plans.

27

The Chronic Delinquent during Adolescence: A New Opportunity for Intervention

Milton F. Shore and Joseph L. Massimo

One of the major theoretical trends in the mental health field over the last few years has been a growing concern with the situations that produce marked disequilibriums in a person's psychosocial adjustment. These "crisis situations" have their origin either in external sources, such as natural disasters, deaths of family members, marriage, changing jobs or residence, entering or leaving school, or retirement, or in internal sources, such as the changes resulting from illness, pregnancy, menopause, or puberty. These situations have attracted much attention recently because they have been shown to be especially opportune times for actively intervening to effect constructive changes in personality functioning.[8] What has been lacking, however, is a clear theoretical understanding of the forces operating in a particular crisis from which there can then be derived those strategies for therapeutic intervention appropriate to the specific situation.

The need to intervene actively in order to bring about personality change rather than waiting for the individual to seek assistance on his own has arisen from the recent concern with individuals manifesting severe social problems such as delinquency, addiction, and marginal living. In these cases, often because of the characterological nature of the problem, new psychotherapeutic techniques have had to be devised.

Developmental theorists, both dynamic and nondynamic, have always been concerned with the maturational factors, physiological and psychological, that affect a person's behavior at a given time. General agreement exists among all developmental theorists that the rapid biological and social changes occurring during adolescence result in a period of intense psychological disruption (so much so, in fact, that Anna Freud [3] has suggested that the lack of such disruption during adolescence may be symptomatic of a premature and inadequate resolution of certain developmental issues). This intense disruption during adolescence is characterized by the appearance of a variety of elements, some of which resemble material of earlier stages of psychological development and some of which appear to be new and emergent aspects specific to the adolescent period. Developmental theorists have attempted to identify and integrate these elements in two principal ways.

One group has stressed primarily the earlier material, especially the unresolved sexual and aggressive conflicts revived during adolescence. The other has focused chiefly on the unique tasks and emerging elements of the adolescent period.

The recapitulative theories of the first group are best exemplified by Freud and Blos. Freud saw in adolescence the revival of the oedipus complex and the reawakening of castration fears. More recent is the theory proposed by Blos,[1] who stresses the separation experience in adolescence in what he has called the "second individuation stage." It should be remembered that neither Freud nor Blos ignores the new elements of the adolescent period. However, they conceive of the recapitulative aspects of the adolescent period as most important in determining the nature of the adolescent experience.

The emergent theories developed by the second group focus primarily on the new structures that are evolving during the adolescent period. They are best exemplified by Inhelder and Piaget,[5] who have delineated the new cognitive features present in the adolescent, and Erikson,[2] who identifies the struggle for identity as the unique and major feature of the adolescent period.

The particular theoretical direction, recapitulative or emergent, clearly determines the specific techniques used to treat adolescents and how these techniques are employed. It determines whether one directs attention primarily to the unresolved elements and works them through, or whether the focus is mainly on the features that are maturing and developing. Spiegel,[15] noting the importance for intervention of our theoretical direction, has stated that although we usually conceive of one of the tasks of adolescence as the development of the capacity to find a nonincestuous object, our concerns with the contaminations of object relations in adolescence often prevent us from defining what constitutes a nonincestuous object and encouraging these new object relations when they appear.

The development of a program for therapeutic intervention during adolescence depends, however, not only on our understanding of the maturational crisis of adolescence but also on those particular social and personal factors that are operating in the individual adolescent to influence the direction of his resolution of the crisis.

Three elements operate to limit the available alternatives for reducing the maturational pressures and conflicts. These are:

(1) The sociocultural factors which influence both the cognitive and affective development of the personality, offering only certain opportunities for identity formation. Thus, it has been found that there is often a severe identity crisis in lower-class youth during adolescence when they become aware of the limited social opportunities available to them. Despair sets in, and a resolution to the identity crisis is often made along antisocial lines.

(2) The psychopathological elements of the affective system which often reflect sociocultural origins, but are primarily determined by the nature of early object relationships. Thus, the character of the unresolved conflicts, as well as the defensive structure, will serve to limit the alternatives for resolving the adolescent crisis. These affective elements, of course, also have a profound influence on cognitive development.

(3) Specific situational events often of an external kind (such as suspension from school or removal from home) which block certain directions and avenues for the resolution of the struggle for identity.

The conceptual outline described above formed the basis for our special treatment program for adolescent chronic delinquents (that is, boys with a long history of antisocial behavior who have had contact with the police and the courts). The boys were in the low socioeconomic groups living in a middle-class, suburban neighborhood. They were no longer in school, either because they had been suspended or because they had voluntarily decided to withdraw. In describing this program, the emphasis will be on the relationship of the strategy and techniques of therapeutic intervention with this group to the understanding of adolescence as related to the sociocultural, psychopathological, and situational aspects mentioned earlier.

One of the sources of major concern unique to the adolescent in his struggle for identity is the emergence for the first time of realistic attempts to define vocational interests and goals. Conceptually, this area might be seen as one which, initially, though not entirely devoid of attitudes derived from early family experiences, is relatively new and free of major conflict. Although the adolescent, especially the male, has preconceived notions about the working world, these notions have yet to be tested out in experience. It is only when the frustrations in testing out one's vocational wishes with reality occur that severe contaminations of the vocational area with the individual's conflict system results. Many years later, therefore, it is often difficult even to approach the area of work with adult males because it is so closely tied with guilt, shame, and other intense emotions. Although we have long been aware of the vocational area as newly emergent in the adolescent, we have often ignored it as an opportunity for intervention in bringing about change in other aspects of the personality, those riddled with conflict. Only recently, when we have been faced with helping the lower-income groups, has there been a revival of interest in the significance of employment in the psychological life of the individual, especially the male. This revived interest has led to a new awareness of the importance Freud had originally placed on work. It has also led to new efforts to integrate the work experience into psychoanalytic theory with particular emphasis on the role employment plays in the development of certain ego functions.[4, 6] In a recent article of our own,[10] we have attempted to describe the psychological significance of work specifically for the adolescent.

The basic assumption of our treatment program for chronic antisocial adolescents was that employment could be used as a way of reaching these consistently unreachable boys. We believed that through the job one could indirectly introduce services that are known to be necessary, but are often rejected when offered early because they are so closely related to the intense conflictual elements of the adolescent. (Obtaining help, for example, being tied to being overpowered, and learning being related to accepting authority, both of which are especially frightening to these youths.) In other words, it was our belief that by a focus on the use of new emerging energies, one could later aim toward the freeing of energies that were locked in conflict.

However, the chronic delinquent has difficulty in choosing a job, even if he desires one very much. He often wants a job more in line with his omnipotent fantasies than with the realities of his capacity and talents. On such a job he is easily disappointed and bound to fail, confirming his belief that he is inadequate, which is then translated into a characteristic pattern of projection and retaliation for what he feels is being done to him, in this way triggering more conflict and a rash of antisocial behavior. Any program for adolescents using the job as an entree for intervention, therefore, must deal with preparation and job readiness. This was incorporated into our program through exploring the boys' job interests, helping the boys fill out forms, role play of employment interviews, and going out with the boys in search of jobs.

Not only were these chronic delinquents not psychologically ready for employment, they often did not have the basic academic skills required for even the least demanding jobs. Although the schools where they had matriculated were among the best in the country and although many attempts were made to get them into remedial education programs, they were still only able to achieve at a second- or third-grade level. These are the boys who eagerly await their sixteenth birthday so they can legally leave school on their own, if they have not been suspended earlier because of their extremely provocative behavior and poor academic achievement. The schools themselves are often pleased when these boys leave, for they are the source of much difficulty and take a great deal of the school's time and energy.

Recent work has suggested that the academic deficiencies in antisocial youth are not so much a failure due to neurotic conflicts as an angry rejection of any of the socializing influences, one of which is learning. Because of this, an effort was made to make learning more meaningful by directing it to the boys' individual concerns and interests, especially in the vocational area (one boy learned to read by studying the driving manual because he wanted a job driving a car; a second learned through menus because he was eager to learn how to order food in a restaurant; and a third, while working in a gasoline station, began by reading labels on oil cans). Soon the boys began to show greater motivation to learn.

Job placement and remedial education, however, are not enough. The early object relationships for these adolescents with chronic antisocial problems were often extremely disturbed. Therefore, psychotherapy became essential. Because of the special needs of this group, the psychotherapy had to take a new and different form. The fears of dependency and homosexuality which are characteristic of adolescents in general were intensified in this group because of their connection with intense annihilation anxiety. It was for that reason that the focus was on the reality situation of the job, on the maintenance of psychological distance between the therapist and the boy, and on the self-initiating aspects of the program. For example, rather than permitting the boy to indulge in wild fantasies of destruction and violence, which are known to lead often to flight out of fear, the focus was on what was going on in reality (How do you look for a job?) and on how the boy could master the situation on his own. Thus, success on the job itself offered the boy a great deal of independence, permitted realistic gratification, and gave both the boy and the therapist a task on which to work together. It was when the boy failed on the job or had difficulty with his fellow workers or superior that the therapist began to explore in detail the reasons behind the inappropriate behavior.

The psychotherapy was also characterized by its intimate connection with the cognitive development of these adolescent delinquents. Whether caused by sociocultural or psychodynamic factors, the cognitive functioning of these boys had four major characteristics, each of which had to be taken into account in a program of intervention:

(1) Motoric orientation.
(2) Concrete thinking rather than symbolizing.
(3) Present time orientation.
(4) Desire for immediate gratification.

In recognition of these characteristics, the therapist made himself available any time, day or night, whenever the boy needed him, rather than at regular hours by appointment. The boy was not seen at an office, but on the job or in other places in the community. The therapist did not limit the length of his contact with the boy. The therapist showed his concrete support by such activities as accompanying the boy to job interviews, helping the boy shop for clothes or a car, or going to court with him. (No effort was made to influence the court. Court appearances were seen as part of the reality which the boy had to learn to handle.) This relationship was not that of a pal or a friend, but was professional in character. The therapist was always clear as to why he was undertaking a particular action and its possible significance to his relationship with the boy.

Specific situational factors were also of great significance in this program. No matter how much denial is present in the boys or their families, recent work has shown that leaving school for whatever reason is anxiety-provoking for both the boys and their families. Although the adolescent can legally leave school at age 16, it was felt that the boy who does so is in a period of intense distress and discomfort. This discomfort is particularly evident in suburban areas where frequently there are no organized gangs in which these dropouts can find a place and gain status. The act of leaving school thus serves only to increase the boy's alienation from the community and from others. The anxiety generated by the crisis of leaving school, added to that produced by adolescence itself, we felt, would make the boy more amenable to intervention.

Within twenty-four hours after the boy had left school, he was contacted and met anywhere and at any time and offered help in getting a job. (No attempts were made to get the boy to return to school unless he expressed such a desire.) Under these circumstances, none of the boys rejected this help.

A major feature of this program was that comprehensive, vocationally oriented psychotherapy was administered by a single person who offered job assistance, remedial education, and psychotherapy when they were needed, a factor that we feel was essential for these boys who needed an integrated, multidisciplined set of services in one person rather than in the characteristically departmental framework of the typical agency or institution. It was our belief that the undifferentiated ego functioning in these boys made it very difficult for them to understand the divisions in roles and functions that have become so characteristic of our mental health services and that such separations of services would serve only to complicate treatment unnecessarily.

This program for chronic, adolescent delinquent boys was evaluated by comparing a group of treated boys with a matched group of delinquents who were not treated.[7] In the treated group profound changes in ego functioning occurred which could be reliably identified: guilt increased and seemed more available as a deterrent to antisocial behavior,[12] object relations improved,[14] people were described in less personalized fashion,[13] and time perception showed a greater future orientation.[9] Along with these changes there were also major improvements in general behavior (marked reduction in delinquent activity and improved job performance) as well as significant positive changes in academic learning (vocabulary, reading, and arithmetic). These changes not only occurred during the treatment period of ten months but were found to continue two and three years after treatment was terminated.[11] The changes were found to be independent of the boy's intelligence and were greater than those found in a group of nondelinquent boys studied over the same period.

In summary, the recent theoretical emphasis on crises as opportunities for active intervention should lead us to specify more clearly the strategies and techniques we can use to treat a variety of problem groups. Developmental crises, such as during adolescence, tax our ingenuity because they require an understanding not only of the forces that are operating to perpetuate the pathology but also of the emerging forces that are pushing toward change and growth, thus offering new directions for intervention. It is only when we are able to understand all these forces and to utilize them appropriately in our program planning that we can feel confident that our therapeutic efforts are effecting significant and lasting change, especially with people who have been characteristically labeled as the "hard to reach."

References

1. Blos, P. On Adolescence. New York: Free Press of Glencoe, 1962.
2. Erikson, E. Identity and the Life Cycle. Psychological Issues No. 1. New York: International Universities Press, 1959.
3. Freud, A. "Adolescence," in J. Weinreb, ed., Recent Developments in Psychoanalytic Child Therapy. New York: International Universities Press, 1960, p. 1.
4. Holmes, D. "A Contribution to a Psychoanalytic Theory of Work," in A. Freud et al., eds., Psychoanalytic Study of the Child, Vol. XX. New York: International Universities Press, 1965.
5. Inhelder, B., and J. Piaget. The Growth of Logical Thinking from Childhood to Adolescence. New York: Basic Books, 1958.
6. Jahoda, M. "Notes on Work," in R. M. Lowenstein et al., eds., Psychoanalysis—A General Psychology. New York: International Universities Press, 1966.
7. Massimo, J. L., and M. F. Shore. "The Effectiveness of a Vocationally Oriented Psychotherapy Program for Adolescent Delinquent Boys," American Journal of Orthopsychiatry, XXXIII (1963), 634. Reprinted in F. Riessman, J. Cohen, and A. Pearl, eds., Mental Health of the Poor. New York: Free Press of Glencoe, 1964, p. 540.
8. Parad, H., ed. Crisis Intervention: Selected Readings. New York: Family Service Association, 1965.
9. Ricks, D. F., C. Umbarger, and R. Mack. "A Measure of Increased Temporal Perspective in Successfully Treated Adolescent Delinquent Boys," Journal of Abnormal and Social Psychology, LXIX (1964), 685.
10. Shore, M. F., and J. L. Massimo. "Employment as a Therapeutic Tool with Delinquent Adolescent Boys," Rehabilitation Counseling Bulletin, IX (1965), 1.
11. Shore, M. F. and J. L. Massimo, "Comprehensive Vocationally Oriented

Psychotherapy for Adolescent Delinquent Boys: A Follow-up Study," *American Journal of Orthopsychiatry,* XXXVI (1966), 609.

12. SHORE, M. F., J. L. MASSIMO, and R. MACK. "The Relationship between Levels of Guilt in Thematic Stories and Unsocialized Behavior," *Journal of Protective Techniques,* XXVIII (1964), 346.

13. SHORE, M. F., J. L. MASSIMO, and R. Mack. "Changes in the Perception of Interpersonal Relationships in Successfully Treated Adolescent Delinquent Boys," *Journal of Consulting Psychology,* XXIX (1965), 213.

14. SHORE, M. F., *et al.* "Object Relations Changes Resulting from Successful Pyschotherapy and Adolescent Delinquents and Their Relationship to Academic Performance," *Journal of the American Academy of Child Psychiatry,* V (1966), 93.

15. SPIEGEL, L. "Comments on the Psychoanalytic Psychology of Adolescence," in A. FREUD *et al.,* eds., *Psychoanalytic Study of the Child.* New York: International Universities Press, 1958, XIII, 296.

28

Changing Concepts and Changing Models of Residential Treatment

Edgar H. Auerswald

I. TRENDS IN THEORY AND PRACTICE

The explosion of scientific knowledge, technology, and population in the middle third of this century, and the effects of this explosion on the human condition, have posed a number of challenges for the behavioral sciences that most agree are yet to be met. The overriding challenge is, of course, the prevention of nuclear holocaust, but such related problems as self-perpetuating poverty, crime and delinquency, drug addiction, senseless violence, refractive learning problems, destructive prejudice, "functional" psychosis, childhood autism, and the like follow close behind.

To those who have been concerned with the failure of the behavioral sciences to meet these challenges, the conclusion has been inescapable that the issues raised defy solution within any single disciplinary framework. A revived interest in attempts to link the knowledge of all disciplines in a unified holistic theory has resulted, and the focus of these behavioral scientists as a group has begun to shift from the previous emphasis on the adaptation or maladaptation of the individual man or growing child to a relatively stable environment to an emphasis on the phenomenology of individual human ecology.

As a result, the vantage point of the behavioral scientist from which the growth and development of the individual is viewed has tended to move outward from its circumscribed focus on intrapsychic phenomena, past the point of parent-child interaction, and even past the full family arena to a point where the horizons of scientific concern have expanded to include a view of the infinite variety of interaction between the child and the various objects, people, and functional systems filling the space around him as he grows and develops through time.

In recent years, a conceptual framework usable in organizing this ecological field has been taking form. General systems theory has been used to identify the hierarchical systems which make it up. General communications theory, information theory, game theory, theory of small-group processes, and insights gained from study of decision-making processes, non-verbal communication, and psycholinguistics have provided ways of studying and conceptualizing interactional processes between systems. The time dimension has been clarified by attention to key periods in the life cycle, the theory of crisis, and the study of time itself. This holistic framework provides a theoretical structure for an over-all realignment of current knowledge and a latticework on which broad spectrum data collected on the operations of key systems and at the interfaces between systems in any given community can be hung.

These developments, together with the evolution of techniques of electronic storage and processing of mass data, have brought us to the threshold of revolutionary changes in man's view of himself and the means he uses to foster and maintain his biopsychosocial well-being.

No longer will behavioral scientists be forced to confine themselves to the study of isolated phenomena or to the diagnosis and treatment of the individual with such models as that of so-called functional illness that assumes an unknown etiology hiding somewhere within him. And no longer will our pursuit of knowledge of man's complex social organization be confined to collective appraisals that cannot encompass individual differences.

We are rapidly acquiring the means to evolve a template of the idiosyncratic structure and operations of any community we wish in some detail, to identify the forces producing change in that community and the nature of that change, and, by focusing on the interfaces between this mapped environment and the individual infant-child-adolescent-adult over a time span, to identify the sources and pathways of messages and forces which control the direction and shape of his psychobiological growth, the process of his socialization, and the development of his capacities to cope with his physical environment.

Many important developments of significance to residential treatment of children have occurred within and contributed to this broad trend. In the service of brevity only three will be described.

One has been the elevation of the cognitive aspects of child development to a position of importance equal to that of instinctual and emotional aspects. In addition to the well-known advances in ego psychology, a particularly significant body of knowledge has been accumulating which strongly suggests that the development of intelligence and coping skills in children is not limited by a fixed genetically determined central nervous system capacity, but rather depends to a large extent on the quantity, quality, and organization of stimuli which impinge on the developing central nervous system during the first few years of life.

And, even if one accepts the criticisms leveled at the monumental work of Piaget and his followers as to the general applicability of their model, they have demonstrated the necessity of sequential exposure of the child to experiences providing the informational building blocks necessary for the development of the well-defined and differentiated operational concepts, the language, and the symbolic internal representations of outer reality needed for successful performance of the increasingly complex tasks of living.

It has become clear that the sequential process of development of a child's psychobiological apparatus must be understood not only in terms of emotions and of phylogenetically inherited mechanisms of individual and species survival but also in terms of the source, formation, and transmission of messages received, the structure and content of the messages themselves, and the reception, assimilation, and integrative functions of those messages and their inclusion in cognitive structures. Instruments for mapping cognitive lacks and distortions in individuals are being developed. A kind of "curriculum for living" in a given community can evolve from this work, appropriate segments of which can be used to correct these lacks and distortions.

A second development is that, with the identification of ecological systems, more widespread recognition that the family, long recognized as the most generic system of all in the provision of the experiences necessary for healthy growth and socialization of children, has been studied very little as a system in and of itself. Each discipline in the behavioral sciences has tended to study the family within its own frame of reference so that choice of what data to collect and the interpretations of those data were made within the limited context of that discipline. The psychologist or psychiatrist, for example, might study mother-child interaction which, though certainly a part of the operations taking place in a family, constitutes a dyadic relationship which excludes full cognizance of other factors in family operations which influence that dyad. And the sociologist was more likely to study the family as an institution, the configurations of which are defined according to a given culture. Neither deals with the family as a system that performs certain defined tasks, one of which is to act as the transmitter of messages and arbiter of experience necessary for the health and socialization of its children (Parsons). There had been no discipline of familiology and thus no body of knowledge constituting a theory of the family as a system in itself. Fortunately, in the last decade such a theory has been rapidly evolving.

Third, when viewed in this holistic framework, common situations which have been treated as results of individual "pathology" emerge as "crises" in a sequence of interlocking events in a field of forces in which the individual is only viewed as central because it is he who, because his behavior is deviant enough to be labeled or because it is he who develops a symptom picture, comes to the attention of some agency of society that deems his behavior strange or intolerable or his symptoms in need of treatment. The point or points in the total field which need to be influenced by "helping" people is often to be found in some system contiguous to, or even seemingly distant from, the individual in trouble, most often in the family system, including the extended family, but frequently in other systems such as a neighborhood, a public school, or a Department of Welfare as well.

A whole new technology of prevention, diagnosis, and treatment is taking shape. For example, labels which describe syndromes, the etiology of which is multidetermined and may vary from case to case, need no longer be the focus of diagnosis, which will consist instead of identification in the total ecological field of the various etiological vectors in each case. Treatment, following this form of diagnosis, will consist of the production of change through an attack on these vectors in vivo. Treatment effort confined to work in one location during fixed segments of time called appointments will, as time goes on, be used much more selectively. The agent of change will need to be mobile, to move freely from system to system in the pursuit of his goals. Thus the impact of his skills, though primarily applied to alleviation of an identified problem in an individual, will be felt in a much broader arena. He becomes an ongoing agent of community enhancement.

Under the impact of these trends a fundamental shift is taking place in role functions and in assignments of responsibility for tasks aimed at therapeutic change. In the technical sense a game is emerging which is not just an extension of the old one. It is a new game, based on different premises and with a new set of rules, within which the highly trained professional becomes the engineer in the production of change, but various systems in the community are asked to assume responsibility for the various tasks involved. The model of the therapeutic community with which residential treatment centers have struggled for a few decades now has come home to roost where it belongs: in the families and communities which produce our children in the first place.

II. TWO STRATEGIES, THE OLD AND THE NEW—A CLINICAL EXAMPLE

The contrast in practice between the two strategies, the old and the new, which results from the shifts in theory described above, is not easy to demonstrate, since the two strategies must be used separately. This is to say, a symptom picture, for example, is defined either as an illness or as an ecological phenomenon. It can be seen as both, according to which definition one wishes to use; but in the process of attempting to change it, the rules under which decisions are made and remedial action taken will depend on which definition one chooses to use operationally from the start.

At this writing, data to demonstrate that one strategy produces better outcomes than the other are not available. Indeed, it would be difficult to design a study toward this goal, since the over-all goals of the new strategy include change in many community systems not considered within the realm of the old strategy.

Despite the recognition of this difficulty, the practical significance of the theoretical points made above will gain clarity with a hypothetical description of how a case might be handled when the problem is defined as illness and, in contrast, how the same situation might be handled by a helping system using the "ecological systems" frame of reference. The family described, at least, is an actual family.

The Family: Jose Rivera is a 13-year-old, the oldest boy from a Puerto Rican family consisting of mother, father, three girls, and two boys, all living in New York City. He did passably well in school through the elementary grades, but shortly after entering junior high school, he began rather suddenly to seem restless and preoccupied. He seemed unable to concentrate on his schoolwork, ceased to learn, and became involved in frequent outbursts of temper leading to a series of fights with his classmates. His behavior frustrated and baffled his teachers, who, in attempts to discipline him and maintain order in class, sent him frequently to the principal's office. Eventually, he wound up in the office of the school guidance counselor, whose efforts to understand the problem and deal with it were also frustrated, despite consultation with Jose's mother, whose only response was surprise. She had not noted much change in his behavior at home, but admitted she had been preoccupied with other problems.

Strategy One—The "Illness" Strategy

First, let us use the model of care which defines Jose's problem as an illness and describe what might happen.

The boy is referred to the school psychiatrist, who interviews him and his mother for diagnostic purposes.

In his report, the psychiatrist notes that the boy seems very angry at his mother, and, coupling this observation with the guidance counselor's report that the mother seems unrelated to the boy, since she has been unaware that the boy was in trouble, suggests that inadequacies in mothering may have deprived the boy of supplies and supports he needed over many years and that his present behavior represents the end result of that deprivation. He goes on to state that the events which triggered the boy's recent behavior were his entry into junior high school, where he was expected to be more autonomous than in elementary school, and his movement into adolescence, with the consequent reawakening of sexual drives and the dependency-autonomy conflict characteristic of adolescent years. The psychiatrist notes that he has learned from the mother that she and the boy's father have been fighting for the last six months or so, especially over money, that the father is out of work, that he has been suffering from incapacitating headaches, and that he has been spending less and less time with his family of late. He speculates that the boy's disturbance has been compounded by the lack of an adequate model of male identification, since the father is himself "disturbed." To check his speculations, he sees the father, who confirms what the mother has reported about him. He expresses his anger at his errant son, but disputes the psychiatrist's contention that the boy is sick, although he has no alternative explanation for his behavior except "bad company."

In the course of his diagnostic write-up the psychiatrist refers to Jose's "emotional disturbance" and makes, in the end, a diagnosis of "Behavior Disorder."

Jose is also tested by a psychologist, who finds that his I.Q. is within the limits of normal, but that projective testing yields similar information to that obtained in the psychiatrist's clinical interview, indicating the boy's rage at his mother, sexual fantasies which take on a "sadistic" quality, and anxiety related to a receding male figure, presumably his father. There is also considerable sibling rivalry apparent in his projections.

The psychologist agrees in his report with the psychiatrist's diagnosis of "Behavior Disorder." However, based on the seeming suddenness of onset of the boy's behavior, the findings of performance scatter, and some fantasy tapped by the T.A.T. having to do with magic and witchcraft which seem rather bizarre, he adds a note that there remains the possibility of an "underlying schizophrenic process."

The psychiatrist and psychologist both recommend psychotherapy for Jose and counseling for his mother and father. The psychiatrist also suggests that Jose be given tranquilizers on a trial basis to see if they will quiet his behavior in the classroom.

Jose is lucky, and, despite the critical shortage of skilled professionals, a group is found to begin working with him and his family within a few weeks. Things seemingly go well for a while. His behavior improves in school, although the tranquilizers make him sleepy, and he learns little. But some new developments occur which rapidly destroy the optimism of those concerned.

First, Jose begins to truant, not every day, but with increasing frequency. He complains that his teachers blame him incorrectly for starting trouble. Then, Jose's father, after a period of initial restraint resulting from the advice of the parental counselor, explodes in anger and beats the boy severely. Finally, within a few days after the beating, Jose is apprehended while truanting with two other boys by the police who spot the trio attempting to pry open a parking meter. Nothing has actually been stolen, so the police officer compassionately returns the boy to his family for discipline.

But the die is cast. Jose, a "disturbed" boy who lives in a "disturbed" family with a "depriving" mother and a "punitive" father who seem unable to control him, is now behaving in a way which is sufficiently "delinquent" to endanger both his own future and the property rights of others. It seems unwise and uncaring to allow him to remain at large in his community under those circumstances. The decision is made that he must be "placed." There is some haggling at the conference where this decision is made over the question of where he should go. Some feel, since the question of possible "underlying schizophrenia" has been raised, he should perhaps go to a psychiatric hospital, but it is subsequently decided that a residential treatment center is more appropriate since he needs "long-term" treatment.

Again, Jose is lucky. A place for him in such a center is found within a short time, and he is admitted. The locus of responsibility for Jose's well-being changes. The residential treatment center, which is some distance from his home and community, takes over. It happens to be a center with a stable program and staff, and his treatment proceeds. An effort is made to work with his family as well, but distance intervenes, and the preoccupation of Mr. and Mrs. Rivera with their economic and social problems makes discussion of their inner life difficult. However, work with the family is seen as necessary as a preparatory move to Joses' return home once his illness has been treated, in the hope that the family will be able to reinforce rather than undermine the changes that his treatment has produced in him.

Strategy Two—The "Ecological Systems" Strategy

Now, let us describe the case as it might evolve using a different model of care—a model based on a definition of Jose's difficulty as an ecological phenomenon, not an illness.

In order that this can be done, the reader must first envision a newly structured system of service delivery which I shall call a Neighborhood Family Health* Center. This is a unit consisting of various front-line "helping" people—physicians (G.P.'s, internists, pediatricians, obstetricians, psychiatrists, and so on), nurses (public health nurses, R.N.'s), psychologists, social workers, clerical staff, and aides possessing various task skills, all functioning under one director and tied together by a system of procedures and case recording that forces constant communication, consultation, and case planning among those of the group dealing with each family. There are several General Service Workers ("generalist" workers of varying disciplines) who are charged with initial exploration and problem analysis of each situation that arises and with the ongoing "chairmanship" of the plan for care for the families to which they are assigned. There is a Mobile Crisis Team operating out of the Center which will go on call to whoever so requests. The unit is geographically based in the community it serves and thus easily accessible. It is designed to be one of several "front line" units, each with its umbilical communications and transportation connections to a central unit embodying over-all administrative functions, training and research operations, and those services which are either not

---

* Health is herein defined according to the World Health Organization definition: physical, mental, and social "well-being."

needed in the front line unit or economically less costly when centrally combined.*

The Rivera family moved into the helping arena of the Neighborhood Family Health Center through two points of entree. The father first appeared with the complaint of headaches of six months' duration, which, of late, had become severe enough to cause him to miss work frequently, with the result that his job as an elevator operator was in jeopardy. He was routed by the General Service Worker to the family physician, in this case an internist. After a thorough medical "work-up" which took a couple of weeks, the doctor reported to the General Service Worker that he could find no clear biological etiology for the headaches. He had made a tentative diagnosis of "Atypical Migraine," but, recognizing the presumptive nature of this diagnosis, he suggested that psychological factors might be at work. The General Service Worker took the case to the unit's psychiatrist, who suggested that he see Mr. Rivera alone and together with his family to see if the source of the symptom might be clarified by an exploration of Mr. Rivera's psychological state and of the larger social system of the family of which he was an integral part.

Before the family session could be arranged, however, the Mobile Crisis Team reported that they had been called by the Guidance Counselor at a local school to discuss Jose Rivera, who for several weeks had been increasingly difficult in the classroom. The Crisis Team had already visited the Riveras at home and reported that the entire family was in a state of crisis since Mr. Rivera had lost his job the day before. In the process of exploration they learned that the family had been receiving supplementary ADC support from the Department of Welfare, since Mr. Rivera's salary had been insufficient to provide for his large family. An aide from the Crisis Team had seen to it that full ADC support would be provided until Mr. Rivera had found another job with help, if necessary.

Recognizing that there were multiple signals of distress coming from the Riveras, the General Service Worker decided that it would be necessary to explore the total ecology of the situation, and, accordingly, she scheduled a conference which included not only Mr. Rivera, Jose, and their family but also representatives of each community system with an interest in the family. Thus a meeting was arranged to include the family, the General Service Worker, the psychiatrist, the internist, and a member of the Mobile Crisis Team—in this case, a public health nurse—from the Neighborhood Family Health Center, the guidance counselor from the school, and the worker from the Department of Welfare and her supervisor.

---

* The Riveras' difficulties actually were handled by a unit with a structure similar to that described. The actual Family Health Unit, however, is in experimental operation and is not yet part of the over-all community system, which is still in the planning stages. The liberties taken in the case description describe the way the case *could* have been handled if the full model had been in operation.

The purpose of the meeting was defined as exploration of the family's current situation and construction of a remedial plan.

Before the meeting could take place, Jose, who had begun to truant, was apprehended by the police along with two other truanting boys while attempting to break into a parking meter. The Youth Squad policeman to whom he was taken called the Mobile Crisis Unit for help in deciding what course of action to take with him. The Crisis Team worker and the Youth Squad officer took the boy to his own home and met with his parents. When he was informed of his son's behavior, Mr. Rivera flew into a rage and threatened to beat his son, who became sullen and defiant. Mr. Rivera then accused his wife of undermining the boy's respect for him. The immediate decision reached through discussion and consensus among the adults involved, including Jose's parents, was that he should be admitted to the Residential Unit* serving the neighborhood until the situation "cooled off" and while more exploration could be done to determine what was creating the crisis.

The scheduled meeting took place two days later. The Youth Squad officer and a worker from the Residential Unit had been added to the roster of those attending.

In the process of exploration of the family's difficulties the first issue that came up was a recent but ongoing battle between Mr. and Mrs. Rivera. Mr. Rivera accused his wife of unwillingness to let him "be the boss" in their family, using as evidence her refusal to turn over the check she had been receiving from the Department of Welfare. The battle over the check had begun several months before when Mr. Rivera had become aware that since his own salary went entirely for rent and utility payments, the children saw his wife, who used the welfare check to buy food, clothing, and an occasional treat, as the dispenser of sustenance. His own contribution, which they never saw, had little meaning to them. At the time this realization struck him, Mr. Rivera had asked his wife to turn over the checks to him, so he could visibly dispense all the money. She had refused.

At this point in the meeting, Mrs. Rivera spoke defensively, announcing that she was not averse to his having the check if she could be sure of his over-all commitment to her and to his family. She related that she had never doubted his commitment very seriously until the day he had asked her to turn over the check. It was the *way* he asked that had disturbed her, since he had threatened to leave her if she did not give him the check. Since the ownership of the check really had little meaning to her as long as it was in the family, she could see no reason why he would threaten to leave over just

---

* This is a hypothetical unit that does not yet really exist in Jose's community. In the actual handling of this case Jose was admitted to the inpatient adult psychiatric unit of a nearby general hospital. The unit was not geared to this style of handling the case, and many problems ensued which would not have arisen had a residential treatment unit existed in his community.

that issue, and she had begun to wonder if he might have another reason for wanting to leave. If such were the case, she had reasoned, she would be a fool to turn over to him what might prove to be her only source of income. Thus, she refused his request, and the battle was joined. Mr. Rivera's threats to leave had become more numerous and strident as time went on.

Further exploration revealed the source of each parent's intense feeling over this issue.

Mr. Rivera was, it turned out, the second of five brothers and felt as he grew that his oldest and youngest brothers were the favored recipients of love and attention from his own parents. He desperately longed for the position of the central figure. In addition, the culturally determined emphasis on the father as ruler in Puerto Rican families had contributed to his view of his role.

Mrs. Rivera, on the other hand, had been overly sensitive to any threat of abandonment since the day in her tenth year when her own father had abandoned his family.

When attention was focused during the conference on the timing of these events vis-à-vis Jose's behavior in school, it was possible to show that Jose had become preoccupied and unruly at precisely the time that Mr. Rivera had begun to voice his threats to leave. When Jose was questioned he confirmed that he had been very upset by these events, adding that his worry was not only that he might lose his father but also, since he was the oldest son, that he would be expected without preparation to take over his father's position in the family. He angrily accused his mother of driving his father away by refusing to "let him be boss." His father responded to his son with reassurances that he was never *really* serious about leaving, and, in the course of his explanation, also reassured his wife, who promptly agreed to give him the checks.

At this point the welfare worker chimed in to say that there was no reason that the checks had to go to the mother in the first place and suggested that they be sent instead directly to Mr. Rivera.

In addition to the self-defined task of the welfare worker, other functions were defined and assigned. The guidance counselor took on the task of explaining the causes of Jose's disturbance to his teachers, who she felt were contributing to Jose's troubles. Their behavior, she observed, seemed to reflect angry frustration over their inability to handle him, and they had begun to label him a troublemaker.

The aide from the Neighborhood Family Health Center agreed to assist Mr. Rivera in finding a new job and, if he wished, to guide him into a program which could teach him skills that he could use in a better-paying position. Mr. and Mrs. Rivera were to make a point of communicating their thoughts and feelings more thoroughly with each other, and the psychiatrist agreed to meet with them as a family as long as necessary. The General Service Worker agreed to act as "chairman" of the execution of the plan.

It was decided that Jose should remain in the Residential Unit temporarily, but that he should return home as soon as the school reported improvement in his behavior and his parents resolved their battle.

Jose's behavior in school changed immediately. It took almost two weeks, however, and another family session before sufficient dialogue had gone on between Mr. and Mrs. Rivera to allow them to resolve their conflict. Mr. Rivera's headaches were relieved almost at once when this occurred. He found another job within a week thereafter without help. He was, however, encouraged to plan for upgrading his job skills, and he applied to a training program in elevator repair. Since he lacked the prerequisite of a high-school diploma, he was not accepted. However, again with help, he registered for evening courses to prepare himself for high-school equivalent examinations to overcome this obstacle.

During the second family session, a family myth emerged which added to the understanding of Jose's anxiety. It turned out that at one time the women of Mrs. Rivera's extended family had a reputation in their village in rural Puerto Rico as spiritualists capable of vague occult powers. Half in jest, during one of his arguments with his wife, Mr. Rivera had referred to her as such a person, suggesting that she had put a spell on him and caused his headache. Jose had heard the reference and wondered whether his father was serious. He was inclined to think he might have been and had the thought that if his father left, perhaps he might be next. He was easily dissuaded in the session by his laughing parents.

Jose returned home three weeks after the initial meeting had been held, his behavior in school much improved. He had been helped by the staff of the Residential Unit to catch up on schoolwork he had missed, and he was able to resume learning.

Work with the Rivera family, however, was not yet finished.*

After the immediate crisis had subsided, since the Riveras were now registered in the Neighborhood Family Health Center, a number of routine procedures could be carried out in order that base-line family data could be accumulated and computer-stored that would ensure that preventive work with them could be done where necessary and that future problems as they might arise would be fully understood.

Each member of the family was given a thorough physical examination, and the advantages of routine checkups and preventive procedures such as immunizations were explained to them.

But, in addition, each member of the family was given a series of short tests as a spot check of those cognitive capacities they needed for successful participant functioning in any community and also those needed in the particular community in which they had chosen to live.

Their knowledge of the anatomy and physiology of their own bodies and their sense of their relationship to objects in space and to time were tested, along with the degree to which they were able to differentiate and under-

---

* The case description from this point on is purely hypothetical.

stand the various transactional arenas in which they needed to function in order to ensure their sense of belonging and participation in the everyday life of their community. The level of development in each family member of the concepts necessary to ensure thinking skills adequate for function in the roles they would need to play according to age, sex, and so on was determined.

A curriculum, worked out co-operatively by the educators and behavioral scientists in the community, designed to correct lacks and distortions picked up by such testing, was in use in training programs available selectively to all people in the community who needed them.

Such training was helpful to the Riveras in several ways. After three years in their community they still remained relatively isolated. Coming as they had from rural Puerto Rico, they were unprepared for the complexities of urban life in the city to which they moved. In many areas of function they were still unprepared.

Mrs. Rivera's shopping habits provide one example. Although supermarkets close to their home offered many food items much cheaper than they could be had in the local Spanish-speaking store, Mrs. Rivera found the supermarket routine beyond her scope and paid more for a limited selection of food as a result. More important than the possibility of saving money, however, was her tendency to see the supermarket as a hostile place and the Spanish store as a friendly haven. Even that perception would pose no serious problem, were it not for her feeling that most of the community around her, the ingredients of which she could not differentiate, was equally hostile. Her children were learning this attitude from her.

Mr. Rivera, on the other hand, had seen little hope for upgrading his capacity as breadwinner since he lacked even the basic credentials he needed to get into training programs that could give him skills. Without such hope, he had begun to feel his efforts meaningless, and his anger at his wife over the welfare check and his fantasies of leaving his family had gained intensity in this context.

The children, with one exception, had learned English and seemed to be making the cultural transition fairly well. The exception was not Jose; it was his younger brother, Julio, aged 5.

Julio had moved with his family from rural Puerto Rico to urban United States at an age when his thinking processes were developmentally not sufficiently abstract to allow him to encompass the shift. He had just begun to develop language skills in Spanish. The shift to an English-speaking environment, with all its gross and subtle differences in word usage and cultural connotations, was sufficiently disruptive to slow down his language development considerably. Since he had only just begun to develop a differentiated view of himself in a stable environment in which objects and transactions had their labels, the shock of the change brought this process to an abrupt halt. The development of his capacities for logical thought oriented to the nature of his world and the flow of events in time had been interrupted, and he had remained rooted in the search for high-level stimuli through action characteristic of very early childhood. He was not developing the capacity to think before acting and, as a result, was acquiring a style of behavior that would bring him into serious conflict with the society he now lived in as he grew older.

Julio needed some very specialized help. He needed organizing experiences, in addition to training in specific thinking skills and language usage.

A curriculum flowing from a battery of tests designed to map his cognitive capacities was needed which could prepare him for a co-operative venture with the local schools. Part of the curriculum could be delivered to him in school, part in an afterschool program, and part at home by his parents, who could be provided with drills to give him along with an explanation of what they were for. In school and afterschool programs, computerized systems could be used for the delivery of some experiences.

Julio's parents were sufficiently in control of their family, well enough organized, and conceptually capable of understanding their part in such a plan. If such had not been the case, it might have been necessary to remove Julio to the community Residential Unit in order that others could take over the parental training tasks until the chaotic family situation could be overcome through work done in an additional plan to help organize the family and educate the parents.

Once all this had been accomplished, the Neighborhood Family Health Center would continue to accept responsibility for the provision of the comprehensive health need of the Rivera family for as long as they so wished.

III. NEW WAYS OF DEFINING OLD TASKS

Out of experience in the use of the "ecological systems" frame of reference as described, the outlines of a new model of the "residential treatment center" are beginning to emerge. The model is that of a single unit embedded geographically and programmatically in the ecological field of the community it serves which performs certain assigned tasks in an integrated system of local delivery of comprehensive biopsychosocial health care for members of that community who, despite a shift in where they sleep, maintain their "residency" in that community. These tasks, I believe, can already be discerned. They will be, I think, fourfold, as follows.

A. Alleviation of Danger

The first category of task is that of alleviation of immediate or rapidly developing danger to life, limb, or property that mitigates against allowing the child or adolescent to remain at home. This task definition contains, I must admit, a certain irony in its familiarity. It now comes up, however, in a new context. Separation of the child for this reason will come during the course of intensive efforts to prevent it through work which will continue to involve the child during the period of residence. Such work will be done by helping people whose task assignments do not emanate from the residential center, the staff of which, under these circumstances, will be charged with the temporary provision of the supportive caring and teaching ingredients of the home. As soon as the immediate threat of danger has been alleviated, the process of returning the child to his home will furnish a concrete issue around which further work in family and community can be accomplished.

B. Cognitive Training

The second category of task for the Residential Center will be the provision of growth experience for certain types of problems in children requiring tight controls and intensive experience not fully obtainable in their family or in the usual day-to-day life of their community. Special programs of cognitive training for dissocial children from highly disorganized families who have not developed the cognitive tools that allow them to think before acting, for example, entail highly specialized work which includes such program ingredients as training in the capacity to categorize experience and to organize the flow of events in time. At the time of this writing, it is hard to see how such work can be accomplished effectively outside of a twenty-four-hour-a-day program, especially for children who need help in such basic areas as the organization and differentiation of time and space.

C. Extended Nursing Care

The third category of problem demanding twenty-four-hour attention is care of children with severe biological problems requiring special nursing care beyond that which can be sustained by a family—the brain-damaged child with severe motor dyscontrol, for example. Again among the tasks assigned are familiar ones, but, again, they emerge with more specific definition in a comprehensive effort centered on the ecological model of child in family in community.

D. Research

Finally, the fourth category of task assignment for the Residential Center in this model is that of research. Children of certain kinds may have to be kept in residence for varying periods if biological tests or longitudinal observations, for example, are needed. Hypotheses calling for such research will arise, I believe, from analysis of data collected from the key systems and interfaces between systems in the total ecological field of the child's environment, not from the narrower framework of a dominant discipline or school of thought. When the holistic behavioral scientist spots something in his wide-angle motion picture of the total community field that requires stop-action or slow-motion examination through a magnifying glass, it can be done in this way.

IV. CONCLUSION

The realignments of organizational structure and disciplinary task assignments suggested by the new strategy will come painfully and slowly. I believe, however, that they will come, since they must. The needs of people will demand them. Furthermore, these developments really should come as no surprise to behavioral scientists. Science has always developed cyclically. With each cycle of specialization man gains more knowledge, and with each cycle of integration he learns how to use it. Bit by bit we edge our way a little closer to the self-understanding that can give us the capacity to choose our destiny.

Let us hope that behavioral scientists will take the lead in making these needed changes, as the latest cycles of specialization give way to integration. If they do not, it is likely that others, who lack the specific knowledge needed, will.

EDITORS' INTRODUCTION   This section is introduced by Buckle, who reviews the complicated array of problems presented by adolescents, both healthy and sick, and emphasizes our current lack of diagnostic and therapeutic knowledge. This leads him to the conclusion that our fundamental need is for research to guide our service efforts, particularly in the field of prevention. The difficulty is that we are not able to wait for the results of this research. We must act now to deal with present burdens even on the basis of our inadequate knowledge. Because of this, the demand for research may become a pious platitude, since the urgent preventive and remedial service demands already outstrip our resources, and both practitioners and community leaders may feel that these concrete demands have higher priority than the abstract needs to develop research and theory. Buckle provides information to corroborate this by analyzing the likely requirements for institutions and specialized professionals to deal with the expectable mental health service demands for adolescents in a European city with a population of 100,000. His figures dramatically emphasize the discrepancy of minimal demands and the likely availability of trained professionals in most countries. He concludes that planners should therefore place first priority on programs of professional education.

Although we do not disagree with Buckle's thesis, it might be as well to mention that professional recruitment must precede training, and we are beginning to realize that the pool from which we recruit mental health professionals is not unlimited. In the United States, for example, we have almost reached the expectable limit of increase in the proportion of such professionals in the population because of competition from other essential activities for segments of the appropriate and available man-power pool.

Buckle goes on to discuss the problems posed for the organization of treatment services for psychiatrically disturbed adolescents by their continuing need for the benefits of home and education. This point is also emphasized by Caplan and by Lafon. We should not see the treatment needs of the sick adolescent in isolation from all his other needs. Since the satisfaction of these involves a complex of educational, social, and vocational services, as well as the existence, bolstering, or replacement of family care and protection, mental health services must be organized in such a way that they have multiple articulations with other services and agencies, or in certain cases that they incorporate within their own framework elements from such fields as education, vocational guidance, and vocational training.

Finally, Buckle takes up the question of whether there should be separate services for adolescents or whether adolescents should be handled within the framework of child psychiatry or adult psychiatry services. He comes to the same conclusion as Caplan in the following chapter, namely, that all three patterns are needed in order to cater to the differential needs of adolescents of different diagnoses and stages of development. He deals along similar lines with the question of whether specialists in adolescent psychiatry should be drawn from child psychiatry or adult psychiatry. He points to the trend in European child psychiatry to focus increasingly on infancy and early childhood, and he emphasizes the necessity for specialists in adolescence to be competent not only in problems of early personality development but also in social aspects of psychiatry, such as milieu therapy, which occupy a more central position in the interests of adult psychiatry. The implication is that for a psychiatrist who specializes in problems of adolescence it matters less whether he originally comes from the child or adult field than that he should also get adequate complementary training in the other field.

In the following chapter, Caplan discusses the role of the specialist in adolescent psychiatry in relation to the roles of psychiatrists in the child and adult fields. He feels that psychiatric problems in adolescence are too numerous to be dealt with only by specialists, and he therefore proposes that they be shared among child, adult, and adolescent psychiatrists. The most complicated problems would ideally be dealt with by those specializing in adolescence, who would mainly be responsible for research in this sector of the field and also for offering consultation to their colleagues in child and adult psychiatry on the diagnostic and treatment problems that they encounter in handling their adolescent patients. This view is in line with Caplan's general orientation to the organization of community services for adolescents. He advocates that on the one hand these should be integrated within the over-all program of community mental health for the population, while on the other hand they should include specialized agencies and services to cater to the idiosyncratic needs of adolescents. This demands a quite complicated set of services, and Caplan's chapter is mainly devoted to describing the basic elements of the system, although, as he points out, it is impossible to prescribe how these elements should be combined because the optimal pattern of organization must depend on local sociopolitical traditions and ways of organization of the human services network in a particular community.

The final chapter in this section, by Lafon, discusses the services needed to cater to the special needs of adolescents who are mentally subnormal or suffer from the various common forms of physical handicap. Lafon points out that in planning such community services in health, education, welfare, and occupational training and placement, it must be remembered that although, as Buckle also emphasized, the handicapped adolescent requires the continuing care and supervision of his family, it is unlikely that even a well-endowed family will be able with its own resources to satisfy all his needs. Lafon warns that the organizers of community services should never usurp the essential primacy of the family and should not erode its sense of responsibility. Often, however, the incapacity of the adolescent is complicated by an incapacity of the family, and this presents the community workers with special problems. He, like Buckle and Caplan, and in line with other contributors to this book, emphasizes that disturbance or handicap in an adolescent does not mean that his ordinary needs for education, family care and affection, and vocational guidance, training, and placement are less, but on the contrary that there are likely to be extra problems in all these areas which mean that he needs more help than the healthy child. Lafon discusses the detailed implications of this for the organization of community services, using for his examples the patterns that have been developed in France, where services in public health, population, labor, and social security are integrated within a single governmental Ministry of Social Affairs. Within this setting, he describes the range of detailed services that have been organized to cater to the needs of the different categories of handicapped adolescents. His account is notable for its discussion of rational governmental planning with a constant sensitive awareness of the special human needs and expectable predicaments of individuals who are not only passing through the usual complications of adolescent transition but whose present and future are also burdened by their psychological or physical handicaps. For instance, he stresses the need for special services to stimulate handicapped adolescents to prepare themselves for maximal social participation in adult life, and yet this must be accompanied by a realistic appraisal and prediction of an individual's actual potential, so that sheltered work and social settings can be made available and so that the adolescent can be guided and trained to adjust to these. Particularly poignant is the anxiety shared by many subnormal and handicapped adolescents who fear the eventual death of their parents when they may be left without personalized family care and be forced to enter an institution for the remainder of their lives.

29

Mental Health Services for Adolescents—An Introduction

Donald F. Buckle

I. PROBLEMS

To depict a mental health service for adolescents which might be provided by any reasonably well-endowed community would be to describe something far in the future. In scarcely any country are even the manifest needs of psychiatrically disturbed adolescents catered for. A 15-year-old schizophrenic finds himself in a closed mental hospital with confused and excited psychotic and geriatric patients; another finds himself wandering around in a beautifully equipped but sterile hospital full of toys more suitable for children ten years younger. In countries which are oversupplied with psychiatric buildings, a mildly subnormal adolescent is likely to find himself living in one, together with idiots and imbeciles. If he is biddable he will work on the farm. A girl will learn to be a hospital housemaid. Really good residential schools providing proper apprenticeship training in skilled trades for the adolescent subnormal are extremely rare.

In the open community, school failures, job failures, unwanted pregnancies, social nonconformity, become matters of conflict between parents and children. School failures are not often blamed on poor teachers (although sometimes they are blamed on poor parents), but are considered as laziness or naughtiness or delinquency. In European cultures and, as far as I know, in American, it is modish for young persons to appear to be tough and cool; consequently, the anxieties that accompany their behaviors are not easily evident to investigators; the unwanted behavior provides "evidence" for the myth of the "psychopath." It does not often occur to worried parents that laziness is sometimes the practice of leisure, that sex behavior is perfectly

363

normal, that delinquency is simply doing what their elders do, even their kings and presidents.

I have often been struck by the apparent absence of psychopathology in older children and by the fact that their disturbances are rather pleasant and exciting difficulties to be overcome, rather than the contrary. Studies of adolescents may reveal very little pathology at all, particularly among the socially and educationally competent. University students are, by and large, socially healthy.

I mention these matters in order to emphasize the very real professional difficulties in determining whether or not an adolescent's behavior is normal or abnormal, whether or not it is healthy or unhealthy, and whether or not treatment should be given.

As to the question of treatability, it is always crucial to determine whether or not a potential patient is psychoneurotic, preneurotic, or pre-schizophrenic, and this cannot be determined by a superficial study of his overt behavior. Misbehavior and social nonconformity are not necessarily unhealthy. In order to determine in a practical way the real mental health needs of adolescents, we should turn our attention to establishing valid theories as to the basic nature of adult mental disorders and to the influences which, at the adolescent period, may lead to their progress or to their prevention.

The genesis of psychoneurosis lies in the experiences of infantile sexuality and the outcome of the oedipus complex; the way in which the adolescent removes himself from his family situation will determine, to a great extent, the fixity and pervasiveness of his neurotic patterns. Thus relationships with other people, which begin as transferences, later have a more independent form. True, the adolescent's love objects are colored by his parental figures or his ideals or by his narcissism; this is a question of degree. The actual persons with whom he happens to be in contact may be all-important for the outcome of this process.

Residential milieu therapy, as practiced with children, is an education in relationships, achieved by exemplary reactions on the part of a professionally trained staff, assisted by other techniques, such as interpretation and group discussion. A series of interpersonal relationships are set up, and to some extent structured by the manifest roles of each person in the institutional society. Insofar as a child is influenced through the method, it is a professionalized extension of growth and development through adult example. Thus one may picture an adolescent as living in a community milieu and envisage a task for social psychiatry to control this milieu so it becomes therapeutic or, at least, developmental in a healthy way.

However, it is not my intention here to discuss in any detail problems of psychopathology and treatment, but rather to note that they exist and are unsolved and that, in my opinion, they need to be solved before we can determine just what should be done and precisely what new services should be set up.

Therefore the first priorities in planning services for the future include research services oriented toward finding out the processes which lead finally to serious psychiatric disease, to determine if these processes are apparent at the time of adolescence. Solutions are aimed at preventing schizophrenia, preventing melancholia, and preventing family psychoneurotic disturbances which may be reflected in the next generation; one can hope to detect which adolescents are at risk and to decide what might be done about them.

But preventive services, also in the first rank of priorities, cannot be suspended until final answers are given. Prevention of mental illness is, for children, a continuing process. It is not a question of preventing anxiety or preventing unhappiness—these feelings may indeed be valuable; it is a question of preventing the complications of anxiety which may lead to further difficulties and stresses and to inhibitions in development. Here, at the strictly practical level, we are in an area where sexual anxieties can be relieved by enlightenment, where occupational failures can be helped by processes of vocational guidance, where inability to communicate with adults can be overcome by the training of the adults themselves. I see primary prevention as a service offering continuous assistance to development and continuous removal of potentially inhibiting environmental factors and able to deal *by professional techniques* with children, adults, and environments, as individuals, groups, and communities.

The preventive services will include the education of the public in mental health principles, about the healthy development of children, the relation of child development to mental illness, the recognition of early signs of mental disorder, and the correct attitudes to be adopted toward the mentally ill. The educational methods employed will be not only through mass media— newspapers, magazines, films, television, lectures—but also through groups where education by discussion can take place, with children, adolescents, family groups, relatives of the mentally ill, and so on.

Effort is needed now to establish common goals, in practice, with persons or groups from other professions concerned with mental health: schoolteachers, clergymen, social administrators, public health nurses, and others.

II. PLANNING GENERAL MENTAL HEALTH SERVICES

In planning a comprehensive mental health service for a given population, one must consider first the needs of this population and the resources available to meet those needs, and then match the two. In psychiatry there is the additional problem that the number of persons in need cannot be accurately assessed because of differences in opinion as to who and what should be treated. The continuum from the normal to the abnormal has no clearly marked boundary, because we are not at all sure of the prognosis in certain types of cases. Furthermore, to add to the uncertainty one is never dealing with the present because the number of professional workers available is not sufficient.

Treatment services needed in a community will cover the whole range of outpatient services, from the comprehensive mental health center to specialized centers; different kinds of psychiatric outpatient departments set up in connection with hospitals or polyclinics; whole-day centers, specialized for the neurotic, the psychotic, the elderly, and the subnormal; a variety of night hospitals and evening units, hostels, sheltered workshops, and the necessary employment provisions which may be required to set them up; inpatient services: psychiatric wards in general hospitals, psychiatric hospitals, specialized psychiatric hospitals, including those for children and for the subnormal. Psychiatric consultations should be made available to a wide variety of medical and social services, including services for infants, school health, rehabilitation, special school services for delinquency and criminality, for divorce, adoption, social service, and—extremely important from the point of view of adolescents—vocational guidance.

It is a useful exercise to look into the numerical needs of a hypothetical European population of 100,000. There will be about 1,800 births per year; these will inevitably give rise to certain mental health problems: antenatal anxieties, psychiatric disorders of pregnancy, problems of family planning, illegitimacy, illegal abortion, and so on. Of these 1,800 births, 30 will be stillbirths, and another 30 will die under one month. Between 10 and 20 will be mentally handicapped.

In this hypothetical population, there will be perhaps 800 or 900 deaths per year, of which 45 will be accidental (many of them young people); perhaps 20 of them will be due to suicide. There will be about 800 marriages, about 100 divorces. Of the 20,000 school children in the population there will be at least 300 per year presenting with mental health problems, and, judging by various investigations that have been made from time to time by survey methods, psychiatrists believe that more than 300 per year ought to present themselves and would do so if one took more effort to work in consultation with their schools. About 1,200 of these as adolescents will leave school each year, probably nearly all of them having vocational problems, many of them having some kind of medical difficulties which ought to be considered in connection with the future.

As far as straight psychiatry is concerned there will be, out of this population, more than 100 subnormal in institutions, about 250 long-stay patients in psychiatric hospitals, and an admission rate of about 250 each year. Of these 250 there will be about 100 cases of schizophrenia.

When one looks into the question of man power, one finds immediately that numbers are insufficient. It is true that some countries have perhaps enough psychiatrists, in the sense that if they were all put to work in a proper plan they could cover the needs, providing they had sufficient collaboration from other mental health professions. But there are few clinical psychologists in mental health work in Europe, only one country, Poland, having a number comparable to its psychiatrists. Some European countries have virtually no clinical psychologists at all; some have no undergraduate university psychology courses. The number of social workers and, particularly, social workers with special education in psychiatry is also very few.

Reverting to our hypothetical population of 100,000, a minimum number of professional positions might be about 150, which should include at least 10 psychiatrists, 10 clinical psychologists, 20 psychiatric social workers, 5 specialist psychotherapists, 5 occupational therapists, and 100 psychiatric nurses, to cover both residential and community care. If one considers the *ideal* needs of this population according to an elaboration of the scheme which I have just described, one might well double this number. Even this would rely on community work done by public health nurses and on general medical practitioners' pulling their weight.

It is not always realized that these professionally trained workers cannot be produced immediately; in planning for national mental health services one must put professional education as first priority because the necessary products will not be available for some years. People are much more important than buildings.

III. PSYCHIATRY FOR ADOLESCENTS

Much of the mental illness alluded to above will concern adolescents because they are members of families whose relatives are in psychiatric difficulties or whose parents are having marital problems. The experiences of adolescents with psychiatric problems in their families can make for difficulties, or they can create healthy attitudes for the future.

Let us remind ourselves of the range of psychiatry in the adolescent age group. Social disorders are prominent: stealing, burglary—at an ever younger age—disorderly behavior in groups, prostitution. In the psychosomatic field, smoking, dependence on drugs, somatic disorders, and physical handicaps with a treatable psychological component, disorders of sex expression, accidents. Psychoneuroses, early manifestations of schizophrenia and depressions, may be expressed as problems in family relations—complicated by family circumstances, adoption, incomplete families, parental illness—or as school problems or as problems in employment. The expression of symptoms in the two areas—home and work—is of course intimately connected psychologically, but the common fact that children may exhibit troubles in one place but not the other carries important implications for case-finding and the setting up of services.

Sex differences in prevalence of disorders, little understood, but consistently in favor of the more healthy feminine sex, will influence both case-finding and provisions.

Immaturity may be a useful diagnostic category, indicating certain aims in treatment. The mental health worker may be legitimately concerned with education insofar as it is a process enhancing or inhibiting psychological and social development.

Subnormality in all its degrees and complications requires much attention. In European centers more than one-half of the children labeled as subnormal because they cannot follow the inappropriate requirements of schools are subsequently able to obtain normally paid employment. The discrepancy between school performance and work performance points to the need for accurate psychiatric assessment and for psychological, educational, and vocational guidance at this adolescent age.

A developing child requires a home—love, parents, human interaction with a minimum of anxiety—and a formal education to equip him for the future, to form his identity, and so to become independent of his childish needs.[3] *If he is psychiatrically ill he may need, in addition, treatment, but he may well, in comparison with the healthy ones, need a home and education all the more.* This statement is the basis for three guiding principles in setting up therapeutic services for adolescents. They are:

(1) Services that maintain home contacts, or that improve the psychosocial climate of the patient's home, are to be preferred to those that cannot provide the advantages of a family. Thus, in the individual case, outpatient services are, in general, to be preferred to inpatient services.

(2) Residential psychiatric services for adolescents should include elements to offset their basic disadvantages. In particular they should either include a professional educational service or enable their patients to attend properly selected schools, even in the case of the older age groups. They should provide a staff capable of substituting, in the child's developmental processes, for his familial figures.

(3) Therapeutic services should be developmental in aim and, when necessary, rehabilitative. This principle demands a detailed psychiatric analysis of etiology, including both psychogenetic factors and recent environments, followed by an analysis of the child's future environments, so that his guidance or his placement after treatment may enhance his development. That is to say, psychotherapy, individual, group or milieu, is not enough. Future environments must be prepared, and both child and environment must be the subject of follow-up action.

With these provisos met, there may be secondary reasons why separate *residential* services for adolescents should be considered. There will be questions of size of the staff, especially to meet the educational provision and the possibility of homogeneity and continuity of care when discharged; mostly these factors will weigh in favor of specialized residential services; against, will be questions of cost and the probable availability of all varieties of parapsychiatric staff and community services in a more general-purpose approach. Homogeneity of patient population is, in my opinion, a relatively weak argument for segregation when institutional staffs are sufficient to offer adequate care. The wider experience of the patient, as a patient, in a therapeutic community may be an advantage—for younger adolescents to be with younger children, and for the older adolescents to be with adults. The decision about special provision for adolescents rests rather on specialization because of type of disorder, and *the therapy required,* than on age; one type of inpatient institution much needed being something like a special school, with a strong psychotherapeutic practice.

As for *outpatient* services for adolescents, there will surely be great differences between one community's acceptance of a type of service and another's. Apart from cases directed to a treatment center by a court, acceptance of a mental health center determines the number of persons who come to it. The number can be increased by referral from other medical and social agencies, and the referrals, in turn, will depend on the stimulus, education, and effects of the community mental health work. The effect of mental health work with other agencies in bringing under care a larger proportion of those in need will in turn depend on the way in which the needs can be met. There are many examples of this process in attempting to find cases through schools. Disturbances in this process occur when teamwork, in the sense of having common aims, between mental health workers and schoolteachers is not achieved or when treatment cannot be applied owing to insufficiency of the mental health services.[2] The rule, "no diagnosis without therapy," applies.

There is no reason to advocate special outpatient services for adolescents, apart from a walk-in counseling center, perhaps; they should be assimilated into the mental health services for school children which should include health education, sex education, the experience of school as a community, educational guidance, vocational guidance, special education, counseling of school staff, and finally, referral to child guidance centers. Today, even child guidance centers are situated as part of a larger mental health service.

There is, however, some scope for special mental health work with young school-leavers in industry, and in Great Britain the role of the Appointed Factory Doctor will include attention to adolescents in the first year of their work. Adolescents in this situation require not only protection from mental illness but opportunities to discuss their educational and vocational futures. The medical role will be all the more important where there are physical handicaps.

Needless to say, continuity of care is important at this age, and in organizing services, the possibility of dislocation between school and industrial medical services should be borne in mind. It has been advocated that physicians might hold double appointments in the same district in order to maintain this continuity.

With regard to community services for adolescents—social services, clubs, and the like—I have often advocated that professional mental health specialists should actively work in these naturally occurring social groups.[1] At the same time the social and welfare workers in charge of the organization of these groups may need to be offered refresher courses in mental health.

IV. PROFESSIONAL EDUCATION

Before deciding on the professional man power which might be occupied with adolescents, it will be necessary to make decisions about organization and techniques used in the mental health services and to require the appropriate training. The difference in training between an "adult" psychiatrist and a "child" psychiatrist in many European countries may be enormous. So long as psychiatric theory and psychiatric treatment are concerned with the immediate treatment of an individual in a consultation room or in a hospital, this division can be maintained, but now we see both in etiology and in treatment so many social factors that it is clearly necessary to understand younger and older persons in order to understand the situation of any adolescent. It is frequently necessary to treat people of different ages together; for instance, families. Furthermore, in institutional settings the relationship between adults and children is of such crucial importance that a therapist who only understands the psychopathology of children is not able really to deal with milieu therapy at all.

Psychiatric services for the young adolescent are usually thought of as belonging to child psychiatry, but child psychiatrists today are becoming more and more interested in the earliest genesis of childhood disorders and are becoming more and more preoccupied with the psychopathology of infancy and preschool children. Thus many professional people engaged in child psychiatric services are somewhat specialized in the early age groups and are more akin to the pediatrician than to the psychiatrist.

In all cases the training of psychiatrists and psychologists for work with adolescents should include a strong emphasis on child development, psychogenetics, psychotherapy, and social psychology. Because the age of adolescence is one in which psychological disturbances may flare up, mental health specialists must have a sensitivity to this process of development and to the possibilities of influencing it. In the last decades we have often emphasized the necessity for special training in child psychiatry to fill a community's need. The pendulum is now swinging back, as more understanding is gained about the importance of social influence for mental health so it is no longer possible to specialize with age groups without a profound knowledge of psychology and psychiatry of all ages. As gerontology becomes of more and more concern to the psychiatrist, he is discovering again that mental development continues beyond childhood, so that ill-health in the old can be prevented by ensuring a healthier development in adolescent years.

Today, in sharp contrast to the medical scene of thirty years ago, deaths in the developed countries are largely due to chronic disease—cardiovascular, cancer, diabetes. The patient presents when he is already advanced in illness; yet our knowledge of pathological processes tells us that he has been ill, perhaps without symptoms, for many years. And anterior to his physical pathology is a way of life which he has assumed in childhood, which has predisposed him, not necessarily inevitably, to the future. Should it not be a proper task for the mental health professions to help counter unhealthy habits of living, and should not services for adolescents recognize through action what we have, with the poet, already known, that the child is father to the man?

References

1. BUCKLE, D. F. "Growing Up with the Normal Family," in *Growing Up in a Changing World*. London: World Federation for Mental Health, 1961.
2. BUCKLE, D. F. "Children and Schools: A Reaction," in H. P. DAVID, ed. *International Trends in Mental Health*. New York: McGraw-Hill, 1966, p. 223.
3. BUCKLE, D. F., S. LEBOVICI, and J. TIZARD. "The Inpatient Psychiatric Treatment of Children in Europe," in DAVID, *op. cit.*, p. 245.

30

Elements of a Comprehensive Community Mental Health Program for Adolescents

Gerald Caplan

This chapter will deal with the elements which should ideally be incorporated into a comprehensive program to cater for the mental health needs of normal and disordered adolescents. Such a program must in turn be planned and operated within the over-all framework of the local community mental health services, which prevent, treat, and rehabilitate mental disorders of all types in people of all ages who reside in the community. These services are organized very differently in different places not only in regard to their auspices, whether governmental, voluntary, or private, but also in regard to their methods of policy making, administration, and co-ordination. Because of this, I shall restrict my discussion to those fundamental issues which may have general applicability and will avoid going into detail about patterns of organization which have relevance only in certain localities of the United States with which I am particularly familiar. As a way of communicating my ideas about the essential building blocks of a program without prejudging how these may be put together in different patterns to conform with local styles of providing mental health services, I shall describe a series of "program elements." If these elements are available in one form or another, the mental health needs of the adolescent population may be satisfied.

The program should be so organized that each adolescent can be handled as an individual with his own idiosyncratic pattern of needs which must be dealt with by a special combination of services, rather than arranging a series of institutions for which we recruit appropriate candidates, rejecting those who are unsuitable. The latter approach is based on the traditional assumption that we are concerned only with those individuals whom we accept as our patients. We therefore screen candidates and select for admission to our clinics only those who fit our research or clinical interests, or with whom we feel our current methods are likely to succeed. The remainder, which unfortunately includes the vast majority of the psychologically disturbed in the population, are not considered our responsibility.*

I am convinced that we psychiatrists should accept a concern for the total population in our community and should devote our efforts to working out ways of serving all of them, either by direct personal contact or else indirectly through the intermediation of other professional and nonprofessional care-givers whom we support by education and consultation. It is because of this that I advocate the inclusion of a comprehensive set of program elements in each community. This will provide a basis for satisfying the needs of all the adolescent population in a way that can be tailored to each individual case. These elements may occasionally be combined in a unified mental health system under one administration, or more usually they may be divided among a series of mental health and nonmental health agencies and institutions, each with its independent administration, but willing to co-ordinate its activities with the rest so that an adolescent may move freely from one to another in line with his needs of the moment.

I am interested not only in catering to *all* the adolescents in the population who are in need of service but also in providing services for the broad range of needs which are thought of at the present time as falling within the sphere of mental health. This range will vary from place to place in line with how the public and the professionals define the role of psychiatrists. The broadest definition is probably found in the United States, where psychiatrists are currently being called upon to assist educators and others to help healthy adolescents achieve greater maturity and positive mental health; to diagnose and treat minor temporary disturbances in normal adolescents; and to diagnose, treat, and rehabilitate behavior disorders such as delinquency, alcoholism, drug addiction, and prostitution, as well as the traditional textbook disorders of psychiatry—mental subnormalities, neuroses, psychoses, psychosomatic illnesses, and the psychological complications of physical illnesses and disabilities. I shall not consider the problem of delinquency, in spite of its importance. Apart from this omission, I shall deal with services to satisfy the entire range of mental health needs of adolescents as currently defined in the United States.

A matter of particular importance is the need for *specialized* knowledge and skills in assessing and handling the mental health dimension of adolescence. The reason for this is that adolescence is a transitional and tumultuous period of development in the life of an individual, and the stable pat-

---

* L. Srole et al.[9] have shown that of the approximately 3 per cent of the total adult population of Manhattan whom they judge to be severely incapacitated because of mental disorders, only about one-third have ever been seen by a psychiatrist.

terns of behavior and mental functioning with which we are familiar in childhood and adult life are upset. The difficulty is to differentiate the normal variations in this period of turmoil from those superficially similar upsets which presage the development of deep disorders such as schizophrenia or personality defects. Moreover, the routine treatment practices of child psychiatry and adult psychotherapy are often unavailing with adolescents because of difficulties in communication and perception between them and adults and because many of them feel they should be treated very differently and in different surroundings from both children and adults. We therefore need the services of psychiatrists with specialist knowledge and skills in dealing with adolescents. But the range and magnitude of the problems of adolescents in the population clearly necessitate more than a series of circumscribed adolescent units manned by specialists. The latter should be available in each large community as a locus for research and for the treatment of especially difficult cases, but they should not be expected to deal with the whole problem. Instead, they should be a resource for the education of child and adult psychiatrists and for other professionals in the community who will inevitably have to handle the majority of adolescent problem cases in their own programs and institutions; and the specialists should spend a significant part of their time offering consultation to these other workers on their handling of particularly complicated cases. My reply to the question as to whether disturbed adolescents should be diagnosed and treated in child psychiatry, adult psychiatry, or adolescent psychiatry units is that each of these should ideally be available for handling adolescents. Certain cases will be most suitable for each.

The following is a list of the major program elements which recent experience indicates to be desirable. Few communities at present possess all of them, but each of the elements has been tried and found of value in a number of places.

I. DIAGNOSIS, COUNSELING, AND DISPOSITION

These three functions should be inseparable. They cater to adolescents who feel themselves or are felt by others to be possibly disturbed. In order to reduce the duration of mental disorders, this service should be readily available to adolescents so that attention can be given as early as possible. Self-referral should be encouraged by dissemination of information to the population of adolescents and their families, and early referral by professional care-givers should be encouraged by building up relationships with the community professionals, who should be offered consultation to help them decide whether or not to refer questionable cases.

There are three major sites for these units, and each of them taps a somewhat different population, so that an optimal program should have all three.

A. Inside the Community Mental Health System

A general diagnostic service and a specialist service for adolescents to be invoked in case of complications which cannot be clarified by the generalist workers should both be represented in the ambulatory clinic. The staffs of each service optimally should have access to a residential facility, where observation of adolescents over a period of time in individual, group, and social situations may provide data for diagnostic and dispositional judgments.

B. In the School System

In this situation the total population of early adolescents is available for routine screening; for example, in line with the work of Bower[4] in California. Supplementary to such an approach is the organization of a counseling service by a school psychologist or the operations of guidance counselors to whom students have ready access and who can appraise the level and nature of possible disturbance and make appropriate referrals. Schoolteachers are the professional workers in most direct and regular contact with young adolescents. In their preprofessional and inservice training, teachers should become familiar with broad categories of disturbance in adolescents and of appropriate channels of communication and referral for specialized professional help. A mental health consultation service should also be provided so that a teacher who becomes concerned about the mental health of one of his students may have a ready opportunity to discuss the case with a specialist and clarify the nature of the student's difficulty and how best to handle it both within the school framework and by invoking the aid of other community services.

C. In the Community

Adolescents in difficulty often turn for help and guidance to professional care-givers such as clergymen, family doctors, pediatricians, social workers, and public health nurses. They may also ask for advice from adults with whom they build up relationships in political, social, recreational, and religious organizations such as social group workers, Boy Scout leaders, church elders, football coaches, political youth club leaders, and others. Programs of education and consultation similar to those for teachers should be provided to help these key persons improve their effectiveness in offering guidance.

In addition, the need of adolescents to feel they are being treated as a separate group, and their rebellion against operating through channels which bear the label "adult" or "child," have been satisfied in some localities by setting up special "Youth Advisory Centers" or "Youth Consultation Centers," to which adolescents can turn directly for advice on life adjustment. These centers often include mental health specialists on their staffs who are able to carry out diagnostic investigations and make judgments on disposition in this explicitly nonmedical setting. It appears that many adolescents feel free to ask for help in such a setting without the loss of face which prevents them from seeking assistance within the framework of the school or the usual community mental health services.

Services concerned with diagnosis, counseling, and disposition, wherever they are located, need to maintain close relations on the one hand with sources of medical consultation and vocational guidance and on the other with community agencies whose co-operation they require in providing for the needs of adolescents. As regards consultation, they particularly need ready access to physicians who can advise on the diagnosis and treatment of skin, endocrine, metabolic, and gynecological conditions. Such problems as acne, weight disorders, and menstrual difficulties are common complications of the psychosocial disorders of adolescence, and services which restrict their focus to the psychological plane are more obviously undesirable at this than at other phases of the life cycle.

As regards community resources, diagnostic units should not only be well informed about medical, psychological, social, educational, vocational, recreational, and religious agencies but should also establish a network of personal relationships with their members. They should maintain contact with every worker in these services to whom they refer an adolescent, with an offer of continuing collaboration and consultation. This will assist them to evaluate the efficacy of the disposition; it will also prevent the other worker from feeling that the case has been "dumped" on him and will thus ensure better co-operation. Psychiatrists in diagnostic units should feel as much responsibility for the future welfare of adolescents they refer to outside units as for those they are able to handle mainly or entirely within the framework of their own organization. This is a crucial element in the philosophy of community-oriented psychiatry, in which we accept a measure of responsibility for the mental health of the entire population and not just for "our own" patients.

II. TREATMENT FACILITIES

The provision of treatment for the short-term and long-term disorders of adolescence should take into account the special needs of the different diagnostic categories, although in practice a particular unit may cater to patients of many types.

Whenever possible the family as a whole should be involved in the therapeutic intervention. The old therapeutic fashion to isolate adolescents from their families during treatment, because of the well-known tensions between adolescents and their parents, is becoming rapidly outmoded. We are beginning to realize that usually the best way of handling this problem is to focus directly on it in joint or concurrent therapeutic meetings. Similarly, therapeutic intervention with the adolescent should be accompanied by a collaborative plan involving the other care-giving professionals in his milieu such as clergymen, schoolteachers, social workers, policemen, probation officers, and youth leaders.

Both outpatient and residential institutions are needed for adolescents, in each of which a wide range of individual, group, and milieu therapies can be provided. In addition to the classical outpatient department or polyclinic and the mental hospital or residential treatment center, the experience of recent years has demonstrated the special value of day treatment centers and transitional institutions, such as night hospitals, week-end hospitals, halfway houses, and hostels. The unit which caters for adolescents may be part of a general child or adult therapeutic institution, or it may be a separate adolescent ward, department, or institution. The following are examples of separate units for adolescents which have already demonstrated their value.

A. Treatment Schools

Treatment schools may be complete entities or in the form of special classes for adolescents in schools which cater also for younger children. These may be day schools, but more usually they are residential institutions. In addition to a staff of educators who have special training and experience in teaching emotionally disturbed students, these schools employ psychologists, psychiatrists, and psychiatric social workers who provide individual and group treatment and offer consultation to the teachers on classroom and extracurricular milieu management problems. The amalgam of an educational, a medical, and an individual and group psychotherapeutic approach which characterizes a good treatment school owes much to pioneers like Aichhorn,[1] Redl and Wineman,[8] and Bettelheim[3] and to the Heilpedagogues and Educateurs of Europe.

B. Treatment Camps

Treatment camps are usually isolated therapeutic communities in rural settings, in which the major emphasis is on a character-building milieu therapy and in which the adolescents learn to improve their individual and group performance in gaining mastery over natural obstacles in agriculture, afforestation, building roads and bridges, establishing drainage and water supply systems, and the like. The staff is composed of educators and craftsmen with special education and experience, supported by mental health specialists who offer consultation on intercurrent problem situations and provide some individual and group treatment for particular cases.

The treatment camps owe much to the work of pioneers like Makarenko,[7] of Russia, and Aichhorn,[1] of Austria, who worked with "wayward youth," and to correctional institutions, such as the Q-camps of

England, which dealt with juvenile delinquents. They also derive some of their methods from group work practice in summer camps in the United States, some of which have specialized over many years in providing summer camping experience for disturbed children and have been staffed by mental health specialists as well as by the usual camping counselors. These summer camps have proved their worth and should be organized wherever possible as a supplementary service to the year-long establishments.

C. Units for Special Diagnostic Groups

Particular provision must be made for the long-term treatment and management of adolescent psychotics, epileptics, and mentally subnormal cases. These units will usually be developed within the framework of child psychiatry or pediatric institutions, but special staffing is called for because of the characteristic problems of dealing with adolescents related to their greater behavioral instability and physical strength and to the development of their sexual impulses, with attendant problems of control. Sexual problems represent a special challenge in dealing with mentally subnormal adolescents. Mentally disturbed adolescents with physical handicaps, such as blindness or orthopedic defects, are a subgroup which demands specialized attention in a therapeutic program which is welded into an active vocational training and special occupational placement service either in sheltered workshops or in supervised units in industry.

D. The Treatment of Adolescents in Mental Hospitals

In most communities severely disturbed adolescents who need inpatient treatment will be treated in mental hospitals, either as patients in adult wards or in separate wards for adolescents. A recent review by Beskind [2] examines the evidence about the advantages and disadvantages of these alternatives. He finds that moderately disturbed patients seem to do better in adolescent wards, but that severely disturbed adolescents seem to benefit from treatment in adult wards as long as the ratio of adolescents to adult patients is kept low. Inclusion in an adult group stimulates the adolescent to mature by providing opportunities for identification, and it reduces acting-out behavior. Because of the latter, this setting is indicated for aggressive adolescents with poor impulse control. In such cases an adolescent group retards maturation and often provides a group atmosphere which fosters acting-out by contagion.

Whether or not the adolescents are treated in separate wards, the hospital should provide appropriate schooling and activity programs for them, and there should be adequate staff in the adolescent units not only to treat their own cases but to offer consultation and collaboration in the treatment of adolescents in the adult wards.

III. VOCATIONAL GUIDANCE, TRAINING, AND REHABILITATION

Mental disorders in adolescence interfere with the orderly development of the occupational career both by inhibiting learning of socially and occupationally required skills and by removing the sufferer from the normal channels of communication which usually determine job choice by arousing appropriate interests and by providing the opportunity for identification with role models. Once a disturbance has occurred in this complicated process and the adolescent has got "out of step," his return to a normal occupational path becomes very difficult.

In a stable society and one not involved in rapid technological change, adolescents move from the school to the work fields with a minimum of strain and self-consciousness. In our society, where the patterns of utilization of man power are changing rapidly and where progressively fewer boys and girls take up work similar to that of their parents or other familiar adults than in previous generations, the educational and vocational training systems are developing special resources to cope with the problem. These resources need the consultant help of specialists in the mental health of adolescents in order to deal with the normal psychosocial complications of their work. This collaboration may form an appropriate basis for our invoking their help in fulfilling our responsibilities in the rehabilitation of our patients.

This is best achieved if workers from each system penetrate the other in order to obtain an identification with the other's point of view and learn to appreciate the nature and boundaries of the collaborators' expertness. This means that vocational selection and training personnel should be brought as consultants and collaborators into rehabilitation units within the community mental health program, for example, in mental hospitals and day treatment centers; and that psychiatrists, social workers, and counseling psychologists should go as consultants into the institutions organized by the departments of youth education and vocational selection and training, such as craft and technical schools and apprenticeship training programs.

A number of special services have proved of particular value in the rehabilitation of disturbed adolescents. These include *sheltered workshops* for former patients with chronic residual defects, *supervised industrial placements* for those who can work in normal settings if they and their foremen are given special supervision, and *selective placement,* whereby a skilled attempt is made to find a special niche in some low-demand job for the person with reduced capacities. In an effective rehabilitation program the adolescent is moved in a graduated manner into occupational situations of progressively increased challenge and burden, and parallel to this he is moved to social situations which demand increasing independence, that is, from inpatient wards with maximum supervision to those with minimum supervision, and on to transitional institutions such as day hospital, night hospital, and week-end hospital, halfway house, and then home to his family or a foster family or residential hostel.

In most communities it is not sufficient for the mental health workers to focus only on the adolescents; they must also work with the employers in such organizations as Rotary and the other service clubs and the chamber of commerce, as well as with the trade-unions, so as to stimulate the provision of an increased range of jobs which are suitable for the rehabilitated adolescents.

IV. EDUCATION OF DISTURBED ADOLESCENTS WITHIN THE SCHOOL SYSTEM

Disturbed adolescents may continue at school during their period of treatment or may be excluded and must then return when their treatment has progressed to a suitable stage. Provisions for the schooling of disturbed adolescents include the following.

A. Specialized Technical Supervision and Mental Health Consultation for Teachers

As far as possible, disturbed adolescents should be educated in the normal setting so as to combat mutual alienation between them and their social milieu. In school systems such as those in the United States, high schools operate on an educational unit system in which each subject is taught in separate classes, and the student population is divided into a larger number of functional groups so that each student can choose from a variety of subject patterns, and he belongs at any time to several different classroom groups. There is thus a good opportunity to match a disturbed adolescent's needs with the capacities of suitable teachers and settings and with appropriately chosen peer groups. This ideally allows administrative regulation of the number and type of students in each classroom group and means, for example, that students who are emotionally disturbed but still well enough to attend a regular school can be spread throughout the system, rather than being concentrated all the time in one class where they may overburden the tolerance of a teacher and of fellow students.

Despite each arrangements, a disturbed student is likely to present his teacher with a variety of unusual problems in education and management for which the teacher's training and experience do not readily suggest a range of solutions. A school system should provide ways of dealing with this expectable situation by offering the consultative or supervisory services of educators with special training in dealing with emotionally disturbed students and also a mental health consultation service staffed by mental health specialists. The special educators can help the classroom teacher learn new educational skills for classroom teaching and extracurricular management. The mental health consultants can help the teacher gain effective understanding of current cases and maintain professional objectivity in the face of emotionally disturbing elements in work situations—a potent cause of difficulty in view of the impossibility of providing teachers with lengthy and expensive training, such as that given to mental health specialists, in the mastering of countertransference forces.

B. Special Classes

Some severely disturbed adolescents can be maintained in the normal school setting if a special class can be organized within its framework, to which they can go for a few hours a week for special emotional and educational attention. Some students may have to attend the special class full time for a period, and then may progressively return to ordinary classes.

The special classes should be taught by teachers with appropriate training and experience, who are helped by mental health specialists, usually psychologists and social workers. The latter collaborate with the teachers in conducting certain classroom sessions or tutoring or treating individual cases; and they offer consultation to the teachers on problems encountered in their teaching. The teachers of the special classes should spend part of their time in supervising the progress of their students who have returned to the regular classes and in helping the ordinary teachers improve their skills with disturbed youngsters.

C. Special Schooling

The most severely disturbed adolescents, or those suffering from particular disturbances such as mental subnormality or physical disabilities like epilepsy, blindness, and crippling, or illegitimate pregnancy, may for a longer or shorter period of time be unacceptable in normal schools. Teachers should be available to visit them for individual tutoring in their homes, or special schooling should be provided by the educational system. This may take the form of a separate class or school, or a unit within the framework of an ambulatory or residential treatment institution. If such units are part of the over-all community educational system, there is a greater likelihood of facilitating the rapid return of each adolescent to the normal educational setting as soon as he is fit to go back.

V. PREVENTIVE SERVICES

The effective operation of all the previously discussed program elements should have a preventive effect at the secondary and tertiary levels, that is, the prevalence of mental disorders in adolescence will be reduced by early diagnosis and prompt treatment to shorten duration of existing cases (secondary prevention) and the rate of residual defect will be lowered by the concurrent and follow-up rehabilitation of patients who are treated (tertiary prevention). Significant changes in these community rates will obviously depend on services being provided for a substantial proportion of the population of disturbed adolescents. Services may be very effective in individual cases, but if they are restricted to a few carefully selected patients of high intelligence and upper or middle socioeconomic class, the over-all community statistics will not show much improvement. This emphasizes the necessity to plan the deployment of community supplies of workers, money, and methods in relation to a meaningful priority system so that the wishes and needs of the people are satisfied as much as is practically feasible with the resources available. This implies close collaboration between the professional workers and civic leaders, so that policy decisions can take full account of how the situations are perceived from the two vantage points of the demands for high-quality professional operations and the needs and resources of the population.

In addition, the range of community services should include program elements specifically geared to *primary prevention*—the promotion of mental health or optimal potential for creative living and reality-based mastery of life's problems by adolescents and also the reduction of the risk of new cases of mental disorder occurring in the adolescent population.

Primary prevention focuses not on individual cases of emotional disturbance, but on the total population of adolescents, some of whom are not at special risk, but may be helped to achieve a fuller life, while others may develop a mental disorder unless this is forestalled by preventive activity.

The promotion of mental health in the adolescent population depends on improving biopsychosocial supplies so as to provide the best possible circumstances in which to grow up. Improvement of these supplies is likely to be especially important in sections of the population which are currently deprived and disadvantaged due to poverty or prejudice. Improvement, for example, in living conditions, medical care, and level of education for lower-class Negroes in the slums of big cities in the United States will probably have important effects on their present and future mental health. This will also be helped by extending their social, political, and occupational horizons while at the same time raising their expectations and those of their families in regard to what they can accomplish if they accept the challenges of a new way of life. Clearly, such a program demands a major campaign of social action, in which the mental health issues and their protagonists are only one of the leverage points. This is the general rule in the field of primary prevention.

Another example of mental health promotion is the so-called "character-building" aspect of the education of adolescents. Educators such as Kurt Hahn,[5] originally of Germany and later of Great Britain, and the British Outward Bound Movement,[6] which exercised so profound an influence on the shaping of the U.S. Peace Corps, have emphasized the value of the experiential side of education, particularly for adolescents. They expose students to situations of challenge such as the rigors of nature in mountaineering or ocean sailing, or psychosocial stresses such as public speaking or culture shock, and they dose the stress so that it just overtaxes the current resources of the student. This precipitates a crisis in the student. The educator supports the student in working his way through the artificially induced and controlled crisis and helps him find a healthy adaptive solution. The new coping patterns which he develops during this process are then incorporated by the student in his ongoing repertoire of psychosocial skills, and the result is that his capacity for a mentally healthy or more "mature" response to future crises is enhanced.

Students who successfully undergo such educational experiences show an increased ability to handle unexpected life problems and an increased capacity to tolerate confusion and emotional frustration. These are signs of improved positive mental health. They are also likely to reduce the risk of dealing with a life crisis by ego regression or magical and symbolic psychic manipulations which lead to symptom formation instead of by actively modifying the real life situation in line with cultural prescriptions and expectations.

Workers dealing with primary prevention will focus much of their efforts on helping adolescents to cope adequately with the life crises which are so common at their age. Mental health workers will survey the forces impinging on adolescents in their community and list the hazardous situations which provoke crises in a significant proportion of the adolescent population. Studies are replete with examples of such factors deriving from the development of the adolescents themselves and also from the attitudes and behavior of the adult world. These stress factors cannot usually be entirely avoided, but they can often be weakened by individual or social action. For instance, the shock of menarche can be reduced by anticipatory education of young teen-agers and by counseling mothers to talk about menstruation in a positive manner as a sign of valued femininity and maturity and not negatively as a "curse" and a disability; attitudes of fear and punitiveness of the adults in relation to the difficulties of adolescents in impulse control can be reduced by parent-education groups and through explaining the psychology of adolescence in the mass media; unemployment and redundancy of adolescents can be reduced by public work programs, by better town planning and industrial, man-power, and educational planning, so that local industry provides apprenticeship opportunities and so that schools and trade schools teach the skills which will be needed in our automated society, in order that fewer unskilled adolescents enter the labor market searching for jobs that no longer exist; the special stress for adolescents whose same-sex parent dies or is separated by job demands, divorce, or chronic illness and long-term hospitalization may be reduced by mobilizing or strengthening the efforts of social welfare and recreational agencies such as Boys Clubs and Girls Clubs, Family Agencies, and Big Brother and Big Sister Organizations, to provide adult substitutes as identification figures.

Finally, services should be provided to help adolescents in crisis choose healthy ways of adapting. This can be done by organizing *anticipatory guidance* discussions for groups of adolescents just before an expected crisis strikes, for example, on the eve of school-leaving, or in the early stages of a residential training course, or before going out into the stress of the adult work situation as an apprentice, and so forth. It can also be accomplished through *preventive intervention* with adolescents and their families by mental health specialists in individual crisis situations, or on a much wider scale by fostering the intervention of community care-givers who are likely to be on the spot during the short period of the crisis upset and to whom the adolescents are likely to turn for assistance—the clergymen, teachers, youth leaders, public health nurses, family doctors, and the like. These helpful efforts will be fostered by the mental health workers taking part in the professional and in-service training of the local professionals and also by offering them mental health consultation to assist in dealing with particularly difficult or troublesome cases.

VI. RESEARCH

Community services for adolescents are not complete without an active research program. Our knowledge of variations of normal personality development must be extended by longitudinal studies of ordinary adolescents if we are to improve our diagnostic ability to differentiate patterns of disturbed behavior which are likely to lead to serious illness. We must also organize an effective follow-up program for our patients so that we can correlate their eventual course with our clinical predictions and thus improve our knowledge of the natural history of mental disorders in adolescence. This involves setting up an effective records system, which can also monitor the flow of patients in and out of our programs and from unit to unit. Such a system will permit a continuing evaluation of the operations and results of different elements of the program and a feedback from this to improve both its *efficiency* in respect to the cost of its various parts in terms of workers and materials and also its *effectiveness* in respect to improvement in incidence, prevalence, and residual defect rates of adolescent mental disorders in the community. This data collection and analysis system will help to foster collaboration among the different units, all of which will benefit from its reports. Wherever there is a nearby university, the collaboration of its researchers in departments of psychiatry, psychology, and social science should be invoked by a community program for mutual benefit.

CONCLUSION

The list of program elements in this chapter represents a set of guidelines for mental health planners. Wherever an element is missing, attempts should be made to introduce it either as a separate unit or as a new element in an existing service. I wish to re-emphasize that I do not advocate any particular administrative pattern for welding these elements into a functioning system. I believe there are innumerable ways of achieving this, so as to be compatible with the general patterns of services in different communities. The main point is not who controls the organization or how it is financed and administered, but how to ensure that there is free communication among the workers responsible for the various program elements and that adolescents can move easily and at rates to suit their own needs from unit to unit, so that they receive care appropriate to their current situation.

Last, I believe that specialists in adolescent psychiatry should be involved in this system in a variety of ways and with varying degrees of responsibility. Sometimes they will have complete clinical responsibility for the diagnosis and treatment of their own patients. Sometimes they will share responsibility with child psychiatrist and adult psychiatrist colleagues in whose cases they collaborate. Sometimes they will have only partial responsibility when they offer consultation and education to psychiatrists, family doctors, educators, clergymen, legislators, and other professional caregivers and administrators on their own handling of the mental health dimension of their work with adolescents. A concern for the total population of adolescents in the community thus involves the psychiatrist in a range of roles which he must learn to identify and fulfill by differentiated professional activity. If he does so, he will add a new and more complicated dimension to his previous work as a clinician whose focus was confined to his own patients—a *community* dimension. He will be only one of the elements in the community program I have described, but a very important one.

References

1. AICHHORN, A. *Wayward Youth*. New York: Viking, 1953.
2. BESKIND, H. "Psychiatric Inpatient Treatment of Adolescents: A Review of Clinical Experience," *Comprehensive Psychiatry*, III (1962), 354.
3. BETTELHEIM, B. *Love Is Not Enough*. Glencoe, Ill.: The Free Press, 1950
4. BOWER, E. M. "Primary Prevention in a School Setting," in G. CAPLAN, ed., *Prevention of Mental Disorders in Children*. New York: Basic Books, 1961, p. 353.

386   *A Community Mental Health Program for Adolescents*

5. HAHN, K. "Outward Bound," in G. Z. F. BEREDAY and J. A. LAUWERYS, eds. *Education and Philosophy, The Year Book of Education.* New York: World Book, 1957, p. 436.
6. JAMES, D., ed. *Outward Bound.* London: Routledge and Kegan Paul, 1957.
7. MAKARENKO, A. S. *The Road to Life,* trans. S. GARRY. London: Stanley Nott, 1936. Vol. I.
8. REDL, F., and D. WINEMAN. *The Aggressive Child.* Glencoe, Ill.: The Free Press, 1957.
9. SROLE, L., et al. *Mental Health in the Metropolis.* New York: McGraw-Hill, 1962, p. 147.

31

Services and Mental Health
Activities for
Handicapped Adolescents

Robert Lafon

In this chapter I shall limit my remarks to adolescents who are either mentally retarded or suffering from motor, sensory, or speech handicaps (all of whom I shall classify by the more general term of adolescent handicapped). Even then the subject remains extremely broad and complex. I shall discuss it in the context of extant services and programs and indicate the aspects peculiar to these handicaps during adolescence.

I. GENERAL REMARKS

The course of action to be followed with handicapped adolescents is only part of a broader plan which should be followed throughout the handicapped person's life, from his birth to his death, and even before and after, if we consider genetic factors involving his relatives and descendants.

This concept of prevention, detection, diagnosis, treatment, and aftercare is overwhelmingly complex. It pertains not only to mental health services and sciences but also to the interaction of such diverse administrative bodies as the offices of public health, social welfare, education, labor, youth, and justice; it involves different social and political organizations in various countries; it encompasses interactions between the pure and social sciences (biology, psychology, education, pediatrics, psychiatry, sociology, the judicial and administrative branches of government, and so on); and it includes the relationship between multiple family units, on the one hand, and public, semipublic, and private community interests on the other.

387

The political structures and social evolution of each country will determine the actual form of the services and programs, the level of their development, the ability to initiate such a program and the advantages obtained, and the priorities among more or less limited possibilities. I shall deal here with information gathered from developed and industrialized countries, although it should be borne in mind that the rights of the infant and adolescent handicapped are universal. These rights were clearly defined at the Beirut Congress in April 1963:

(1) An unconditional right to life.

(2) The right to respect.

(3) The right to a certain priority concerning treatment and education.

(4) The right to know the truth about the handicap as soon as possible.

(5) The right to a family and the natural affection obtained from it.

(6) The right to special work that does not degrade.

Services should be organized to fit in with the vertical framework of the power structure in each country and with the horizontal framework of institutions and services involved in direct action. This should be encouraged and accompanied by the co-ordination and co-operation of the systems involved and by multidisciplinary and multiprofessional teamwork. These efforts are already too thin; any further division and dispersion is unacceptable.

Single families, even when wealthy, are unable to assume the heavy financial and educational responsibility of rearing handicapped children. Collective participation is indispensable, but it should never usurp the essential primacy and collaboration of the family. The family is the natural tutor of every child and adolescent. Its role should be to give as much individual attention as often as possible and to establish permanent bonds of respect between the child and his family.

However, the child's incapacity is often accompanied by a familial incapacity. In this case, family associations and health services should combine their efforts and strive to help the family as well as the child.

Modern social and socioeconomic organizations are becoming increasingly averse to anything which cannot be poured into a "normal" mold, a fact clearly exposed by familial abdication—much to the benefit of private foundations, insurance or social security groups, and public services. This tendency offers a course of action which is dangerously easy for both parties. The family gets rid of the child, and the service is freed from its responsibility toward the family and its obligation to co-operate with it. The child is placed in a neatly organized, conditioned, and secure environment which is comforting to the service and comforting to the child.

It is incumbent on the nation and the community to do even more for the handicapped than for its normal citizens if the family is to be able to assume its responsibilities. Some time ago I wrote "that if we wish to respect the principle of equality, we need something more than equality to raise the handicapped to the level of the others." Although some states are beginning to recognize this obligation, the public at large needs to be educated further in the subject of mental health. Public education should be part of mental health programs.

The battle waged for the handicapped is the responsibility of departments of public health and social welfare in some countries and of departments of education in others; sometimes it is the responsibility of both departments. Space does not permit a detailed comparison of these systems, but it should be noted that during adolescence two other vertical organizations enter the picture: departments of labor and youth and, occasionally, justice and the police who may deal with handicapped adolescents in reformatories or through probation officers.

By creating a Ministry of Social Affairs, and by regrouping the Office of Public Health, Population, Labor, and Social Security, France has taken a step in the direction of an effective co-ordination among the services concerned. This topic can be schematized.

If we consider the length and extent of the work undertaken by each of these vertical organizations, we see that only the Ministry of Social Affairs (health, population, and welfare) has a permanent function. It is responsible for the welfare of the following:

(1) The handicapped, for as long as he lives.

(2) His lineage (living family and descendants) of which he is but one link.

(3) The family and social group to which he belongs and which he frequently disturbs.

Other organizations enter in specific ways:

(1) The department of education, during the handicapped person's formal, or special, education.

(2) The department of labor, when he reaches adolescence and receives help in finding employment.

(3) The department of youth, which deals with problems peculiar to this age group, leisure and sport.

(4) The police and the courts, should the occasion arise, may assure legal protection, respect for law and order, and respect for other individuals; or they may have to authorize permanent guardianship.

Whatever the outcome of his education and period of rehabilitation, the person involved will sooner or later improve or remain a ward forever—either completely or in part—of the Department of Social Affairs. This De-

partment exerts what could be called authority over health and social problems. It should have the right to take any necessary financial or institutional
action (whether it concerns the services, personnel, or institutions themselves).

All of this necessarily implies that the various programs will possess a
preventive function as well as a general, and particularly educational, function. They should have the means and organizations to detect, diagnose,
treat, and give aftercare; they should have decision-making bodies (like
medical and psychopedagogical committees, social and educational committees, committees for the guardianship of children, rehabilitation committees, and so on); organizations to assist the adult handicapped; training
centers for personnel; research groups; and so forth. These will vary, of
course, from country to country, as will the collective concepts regarding
economic and humane treatment. The very nature of the handicap will
vary. Thirty years of experience has shown me that whatever the specific
procedures adopted, co-operation, and especially co-operation between
the public and private sectors at both the administrative and technical
levels, is necessary for the program to be efficient. In most countries, controlling the action of certain sectors may make more efficient and broader
efforts possible.

II. PECULIARITIES OF ADOLESCENCE

(1) It is advisable to begin the process of education and rehabilitation
at the beginning of adolescence, although it will often be necessary to give
this process a new orientation.

For some of the handicapped, rehabilitation will have achieved all it can
by the end of childhood, and there will be less need for special arrangements. Others, on the contrary, will need little but schooling, although this
will continue beyond the age where it normally ends.

We may have to reconsider whether cases where both sexes have mixed
freely during childhood should continue to do so during adolescence.

(2) This leads us to a consideration of the influence on adolescents of
the appearance of secondary sexual characteristics.

A first point, to be borne constantly in mind, is classic: one should not
expect a revolutionary improvement or an end to the handicap itself with
the arrival of puberty. "It's not just a matter of sex," despite the many
assurances, some of them even medical, to the contrary. What all too often
does end with puberty is that period during which something valuable might
have been done. Puberty often marks the end of the "apprenticeship" and
the possibility of making any further progress.

The next point is common to all adolescents, but it is one which is often
exceptionally painful to the handicapped and often more complex. The
handicapped person has a heightened awareness and sense of disgrace
about normal development. Disturbing physiological changes may be

marked by feelings of anxiety. Psychological disturbances such as hyper-emotion, agitation, sexual fantasies, auto- or heteroerotic preoccupation, and the like may lead to behavior patterns as diverse as asthenic depression and hyperasthenic aggression. Sexual education will be more difficult. Occasionally it may be impossible.

The attitude of parents during this period should also be analyzed. The normal, stereotyped reaction to adolescence will tend to be more emotional and anguished. Deception, humiliation, overprotection, confinement, irrational hopes and demands, resignation, and despair will all be expressed by ambivalent attitudes. The distressing circumstances surrounding the first appearance of the handicap will be relived, and often in an even more painful way.

(3) The handicapped adolescent's anticipated drama concerning the death of his parents appears, in a more acute form. From the first, the handicapped person resents his envisaged abandonment to an anonymous society, which all too frequently offers nothing but an institutionalized solution and the existence of a vegetable. These reactions are common to many normal adolescents, but the feelings of insecurity experienced by the handicapped adolescent are especially acute.

(4) The preparation for the period of follow-up rehabilitation is even more necessary during adolescence. This should be examined most carefully with regard to vocational training and social life.

Vocational training is an essential goal and one of the major means of rehabilitation. It confronts us with two differing conceptions: one, that schooling should be prolonged longer than is normal; the other, that on the contrary the handicapped should be placed in a vocational school very early, with real tools and real materials with which to work, the idea being that handicapped people must get a head start on the others in order not to miss the boat of employment. No doubt the best solution is a combination of the two: early entry into vocational school *and* prolonged schooling.

The end of adolescence will usually be marked by the handicapped person's acquisition of a noncompetitive job. This poses various problems that depend on the nature of the handicap. Possibilities of normal kinds of work should be considered. In some cases, the handicapped worker may be able to compete with normal workers, but this does not mean that he loses the right to special consideration and to easier working conditions.

The maximum effort to explore the individual's capacities so that he can receive appropriate vocational training should be made throughout adolescence; but there are cases in which the family, to reap immediate benefits, foregoes this necessary training and withdraws the handicapped person in order to place him in a job situation which is both precarious and beneath his capacity. The rehabilitation and the handicapped person's future are compromised. Here we are faced with the question of the right of the family, qua family, to stop the process of rehabilitation of its own free will.

This decision by the family is often made without good reason, although the family may already have asked the Department of Social Affairs for assistance in rehabilitating the adolescent. When this happens, perhaps the Department should be authorized to protect the adolescent and to insist on his continued rehabilitation.

Employment in noncompetitive work, especially in sparsely populated areas, will occasionally lead to a situation in which the young workers, handicapped or not, live together. Problems of various kinds will arise, some connected with group living, which we shall examine below, and some relating to the contribution in terms of salary made by the handicapped person toward his own living expenses. In many cases society will have to meet part of these expenses.

Some difficulties regarding noncompetitive work, and the absorption of handicapped workers into the national labor force, may arise in countries plagued by chronic and extensive unemployment problems. In such countries there may be a tendency to minimize any extra effort made in favor of the handicapped and to impede what is considered an onerous, because special, treatment.

During adolescence the handicapped person should be prepared for social life. He should be taught the desire to leave the family—or the institutional group—where, more often than not, he is overprotected. He should be free to go out frequently; he should travel normally, using public transportation; he should be permitted simple purchases, take excursions, learn the rudiments of traffic laws, and so forth.

While the idea of coeducational institutions is readily accepted during childhood, there is a tendency to separate the sexes in adolescence, although if certain precautions are taken, some benefits may be derived from maintaining normal coeducational relationships during this period. This is easily accomplished in day schools, but is more difficult, or generally not advised, in boarding schools. The organization of leisure can provide occasions for bringing the sexes together. One should not lose sight of the fact that, if the goal is the genuine integration of the handicapped into society, any segregation of the sexes will ultimately be impossible. The sexes will inevitably mix when they begin work. Experience has shown that when adolescents who have been educated in sexually segregated institutions are placed in mixed vocational schools or working environments they are much more disturbed, both sexually and in their normal relations, than are the others.

While on the subject of this preparation for society and the period of follow-up rehabilitation, another point relevant to the comments made in II(a) arises. We should try to discover whether the adolescents benefit from a change to an environment different from that in which their childhood rehabilitation was conducted. For some time there has been an insistence on the necessary continuity of place, general atmosphere, and social contacts. There has been speculation about the creation and development of institutions in which the handicapped person would pass his entire life, from birth to death, and where adolescence itself would consequently be nothing more than a biopsychological phenomenon, occurring without any alteration or expansion of either environment or social possibilities. Experience has shown that the stagnation which takes place within the same secure and conditioned environment inhibits development and even leads to regression, which can be corrected only by changing the environment, methods, and personnel. I personally would recommend combinations or complexes of progressive and complementary institutions, rather than large and self-contained institutions designed to accommodate all age groups.

The journey toward communal living will be greatly facilitated each time the handicapped person is able to participate in a normal educational experience, involving normal students, coeducational classes, and ordinary schools. The same can be said about participation in clubs, sports, and leisure activities. The physically handicapped may well be able to withstand cultural or musical competition, for example; the intellectually handicapped may be able to compete in certain sports.

If the handicapped person is unable to attend an ordinary school, or to participate in normal classroom situations or activities, the doors of the institutions for the handicapped should occasionally be opened to the normal, neighboring adolescents so that they can organize various educational and leisure activities or sports (swimming, track events, or organized games).

In boarding schools, vacations and family week ends are good ways to maintain contact with the family and society.

The end of adolescence with the affirmation of marriage possibilities, the orientation of the sexual drive, and the approach of adulthood poses the problem of the right of the handicapped to love and marriage, freedom, and the exercise of civil rights. Mental health services cannot remain indifferent to these problems both because parents feel concerned and seek advice and solutions and because those among the handicapped themselves who are more alert and open now begin to put questions to their doctors and teachers.

These services are involved in various other ways. They have the responsibility to study a number of issues: the consequences—and the prevention —of procreation by the handicapped and the difficulties that some handicapped people will have in living a conjugal life, in educating their own children normally, and in fully assuming their family responsibilities. (These studies should also examine hereditary repercussions as well as those felt by the entire family group.) Finally, these services play a role in the possible application of measures concerning guardianship.

III. ASPECTS OF MENTAL HEALTH SERVICE PERTAINING TO THE NATURE OF THE HANDICAP AT THE ONSET OF ADOLESCENCE

Space will not permit a complete development of this topic, especially as most of these services, with but few exceptions, are not specifically mental health services. They tend to work in conjunction with other groups, such as counseling services, vocational centers, and various labor groups, on the one hand, and on the other, with specialized medical services such as orthopedics, prosthetics, ophthalmology, otorhinolaryngology, orthophonics, neurology, physical therapy, and so forth.

Because of psychological, psychosocial, and psychiatric repercussions emanating from the handicapped person's individuality and particular situation, these services must work in very close collaboration with the medico-social psychopedagogical teams and particularly with the child neuropsychiatrists. However, these services exist primarily to treat the mentally retarded. Some specific comments are called for.

A. The Mentally Deficient

This is, admittedly, a difficult classification to make. Intelligence quotients have the apparent advantage of measuring objectively and exactly, but they are dangerous when accepted as inflexible. They are only one method of evaluation, which should be correlated with other equally important data, such as the social environment and emotional disturbances. These other deficiences, by constituting a different sort of handicap, make every classification imprecise and every situation relative.

The study of mental deficiency must be undertaken not only in a clinical and sociological frame of reference but from an ethnological one as well.

To clarify the topic, I cite the following medical, social, and administrative classification adopted by the French team as a common reference, though it should not be imposed universally.

(1) *The slightly handicapped,* who are capable of enjoying an autonomous life, and of adapting to the working world. Their I.Q.'s are no lower than 65.

(2) *The slightly handicapped who present associated emotional problems.* Strictly speaking, these are not intellectually inferior to the preceding group, but they are additionally handicapped either in their motor capacities or by "emotive overloads" (affective disturbances and reactions to their social environment) which aggravate their general inability to adapt.

As with the above, they are capable of leading autonomous lives and of adjusting to the working world.

(3) *The average handicapped* are capable, after their rehabilitation, of partial independence, of performing simple work, but throughout their lives they will need a special environment. Their I.Q.'s are 50 or slightly above.

(4) *The seriously, although "semieducable," handicapped* are capable only of a collective and sheltered existence. Their I.Q.'s fall between 30 and 50.

(5) *The seriously handicapped, or seriously retarded,* are those whose ability to learn is slight or nonexistent and whose ability to adapt to a communal life is problematical and hazardous. Their I.Q.'s are less than 30 and have no minimum.

To begin by examining the more serious cases, the seriously retarded will be placed in institutions which are, essentially, hospitals: psychiatric wards, wards working in conjunction with psychiatric clinics, or clinics for the incurably retarded, and institutions working with staffs who are specialists in mental defect. Most of these will be of a residential nature, but upon the request of certain parents, outpatient wings could be established, to be used especially while the parents are still alive and possibly as part of a larger community social center, which would be open to the public.

In private institutions the community will usually have to provide either a subsidy or pensions.

Adolescents will have to be placed in sections appropriate to their age, although their therapy and education will remain largely unchanged.

Certain doctors have been led to suppress menstruation by pharmacological means in cases where the girl is incapable of practicing a minimal physical hygiene or exercising precaution.

With adolescence, both the seriously and the average handicapped are placed in educational institutions with medical staffs. Later, if they cannot be kept in the family, they are placed either in vocational centers, in noncompetitive work, or in centers or homes for young workers who are mentally retarded.

Theoretically, a distinction should be made between institutions for the seriously handicapped and those for the average handicapped. Actually, it is very difficult to draw a line between these two groups, and classification is often very delicate and more circumstantial than definitive. It has even been found that during rehabilitation, because of adolescence and the activity of their immediate environment, some patients previously considered to be seriously handicapped exhibit efficiency and behavior only slightly inferior to that of the average handicapped.

For the majority in these two categories, the atmosphere of the vocational school and the opportunity to work give them a sense of compensation and satisfaction and generally lead to a flowering of personality. This is all the more true, and more readily observable, where a sense of teamwork and discipline exists and where work is suited to capacities.

The vocational school is often a door opening onto society. To the young mentally retarded, however, some aspects of society will still appear insurmountable obstacles with which they must collide. These include, for the boys, military service (if it is obligatory in their country), driving licenses, and marriage. With adolescence and marriageability, the sexual drive is established; with work, the horizon is enlarged; but now certain freedoms are exhibited and certain desires incapable of fulfillment are born. It becomes difficult to make handicapped youths understand and accept the rules governing society without relying on the old standbys—"later," or, "you're still too young"—and without issuing refusals which, because not understood, place them once again in a position of inferiority and incapacity.

One of my collaborators, Dr. Bascou, has suggested a process of "adultation" to lift handicapped adolescents out of the social puerility in which most of them have been sheltered and conditioned. Unfortunately, although "adultation" is certainly necessary, it has certain limits and risks becoming nothing more than a sham if the ultimate goal is a genuine and happy confrontation with the norms of society.

It is clear to what extent this preparation for a social life, this introduction into so-called "normal" living, poses problems peculiar to each case, and especially for the more seriously handicapped. The seriously handicapped principally seek the protection furnished by the mother image and exhibit few signs of heterosexuality (Dawn's disease, for example, is characterized by an almost complete absence of heterosexuality; the handicapped person desires nothing more than maternal contact and care and is especially frightened by the prospect of being left alone after the death of his parents). But the situation of the average handicapped is very different. He is often physically attracted to the opposite sex, engages rather frequently in autoerotic or homosexual activities, and desires something more than maternal affection.

It is true that many handicapped people experience a late arrival of puberty, are emotionally immature, and lack normal sexual potency, but it is also precisely here that the compensation provided by military service and the opportunity to drive automobiles is usually significant.

These few points clearly illustrate how a recognition of the many serious problems raised by particular adolescent cases must necessarily expand the range of activity in which mental health services are now involved.

Similarly, the type of work actually performed will depend on the nature of the handicap. For the seriously handicapped and the near-average handicapped, this work should be performed in centers completely subsidized by the Department of Labor, rather than in purely noncompetitive centers. The following standards should be observed:

(1) A designated, but reduced, output.

(2) Safe and supervised working conditions.

(3) A continuation of therapy and the process of social adaptation begun in the rehabilitation centers.

An on-the-job training period without regard to profit should be conducted for three to six months.

An in-depth study has shown that semi-industrial mass production would seem generally to offer the best prospects, on condition that this work is easy and divided into simple tasks, is not excessively strenuous, and is performed by teams.

There still remains a place in our highly industrialized world for certain kinds of work that allow emphasis on good human relations and thereby constitute a real therapy. The vocational center should achieve this consolidation of effort through the manufacture of an immediately useful and consumable product.

Experience permits us to consider four categories of work suited to the capacity of these handicapped people:

(1) Wrapping and packing.

(2) Assembly work.

(3) Work dealing with products made by the transformation of raw materials.

(4) Various services.

The salary received by the handicapped worker should be based on his productivity and effort. His salary scale should provide him with healthy competition and the possibility of a promotion or raise in pay.

Laws concerning the employment of the handicapped in industry should favor companies that contract work to subsidized centers. These companies could be exempted from employing the handicapped in their own shops.

The efficiency of these centers could be considerably increased if they could hire a reasonable proportion of normal workers without losing their status as essentially subsidized centers. A proportion of 25 per cent of the total work force does not seem unreasonable.

The Department of Education should be responsible for the education of the slightly handicapped; however, the mental health services should participate in the detection, diagnosis, and supervision of rehabilitation.

In cases where the slightly handicapped suffer from associated disturbances, mental health services should have the decisive voice on treatment, whether through consultations and the use of their child psychiatry clinics, or through their counseling services and medical and educational consultations, or, finally, through institutes designed exclusively for these cases.

B. Motor Handicaps

These take many forms. Mental health services have an important role to play regarding the more seriously handicapped.

(1) Those with *cerebral motor handicaps* (both the classification and the specific name are the work of French doctors, Tardieu in particular) are those who have been stricken by a cerebral lesion involving motor deficits, but whose intelligence is not generally affected. These cases should first be treated in centers for specialized rehabilitation, located near well-equipped hospitals. Then, at about 10 to 13 years of age, they should move on to institutes for motor education (which may be either autonomous or incorporated in the above-mentioned centers). By offering appropriate mechanical treatment and a psychomotor education, these institutes should prepare the adolescent for occupations that could be conducted either in a normal social environment or in the various vocational centers. They may even be able to finish or go beyond their secondary education.

Because of problems peculiarly their own—their tendency to tire quickly, their need for special equipment, and their difficulty in maintaining any rhythm of work—it may not always be possible to place them in scholastic institutions designed for cases presenting other motor handicaps.

According to the plan adopted by the French, a small number of institutions staffed with very specialized instructors should be able to satisfy this specific need.

In addition to treatment given by neurologists, orthopedists, and physical therapists, psychiatric treatment will also often be necessary because of the many psychological disturbances manifested by these cases, despite their well-known capacity for overcompensation.

(2) The mentally handicapped with *physical motor problems* can only rarely be rehabilitated with the cerebral motor cases or with the mentally retarded whose degree of retardation is equal to their own. Various methods should be combined and adapted to these special cases. Institutions capable of handling them when they reach adolescence, and later when they begin work, should be created.

Most of the mentally handicapped will have to be placed in institutions for the mentally retarded.

(3) Those with *other motor handicaps* present cases with various etiologies: congenital malformations, amputations, poliomyelitis, medullary trauma, peripheral lesions, and so forth. They often need associated treatment (prosthetic, orthopedic, neurological, therapeutic, and so on) and present such various institutional problems that this subject cannot be treated adequately in this chapter. Here, medicine and education should combine their efforts, for some of these handicapped people are capable

of pursuing advanced studies and of obtaining diplomas and degrees that would further their careers and their futures.

We should therefore envisage the establishment of training centers as well as special schools and colleges, all of these possessing placement bureaus.

(4) The last category consists of *serious hereditary cases:* myopathy, degenerative medullar disturbances, paraplegia with sphincteral or respiratory problems. Although in these cases neurological treatment is of more importance than psychiatric treatment, special psychological attention is still necessary. For these adolescents, we should plan the establishment of institutions or special wards located near rehabilitation centers or adult paraplegic centers.

C. Sensory and Speech Handicaps

These also pose mental health problems, but are rarely treated in mental health clinics. They will have to be referred to the psychiatrist or the psychologist in consultation with the institution's therapist and others concerned.

D. Associated Handicaps

Although we have already mentioned those related to the mentally retarded and the physically handicapped, there are other cases which remain rarely or poorly treated:

(1) The mentally retarded who are deaf-mute.

(2) The mentally retarded who are blind.

(3) The motor handicapped who are blind.

(4) The blind deaf-mute.

Some of these have been treated with astonishing results.

The frequent overlapping of various handicaps thus demonstrates both the complexity and the similarities of the mental health problems raised by the emotionally disturbed or handicapped adolescent. The points made by Buckle are relevant to this frequent overlapping.

These problems therefore demand the creation and development of a vast network of institutions, specialized services, detection centers, administrative bodies, community financing, special financial allocations and pensions, specially trained personnel permitting multidisciplinary and multiprofessional team-work, medical research, and educational, psychological, and sociological research. Such a network would open new perspectives on different means of treatment.

This essentially humanitarian program risks being compromised by a shortage of personnel and particularly of competent neuropsychiatrists.

Adolescence marks an important turning point for the handicapped. According to the means at our disposal, he will either remain uncured in an asylum or may hope for an active and productive life and the possibility of developing latent capacities.

OFFICERS OF THE INTERNATIONAL CONGRESS AND MEMBERS OF THE INTERNATIONAL STUDY GROUP

International Association for Child Psychiatry and Allied Professions

INTERNATIONAL CONGRESS: EDINBURGH, JULY 1966

President: John Bowlby (United Kingdom); *Vice-Presidents:* Anna-Lisa Annell (Sweden), E. James Anthony (U.S.A.), D. J. Duché (France), D. Arn. Van Krevelen (Holland), Serge Lebovici (France), Kirsten V. Rasmussen (Denmark); *Treasurer:* Gerald Caplan (U.S.A.); *Secretary-General:* Frederick A. Stone (United Kingdom); *Assistant Secretaries-General:* Leonard J. Duhl (U.S.A.), Cyrille Koupernik (France), Walter Spiel (Austria).

INTERNATIONAL STUDY GROUP

Chairman: Serge Lebovici (France); *Secretary:* Cyrille Koupernik (France); *Members:* Anna-Lisa Annell (Sweden), E. James Anthony (U.S.A.), John Bowlby (United Kingdom), Mary Capes (United Kingdom), Gerald Caplan (U.S.A.), D. J. Duché (France), Leonard J. Duhl (U.S.A.), Elizabeth Irvine (United Kingdom), Kirsten V. Rasmussen (Denmark), Walter Spiel (Austria), Frederick A. Stone (United Kingdom), D. Arn. Van Krevelen (Holland).

INDEX

Abse, D. W., 186, 193
absenteeism, job, neurosis and, 155
absolute novelties, 22
abstract concepts, 23; delinquents and, 288, 304–308, 312
abstract reasoning, 1, 2
abstract theories, 23
abstract thinking, 2, 16, 114, 307
abstract verbalization, 305, 312
abstraction, development of, 15, 18
academic achievement, 9; and job opportunities, 145–146, 175–180, 332, 338; parental emphasis on, 129, 159, 200, 300
Ackerman, N. W., 45, 316
acne, 36, 376
acting out: autoerotic, 63; as delinquency, 265–266, 305; heterosexual, 63; *see also* sexual acting out
action behavior, internalization of, 22, 300
adolescence: adult reactions to, 54–75; ages at onset of, 28, 38; beginning of, 11–13, 28–29; body-image and (*see* body-image); climate and, 29, 32; constitutional differences in, 38–44; definition of, 28; delayed, 39–41, 43; and delinquency, 55, 76, 79; early sexual maturation in, 38; endocrinological mechanisms of, 7, 36–38; ethnic differences in, 31, 32; "good" reaction to, 75–76; latency concept of, 80–81, 83, 106; maturational crisis of, 335–337; nutrition and, 29, 32, 35, 39, 40; Oedipal period (*see* Oedipal transition); parental reactions to, 54–70; phases of, 28, 80–83; primary and secondary sexual characteristics in, 29–33, 43–44; race and, 29, 32; research and, 74–75; sexual incongruities in, 41, 44; societal reactions to, 72–74; socioeconomic factors in onset of, 29, 32; stereotypic reactions to, 54–75; youngsters' reactions to, 83–87, 390; *see also* physical development
adolescent psychiatry, 360–361, 367–370, 374, 385; *see also* community mental health services

adolescent transition, 149–150
adopted children, 104, 133–141; ambivalence in, 137, 138; anxiety in, 135–136; and delinquency, 136; fantasies in, 136, 139; and search for identity, 104, 134, 135, 141; therapy of, 139–141
adrenal cortical trophic hormone (ACTH), 37
adult authority, revolt against, 8, 17, 19, 45, 101, 102, 107–111, 130, 158, 160–161
adult psychiatry, 360, 370, 374, 385
adult reactions to adolescence, 54–75
adultation, process of, 396
aggressive impulses, suicide and, 257–258
Aichhorn, A., 377
alcoholism, 59; suicide and, 229, 248
Allchin, W. H., 290–291, 322, 333
ambivalence, 17, 57, 59, 68, 70, 71, 81, 108; in adopted children, 137, 138; anorexia nervosa and, 193, 204; and job choice, 158
amenorrhea, 40; anorexia nervosa and, 186, 188–190, 192, 196; hypothalamic, 186, 190
amnesia, 130
amorphous self-concept, 48
amphetamines, 40, 272, 273, 281–284
anal defiance, displacement of, 193
anal fixation, 58–59
anal-muscular developmental phase, 203
anamnesis, body-image and, 43
androgen-producing cells, 30
androgenic hormones, 40
androgens, 37, 38
anger, depression and, 266, 267, 269
annihilation anxiety, 339
anorexia nervosa, 39, 129, 181, 185–207; ambivalence and, 193, 204; anxiety in, 198, 200, 201, 203; appetite and, 190–192, 196; body-image and, 182, 188, 193–196, 202; cognitive-perceptual disturbances in, 182, 188, 194–196, 198, 201–203; defenses in, 192, 200–201; depression and, 193–195; developmental patterns, 198–203; diagnosis and nosology, 187–189; differential diag-

402